THE DOWNTOWN ANTHOLOGY

6 Hit Plays from New York's
Downtown Theaters

THE DOWNTOWN ANTHOLOGY

6 Hit Plays from New York's
Downtown Theaters

Edited by
Morgan Gould & Erin Salvi

New York, New York

Published by Playscripts, Inc.
7 Penn Plaza, Suite 904
New York, New York, 10001
www.playscripts.com

Cover Design by Noah Scalin
Cover Image by Chuck Scalin
Map Illustration by Gabriella Miyares
Text Design and Layout by Erin Salvi

First Edition: May 2015
10 9 8 7 6 5 4 3 2 1

ISBN-13: 978-1-62384-003-7

Praise for the Plays:

A Map of Virtue

"With a Hitchcockian sensibility, [Courtney] makes psychodrama out of the mystery of what keeps people together even as imaginations and egos push them apart. Like a souvenir from a fleeting dream, this play will pass over you painlessly, and then it will linger."

—*Backstage*

We Are Proud to Present a Presentation...

"Impressively navigates the tricky boundaries that separate art and life, the haunted present and the haunting historical past."

—*The New York Times*

Trevor

"Hugely entertaining tragicomedy...the genius of [Jones's] play is how he has so cleverly humanized both characters."

—*Chicago Sun Times*

The Lily's Revenge

"...offers so many incidental pleasures that theatrical time—always a curiously malleable element—seems to contract."

—*The New York Times*

Alice in Slasherland

"A geek kid's theater dream come true!"

—*Show Business Weekly*

Phoebe in Winter

"Gives new meaning to the phrase 'the war at home'...every other line comes out as a smartly put, hard-won truth you want to hold on to for later rumination."

—*New York Theatre Review*

Praise for the Theaters:

13P

"Playwrights need more than staged readings, more than productions. Playwrights need other writers to drink with, to fight with, to challenge, to respond to, to inspire. Not since Circle Repertory have we seen playwrights in New York forging a home for each other."

—*The Village Voice*

Soho Rep.

"After 35 years of anchoring the downtown theater scene, Soho Rep. is still living up to its mandate of producing bold work by brave pioneers."

—*Variety*

Lesser America

"The Lesser sensibility has an edge to it, but one that is matched by a passionate sense of storytelling."

—*New York Press*

HERE Arts Center

"HERE is one of the country's premiere venues for theatrical oddities, a real Frankenstein's lab. And every year, they haul their wonderful creations out of the dark. It's a fun, easy way to see the hungriest artists imagine the future of American theater."

—*New York Metromix*

Vampire Cowboys

"Gleefully lowbrow entertainment for overgrown adults"

—*The New York Times*

Clubbed Thumb

"More than just a producer of quality theatre, the 13-year-old New York City-based company is a nexus for actors, writers and directors."

—*American Theatre*

Contents

Acknowledgments

First and foremost, the editors wish to thank the exceptionally talented playwrights who generously allowed us to include their work in this book, as well as the incredible theater companies who have worked with us to make this volume possible.

Special thanks is due to Jason Pizzarello, without whom the idea for this book might never have come to light.

The editors would also like to thank Lane Bernes, Brendan Conheady, Billie Davis, Cate Fricke, Lizzie Martinez, Lysna Marzani, John O'Connor, and Teresa Sanpietro for their essential contributions to the creation of this anthology and their unflagging support throughout the process.

Many thanks also to Mark Subias, Rachel Viola, Antje Oegel, Kate Navin, and Mark Orsini for their efforts and assistance in compiling this book.

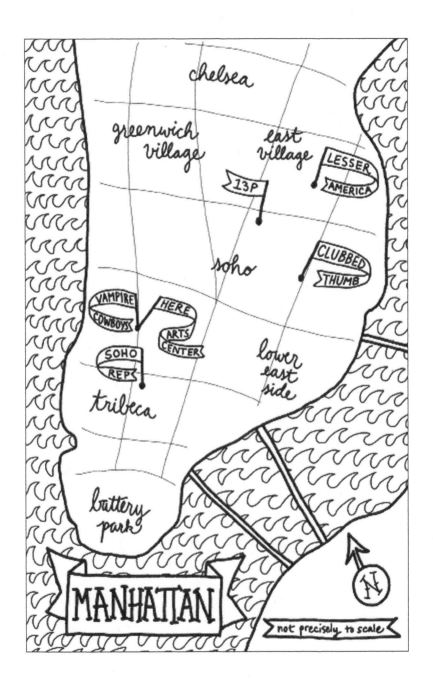

Foreword

Erin Courtney, Jackie Sibblies Drury, Nick Jones, Taylor Mac, Qui Nguyen, and Jen Silverman have each written a startling and wildly imaginative play—each like a strange, found object, and each a true document of our own strange and troubling times.

Erin Salvi and Morgan Gould have chosen wickedly and wisely, in my opinion. Anthologies of plays would seem to be an afterthought in the highly transformative and ever-transitional world of the theater, especially in the more daring and unpredictable purlieus of what is known as downtown theater—ever a sinister place for the snarky wiseacres of the mainstream, ever spiteful and corporate despite their preaching.

I've edited seven, and am proud to have done so: the first came out on cassette tapes and featured John Cage and several of the Language Poets. *From The Other Side Of The Century II* (edited with Douglas Messerli of Sun & Moon Press) was touted as the most comprehensive anthology of new American Drama ever published, and *New Downtown Now*, my most recent, is one I'm still pleased with. These books are important because the times and tastes change so rapidly; it is damned important to be able to consult what is new, newer, and newest. When I started in New York in the late 70s there were *no* recent collections of plays—a sad commentary on the times, and the smugness of the prevailing 60s mindset.

Each of these six plays strikes me as a carefully articulated world with a mind of its own, a landscape that doesn't know how to stay put: from Erin Courtney's, where two and two make five, and Jackie Sibblies Drury's mad choruses of a lost Herero legacy to Taylor Mac's happy world of flowers —so happy they are terrifying; from the apish miscreants of Nick Jones, to the slasherdom of Qui Nguyen and the terrors of Jen Silverman's nightmare land. Six strange worlds, all very germane to the one we think we know. The seventh is this book itself, glowing in the dark of the night.

—*Mac Wellman*
Award-Winning Playwright and
Chair of Playwriting at Brooklyn College
March 24th, 2015

Editors' Note

When we began conceiving of this anthology, we felt there was a lot of significant work that wasn't being circulated to anyone outside of a small segment of New Yorkers—those few people who have the opportunity and the means to frequent theaters below 14th Street in Manhattan. With this in mind, we set out to create an anthology of work that would serve as a kind of sampler platter for readers wanting to learn more about the landscape of New York theater that sits apart from Broadway. Our hope is that this book will enable more people to discover writers and theaters that are redefining theatrical storytelling and championing new, exciting models for collaboration. We selected six plays that we feel exemplify a wide range of downtown work—language-bending, rule-busting, form-shattering, truly wild theater that represents a wave of adventurous work that New Yorkers have come to actively seek out. While "downtown" is a literal place in New York City, it is also an aesthetic movement that has and will continue to shape modern drama for decades to come.

Defining what makes a "Downtown Play" is tricky. It's not always about the geographic location of the theater (though that is often a factor), and the types of plays that represent the essence of downtown theater elude simple categorization. Perhaps the best way to begin a discussion of downtown theater is by exploring what led us to choose the individual plays that make up this collection in the first place.

When Erin Courtney and 13P presented the Obie-winning *A Map of Virtue* at the 4th Street Theatre, it scared the living daylights out of every theatergoer who dared to buy a ticket. Her spooky tale about bird statues, tiny child ghosts, masked men, mysterious fires, and the pitch-black void of the middle of the night carved out a story about innate human fear and the deceptive ways in which our memories fail us.

Jackie Sibblies Drury's *We Are Proud to Present...* had the whole community talking. Lines formed outside Soho Rep.'s space on Walker Street as people clamored for tickets. Her subversive, devilishly funny, painfully honest, and dizzyingly meta-theatrical piece about race, ownership, and how we inherit and pass down the stories of our past vibrated the theater season and cemented her as a force in the downtown theater and beyond.

What surprised most theatergoers about Nick Jones' *Trevor,* presented by Lesser America at Theater for the New City, was not how hysterically funny the show was (it did, after all, feature an actor playing a former showbiz chimpanzee), but how that humor was balanced out by an almost achingly sad tale. It was a nimble maneuver on the part of Jones and Lesser America—to not play the story only for laughs, but to root out the intense relatability of an animal haunted by failure and longing. The result was an unexpected exploration of what it really means to be human.

When it opened, Taylor Mac's *The Lily's Revenge* rocked HERE Arts Center. A fully immersive, epic party for freaks, weirdos, and their allies, Taylor, known for his lavish design aesthetic and queer-centered performance focus, threw a full-on, five-hour, multi-floored theater bash. He pulled together people from all aspects of performance—dance, cabaret, burlesque, theater, drag, and more—and told an unparalleled story of outsiderness. He didn't play the victim, but he did play songs and movies, and in the end, the result was a brilliantly homespun shining star of an epic theater piece.

With *Alice in Slasherland*, Qui Nguyen and the Vampire Cowboys dared to go where few stage plays have gone before: into the realm of the horror film genre by way of Lewis Carroll's *Alice in Wonderland*, rounded out with bouts of exquisite fight choreography and self-referential humor. Surprised and delighted audiences came out in droves to see what appeared to be an entirely new form of theater, combining the tropes and concerns of modern pop culture into a gleeful, action-packed live performance.

Clubbed Thumb's presentation of Jen Silverman's *Phoebe in Winter* at The Wild Project was a mythic, haunting production—a story of the aftermath of war that seemed at once to stand outside of time and to be born very much of our present-day concerns with retribution and responsibility. The characters played musical chairs with names and identity and enacted an elaborate and dangerous battle for control that rendered the family structure as twisted and complex as the wider sociopolitical landscape.

When curating this book, it was important to us not only to honor these writers, who are reimagining, warping, and even exploding the rules of traditional fourth-wall, "well-made play" theater, but also to recognize their collaborators. It often takes years between the moment a playwright sits down to write the first words of a play and the moment that play is actually presented before an audience. Many hands contribute to a *play* (as opposed to simply a script) being born. And in many cases, that road starts with an artistic leader who decides they want to make it happen.

These artistic vanguards are really the theatrical party hosts of the downtown theater. The Vampire Cowboys—those goofy, playful geniuses Qui Nguyen and Robert Ross Parker—decided to make unapologetic geek theater on their own terms. In 2010, Laura Ramadei, Daniel Abeles, and Nate Miller, the founders of Lesser America, created a home that would make space for young and emerging artists to generate boldly entertaining work. Sarah Benson and her team at Soho Rep. continuously set the bar for challenging and delighting audiences with their formally expansive, artistically excellent seasons. Kristin Marting of HERE Arts Center dares to program some of the most aesthetically diverse and adventurous work out there. Whether it's puppets, opera, or multimedia, Marting doesn't back away from any project, no matter how daunting. Maria Striar of Clubbed Thumb is a fierce, no-nonsense champion of writers. She takes a play that others would shy away from and finds the best artists in the country to work all summer every summer to bring it to life. The 13 playwrights of the award-winning company 13P decided not to wait for an institution to green-light their work, so they resolved to make their own. And ironically, they created one of the most seminal institutions of the decade—one that others, we suspect, will continue to emulate for years to come. These tastemakers, gatekeepers, and trendsetters are part of a very vital artistic scene in America. And yet, so many don't even know their names. But these artistic leaders, who regularly dive in and make theater happen, are part of a network that supports the creation of new work and the constant reinvigoration of the way we tell stories on stage.

We are so grateful to these visionary writers, collaborators, and artistic leaders for coming together to create this book. We're excited to share with you, the reader, a small piece of the picture that is downtown theater and to equip you to imagine a theater that challenges the notions of what a play is and what a theatrical experience can do. All six of these pieces push current boundaries of theater and performance. These artists charged forward with something untested, untried, and unknown. We hope this book will inspire others to do the same.

—Morgan Gould & Erin Salvi

A Map
of Virtue

Erin
Courtney

About the Collaboration
Mapping Out a Model for Self-Produced Theater

13P changed the landscape of downtown theater in New York. By formalizing self-producing, and using the model of artists helping other artists to produce and realize their respective works, Erin Courtney and the other members of 13P (Anne Washburn, Winter Miller, Rob Handel, Gary Winter, Kate E. Ryan, Ann Marie Healy, Sheila Callaghan, Lucy Thurber, Julia Jarcho, Madeleine George, Young Jean Lee, and Sarah Ruhl), along with Executive Producer Maria Goyanes, dared to imagine a world where artists could control their own work and give their careers a launching pad without waiting for other institutions to pave the way. Aesthetically, these fiercely fun, wild and imaginative plays helped spearhead a movement in the downtown theater world of creating and supporting challenging, difficult, unruly plays.

These 13 writers have gone on to earn countless awards and accolades, and are among the most lauded writers in the country. And 13P, which always intended to end after producing 13 plays, will remain a vanguard of the downtown experimental theater movement. An extensive archive of materials you can use to create your own version of the 13P producing model can be accessed at 13p.org.

§

Resources for 13P shows were modest. The staging of A Map of Virtue *was arrived at through simplicity and practicality. Even people who knew the 4th Street Theater were tricked by Marsha Ginsberg's subtly angled and oddly textured set. The walls absorbed Tyler Micoleau's light; they were almost voids. It all looked like nothing. There was a sudden burst of many canaries chirping, courtesy of sound designer Daniel Kluger, that haunts me to this day. The scenes of the play are very short. We rehearsed each one thousands of times. The actors were steeped in the play. The first preview was dreadful because the actors Maria Striar and Jon Norman Schneider were sitting silently way downstage as the audience came in, very doom and gloomy. We fixed that immediately. The success of the play was unexpected. Some audience members were terrified; I would sit in the back of the house and watch them jump. It was an emotional experience, making Erin's play.*

—Ken Rus Schmoll, Director

Mission Statement: 13P

13P (Thirteen Playwrights, Inc.) was formed in 2003 by 13 mid-career playwrights concerned about what the trend of endless readings and new play development programs was doing to the texture and ambition of new American plays. Together they took matters into their own hands, producing one play by each member playwright. They presented their final production in the summer of 2012 and then immediately imploded.

About the Author

Erin Courtney's play *A Map of Virtue,* produced by 13P and directed by Ken Rus Schmoll, was awarded an Obie and described as "one of the most terrifying plays of the past decade" by Alexis Soloski in the *New York Times.* Ms. Courtney's other plays include *I Will Be Gone, Honey Drop, Black Cat Lost, Alice the Magnet, Quiver and Twitch,* and *Demon Baby.* Her work has been produced and developed by Clubbed Thumb, Atlantic Theater Company, The Flea, New York Stage and Film, Adhesive Theater Project, Soho Rep., Vineyard Theatre, and The Public Theater. She has collaborated with Elizabeth Swados on the opera *Kaspar Hauser* and is starting work on a new musical with Ms. Swados on the life of Isabelle Eberhardt. She has been a resident at the MacDowell Colony, a recipient of a New York State Council on the Arts grant and two MAP Fund grants from the Rockefeller Foundation. She is an affiliated artist with Clubbed Thumb, a member of 13P, and a member of New Dramatists. She teaches in the MFA playwriting program at Brooklyn College and is a co-founder of the Brooklyn Writers Space. Mac Wellman's MFA program at Brooklyn College, 2003. BA, Brown University, 1990.

"In addition symmetry principles are characterized by a quietude, a stillness that is somehow beyond the bustling world; yet in one way or another, they are almost always involved with transformation or disturbance, or movement."

-David Wade,
Symmetry: the Ordering Principle

Cast of Characters

BIRD STATUE, our guide through the story

SARAH
MARK

NATE, married to Sarah
VICTOR, Mark's boyfriend

JUNE, dresses like a headmistress
RAY, dresses like a headmaster

Parts

One: Curiosity
Two: Loyalty
Three: Empathy
Four: Honesty
Five: Integrity
Six: Love
Seven: Intuition

Middle of the Night: when bad things sometimes happen

Seven: Intuition
Six: Love
Five: Integrity
Four: Honesty
Three: Empathy
Two: Loyalty
One: Curiosity

Acknowledgments

The premiere production of *A Map of Virtue* was produced by 13P at the 4th Street Theatre in New York City, February 2012. The production was directed by Ken Rus Schmoll, with the following cast and production staff:

NATE . . . . .Alex Draper
BIRD STATUE . . . . Birgit Huppuch
RAY. . . . . .Jesse Lenat
JUNE. . . . . .Annie McNamara
VICTOR . . . . Hubert Point-Du Jour
MARK. . . . . .Jon Norman Schneider
SARAH. . . . . Maria Striar

Set and Costume Designer. . . . . Marsha Ginsberg
Lighting Designer. . . . . .Tyler Micoleau
Sound Designer. . . . . Daniel Kluger
Songs . . . . .Jesse Lenat
Casting Director . . . . .Kelly Gillespie
Producer . . . . Maria Goyanes
Associate Producer . . . . Rachel Silverman
Production Stage Manager. . . . . Megan Schwarz Dickert
Production Manager. . . . . Jason Goedken
Technical Director . . . . David Ogle

The production was made possible in part by a grant from the MAP Fund, a program of Creative Capital supported by the Doris Duke Charitable Foundation and the Andrew W. Mellon Foundation.

Special Thanks

To all of the staff and playwrights of 13P, Anne Kauffman and New George's, Pam MacKinnon and Clubbed Thumb in residence at Fordham University, Sarah Krohn and Williamstown Theatre Festival, Erik Ehn and the Pataphysics crew, the ladies and gentlemen of Cho-Chiqq, Edmond Jabès, Mac Wellman, Antje Oegel, and Scott Adkins.

A Map of Virtue, 13P, New York, New York (2012). Photo: Blaine Davis.

A MAP OF VIRTUE
by Erin Courtney

Scene One

(SARAH and MARK are in different rooms.
They do not hear each other.
They are being interviewed for a documentary film.
It should feel like their interviews have been edited together.)

BIRD STATUE. Part One: Curiosity.

SARAH. He seemed so kind to me. Gentle. I saw him in a diner. I was sitting in a booth near a window.

MARK. I was sitting at the counter. I was drinking tea and water without ice.

SARAH. My coffee cup was neatly placed between my two hands. I stared straight ahead, trying to keep my face relaxed. He stared at me from a bar stool at the counter.

MARK. I noticed her sitting there because she had two birds tattooed on her chest. They were symmetrical and her hands were symmetrically placed on either side of her cup. I love symmetry so I was drawn to her. She was very still and so I kept looking right at her, patiently, because she didn't mind me looking at her. She was there and I was there and for a long time there was no movement in the diner. Until the sounds of birds.

SARAH. Suddenly, there was the sound of birds. Seemed like a thousand birds—everywhere—it was just like that Hitchcock movie but it wasn't a movie, it was happening and it was really frightening. I felt frightened. I decided to hide in the bathroom of the diner. I waited there until I could not hear the birds anymore. When I came out, the man was gone. I remembered he had a notebook. I wondered what was in the notebook.

MARK. Thousands of birds. Frightening. Now, I was carrying a small bird statue in my pocket and she had the bird tattoos and suddenly this swarm of birds was surrounding us. Some kind of omen, I thought, an omen for sure. She ran to the bathroom. The windows were darkened by the birds, the shadows of the birds, and then I saw my bus. So I ran for it, and the bus driver, who never looks surprised, looked horrified by the birds and he said "Jesus, I fucking hate birds" just as one of them slammed into the windshield.

SARAH. I thought about him all the time and how his face looked young and smooth but his hands were wrinkled and old.

MARK. I thought about what she did in the bathroom. Did she sit on the toilet? Stand over the sink? Did she cover her head?

SARAH. I did not usually go to that diner. I usually went to the bar next door because of the mixed nuts. But that bar had recently been bought by a new owner so they didn't have the nuts anymore.

MARK. About two years later, I am on vacation in Ireland. I am in a very small town called Ballybunion and I am walking along this path right at the edge of a cliff that overlooks the sea. I see a bench and I go to sit on the bench and there is the woman from the diner.

SARAH. I can see that he recognizes me and I recognize him but it's as though we have taken a vow of silence and so we don't speak and it's not strange that we don't speak. I even put my hand on top of his hand but we don't look at each other. We look at the ocean.

MARK. I thought to myself, this is the moment to finally get rid of that bird.

SARAH. Eventually, he gets up and he puts this very tiny bird statue on the bench next to me and he walks away. I sit for a while then I walk away in the opposite direction. Then I went back and put the very tiny bird statue in my pocket.

BIRD STATUE. I am the very tiny bird statue.

MARK. When I moved to Africa, I began to write letters to her. Of course, I didn't know her name or her address so I could not send them. But I found myself searching my memory for details. The blemish on her cheek, her short finger nails, and then I made up a story for her. A story about her childhood, her family, her career, her eating habits, what kind of authors she likes to read—Dostoevsky! Dostoevsky is her absolute favorite! Well, according to my version of her.

SARAH. When I got back home, I began to incessantly draw that bird! Sometimes when I was on the phone, I would look down and see that I had drawn it without realizing it. And of course, I wished I had spoken with him. Asked him his name. Asked him why he liked birds. Asked him if he had been afraid that day in the diner. Asked him why it felt okay to touch his hand in silence. But oddly, I did not care to imagine his day job, or if he was married, or if he had children.

I did wonder about what he dreamt about at night. For some reason, I often tried to imagine that. Oh, last night, I dreamt that I was trapped in some sort of strange school or retreat and we were supposed to have taken a vow of silence but all of these people were talking and that was making me really angry and I started swearing and then I called my sister and told her that I had taken this vow of silence and so I couldn't talk to her. So she panics and she sends her husband—with the police!—to come and get me and I was mad but then it turned out that the evil headmistress had poured gasoline on some of the children, was suffocating some of the children. This was all happening live and on TV at the same time. But then there was hope, a group of children had found an escape tunnel and they were making their way out. Well, it's obvious what I am trying to work out in that one. Right?

MARK. When I was a boy, I was sent to boarding school in Illinois. The headmaster handpicked a few of us—the ones he could tell that he could manipulate—and he had us meet in his library for late night study groups—but instead of studying he had us perform sexual acts on each other while he watched and masturbated. I was 12. It was a very confusing time.
His study was filled with bird statues of all sizes, from all around the world. One day, I put the smallest bird statue in my pocket. I had never stolen anything in my life but I stole it and I ALWAYS carried it with me until that day in Ireland. That little bird was looking over its shoulder. Its beak, up in the air, its head twisted up and back, looking for danger. A meadowlark.

BIRD STATUE. I am a statue of a meadowlark. I have had three owners: the headmaster, Mark, and Sarah.

SARAH. When I got back from Ireland, I decided to go to art school.
I painted that bird and I drew that bird and I began to sell the paintings.
And I began to make a lot of money!
And my friends were freaked out because I had never expressed an interest in being an artist before,
and it happened so fast, and because some of my friends were struggling painters, well, let's just say, I'm not friends with them anymore.

MARK. I walked by an art gallery and there in the window was a giant painting of my bird. I went into the gallery but no one was there. I picked up the bio of the artist. And there was her photo. She was smiling.

I know it was wrong what I did, but I took my Swiss army knife out of my pocket and before I could talk myself out of it,
I slashed the big red painting.

That was my bird.
I had left it in Ireland and she had stolen it.
I've never done anything like that, before or since.
It was so violent.

I slashed her painting. And I ran and ran until I couldn't run anymore.

And then I had to figure out how to get back home because I had run into a neighborhood that I did not recognize.

Scene Two

(SARAH *and* NATE *are at home.*)

BIRD STATUE. Part Two: Loyalty.

SARAH. Some asshole slashed my painting.

NATE. What? No!

SARAH. Yeah.

NATE. Which painting?

SARAH. The one in the window. The red one.

NATE. I loved that one.

SARAH. Me too.

NATE. What kind of a person would do that?

SARAH. Some kind of sick bastard.

NATE. How could that even happen?

SARAH. The intern went out for coffee. They want me to watch the tapes to see if it's somebody I know.

NATE. What if it is someone you know?

SARAH. I hope not. I hope it's a stranger. Some random fucked up kid. You know?

NATE. Maybe it's someone…who hates birds?

SARAH. Don't make jokes. It's probably someone who hates me. Right?

> (SARAH *and* NATE *watch the security tape. She recognizes Mark. She winces as he slashes at her painting.*)

NATE. Do you know him?

> (*Long pause.*)

SARAH. No.

NATE. Are you sure?

SARAH. Yes.

NATE. Are you okay?

SARAH. It's just a painting. It's just a thing.

Scene Three

> (*As the* BIRD *narrates this scene, we also "see" the scene happen on stage.*)

BIRD STATUE. Part Three: Empathy.

Sarah and Mark see each other on a busy city street.
They stop cold and stare, like two wild animals.

He thinks to say "I'm sorry" but he knows it's not enough.
And he is not sure that he is sorry.
She wants to rip his eyes out and then she wants to smother him with kisses.

Is there a truce?
There might be a truce.

Mark's boyfriend, Victor, arrives and looks curiously into Mark's face.
Mark smiles and reaches out for his boyfriend's hand.
Mark and Victor walk past Sarah.

Sarah looks down at her coffee as they pass.
She sort of smiles.

Sort of.

Scene Four

> *(At a zoo in the aviary.*
> MARK *and* SARAH *are both looking at the birds for a long time before they speak.)*

BIRD STATUE. Part Four: Honesty.

MARK. *(With some guilt, but also curiosity:)* Are you painting still?

SARAH. No.

MARK. Do you miss it?

SARAH. No.

> *(Pause.)*

I am writing very short stories.
34 syllables long.

MARK. Like a haiku. No, a haiku is 5-7-5. That's 17 syllables.

SARAH. Like two haikus.
Without the line breaks.

> *(Pause.)*

MARK. What are they about?

> *(SARAH *takes a deep breath. She doesn't really want to say but she decides she owes it to him.)*

SARAH. They are about a man and a bird, and a woman and a bird. The man and the woman are twenty-something and they are also forty-something and seventy-something all at the same time. They are young and childless and they are old and parentless, all at the same time.

MARK. What color is the bird?
In the story?

SARAH. Black.

MARK. It's a meadowlark.

SARAH. I don't know. It's not alive.

MARK. It's dead?

SARAH. No. I mean it was never alive. It's inanimate. A statue.

(Pause. They both look at the birds that are flying about and whistling.)

MARK. *(Pointing to a bird in a tree:)* That's a swallow. You can tell by its call. "Poor Sam Peabody, Peabody, Peabody."

SARAH. You know a lot about birds.

MARK. Unfortunately.

SARAH. I thought you loved birds!
That's what I imagined about you.

MARK. I hate birds.

(Pause.)

Your tattoos on your chest are swallows.

SARAH. I always thought they were blue birds.

MARK. Well, they're drawn with blue ink, but they're swallows. See? Look?

SARAH. I have a hard time remembering the names of things.
I remember shapes and textures but...

MARK. Sailors get two swallows on their chest after they've been at sea for a long time. They get them to mark the fact that they made it home.

SARAH. I'm sorry...well...you were really angry at me weren't you?

MARK. I was angry at that bird because I was ready to let him go.
I didn't want to ever see it again. You brought it back.

BIRD STATUE. I am in her pocket right now! I'm right there!

MARK. I wanted to throw that bird in to the sea.

SARAH. That's strange because I almost threw it into the sea.

BIRD STATUE. I wanted to go into the sea!
I wanted to feel the water.
I wanted to sink to the very bottom or to be carried on a current.

A woman carved me out of cottonwood.
She sold little wooden animals; turtles, birds, horses, on a table on the side of highway in New Mexico.
A boy bought me with his own money while on a cross-country road trip with his parents. He whispered to me during that long trip about all the ways he was planning to run away. When he got older, he used to tell me all the ways he was planning to kill his father, with poison, with rocks, with a gun, with a pillow. But he never did do that. No.

As he grew up, he bought more and more birds. Fossils, skeletons, eggs, sculptures from stone, bronze, terra cotta, some birds that had once been alive and now were stuffed. He became a headmaster and he ran a school and I and all the other birds lined the shelves and tables and desks of his office.

The headmaster, who had once been a boy, also liked to write Terzanelles. And he would recite them for hours on end, walking in circles in his room. The lines of the poem, repeating, he needed to repeat himself.

Some nights, he would bring a group of boys into the room. It was strange, the noises they made. The contortions their bodies got into as they jerk into some kind of position, grunting, sweating, jerk jerk jerking and then a release, a clean up, a shame, a sadness, and then the next attempt at sucking, reaching, grabbing, maneuvering inside.

Mark stole me and always carried me in his pocket, smelly, dark and always moving. His fingers working over my surface, fondling or pinching, enveloping.

And for one moment, he left me on a beautiful cliff overlooking the sea. It was so beautiful. But then Sarah took me and I went back into pockets and nightstand drawers and the bottom of purses with crumbs and old receipts and change.

Scene Five

(At SARAH *and* NATE's *house.)*

BIRD STATUE. Part Five: Integrity.

SARAH. I am having my tattoos removed.

NATE. Don't do that.

SARAH. I already went to my first session and it hurt like a mother fucker. It hurt way more than getting the tattoo.

NATE. Let me see.

(He peeks under the bandages.)

Oh, sweetie, that looks like it really hurts.

SARAH. It does.

(He gives her a gentle hug.)

NATE. Why? I didn't know you wanted to get rid of them.

SARAH. It turns out they are swallows.

NATE. Is there something wrong with swallows?

SARAH. No.

(Silence.)

Do you know why I picked these birds?

Because I saw a picture in a magazine.
A beautiful woman wearing a blue evening gown.
Her hair swept up and two bright, blue birds on her chest.

NATE. I remember that picture.
You had it tucked into your mirror
For a long time
And after you stared at it for a long time
You went and got that tattoo
And I was like, those are sexy.

SARAH. I know. They are. They were. But I didn't earn them.

NATE. Since when do you have to earn a tattoo?

SARAH. I just feel like I stole them. That's all.

NATE. Oh, you paid for them. I was there. You picked a great artist, you picked a great image in a great spot and…

SARAH. I just want to start over.

NATE. Uh-huh.

SARAH. It's not symbolic, Nate! It doesn't mean anything. I just want to be a blank slate.

NATE. Oh-kay.

SARAH. It doesn't mean anything.
It doesn't mean a thing.

Scene Six

(At a cocktail party, MARK, SARAH, *and* NATE *are standing together. A stranger named* JUNE *is standing near them listening.* JUNE *is wearing an outfit that somehow suggests "Headmistress."* JUNE *is very attractive.)*

BIRD STATUE. Part Six: Love.

NATE. *(Talking to* MARK:*)* When I met Sarah, she was at a friend's party.

It was a lot like this party except it was a costume party. She had this circle of people around her and everyone was smiling. She was telling some story and her story had everybody laughing. I was standing across the room so I didn't know that the reason they were all laughing was because she had just told a story about this time in college when she crapped her pants.

I just saw the laughing and I saw her beautiful neck and she seemed giddy.

It was a costume party, so she was dressed up like a 1970s housewife. She had on this polyester pantsuit—purple I think, and a cheap wig and giant sunglasses. I come over (I was dressed like a big banana) and she offers me a pig in a blanket from her tray and she says to me "Have you ever crapped your pants?"

So, she kind of freaked me out.

(To MARK:*)* How do you two know each other?

MARK. We just keep bumping into each other, every few years.
In a diner,
in Ireland,
at a zoo.

SARAH. *(To* NATE:*)* That's not true.

MARK. It is.

SARAH. *(To* NATE:*)* No, the part about how WE met. I met you at a bonfire at the beach. And it was very quiet and we held hands.

NATE. That was the second time we met. And we walked home on that country road that was busy though, it had a fair amount of traffic, and we saw that big, wet dog running down the middle of the road.

MARK. Did it get hit?

SARAH. No, I think it was running towards home. That's how it seemed to me.

JUNE. Do you guys wanna check out this other party? I can drive us.

Scene Seven

*(*MARK, SARAH, *and* NATE *are in the back of a van.*
NATE *is asleep, his head resting on* SARAH's *shoulder.*
JUNE *is driving.*
She keeps her eyes on the road but she speaks to SARAH *and* MARK *in a loud voice so they can hear her.)*

BIRD STATUE. Part Seven: Intuition.

JUNE. You are going to love it! And in the morning we can watch the sunrise and do yoga!

SARAH. I just started doing yoga. I'm not good at it but it's helping me be in my body.

MARK. I know what you mean! I am so rarely in my body.
(To JUNE:*)* So June, how long have you lived outside the city?

JUNE. Oh! A few years. I just got so sick of the city and I wanted the peace and quiet of nature. You have to build a community though or else you get lonely.

SARAH. That's why you invited us out!

JUNE. Exactly!

MARK. *(To* SARAH*:)* I'm so glad we became friends. I mean the kind of friends that actually have conversations in real life. You know I created a fictional version of you.

SARAH. Ooooh. What was my fictional version like?

MARK. You were a single mother.

SARAH. What was it about me that made you think "single mother"?

MARK. Well, the diner was right across the street from a school. And it was 2:30 in the afternoon, so I thought, her daughter goes to that school and she likes to spend 30 minutes in quiet before she has to go be the "mother" so soon, because 3:00 comes so soon, and then you have to be the "mother" again.

SARAH. And what's my daughter's name?

MARK. Maple.

SARAH. Like the syrup?

MARK. Like the tree.

SARAH. Of course!

NATE. *(Waking up:)* Where are we?

SARAH. June is driving us to a party out in the country. Remember?

> *(*SARAH, MARK *and* NATE *all fall asleep in the van.*
> JUNE *is still driving.)*

BIRD STATUE. A TERZANELLE FOR A ROAD TRIP

Here is a song about where we begin
And how we map the trash we leave
The headmistress is drawn to wandering

The wandering are drawn to echo's weave
The man is drawn to the ink on her skin
and how we map the trash we leave

The woman is drawn to a bird within
The husband is drawn to a pretty neck
The man is drawn to the ink on her skin

The headmaster is drawn to meadowlark's peck
The meadowlark is drawn to an old dishrag

The husband is drawn to a pretty neck

Old dishrag is drawn to apple bag
And apple bag is drawn to ants
The meadowlark is drawn to an old dishrag

And ants to spiders to webs to plants
Here is a song about where we begin
And apple bag is drawn to ants
The headmistress is drawn to wandering

> *(The van has stopped.*
> JUNE *pickpockets them.)*

JUNE. We're here!

Scene Eight

> *(MARK, SARAH, NATE, JUNE and RAY are in a strange house out in the woods.*
> *There is a large bird mask on the floor next to RAY.*
> *Everyone sits on mattresses on the floor.)*

BIRD STATUE. In the Middle of the Night…

SARAH. Do you have any beer? Or whiskey?

JUNE. Why do you want a beer?

SARAH. Because it tastes good?

JUNE. Because you are an alcoholic.

SARAH. *(Joking, sort of:)* Ha. Ha. What kind of party is this?

RAY. You can call me Ray but when I wear this bird mask then you can just call me YOU and you can order me around. For example, "You are ugly. You, go get me some soup! You, watch this fire burn. You, read me a story." Etc.

SARAH. You know what? It's late and I think we should get home. Can you give us a ride to a train station? Or can we walk to one?

MARK. Yeah, I got a lot to do tomorrow.

NATE. Yeah. Thanks for inviting us.

JUNE. Well, I'm actually really sleepy. I'm going to take a nap and then I'll drive you to the train. Why don't you all get some rest and then we'll take you to the train.

> *(JUNE and RAY leave the room.)*

NATE. This is not happening.

MARK. Yeah, I think we are stuck here.

SARAH. Come on! Fuck! What the fuck!

MARK. Look out the window, we are in the middle of a freakin' forest.

SARAH. This is bad. Is it like a sexual thing? Like an S and M thing?

MARK. I have no idea.

NATE. Well I'm gonna call a car service. It's gonna cost a fortune to get a car back to the city.

SARAH. *(Overlapping:)* Do they even have car services out here?

MARK. They do, but they are like just some guy and his car.

NATE. Where's my phone?

> *(They all check their pockets for wallets and phones.*
> *They find nothing in their pockets.)*

SARAH. They took our shit!

MARK. Fuck!

> *(MARK tries the door.*
> *It's locked.)*

NATE. Shit. Shit.

SARAH. *(Scared:)* Oh. This is actually really bad.

> *(NATE looks out the window into the big backyard.*
> *RAY is out in the big backyard.)*

NATE. *(Rattling the windows:)* Hey, hey asshole, give us our fucking shit back! Jesus. He's gardening! What?

MARK. They aren't just gonna give it back to us.

SARAH. What are we going to do?

NATE. We have to get out of here and flag down a car.

SARAH. What if they have guns?

MARK. Look. We haven't seen any weapons.

SARAH. That doesn't mean they don't have them.

NATE. But they might not have any.

SARAH. But they might have some.

MARK. Let's calm down. We are going to get out of here. There are three of us and two of them.

> *(They look out the window.)*

SARAH. Oh.

NATE. What?

SARAH. Oh no.

NATE. What?!

SARAH. Ray is holding a rifle.

NATE. Oh.

MARK. Oh.

SARAH. Oh.

> *(They all sit back down.*
> *Lights go out.)*
>
> *(Later.)*

SARAH. This is a creaky old house, little movements sound like giant bangs in here.

MARK. I don't remember what I was dreaming. Do you?

NATE. No.

MARK. I was hoping a dream would be fresh on my mind.

SARAH. Me too. I am starting to feel queasy.

MARK. You'll get...

SARAH. I'm not used to being up in the middle of night. I'm not a night person.

NATE. It is almost morning actually.

SARAH. But not really.

NATE. No, not really.

SARAH. Do you think they have food hidden in this room somewhere?

NATE. Don't do it.

SARAH. Why not?

MARK. It will make too much noise.

SARAH. I don't think they care if we make noise.
Cheese. I wish I could eat some cheese.

> *(SARAH begins looking around the room. There are a few boxes and she looks in them.)*

MARK. I think I saw a piece of cheese.
Where did I see it?

> *(MARK also begins looking around the room.)*

NATE. You must have dreamt the cheese. Have some more soup. It will help you sleep.

SARAH. It's not soup. It's warm water.

NATE. At least we have water.

> *(In one of the boxes, SARAH finds a folded stack of children's clothes.
> She holds up a small pink t-shirt.*
>
> *She finds a child's ball.
> She bounces it.
> She bounces the ball many, many times.)*

NATE. Stop it.

> *(She stops.
> RAY, in another part of the house, picks up his homemade banjo and works on
> a song he has been writing.)*

RAY. *(Singing and playing ukulele:)*
You like to hold this thing
Inside your fist
Your fist protects compactly
Your fist protects itself.

The axe is a fractal repeating
The nutshell might be dead and over with
I think it used to protect the seeds
It's comforting that
I still got the goods.

You like to hold this thing
Inside your fist
Your fist protects compactly
Your fist protects itself.

The axe is a fractal repeating
The nutshell might be dead and over with
I think it used to protect the seeds
It's comforting that
I still got the goods.

I still got the goods.
I still got the goods.
I still got the goods.

> *(Lights go out.
> When the lights come back up in the house, there are blackout drapes that have
> been hammered into the window frames.)*

SARAH. I wonder what day it is?

MARK. I can't tell when it's night or when it's day anymore.

NATE. I think it's Monday.
She took us on Saturday night
And I think today is Monday.

(MARK throws his body against door.
THUD.
MARK throws his body against door.
THUD.
MARK throws his body against door.
THUD.

Later.

MARK is asleep.
SARAH and NATE have sex, quietly.

Then they sit quietly.
There is a squeaking noise in the wall.)

SARAH. That squeaking in the wall is a bat. I thought it was a rat but now I think it's a bat.

(They listen to the bat.
There is the sound of the shotgun being fired outside.

Bang.
Bang.
Bang.

Later.

JUNE is back in the room with MARK, SARAH and NATE.
RAY stands next to JUNE holding the shotgun.
JUNE hands MARK a 3x5 notecard.)

JUNE. Mark, teach us what these words mean.

MARK. I don't understand what this says.

JUNE. Understand it and then teach it to us.
You have one minute to prepare.
You will be evaluated on your ability to get them to understand it.

(JUNE sets a timer.
MARK tries to decode the words on the notecard.
MARK cries and cries.
RAY holds the shotgun.
Buzzer dings.)

JUNE. Okay! Let's hear it!

MARK. *(Reading from notecard:)* Vla.
Baaaaahd.
Dur-en-schmite.

(MARK gestures that they should repeat.)

Vla.

SARAH and NATE. Vla.

MARK. Baaaahd.

SARAH and NATE. Baaaahd.

MARK. Dur-en-schmite.

SARAH and NATE. Dur. En. Schmite.

JUNE. But what does it mean?
Explain the meaning to them!

MARK. I don't know.

JUNE. You are not trying!
You are not trying at all!

MARK. *(Scared:)* Vla is a name?
Vla is a person.
Baaaahd is a verb.
Vla does an action—baaahd.
Dur-en-schmite is an adverb.
It describes the action.
No. NO.
It is a location.
It's a place.

> *(JUNE shakes her head no.*
> *RAY grabs MARK and takes him out of the room.*
>
> *Lights out.*
>
> *In another part of the house.)*

RAY. *(Itching his scalp:)* June? June, I think the head lice are back.

> *(SARAH and NATE are alone in the room.*
> *SARAH has ripped a small corner of the blackout curtain so that she can see the yard.)*

SARAH. What's behind that garden? A fire pit? And a shed.

NATE. Do you see him? Can you see Mark out there?

SARAH. No, it's Ray. He's standing next to some kind of bonfire pit.
But there is something in the fire pit. What's in the fire pit?

> *(NATE looks through the small hole.)*

NATE. Wood. I think. For a fire.

SARAH. It's lumpy though.
Like a blanket.
Is it moving?
It looks like that blanket is squirming.

NATE. It's coal. It's a pile of coal.

(Quiet.)

NATE. I know you never loved me. I know you don't.

SARAH. Don't say that.

NATE. No. It's all right.

> *(Lights out.*
> *Later.*
> *In another part of the house.)*

RAY. *(Picks up his banjo and sings:)*
I just don't got no more
No more
This is the time of night for the
Head lice
I just don't got no more
No more
This is the time of night
For creaking stairs

I just got no more
No more
This is the time of night
For sighing.

> *(Later.*
>
> JUNE *enters the room.*
>
> RAY *brings* MARK *back into the room.*
>
> SARAH *and* NATE *are relieved to see* MARK.
> MARK *will not make eye contact with them.*
>
> JUNE *and* RAY *leave.)*

SARAH. Oh, Mark! Are you okay?

> *(*SARAH *gives* MARK *a big hug.*
> MARK *accepts the hug.*
> *They hug for a long time)*

NATE. What happened?

> *(*MARK *will not answer that question.*
>
> SARAH *and* MARK *and* NATE *lie down on their mattresses with their eyes wide open.*
>
> *Later.*
>
> *After a long time,* SARAH *stands up to look through the small rip in the curtain.)*

SARAH. Nate. Wake up. I think I see a person out there.

NATE. What?

SARAH. Look. Look. What is that?

>   (NATE *looks through the hole.*)

NATE. It looks like smoke. I think it's smoke.

>   (SARAH *squeezing in to look.*)

SARAH. I think it's a child. In just her underwear. Mark. Come here.

>   (MARK *looks.*)

MARK. I can't see anything.

NATE. I think it's just the smoke. The fire's dying down.

SARAH. Look again.

>   (MARK *looks again.*)

MARK. It does look like, a little like, a girl.

>   (SARAH *is looking over his shoulder.*)

SARAH. Is she dancing in the fire?

MARK. If a child were in the fire, she would not be dancing. She would be screaming.

>   (NATE *looks again.*)

NATE. I think there is someone there. I think there is more than one. It looks like children.

>   (JUNE *walks in with the shotgun.*
>   RAY, *wearing his bird mask, hammers the window drape shut.*)

JUNE. (*To* RAY:) You, go get the buckets of water.
(*To* MARK, NATE *and* SARAH:) Left arm. Straight out.

>   (MARK, NATE *and* SARAH *do as they are told.*
>   RAY *places a 5-gallon industrial bucket filled with water in each of their left hands.*)

JUNE. Your arm moves one bit, and I will drown you.
You drop the bucket and I will make you drown the person next to you.

>   (*They stand holding the buckets for a long time.*
>   *Their bodies hurt but they keep still.*
>
>   *Lights out.*
>
>   *A few hours later,* MARK, SARAH, *and* NATE *are staring into their soup bowls.*
>   JUNE *and* RAY *are not in the room.*
>
>   *A man enters wearing Ray's bird mask.*
>   *There is a sound of crying from inside the mask.*)

The man takes off his bird mask and it is VICTOR*!)*

MARK. Victor!

Scene Nine

*(*VICTOR, SARAH, NATE *and* MARK *are driving fast in Victor's car.
They are happily speeding away in the car.)*

BIRD STATUE. Part Seven: Intuition.

MARK. Victor! How did you find us?

VICTOR. GPS! Your phone has GPS.
I guess they forgot to turn off your phones!

NATE. Oh my God! Thank you! Thank you GPS!

SARAH. Thank you, Victor, thank you.

NATE. Thank you, Victor!

MARK. I love you!

SARAH. I love you too!

NATE. We all love you!

VICTOR. So what the fuck happened to you guys?

MARK. It was so stupid. This woman invited us to a party in the country and we went with her but she fucking kidnapped us!

SARAH. I've never been so scared in my life.

NATE. I really thought this is it. We are going to die.

MARK. How did you get in the house?

VICTOR. Well, I had this old pastry box in the car, tied with red and white string, and I carry the box and I go ring the door bell. Ding Dong. And this woman answers the door.
She says "May I help you?" I say "I have a delivery." "Who is it from?" she says.
I wanted to say "It's from the devil" but I can't think of anything else to say so I say nothing and she says she doesn't want to take the package and she slams the door. So, I walk all around the house and I see the blackout drapes on the windows so I am thinking, this is not good. Something weird is going on. And I walk around to the side door and it's locked but next to the side door is this bird mask and so I have no idea WHY I do this, but I put the bird mask on and knock knock knock on the door. Finally she opens the door and says "If your head wasn't attached to your body you would lose it" and she lets me in!

BIRD STATUE. A TERZANELLE FOR A MEADOWLARK

As meadowlark is categorized
A perching bird, her call a whistle sound
"see-you" "see-you" "see-yeer" "see-eyed"

Found on farms, they nest on ground
Their nests destroyed as hay is mowed
A perching bird, her call a whistle sound

In times of danger, meadowlarks shriek and goad,
loud rattle noises form in throat
Their nests destroyed as hay is mowed

They build new nests, all by rote
moving forward, while looking back
loud rattle noises form in throat

But I cannot warn of an attack
I cannot make that sound and call
Moving forward, while looking back.

Because I am not alive at all
as meadowlark is categorized
I cannot make that sound and call
"see-you," "see-you," "see-yeer," "see-eyed"

Scene Ten

(RAY and JUNE are in the room with the mattress on the floor. JUNE is staring out window.)

BIRD STATUE. Part Six: Love.

JUNE. *(Looking out a window:)* There is something not quite right with the garden. The lavender looks a little too tall on this side. You need to maintain the height.

RAY. I'm sorry I didn't notice that.

JUNE. I can't stand to look at it like that. I have a headache.

RAY. I'm sorry. Do you want an Advil?

JUNE. I already took one.

RAY. You might be dehydrated.
Or hungry.
I could make some food for you.

JUNE. No. Thank you.

(Pause.)

JUNE. Do you have any family?

RAY. No. Not really.

JUNE. I came from a huge family.

RAY. Do you miss them?

JUNE. Of course not. They were terrible people.

RAY. It's dry tonight. Clear. Let me go make you a sandwich.

JUNE. No.
They will bring the police.
So you know what we need to do.

RAY. Yes.

JUNE. We've practiced it so it won't be difficult.

RAY. Yes.

> (RAY *looks out the window, up at the stars.*)

Is that Orion's Belt?

JUNE. I never studied the stars.
Go get the gasoline.

RAY. I always thought that I would study them, but I never did.

JUNE. We can't always do everything.

RAY. No.

JUNE. And get the matches.

> (*Pause.*
>
> RAY *hesitates.*)

BIRD STATUE. He is not wearing the bird mask.
He thinks to himself.
I could NOT put it on.

> (RAY *puts on his bird mask.*)

JUNE. You! Go get the gasoline.

RAY. Where is the gasoline?

JUNE. In the shed. Next to the canned goods,
and the first aid kit, and the axe.

> (RAY *goes to get the gasoline and he sings [from inside his mask].*)

RAY.
I still got the goods.
I still got the goods.
I still got the goods.

Scene Eleven

(We "see" the scene as the BIRD STATUE *describes it.)*

BIRD STATUE. Part Five: Integrity.

Ray returns carrying the gasoline.
June and Ray look at each other for a long time.
Ray would like to run but he has come too far to leave.
Ray knows that she knows that he wants to run.
June has no doubt about what is the right thing to do, but she is irritated by Ray's doubt.
June strokes Ray's cheek to reassure him.
June douses the mattress with gasoline.
She sort of smiles.
Sort of.

Scene Twelve

*(*SARAH, NATE, *and* MARK *are all eating fast food.*
VICTOR *is still driving.)*

BIRD STATUE. Part Four: Honesty.

NATE. *(Slurping his soda:)* Okay, wow. A hamburger never tasted so good.

SARAH. *(With a burger in her mouth:)* Is that a mountain range?
What's it called?

NATE. *(Reading a sign:)* Mt. Tremper.

VICTOR. I thought you'd left me.

MARK. You did?

VICTOR. Yeah.

MARK. I wouldn't leave you.

VICTOR. *(Softly:)* I thought it was like that time before.

MARK. Oh Victor. I'm sorry.

VICTOR. I was so mad.
But something told me I should come find you.
Something told me...

SARAH. So we're in the Catskills?

NATE. Hey, if we hadn't just been kidnapped this would be like a great weekend getaway.
Shit. It's even more beautiful though since...you know...since we were kidnapped.
Don't you think so Sarah?

(SARAH *has stopped chewing.*
SARAH *looks horrified.*
SARAH *begins to spit out her food.)*

SARAH. Stop the Car.
Stop the CAR.
Oh God. GOD.
Stop the freakin' car.

NATE. Are you gonna be sick?
Pull over!

VICTOR. I can't pull over here. It's not safe.

MARK. Are you okay? I think she's going to be sick.

SARAH.
STOP THE CAR
STOP THE CAR
STOP THE CAR
STOP THE CAR
STOP THE CAR
STOP THE CAR

BIRD STATUE. In the middle of the night, in the house in the woods, Sarah left me in a pile of clothes. When Nate and Mark were sleeping, she had taken me out of her pocket and she had me climb in and around this mountain of fabric. She remembered how, when she was a girl, she would swirl a blanket and make it into a mountain, a landscape, and she would have her little toys play inside the folds of the fabric. They would climb the mountain and sleep inside the caves and zoom along the roads and carefully navigate the tricky passages that required attention. Oh. Careful there. There's a cliff, walk very carefully there and keep an eye out for loose rocks.

I felt the heat first. The fire started at my base, at my claws and worked its way up my body and it evaporated the water inside me. The heat disturbed my insides so much that everything inside of me reformed. I went from wood to water and air and heat and ash. The part of me as air, flew up and settled in around the ceiling, thick with smoke—and the part of me that was ash, settled down onto the floor. And when the floor collapsed, that part of me settled into the dirt.

Scene Thirteen

(SARAH, NATE, MARK, *and* VICTOR *are all being interviewed.*
Sometimes they are in the same room.
Sometimes they are in different rooms.
It should feel like the interviews are edited together.)

BIRD STATUE. Part Three: Empathy.

SARAH. I had been trying all sorts of things in order to get IN my body. Meditation. Yoga. Chanting: cycling through the vowel sounds in order to take in the earth, so like this—you make a sound and then you say words that have that sound in it. It's about the sound inside the word.

MARK.	**SARAH.**
As a child I was abused by a man	AH: ah, she saw
obsessed with birds.	The law, raw
Hence, I became obsessed with birds	and odd
I became obsessed with this mysterious	all the raw and odd
woman obsessed with birds.	Songs she saw//
	AA: Her anger stays
	Her anger says to stay
Then I destroyed her painting and	away, no play, today
she very painfully erased her bird tattoos.	
Then I was held captive by a bird man.	EE: I see, I see, you
	Are free, I tree,
	I please and tease
It's too much isn't it?	IH: I miss the kiss.
	I miss the lick of the
I mean how can that all happen?	Sick pickle of it.

SARAH. It wasn't working. None of it was working.
But when I saw June. I had this feeling about her, that she had found a better way of living.

NATE. So Victor leads us out the back door and into his car!
And the gratitude
The relief
Was so big.

SARAH. But after we had been driving for like an hour.
I thought, "but what about the children?"
And suddenly I am screaming and screaming
Stop the car
Stop the car
Stop!
And we stopped and we called 911
And Victor gave them the coordinates of the house.

When they got there the house was on fire. I've had to live with this.
We had seen that there were children and we left them.
In that moment when Victor came in, I forgot all about them.

MARK. I feel for her. I do.
I mean I believe that she believes that she saw them.
The smoke looked like a child dancing.

BIRD STATUE. Part Two: Loyalty.

NATE. I'm not going to let her die over this.
I'm worried that her guilt will…that her guilt is…you know…going to consume her…
If they do find that there were children there,
Well if that turns out to be true, then it still won't have been our fault.
We didn't light the match, you know. We didn't kidnap those kids.
We were sleep deprived and they had been feeding us food with no protein.
They were brainwashing us.

SARAH. Still. We had seen the children.
You saw them too!
You said, "It looks like a girl."

MARK. "Looks like" a girl.
It looked like a girl but it wasn't a girl.

NATE. They have not found any remains of children.
If there had been children, they would have found the remains.
They found the remains of June and Ray.

BIRD STATUE. And my remains were there, too!

MARK. —and things come back up and pull us back and something else pushes us forward. We make some kind of association with something and this association becomes a faith—I don't know—just sometimes our faith in something—can lead us down some paths that are bad. And each little mistake or misstep can lead us to the next one until finally, it's the middle of the night out in the woods and you are on a mattress on the floor—trapped.

SARAH. I think it's important to…to own…our behavior. If we don't try to learn from our choices then nothing good comes out of it. What if we could make a map, a map that marks out the terrain we have covered, and the map, like a map of virtues could help guide the next person through a dangerous passage.

(VICTOR *begins humming the tune "Rock Of Ages."*)

MARK. But there is nothing we could have done differently. We didn't do anything wrong.

SARAH. When Victor came, we should have checked for the children.
The police have not searched the entire area for bodies.

Could I have a glass of water?

(MARK *indicates that she has a bottle of water under her chair.*)

Oh! Oh!
Thank you.

VICTOR.
(Sings his own lyrics:)
Map of virtue,
Come to me
Let me find
Myself in thee.

*(She reaches under her chair
and drinks from the bottle of water.)*

Thank you.

MARK. We did go back…I thought she was wrong but even after we had called the police she just kept screaming at us and so…we turned around and drove back, just to see, because she was crying so hard and yelling at us. So we did drive back, but it was too late you know.
I don't know whether or not we—it was a strange bunch of days. We were frightened.

VICTOR. I grew up by the ocean and you learn that if a riptide takes you out, you better just conserve your energy and hope to God—or whatever you believe in—that someone notices you are gone and that that someone has the capability to come and find you and pull you out and bring you back in.

MARK. You hope someone notices you are gone.

SARAH. I saw children.

VICTOR. The evidence shows that there were no children there.

NATE. There were no children there.

Scene Fourteen

BIRD STATUE. PART ONE: CURIOSITY.

VICTOR. When Mark disappeared, he hadn't told me about Sarah.
None of it.
The diner.
Ireland.
I had no idea that Mark had this secret friend, or enemy, or obsession.
I had no idea that she existed and that he had slashed her painting.

He needs some things to be secret.
Or private.
And later when he did tell me the whole thing,
he was so really ashamed about slashing that painting.
That was really hard for him to tell me that.
I don't think he ever wanted me to know about that.

He had told me about the headmaster's office.
He had told me but it's not something that he wanted to talk about too much.
He kept that experience in a little box.
Separate.

MARK. We were at this party and we stayed up all night and this woman who had been talking with us invited us to this other party. She said she could drive us to this other party and she drove us in this van.

NATE. A windowless van.

SARAH. Well, looking back now, I think we followed that woman, or at least I think I followed her because I had a craving for consistency. I thought maybe she had discovered a healthier way to live.

MARK. Let's see. I guess I followed the woman into the windowless van because I had been living too consistently. You know just the opposite to what you are talking about. I was finding myself horrified by the sameness of my days and it's hard for me to admit that because that includes Victor. And in the end, Victor is the one who saved us.

NATE. Why did I get into the van?
God.
I think about that a lot.
Because my wife did?
Because her new friend followed her?
Because I didn't want to get left behind?
Because I was curious.
And I did not want to get left behind
And because she had this new mysterious friend.

MARK. Victor and I met through a mutual friend.
And I wasn't looking to be in a relationship.
I was just doing my thing.
But after two days, I just knew that he was going to be in my life for a long time.
It's weird.

VICTOR. The very first time I saw him, I thought he was praying! We were at this mutual friend's BBQ, and we all sat down at these big picnic tables to eat.
And he bowed his head like this.
And I thought. Wow. This guy is religious. That's interesting.
Although, it turns out he had a migraine headache and the sun was hurting his eyes and he was trying to will his headache away.

A form of prayer but not the kind I had assumed.
Of course, an hour later the migraine had gotten much worse and he was puking into a bush. I went to help him, even though we hadn't been introduced, and he was so sick that he had no guile, you know, there was no mask. He wasn't embarrassed either, he just needed someone to help him. So I helped him get home and got him some painkillers and a wet washcloth to put over his eyes and I turned out all his lights and closed all the curtains. And I told him I would check in on him the next day. Bring him chicken noodle soup if he wanted it.

Then I totally forgot all about him! For like three months.
It was a really busy time.

MARK. I was totally waiting for my chicken noodle soup!

VICTOR. But then we met again at that same friend's house and he was like "Where's my soup?" and we laughed and we have been together ever since. Sometimes you meet someone and that familiarity is just there right away. Like you've known them for a long time even though you haven't.

MARK. I was grateful, you know.
But it wasn't until I met him the second time that I was like, whoa.
He is really attractive.
You know, gorgeous.

VICTOR. Well, I'm glad I got to live up to my name. You have a name like Victor and it's a hard idea to live up to. That's a funny thing about names. A funny thing.
It was an incredible
endorphin rush.
Seeing him ALIVE.

>   *(Silence.*
>
>   *Silence.)*

She says she saw children there.
I can only tell you about what I saw.
And all I saw was three lost and hungry adults
sitting on a mattress.

That's it.
They did find the remains of Ray and June.
In the ashes, on the stones.

SARAH. When you put your hands together like this, you can almost feel the perfect symmetry of your body.

MARK. It looks like you are praying.

SARAH. I am just breathing.

There was a girl.
And she was dancing.

MARK. I think. I think you imagined that.

NATE. After all, there are some things that we can never know,
but my wife has become obsessed with the girl she believes she saw in the bonfire.
She spends her free time checking out lists of missing children to see if she can find her.
To prove that she existed.
To apologize to the parents.
She describes the girl in detail.

Brown, curly hair and about four foot one.
She had round cheeks and big bones and she liked to dance.

According to my wife.

End of Play

We Are Proud to Present a Presentation About the Herero of Namibia, Formerly Known as South West Africa, From the German Südwestafrika, Between the Years 1884-1915

Jackie Sibblies Drury

About the Collaboration
Proud to Present Big Ideas in Small Spaces

Soho Rep. is a very big small theater. The physical space is extremely intimate—accommodating just 73 theatergoers each night, and they have only six full-time staff members. At the same time, their outstanding reputation and the significant contributions they've made to the field far exceed the small size of the company. In the past two seasons alone, their mainstage productions have been recognized with five Obie Awards, a special 2014 Drama Desk Award citing "nearly four decades of artistic distinction, innovative production and provocative play selection," and the *Village Voice's* 2014 Best Theater for New American Plays.

Recent productions include *generations* by debbie tucker green, the World Premiere of Branden Jacobs-Jenkins's *An Octoroon,* the New York Premiere of *Marie Antoinette* by David Adjmi, the World Premiere of *A Public Reading of an Unproduced Screenplay About the Death of Walt Disney* by Lucas Hnath, Nature Theater of Oklahoma's 10-hour epic *Life and Times: Episodes 1-4,* the New York Premiere of Jackie Sibblies Drury's *We Are Proud to Present a Presentation...* and the World Premiere of Annie Baker's adaptation of *Uncle Vanya.*

§

I might be scarred by my experience of having a play produced at Soho Rep. I'm really worried—terrified, actually—that I won't have such an artistically fulfilling process again. I cannot imagine a more ideal process, which is an insane thing to say, since there was a natural disaster (Hurricane Sandy) in the middle of it. Sarah Benson was both incredibly nurturing and shockingly hands off during our process; she was completely available to me and to the rest of my collaborators, for thoughts, for advice, for insight. She spent so much time crafting the reception of the play, thinking of the make-up of the audience, talking with us about their experience entering and leaving the theater. And yet she made no demands. Ever. There was not one time where I felt she made a single suggestion that was not fully in support of the work we were trying to make, and not in consideration of any agenda outside of our attempt to make the best production we could. When she was with us, Sarah was with us, and she advocated for the play. Which was breathtaking, to me. To have such integrity, as an artist, as a producer, as an institution—it's breathtaking.

—Jackie Sibblies Drury

Mission Statement: Soho Rep.

Soho Rep. is a leading hub for innovative contemporary theater in New York City. The company is dedicated to artistic excellence by supporting distinctive, diverse and pioneering theater. They empower artists to make their boldest work and invite audiences to share in that intimate and transformative live experience. Soho Rep. creates a dynamic context for both artists and audiences that promotes and sustains conversation in the field—and the cultural fabric of the city.

About the Author

Jackie Sibblies Drury's play *We Are Proud to Present a Presentation...* received its world premiere at Victory Gardens Theater, and had its New York premiere at Soho Rep. Other productions of the play include The Matrix Theatre Company, InterAct Theatre Company, Undermain Theatre, Woolly Mammoth Theatre Company, Company One and ArtsEmerson, Available Light, and the Bush Theatre. Drury's play *Social Creatures* was commissioned by Trinity Repertory Company, premiering in March 2013. Her work has been developed at the Sundance Institute Theatre Lab, Berkeley Repertory Theatre's Ground Floor, New York Theatre Workshop, the Lark Play Development Center, Prelude.11, the Bay Area Playwrights Festival, the IGNITION Festival, Soho Rep.'s Writer/Director Lab, and The Civilians' R&D Group. Drury is a New York Theatre Workshop Usual Suspect. She was a Van Lier Fellow at New Dramatists, and is the inaugural recipient of the 2012-2014 Jerome New York Fellowship at the Lark.

Cast of Characters

ACTOR 6/BLACK WOMAN

ACTOR 1/WHITE MAN

ACTOR 2/BLACK MAN

ACTOR 3/ANOTHER WHITE MAN

ACTOR 4/ANOTHER BLACK MAN

ACTOR 5/SARAH

All are young, somewhere in their 20s, ish, and they should seem young, open, skilled, playful, and perhaps, at times, a little foolish.

Settings

A large space, a gathering place, a theater:
The Presentation.
In these sections, the performers have an awareness of the audience, or at least An Audience. We see glimpses of a Presentation, occurring in a theatrical space.

And a smaller space, a private place, a rehearsal:
The Process.
In these sections we see glimpses of a rehearsal through the 4th wall. The performers experiment without self-consciousness, rehearsing in the space without an audience, perhaps a bare-bones version of the actual space.

The Presentation sections and the Process sections are distinct at the start, but over time process becomes presentation, the spaces aren't what they appear to be, and boundaries are broken.

The transitions between these sections should be quick & seamless. Each scene begins in the middle of things, and the play is performed continuously, cohesively, without breaks.

Production Notes

About the punctuation:

A slash (/) indicates the interruption of the next line of text.

A set of brackets indicate that the line can either be spoken or, um, indicated.

Line breaks indicate a subtle, internal shift—not a pause.

A dash is an interruption—either by oneself or by someone else.

About the music:

There is music in this text.

Music and rhythm should exist where they are indicated, and it should be added throughout.

About the time:

One can think of the presentation scenes as glimpses from a longer and complete presentation, one that uses a variety of theatrical styles. I've provided the years, roughly, that each scene is representative of. Or, we could say, the year in which the letter that is being presented was written. Please only use these years if / as they are helpful.

About the violence:

The performance calls for real contact, as opposed to realistic contact. Actions that might make an audience wonder how they were done will work against the play. A slap to the shoulder, a loose rope around the neck: these things will feel much more dangerous than elaborate choreography or invisible rigging, in the end.

We Are Proud to Present a Presentation About the Herero of Namibia, Formerly Known as South West Africa, From the German Südwestafrika, Between the Years 1884-1915

by Jackie Sibblies Drury

Prologue:
Intro, Lecture, Lecture/Presentation, Presentation

(ACTOR 6 enters.)

ACTOR 6. Sorry.
We're all ready?

> *(ACTOR 6 greets the audience,*
> *probably with some warmth and casualness,*
> *definitely with some nervousness.*
>
> ACTOR 5 *hands her a stack of note cards.)*

ACTOR 6. Great.

> *(ACTOR 6 glances at the cards, retrieves a pen,*
> *and crosses "Greet Audience" off the list:)*

ACTOR 6. *(To herself:)* Greet audience.
Fire speech.

> *(ACTOR 6 gives the fire speech, complete with cell phone speech, etc.)*

ACTOR 6. *(To herself:)* Fire speech.
Special Announcements.

> *(ACTOR 6 makes any special announcements. She probably reads them off*
> *her papers/cards.*
> *If there are no theater-related special announcements, perhaps there is a drink*
> *special at a nearby bar?*
> *A sale at the store down the street?)*

ACTOR 6. *(To herself:)* Special Announcements.
Ok.

> *(ACTOR 6 reads a prepared speech.*
> *She also interrupts herself to clarify,*

talking directly to the audience.
The lines that are read are italicized,
the parts that are said are not.)

ACTOR 6. *Hello. Thank you for coming.*
Oh, I already did that.
Welcome to our presentation.
We have prepared a lecture to precede the presentation because we feel that you would benefit from some background information so as to give our presentation a greater amount of context.
Yeah. Ok, so, the lecture's a lecture but it's not a lecture lecture.
We made it fun.
Ish.
Sort of.
Anyway.
The lecture's duration should last approximately five minutes.
It might be ten. I'm bad at time.
Because, you know, what's happening is the important thing, it doesn't matter when it happens, or how long it happens for, it's that it's happening. Am I right?

> *(Nervous laugh.)*

This is happening.

> *(Nervous laugh.)*

Ok.
In this lecture— Um… Wait, what?

> *(She flips through the cards.*
> ACTOR 5 *might try to feed her the lines.)*

ACTOR 6. Ok.
(To the ensemble and the audience at the same time:) "We" forgot to write in the part "we" agreed "we'd" write about the overview.
So…
(To the audience:) Ok. So, there's like a lecture that's only sort of a lecture and then we did this thing that is kind of like an overview before the lecture, which is before the presentation.
Does that make sense?
Ok.
Yeah…
I think I'm just going to skip some of this stuff, you know,
since it seems it doesn't actually say what we all agreed that it should say

Even though we went through a lot to figure out how to do this and introduce it properly, but this introduction isn't what it's supposed to be so…
This is what we're doing: Lecture, Overview, Presentation. Super fun, Great.
(To herself:) Skip skip skip.

Helping me to present the lecture to you is our ensemble of actors.
Our ensemble of actors:

ACTOR 1. I'm an actor.

ACTOR 2. I'm an actor.

ACTOR 3. I'm an actor.

ACTOR 4. I'm an actor.

ACTOR 5. I'm an / actor.

ACTOR 6. *And I am an actor.*

ACTORS 1, 2, 3, 4, 5. Hello.

ACTOR 6. I'm also kind of the artistic director of our ensemble, so.
Ok.
In this presentation, which has already started, I know, *I will be playing the part of*
Black Woman.
I am also black, in real life, which you might find confusing.
Please try to think of it like this:
Black Woman is just the name of the character I'm playing.
This actor will be referred to as Black Man.
This actor will be referred to as White Man.
This actor will be referred to as Another Black Man.
This actor will be referred to as Another White Man.
This actor will—

(To ACTOR 5.*)* Actually, we haven't really explained you yet. And they won't
get it, so…
(To the audience:) Just ignore her for right now.
OK.
Another White Man…because this is true in real life and in this
lecture and subsequent
presentation.
Now, without further ado, we present to you a lecture about Namibia.

> *(A lecture shared by the group:*
> *a map, a Powerpoint presentation.)*

ACTOR 6. *A Lecture About Namibia.*
Located in the southernmost section of the African continent,
Namibia is bordered by:
Angola,
Zambia,
Botswana,
Zimbabwe,
South Africa,
and the Atlantic Ocean.
Let me repeat that.
Or—you guys get it: Blah, blah, blah, blah, blah, and the Atlantic Ocean.

Some other facts about Namibia.
Namibia's Official Language is English:

ACTOR 4. Hello.

ACTOR 6. *Namibia's Recognized Regional Languages are Afrikaans:*

ACTOR 1. Hallo.

ACTOR 6. *Oshiwambo:*

ACTOR 2. Ongiini.

ACTOR 6. *and German:*

ACTOR 3. Guten Tag.

ACTOR 6. *There is a reason for this. An historical reason.*
This is really what the lecture is about.
An Explanation For The Recognized Languages In Namibia.
Let us begin with Oshiwambo.

ACTOR 2. Oshiwambo—

ACTOR 6. *Oshiwambo is spoken by a tribe called the Herero:*
The Herero:

ACTORS 1, 2, 3, 4, 5. *(To the audience, with a helpful smile:)* The Her-er-oh.

ACTOR 6. Actually, Oshiwambo was originally spoken by the Ovambo people, but we aren't really talking about them at all so... The Herero.

ACTORS 1, 2, 3, 4, 5. The Herero.

ACTOR 6. *Another of Namibia's languages is English—*

ACTOR 4. English.

ACTOR 6. *English is spoken in Namibia because the English expanded their colonial holdings during World War One—*

ACTOR 3. —World War One.

ACTOR 6. *That is the reason why English is spoken in Namiba.*
The third of Namibia's languages is Afrikaans—

ACTOR 1. —Afrikaans—

ACTOR 6. *—Afrikaans is spoken in Namibia*
because Afrikaans speakers needed to expand their ranches into Namibia
settling permanently around the turn of the 19th century—

ACTOR 4. —that's 1900?

ACTOR 6. 1800.

    (The slide is wrong.)

ACTOR 5. [Oh, fuck.]

(ACTOR 5 fixes the slide.)

ACTOR 3. 1800.

(Ok. Now they start to get it together. They're getting into the section that they rehearsed the most.)

ACTOR 6. *Around the turn of the 19th century, before Namibia became a German colony:*

ACTOR 1. Südwestafrika!

ACTOR 6. *—which is the name for the colony in German—*

ACTOR 4. Oshindowishi!

ACTOR 6. *—which is the name for German in Oshiwambo.*
Namibia became a German colony in 1884.
It stopped being a German colony in 1915, when it was taken by the English:

ACTORS 1, 2, 3, 4. During World War One!

ACTOR 6. *—but between 1884 and 1915, when Namibia was—*

ACTOR 1. Südwestafrika!

ACTOR 6. *—which is where—*which is when?—

(ACTOR 5 disagrees with her when, saying "where.")

ACTOR 6. *Which is when we are concentrating today.*
We have access to:

ACTOR 4. Postcards!

ACTOR 1. Karte!

ACTOR 5. Letters!

ACTOR 3. Stukken van Document!

ACTOR 2. Ombapila!

ACTOR 6. *—a cache of letters from German troops stationed in German South West Africa between the years 1884 and 1915.*
But before we present the presentation of those letters, we have the overview.
Which we don't have an introduction for. So.
This is going to be the overview.
Or, should we say it?

(The ACTORS agree: "Yeah." or "I guess?" or "Yes yes keep going." Etc.)

ACTOR 6. Yeah—let's all say it together.

(A fast-paced cartoonish overview—a romp. They've like actually really memorized this part. They move through it very quickly, at times frantically. If they have simple puppets/illustrations/costumes, ACTOR 5 made the puppets/illustrations/costumes. There's probably slapstick, a prat fall, some hijinks. The announcement of each year is preceded by a sound: punctuation, the

ding of a bell. And with each ding, a brief comic tableau that sums up what was said about the previous year.)

ALL. An Overview of German South West Africa Between the Years 1884 and 1915.

ACTOR 6. 1884

ACTOR 1. Germany is in charge.

ACTOR 3. Sort of. All the tribes are actively not saying they hate us.

ACTORS 2 & 4. Hey Germany. We aren't *saying* we hate you.

ACTOR 6. 1885

ACTOR 2. Agreements are reached with tribal leaders—

ACTOR 1. Germany is totally in charge.

ACTOR 2. Well, some of the tribal leaders.

ACTOR 6. 1886

ACTOR 1. Germany is like actually in charge.

ACTOR 3. Germany is telling other people that they're in charge.

ACTOR 1. Germany is like basically actually in charge.

ACTOR 6. 1887

ACTOR 1. The Germans are impressed by one tribe in particular, the Herero.

ACTORS 2, 3, 4, 5. The Her-er-oh.

ACTOR 6. The Herero.

ACTOR 2. So tall.

ACTOR 4. So muscular.

ACTOR 1. The Germans put—

ACTORS 2, 3, 4, 5. The Her-er-oh.

ACTOR 1. —in charge of all / the tribes—

ACTOR 6. The Germans put the Herero in charge of all the tribes in German South West Africa.

ACTORS 2 & 4. Hurray!

ACTOR 6. 1888

ACTOR 2. The Herero are in charge.

ACTOR 3. Sort of.

ACTOR 6. 1889

ACTOR 1. The Germans are kind of over the Herero.

ACTOR 3. Over the Herero.

ACTOR 2. So childish and ungrateful.

ACTOR 4. So impudent and unwashed.

ACTOR 6. 1890

ACTOR 1. The Germans put the Hottentots—

ACTOR 3. The Nama.

ACTOR 1. The Nama in control. The Germans give a bunch of Herero cattle to the Nama

ACTOR 3. Herero cattle to the Nama.

ACTOR 2. Which, like sucks.

ACTOR 4. Because the Herero love their cows.

ACTOR 2. We do.

ACTOR 6. 1891

ACTOR 1. The Germans are sort of over the Hotten—Nama

ACTOR 3. Over the Nama.

ACTOR 6. 1892

ACTOR 1. The Germans put the Herero back in control.
They give a bunch of Nama cattle to the Herero.

ACTOR 3. Nama cattle to the Herero.

ACTOR 4. Which is sort of stealing.

ACTOR 2. But they were our cows to begin with.

ACTOR 6. 1893

ACTOR 4. The Nama fight the Herero.

ACTOR 2. The Herero fight the Nama

ACTOR 1. The Germans take the cattle—

ACTOR 3. —take care of the cattle—

ACTOR 1. —care for the cattle—

ACTOR 6. 1894

ACTORS 1, 2, 3, 4, 5. Tenuous Peace.

> *(Tableau: Tenuous Peace*
> *Smile: ding!)*

ACTOR 6. 1895

ACTOR 1. The Germans decide to build a railroad into the interior.

ACTORS 1, 2, 3, 4, 5. More resources for everyone.

> (*Tableau: Fiscal Success
> Bigger smile: ding!*)

ACTOR 6. 1896

ACTOR 1. We are building that railroad.

ACTOR 3. We are building that railroad.

ACTOR 2. *We* are building that railroad.

ACTOR 6. 1897

ACTOR 1. We are failing.

ACTOR 3. We are failing.

ACTOR 2. We are building that railroad.

ACTOR 6. 1898

ACTOR 1. We are really failing.

ACTOR 3. Not good.

ACTOR 2. We are building that railroad.

ACTOR 6. 1899

ACTOR 1. We are fucked.

ACTOR 3. So fucked.

ACTOR 2. We are building that fucking railroad.

ACTOR 6. 1900

ACTOR 1. German settlers are getting poorer and poorer—

ACTOR 3. —and madder and madder, and the German government—

ACTOR 1. —is getting madder and madder and poorer and poorer.

ACTOR 3. Because of the fucking railroad.

ACTOR 2. We are building that—

ACTOR 6. 1901

ACTOR 1. Germany tinkers a little with the law.

ACTOR 3. If you are German and a cow wanders on to your land:

ACTOR 4. It's yours!

ACTOR 3. If you try to take a cow from a German and you aren't a German:

ACTOR 2. You get hanged.

ACTOR 1. Problem solved.

ACTOR 6. 1902

ACTOR 1. Germany tinkers a little more with the law.

ACTOR 3. If you are German and you see land that doesn't belong to a German:

ACTOR 4. It's yours!

ACTOR 3. If you contest a German land claim and you aren't German:

ACTOR 2. You get hanged.

ACTOR 3. If you are German and you see cattle on the land you have just claimed:

ACTOR 4. The cattle are yours!

ACTOR 3. If you steal cattle from a German and you aren't German:

ACTOR 2. You get hanged.

ACTOR 6. 1903

ACTOR 4. The Nama rebel against German rule.
It doesn't end well.

ACTOR 3. But it does end quickly.

ACTOR 6. 1904

ACTOR 2. The Herero rebel against German Rule.

ACTOR 1. The Herero are taught a lesson.

ACTOR 3. The Herero are made examples of.

ACTOR 1. The General Issues The Extermination Order.

ACTOR 6. 1905

ACTOR 1. The General Issues The Extermination Order.

ACTOR 3. The Germans imprison thousands of Herero in labor camps.

ACTOR 6. 1906

ACTOR 1. The General Issues The Extermination Order.

ACTOR 3. The Germans force thousands of Herero into the desert.

ACTOR 6. 1907

ACTOR 1. The General Issues The Extermination Order.

ACTOR 3. The Germans erect a wall to keep them in the desert.

ACTOR 6. 1908
The Extermination order has been issued.
The labor camps have closed.
Eighty Percent of the Herero have been Exterminated.

Those that survived the camps
were used as a source of unpaid labor by the German settlers.
And in this way, the German regime continued:

1909

1910

1911

1912

1913

1914

1915.

And then. And only then do the English intervene.

ACTOR 3. World War One.

ACTOR 6. And there you have it.
A history of German Colonial Rule in Namibia.

> *(Big finish:*
> *The formal beginning to the presentation.)*

ALL. We Are Proud to Present a Presentation About the Herero of Namibia, Formerly Known as South West Africa, From the German Südwestafrika, Between the Years 1884 and 1915.

Scene: Process

> *(And BAM: we're in the rehearsal room.*
> *The mood is instantly more casual, but no one takes a breath because everyone is speaking quickly, overlapping, interrupting, having multiple convos at once, moving things around, getting a snack, checking his phone, consulting the research, etc, etc, etc.)*

ACTOR 6. And, what if we ended it right there?

ACTORS 1, 2, 3, 4. What? / Wait. / Whoa. / Umm...?

ACTOR 5. Why?

ACTOR 6. Because. I don't know if we actually need to read the letters.

ACTOR 1 & ACTOR 5. Why not.

ACTOR 6. I think the overview might be enough.

ACTOR 5. But what about my song?

ACTOR 1. I thought the presentation was presenting the letters.

ACTOR 4. That's what we're doing, aren't we?

ACTOR 6. I don't think we should present the letters.

ACTOR 5. You always do this.

ACTOR 6. Do what?

ACTOR 3. Oh come on.

ACTOR 1. You always kind of...take over?

ACTOR 6. I'm not taking over.

ACTOR 5.	**ACTOR 3.**
I want to read the letters.	You're kind of taking over.

ACTOR 4. I thought that was what we were doing.

ACTOR 6. Have you read them?

ACTOR 1.	**ACTOR 5.**
I've read them.	Yes.

ACTOR 3. Me too.

ACTOR 2. All of them?

ACTOR 1.	**ACTOR 5.**
Most of them.	Yes.

ACTOR 6. I don't think we should just stand there and / read these letters.

ACTOR 1. *(To* ACTOR 6*:)*	
We're not going to just	**ACTOR 5.**
stand there.	But I've read the letters and—

ACTOR 3. *(To* ACTOR 6*:)* I don't know if this is your decision to make.

ACTOR 1. *(To* ACTOR 6*:)* It's theater, you know? / You don't just stand there.

ACTOR 5. *(To* ACTOR 6*:)* I thought we were an ensemble.

ACTOR 6. *(To* ACTOR 5*:)* We *are* an ensemble.

ACTOR 2. *(To* ACTOR 1*:)*	**ACTOR 5.**
Well, it's a presentation,	So then—
it's not theater.	

ACTOR 6. *(To* ACTORS 3 / 5*:)* And as a member of our ensemble / I think I have the right to express an opinion.

ACTOR 1. *(To* ACTOR 2*:)* But it's a presentation in a theater.

ACTOR 2. *(To* ACTOR 1*:)*	**ACTOR 3.** *(To* ACTOR 6*:)*
Right.	Right.

ACTOR 1. So it's theater.

ACTOR 4. *(To* ACTOR 1*:)* Well I don't know if it is.

ACTOR 3.
You should absolutely
express an opinion.

ACTOR 1.
What?

ACTOR 6. I know.

ACTOR 4. I don't know if it's theater just because it's *in* a theater.

ACTOR 5. And I have the right to express my opinion too, don't I?

ACTOR 6.
Yes, you can—

ACTOR 1.
Wait, what?

ACTOR 3. This is what I'm saying.

ACTOR 2. *(To* ACTOR 4:*)* He's not asking like theoretically, he's actually *asking*.

ACTOR 3. *(To* ACTOR 5:*)* Why are you asking her for permission to express an opinion?

ACTOR 4. *(Topping everyone:)* Ok, but, regardless, whatever it is that we're trying to do,
I don't understand why we're not reading the letters.

ACTOR 5. *(To herself—a grumble?)* I'm not asking anyone for permission.

ACTOR 3. Well, not all of us are saying that we're not reading the letters.

ACTOR 6. I am saying that I think that the letters are.

ACTOR 3. What?

ACTOR 6. Ok. I'm saying that I think that they're all…kind of the same.

ACTOR 1.
No way.

ACTOR 3.
Oh come on.

ACTOR 4.
Really?

ACTOR 5. But they're by different people.

ACTOR 6. They're all soldiers.

ACTOR 5. Yeah, different soldiers.

ACTOR 6. They're all German soldiers and I'm saying
like dramatically they're all doing the same thing.

ACTOR 5. But I had to like *pick them up*.

ACTOR 6.
I know.

ACTOR 1.
I think that they're different.

ACTOR 5.
Like at the *library*.

ACTOR 2.
They aren't that different.

ACTOR 6.
And it's amazing that you
found them—

ACTOR 1.
But they're different people.

ACTOR 5.	**ACTOR 4.**
Like the *weird* part of the library.	Different people doing the same thing isn't that different.

ACTOR 6. I just don't think we should present them.

ACTOR 2. I don't think so either.

ACTOR 1.	**ACTOR 5.**
You didn't even read them.	Seriously?

ACTOR 2.	**ACTOR 6.**
I read some of them.	It's like letter after letter / soldier after soldier—

ACTOR 1. But they're / the whole center of the piece—I just don't understand why we wouldn't use them.

ACTOR 3. Shouldn't / we try something out? Before we just—

ACTOR 5. But every person is special, can't we agree that every person is—

ACTOR 4. But if we aren't going to read the letters what are we going to do?

ACTOR 3. I really think we should read the letters.

ACTOR 6. Fine. Ok.
You want to read the letters?
Let's read alllll of the letters. Right now.
And then we can decide.

ACTOR 5. Great. Here.

ACTOR 1. Dear—um—uhhh.

ACTOR 6. Read it.

ACTOR 5. He's reading it.

ACTOR 1. I don't know how to pronounce this.

   (It doesn't say Sarah.)

ACTOR 6. Sarah.

ACTOR 1. But it's not an S—it's like a—

ACTOR 6. Just say Sarah. Read the letter.

ACTOR 5. Just say Sarah.

ACTOR 1. Dear Sarah—Dear Sarah,
I miss you like the July sapling misses April rains. And I—

ACTOR 6. *(Sound of disgust.)*

ACTOR 1. But—

ACTOR 6. Seriously, *(another sound of disgust)*.

ACTOR 5. But I think—

ACTOR 6. Don't you see what I'm talking about?

ACTORS 1 & 5. No.

ACTOR 6. It's just so. There's like no violence, there's no anger there's no—

ACTOR 5. Well, it's just like the beginning of—

ACTOR 3. What about this one?
Ok. Dear—um—

ACTOR 6. Just say it's Sarah.

(It really doesn't say Sarah.)

ACTOR 3. I really don't think it's pronounced—

ACTOR 6. They're all the same—the names aren't important.
Let's just say they all start Dear Sarah. Okay?

ACTOR 5. Fine. All the women are Sarah.

ACTOR 3. But—

ACTOR 6. Just read it.

ACTOR 3. That doesn't—

ACTOR 5. Just read it.

ACTOR 3. Ok. God.
Dear Sarah—

ACTOR 5. Omigod.
Wait, can I be Sarah?
No—I'm Sarah.

ACTOR 3. Oh—ok.

ACTOR 5. I am Sarah.

ACTOR 3. Um. Right, ok.
Dear Sarah,
Once night has fallen, I look to the sky and think of you. The stars are—

ACTOR 6. Just like the other ones.

ACTOR 5. No it's not—

ACTOR 4. Wait wait wait—ok guys—listen to this—
Dear—

ACTOR 6. Sarah.

ACTOR 5. I'm Sarah.

ACTOR 4. I know. Dear Sarah, it has been so long since—

ACTOR 6. Blah blah, miss. Blah blah, love.

ACTOR 1. Dear Sarah,

ACTOR 5. I'm Sarah.

ACTOR 1. Tell me of our little—

ACTOR 6. Blah blah. Children. Family. Who cares?

ACTOR 3. Dear Sarah, The camp is not—

ACTOR 6. Home. Warmth. Comfort. They're all the same.

ACTOR 4. Dear Sarah, We have been apart for so long—

ACTOR 6. Whatever. Distance. They're all the same.

ACTOR 5. No they're—

ACTOR 6. They're basically all the same.

ACTOR 5. Sure, basically, but—

Scene: Presentation [1884]

ACTOR 6. Here we have White Man:

WHITE MAN. Guten-tag.

ACTOR 6. A young German Soldier
leaving the mining town of Zwickau for the first time
Traveling for miles and miles—

ANOTHER WHITE MAN. —kilometers and kilometers—

ACTOR 6. Traveling with thousands and thousands of fellow soldiers:

ANOTHER WHITE MAN. Guten-tag.

ACTOR 6. And they travel for weeks
Over land
Over sea
Until finally they arrive at their new home:

WHITE MAN & ANOTHER WHITE MAN. Südwestafrika.

ACTOR 6. And survey their new territory.
To the North:

WHITE MAN. The Interior

SARAH. Das Innenraum

ANOTHER WHITE MAN. Land and materials to be discovered and developed and exported

ACTOR 6. To the South:

WHITE MAN. The Pasture

SARAH. Die Weide

ANOTHER WHITE MAN. Prairie, grasses as far as the eye can see, grazing lands for millions of cattle

ACTOR 6. To the East:

WHITE MAN. The Desert

SARAH. Die Wüste

ANOTHER WHITE MAN. Kilometers and kilometers

WHITE MAN. And miles and miles

ANOTHER WHITE MAN. Dry, hot, arid, barren

WHITE MAN. Unforgiving and inhospitable

ACTOR 6. And to the West:

WHITE MAN. The Ocean

SARAH. Der Ozean

ANOTHER WHITE MAN. The Ocean

ACTOR 6. And all of this:

WHITE MAN & ANOTHER WHITE MAN. Südwestafrika.

ACTOR 6. Is now considered Germany.

SARAH. Deutschland.

ACTOR 6. And from this place that is so unfamiliar,
That has been given the name of his home,
Our young German Soldier:

WHITE MAN. Guten-tag.

ACTOR 6. Writes a letter to his young wife, Sarah:

SARAH. Ach! Liebe!

ACTOR 6. Who waits for him, back in his familiar home,
A home he many never see again:

WHITE MAN. Dear Sarah.
Today is the first of many days
I will spend away from you.
I will travel far away today.
I will mail this letter if I arrive—
I will arrive, and
I will mail this letter to you.
I will think of you always, and
I will be my best, so that
I will know that when I return

I will be the man you have imagined
I will become.

Scene: Process

ACTOR 6. Great. Wow— Really Great.
Moving on.

ACTOR 1. Wait—

ACTOR 6. What?

ACTOR 1. Well, I kind of need to process that?

ACTOR 6. Process what?

ACTOR 1. It's just, I sort of dove in, you know?

ACTOR 6. OK...

ACTOR 1. And it's like, I know that I found something, something real, but it's like, I'm not sure what came across, or—

ACTOR 5. I thought it was kind of sad.

> *(A passive aggressive, fake helpful exchange.*
> ACTOR 1 *&* ACTOR 5 *have had this fight before...*
> *Whatever. Each actor thinks he/she is being the bigger person by helping the other, who is a total idiot.*
> *Everyone else should want to climb out a window.)*

ACTOR 1. Sad? Really?

ACTOR 5. *Kind* of.
Don't worry, we'll find it in improv.

ACTOR 1. No, but I think he's being romantic.

ACTOR 5. Is he?

ACTOR 1. Yeah.

ACTOR 5. Really?

ACTOR 1. Yeah.

ACTOR 5. Huh.

ACTOR 1. He's being romantic and it's like he's reassuring her.

ACTOR 5. Oh, I see.

ACTOR 1. You get it?

ACTOR 5. Totally.
Just, a question?

ACTOR 1. Sure.

ACTOR 5. Why does *she* need to be reassured?

ACTOR 1. Why?

ACTOR 5. Yeah.

ACTOR 1. Um, isn't that kind of obvious?

ACTOR 5. I don't think it is, actually.

ACTOR 1. Well, it's like I thought since he was going to this like distant land, and stuff, that she would be worried about him, you know?

ACTOR 5. Hmm—

ACTOR 1. But that's just one idea.

ACTOR 5. Yeah—

ACTOR 1. Like I know if someone that I loved was going off to maybe *die* I'd be like, worried.

ACTOR 5. Totally.

ACTOR 1. Right?

ACTOR 5. I totally agree.

ACTOR 1. Yeah.

ACTOR 5. But I'm just wondering why you're like *assuming* that she's the only one who's worried.

ACTOR 1. I'm not assuming anything.

ACTOR 5. No, you kind of are, I think?

ACTOR 1. Okay.

ACTOR 5. I'm just saying maybe he should be worried.

ACTOR 1. Great. Well, thanks for the *note*—

ACTOR 5. OK.

ACTOR 1. But I think I got it.

ACTOR 5. You know what?
All I was trying to say was that your reading didn't totally work for me.
That's all.
But I'm only one person. What did everybody else think?

ACTOR 6. I thought it was fine.

ACTOR 5. You did.

ACTOR 6. I thought it was romantic.

ACTOR 1. I thought so too.

ACTOR 6. And scared.

ACTOR 1. Scared.

ACTOR 6. Yeah, like he was scared.
He doesn't know what he's facing, he's going to this crazy place that is so different from where he grew up—

ACTOR 3. I keep hearing that this guy is going to this place that is *so different*.
But what *I'm* wondering is *where* he grew up.
Like *what* is this *different place* so *different from*.

ACTOR 6. That's a good point.

ACTOR 3. And it's like, from what you guys have been talking about
it's like I think I'm going to be like the Best Friend right?
Since you know.
It seems like a decision has already been made that he's the leading man.

ACTOR 6. Oh, I don't know that we've decided that.

ACTOR 3. No no it seems like you *did* decide that *and* it seems like pretty final. So.
It's fine.
I'm just trying to get a sense of where I'm building my Best Friend character from. I'm perfectly comfortable with a character part. Obviously.

ACTOR 1. You're so good at character roles.

ACTOR 3. I know. I do. I know I am.
So. Where did he grow up?

ACTOR 6 & ACTOR 1. Germany.

ACTOR 3. No, *where*. *Where*. The *streets*, the *city*. The *smells*, the *quality of light*.
Now, for my part, I know that I grew up in...Cologne.

ACTOR 2. They pronounce it Köln in German.

> *(Beat.)*

ACTOR 3. I though we weren't doing accents.

ACTOR 6. We're not.

ACTOR 3. Because I can do a German accent. I have / access to several regional accents in Germany, several—

ACTOR 6. We aren't doing accents / we agreed that we aren't doing accents.
No accents.
No one is doing an accent.
We don't need the song.
We don't need the accents.
Oh my god.

ACTOR 5. I can do a great / "Edelweiss":

> *(ACTOR 5 sings, nay, performs, "Edelweiss."
> Everything is kind of a cacophonous mess.)*

ACTOR 2. All I'm saying is if he was from Cologne, wouldn't he call it Köln? Why would he call it Cologne / if he was from Cologne.

ACTOR 3. Because he's not a German German, but he's basically German.

ACTOR 2. If you didn't know that Köln was the right / way to say Cologne there's no shame in that.
I don't know that you knew that.
I know that Cologne is Köln but I'm not sure that you knew Cologne is Köln.
I know we aren't doing accents
I know we aren't doing accents because
I can do a German accent
I can do an African accent
I can do an African accent while speaking German: Ich bin ein Berliner.

ACTOR 3. Of course I knew that: Cologne is Köln Cologne is Köln.
Everybody knows that. But we aren't doing accents
I'm not doing a German accent
You aren't doing an African accent
We aren't doing accents
We aren't doing accents because
if we were doing accents I would be doing an excellent German accent
A regional Rhineland accent: Spreken-ze deutsch?

ACTOR 6. Are you finished?

(Big Finish for ACTOR 5's *"Edelweiss.")*

ACTOR 6. Are you finished?
Because that isn't what this is about.
It's about.

ACTOR 1. It's about touching something real.

(All think about reality.)

ACTOR 5. Like, the horror of our capacity to casually inflict suffering.

ACTOR 1. Well—?

ACTOR 6. Alright. So make it real.
Let's go back to the letter.
Take it from "I will be my best—" when you're ready.

ACTOR 1. Great.
But.

ACTOR 6. Yes?

ACTOR 1. I'd like to take it from a little bit before that just because well it's like in the middle of—

ACTOR 6. Great. Take it from wherever you need. When you're ready.

ACTOR 1. Great.

I will think of you always, and
I will be my best, so that
I will know that when I return
I will be the man you have imagined
I will become.

ACTOR 6. Great.
OK. Sarah—what's going on with you?

ACTOR 5. He's not—I mean I'm trying to be sad
but he's not giving me anything to work with.

ACTOR 1. But I think the letter is supposed to be romantic—

ACTOR 6. We're working with Sarah right now White Man.
Now, Sarah.

ACTOR 5. Yes.

ACTOR 6. When I'm sad, I always end up thinking about the same thing.
Do you have something like that, Sarah?

ACTOR 5. I think of my cat.

ACTOR 6. Your cat?

ACTOR 5. He's dead.

ACTOR 6. That's sad.

ACTOR 5. Yes it is.

ACTOR 6. Great.
Let's go into the cat.

ACTOR 5. Really?

ACTOR 6. Yes.
White Man—give us the end again.

> (ACTOR 5 *goes into her memory. She is very focused.*
> *She doesn't think about her cat, she becomes The Cat.)*

WHITE MAN. I will think of you always, and
I will be my best, so that
I will know that when I return
I will be the man you have imagined
I will become.

ACTOR 6. Great. Sarah.

> (*She is still The Cat.*)

ACTOR 6. Sarah.
Ok, I think we might need to…push that memory. Ok?

ACTOR 5. But I thought—

ACTOR 6. No, you're doing great.
Ok. I want you to think of your cat as though it were still alive today.

ACTOR 5. But he couldn't be. He'd be like a jillion years old.

ACTOR 6. Well, wouldn't you know it,
the saddest thing that I have ever seen was a really old cat.

    (This is probably a lie.)

ACTOR 5. Really?

ACTOR 6. Yup. It was horrible.
It had arthritis.
I could see its knotted stiffened joins.
It didn't move like a cat.
It couldn't jump.

ACTOR 5. *(Sad face ☹)*

ACTOR 6. It couldn't stalk.

ACTOR 5. *(☹)* Aww—

ACTOR 6. It could only eat and shit and cry.

ACTOR 5. *(☹☹)* Aww noo.

ACTOR 6. *(Needing to go further:)* It was missing an eye.

ACTOR 5. *(Actually horrified:)* Oh my god.

ACTOR 6. More than missing.
One of its eyes was already dead. Decomposing.
It would open its mouth to lick at its decomposing eye
And cry "Feed me or kill me."

ACTOR 5. Oh my god.

ACTOR 6. It would look me dead in the eye—with its one good eye—
and watch me watch it make
yet another agonizing shuffle toward food or death.
And it would gather its remaining strength
to cry "Feed me or kill me."

ACTOR 5. Oh God.

ACTOR 6. And I could do neither.
I could not show the cat kindness.
I was too sad. It made me too sad.
How do you feel?
Sarah, how do you feel?

ACTOR 5. So Sad.

ACTOR 6. Great. Hold on to that.
Let's do another letter.

ACTOR 1. Do you have anything for me?

ACTOR 6. Just keep doing what you're doing.

ACTOR 1. Great.

ACTOR 6. Great.

Scene: Presentation [1887]

ACTOR 6. Here we have Black Man:

BLACK MAN. Ongiini.

ACTOR 6. A Herero tribesman,

ACTORS 1, 3, 4, 5. The He-re-ro.

ACTOR 6. Keeping watch over his cattle as they graze.
As he has done his entire life,
And as his father did before him,
And as his grandfather before him,
And as his great-grandfather before him.
Let's see if he will speak with us:
Ongiini, Herero Man.

BLACK MAN. Ongiini.

ACTOR 6. Wonderful, he is feeling sociable.
Herero Man, please tell us about yourself.

BLACK MAN. I am a Herero man.
I am a herdsman.

ACTOR 6. Are cattle very valuable to you?

BLACK MAN. Why yes, yes they are.
Traditionally, the Herero find value in cattle, in land, and in fire.

ACTOR 6. In fire?

BLACK MAN. Yes, fire.

ACTOR 6. How interesting. Tell us more.

BLACK MAN. Each Herero family has a fire in their backyard.
The Herero believe that this fire contains the souls of their ancestors.
Because of this, they believe that the fire must be kept constantly burning or else their ancestors will be destroyed.

ACTOR 6. Thank you for sharing your traditional belief system with us.
And look!
A second Herero Man is approaching.
Our German Soldier—

WHITE MAN. Guten-tag.

> (ACTOR 6 *watches them interact.*)

ANOTHER BLACK MAN. Ongiini.

BLACK MAN. Ongiini.

WHITE MAN. They greet each other.

> (SARAH *moos as Cow.*)

ANOTHER BLACK MAN. What a beautiful cow.

WHITE MAN. A compliment.

ACTOR 6. Our German Soldier documents his discovery in a letter to Sarah:

SARAH. Ach! Liebe!

WHITE MAN. Dear Sarah.
I continue to be impressed by the members of one tribe in particular: the Herero.
Not only are they tall and well-muscled,
They are more sociable and sweet tempered than I had expected—

Scene: Process

ACTOR 5. Stop. Ok? Just stop.

ACTOR 1. What?

> (ACTOR 5 *is having a full-on freak out.*)

ACTOR 5. I don't know what I'm doing.

ACTOR 6. You're doing great—

ACTOR 5. But I don't know who I am supposed to be. Or what I'm allowed to—

ACTOR 6. It's fine. Let's just go back to the letter, and just be yourself, in the moment—

ACTOR 5. NO. Listen to me. *I don't know what my character is doing.*

ACTOR 6. Ok.

ACTOR 5. I don't know what my perspective is to what's happening,
I don't know what my motivation is,
I don't know what my active verb is,
I don't know what my spine is shaped like,
I don't know what my—my me means—

ACTOR 6. Ok. Ok. Sarah.

ACTOR 5. My name is *not* Sarah.

ACTOR 6. Yes it is—

ACTOR 5. No it's not.

ACTOR 6. Your name is Sarah / and you are a German woman—

ACTOR 5. But I'm not. And I don't know how to do this right.

ACTOR 6. Listen to me—

ACTOR 5. Everything I say is somehow wrong,

ACTOR 6. That's not true.

ACTOR 5. Like I'm not allowed to say anything or do anything, and I don't even know what I'm trying to do—

ACTOR 4. You're telling the story of the Herero Genocide. Ok?

ACTOR 5. But I'm—

ACTOR 4. You're trying. Alright?
Now listen to me.
Your name is Sarah. You are a German Woman.

ACTOR 5. I don't know how to do this.

ACTOR 4. Just listen to me and explore. Ok?

ACTOR 5. Ok.

ACTOR 4. *(Painting the picture for her:)*
You grew up someplace remote. Like…Zwickau.
And you moved South, to Munchen,
And saw the Rhine for the first time,
And the new people
And new strassen
And new streudelschnecken
All so exciting.
But still, you missed your parents, your family, your home.

ACTOR 6. Great.

ACTOR 4. Now who are you?

ACTOR 5. I am Sarah.

ACTOR 4. Right.

ACTOR 6. Well, Hello Sarah.

ACTOR 5/SARAH. Hello.

ACTOR 6. Pleased to meet you, Sarah.

ACTOR 5/SARAH. I am pleased to meet you. Pleased as punch.

ACTOR 6. What a delightful expression, Sarah.

ACTOR 5/SARAH. I say it all the time.

ACTOR 6. Who do you say it to, Sarah?

ACTOR 5/SARAH. I say pleased as punch to my children.

ACTOR 6. Oh, I don't think Sarah has children / maybe she's a teacher, or—

ACTOR 5/SARAH.	**ACTOR 4.**
She has two boys.	[Let her do it.]
Two blond little men.	

ACTOR 6. Sarah.

ACTOR 5/SARAH. There is Heiner. And
Leipzig.

> *(ACTOR 5 adopts a "German" accent. It's not ok.*
> ACTOR 4 *might begin to hum "Edelweiss.")*

SARAH. Ach! Leipzig! Liebe Leipzig!
Ze boyz at school are zo mean to mein liebe Leipzig
Until ein tag, I take Leipzig by the shoulders:

> *(She grabs* ACTOR 4.*)*

SARAH. und I look him in ze eyes
und I say to him,
Leipzig,
look at me Leipzig!

> *(ACTOR 4 becomes Leipzig, with "German" accent.)*

ACTOR 4. *(As Leipzig:)* Ach! Mama! Ze Boyz!

SARAH. I know, Leipzig.
You listen to Mama.
Find ze grossest boy und give him ein shtomp:

ACTOR 4. *(As Leipzig:)* Shtomp!

SARAH. Und ein drang:

ACTOR 4. *(As Leipzig:)* Drang!

SARAH. Und the next day, at kindergarten—

ACTOR 6. Sarah.

SARAH. —Leipzig valked up to ze grossest boy,

> *(ACTOR 4 walks over to* ACTOR 3.*)*

ACTOR 4. *(As Leipzig:)* Hallo, Boy.

ACTOR 3. *(As Grossest Boy:)* Hallo, Leipzig.

SARAH. Und shtomp!

> *(ACTOR 4 "shtomps"* ACTOR 3.*)*

ACTOR 3. *(As Grossest Boy:)* Ach!

SARAH. Und drang!

    *(*ACTOR 4 *"drangs"* ACTOR 3.)*

ACTOR 3. *(As Grossest Boy:)* Ach!

SARAH. Und ze boy cried for heez Muter.

ACTOR 3. *(As Grossest Boy:)* Mama!

SARAH. Und Leipzig lift happily eva afta.

SARAH & ACTOR 4. Yay!!!

ACTOR 6. Guys.

SARAH. *(With a smile:)* Da?

ACTOR 6. We've established that Sarah doesn't have children yet.

ACTOR 5/SARAH. I have decided that I have my Leipzig.

ACTOR 6. But you can't.

ACTOR 4. *(As Leipzig being dragged away:)* Mama!

ACTOR 5. What if only I know?

ACTOR 1. The letters we're reading talk about wanting a family, not having one.

ACTOR 5/SARAH. He is your son too.

ACTOR 6. You can be Sarah without him.

ACTOR 5/SARAH. I want my Leipzig.

ACTOR 1. But—

ACTOR 3. Maybe you *have* lost children.

ACTOR 5/SARAH. Liebe Leipzig.

ACTOR 6. No—

ACTOR 3. Maybe she's lost children.

ACTOR 6. But—

ACTOR 3. And they're dead,

ACTOR 5/SARAH. *(A gasp.)*

ACTOR 3. And you're longing for your husband to come back, across the ocean, and make more children.

ACTOR 6. I don't think—

ACTOR 5. Across the sea.

ACTOR 3. *(To* ACTOR 6:*)* The stakes are so high.

ACTOR 5/SARAH. My husband.

ACTOR 3. Right?

ACTOR 5. Yeah.

ACTOR 3. Not just your husband your— Your "future family."

ACTOR 5/SARAH. My future.

ACTOR 3. Right.

ACTOR 6. Ok.

ACTOR 5/SARAH. All Sarah wants is to be impregnated.

ACTOR 6. Um.

ACTOR 3. Yes.

ACTOR 6. Alright.

Scene: Presentation [1888]

> *(SARAH begins to sing a melodramatic folk song with total commitment and sincerity.*
> *It sounds kind of like "Edelweiss.")*

SARAH. To the north, across the sea,
I sit and wait, wait for thee,
Distant husband. Where is he?
I sit and wait, wait for thee.

> *(A beat is introduced, and complicated. The song becomes the dance re-mix of itself.)*

SARAH. With my womb, lying empty,
Like my heart. Come back to me,
My husband. I wait for thee.
I wait for our family.

> *(And then they break it down.*
> *It's pretty awesome.*
> *The actors might spit beats,*
> *and sample a popular song or two.*
> *Aww, yeah.*
> *Out of this,*
> WHITE MAN *kind of raps a letter.*
> BLACK MAN *beat boxes or hypes him or something.)*

WHITE MAN. Dear Sarah.
I have never been in a hotter place in my whole life.
The whole place, as far as I can tell is a desert.
I know there is ocean to the west, but I have never seen it.

All everyone talks about is rain.
Wondering if it will rain, when it will rain, how much it will rain,
This passes for sport in these parts.
There are trees of course, and those with the best shade are hotly contested for.
There is one tree, the best without a doubt,
With shade that is, inexplicably, 5 full degrees cooler than the shade of any other tree.
I have named this tree
Sarah.

Scene: Process

(A shift. Everything is probably less awesome.)

ACTOR 6. Keep going.

ACTOR 1. That's the end of the letter.

ACTOR 6. You're doing so well, just stay with it.
Explore.
Go back to the end of the letter, and give us some more.

*(Uh-oh.
Beat boxing, sort of.)*

ACTOR 1. I have named this tree Sarah.
Because that is your name.
And I like you—I love you—
Like I love... / trees?

ACTOR 6. No no we don't need more
we need deeper.
We need to see more of this world, we need / to see more—

ACTOR 3. We need to set the scene.
It's like, where is he? He's writing this letter but
Where Is He?
What else is happening?
Who is he *with?*
What are *We doing* while he is writing the letter.

ACTOR 6. You're right.

ACTOR 3. I know.
So, we're soldiers, we've spent all day doing like colonial
soldier-y stuff and
we're tired and
we've come back to our—
our bivouac—

ACTOR 1. Our what?

ACTOR 3. Our, like, rustic military tent camp thing.

ACTOR 1. Got it.

ACTOR 3. And it's been a long day, and we get back to the bivouac and we're—
Building a Fire.

ACTOR 6. Try it.

> *(The worst improv ever.*
> ACTOR 1 *&* ACTOR 3 *build a fire.*
> *They light the fire.*
> *They take turns blowing at the fire.*
> *The fire catches.*
> ACTOR 1 *is not a great improv partner.)*

ACTOR 3. Do you know when he'll get here?

ACTOR 1. Who?

ACTOR 3. The General.

ACTOR 1. Oh—I don't know.

ACTOR 3. I thought you said you knew.

ACTOR 1. But I don't.

> *(This isn't working. Can we stop?)*

ACTOR 6. Keep going.

ACTOR 3. Are you hungry?

ACTOR 1. Are you hungry?

ACTOR 3. I could eat something down to the bone.
And you. You must be starving.

ACTOR 1. Meh.
[This is terrible.]

ACTOR 3. Ok, so what are we doing by the fire?

ACTOR 1. Well, I'm…trying to write a letter.

ACTOR 3. Yeah.

ACTOR 1. So I should just write the letter.

ACTOR 3. But that's not—
Ok. Just tell me:
What do you think of the General?

ACTOR 1. I don't know.

ACTOR 3. I think the General is a fine man. Don't you think so?
That's something we soldiers would talk about, 'round the fire.

ACTOR 1. Sure.

ACTOR 3. Ah, The General.
The General—is the reason I joined up.
As a boy growing up in *Cologne,*
I knew that I was meant for greater things—to see the world.
And that starts here.
This is my first assignment.
Is this your first assignment?

ACTOR 1. I'm just trying to write this letter.

ACTOR 3. Yeah.
Who is the letter to?

ACTOR 1. Sarah.

ACTOR 3. Good. Why are you writing it?

ACTOR 1. Why don't I just read it?

ACTOR 3. No.

ACTOR 1. Why not?

ACTOR 3. Well, because I don't think a soldier would share his personal letter with another soldier.

ACTOR 1. But, I don't mind.

ACTOR 3. Go ahead.

Scene: Presentation [1896]

(WHITE MAN & SARAH are dominant in the presentation.
The letter is filled with Romance and Yearning.
There might be some distant representation of African bodies...but the love is foregrounded.)

WHITE MAN. Dear Sarah.
We awoke before dawn again this morning.
And walked, and walked,
And walked until long after dark.
We walk so much even when I sleep
I dream of walking in the heat.
There is so much heat here Sarah.

I saw steam rising from the shoulders of the man in front of me.
It is so hot our very sweat is wrested from our bodies.
I have never experienced such thirst as this.

Dear Sarah, I beg you
for a picture, of you in our garden,
for a picture of you in a cool and living place.
I will hold your picture to my lips and feel refreshed.

Scene: Process

ACTOR 4. Can I ask a question?

ACTOR 6. What is it?

ACTOR 2. Are we just going to sit here and watch some white people fall in love all day?

ACTOR 4. I wasn't going to put it like that—

ACTOR 2. Where are all the Africans?

ACTOR 1. We're just reading the letters.
I'm sure we'll find something that has some more context.

ACTOR 2. I think we should see some Africans in Africa.

ACTOR 1. And I think we have to stick with what we have access to.

ACTOR 2. No no no. This is some
Out-of-Africa-African-Queen-bullshit y'all are pulling right here, OK?
If we are in Africa, I want to see some black people.

ACTOR 6. He's right. We have to see more of the Herero.

ACTOR 4. That's all I was trying to say.

ACTOR 6. We need to see what—

ACTOR 4. We need to see Africa.

ACTOR 2. That's what I'm talking about.

ACTOR 4. You know? These dusty old letters talking about this dusty old place—

ACTOR 2. Yes.

ACTOR 4. I want to see the live Africa.

ACTOR 2. Preach.

ACTOR 4. The Africa that's lush—

ACTOR 2. Um—

ACTOR 4. The Africa that's green

ACTOR 2. Well—

ACTOR 4. With fruit dripping from trees—

ACTOR 6. Dig into it.

ACTOR 2. But the desert—

ACTOR 4. Gold pushing its way out of the ground—

ACTOR 2. That's not—

ACTOR 6. *(To* ACTOR 2:*)* Shh—

ACTOR 4. And so many animals—

ACTOR 6. Yes.

ACTOR 4. Monkeys—

ACTOR 6. Yes.

ACTOR 4. Gibbons—

ACTOR 6. Yes.

ACTOR 4. Elephants and giant snakes—

ACTOR 6. Stick with it.

ACTOR 4/ANOTHER BLACK MAN. And I hunt them.

> *(*ACTOR 4 *adopts an "African" accent. It's not ok.)*

ANOTHER BLACK MAN. I hunt de lion. I hunt de jagua. I hunt de tiegah.

ACTOR 2. But—

ACTORS 3, 5, 6. Shhh.

ANOTHER BLACK MAN. When I kill a tiegah I eat de heart of the animal while it beats.

> *("African" Drums begin, slowly, provided by* ACTOR 6.
> *The beat is felt in a count of 7.*
> *[1-2, 1-2, 1-2-3].)*

ANOTHER BLACK MAN. I push my hands inside the animal, breaking apart bone and sinew, until I reach the heart
and I pull it toward my heart, feeling
the veins stretch and snap, wiping
spurts of blood from my face.

> *(By now,* ACTORS 1 *&* 3 *&* 5, *have found the beat also.*
> *Now it starts to grow.)*

ANOTHER BLACK MAN. I barely have to chew, the heart is tender.
I pull a fang from the animal's mouth and add it to my necklace of teeth—
another kill,
another point of pride,
another day I provide for my family.
My family—we feast on the best parts of the meat,
we feast, and women ululate

(ACTOR 5 ululates.)

ANOTHER BLACK MAN. and dance with naked breasts

(ACTOR 5 performs "African" Dance. Others join.)

ANOTHER BLACK MAN. in front of our fire.
And they are all my wives, the women are all my wives
and I take two of them to my bed,
and I fuck both of the wives I took to bed
and I make them both pregnant because we are all as dark and fertile as
African jungle soil.

("African" Dance and Drumming and joy.
ACTOR 2 breaks in:)

ACTOR 2. Y'all need to stop.

ANOTHER BLACK MAN. I have many children. Many Many Children.

ACTOR 2. For real. Just stop.

ACTOR 5. Keep going!

ANOTHER BLACK MAN. Many children that I love.

ACTOR 2. STOP.

(They stop.)

ACTOR 2. This isn't that kind of Africa.
Ok?
We already Wikipediaed this.

ACTOR 5. Yeah, but—

ACTOR 2. We know it's like desert: dry, hot, arid, barren.
What's he talking about tigers and palm trees—

ACTOR 4. I was making the part my own.

ACTOR 2. Oh come on.

ACTOR 5. You don't want us to do anything.

ACTOR 2. You can't make the part your own so much that you ignore
what's actually there.

ACTOR 1. That's not what he's saying.

ACTOR 2. Oh really?

ACTOR 1. It's not.

ACTOR 2. So why don't you tell me what he's saying.

ACTOR 5. Why are you always so angry all the time?

ACTOR 2. I know you didn't.

ACTOR 5. What?

ACTOR 4. Guys I know that I don't know everything about the Herero but—Will you listen? We have to start somewhere.

ACTOR 2. So start by being black.

(Beat.)

ACTOR 6. Ok guys.

ACTOR 4. What are you trying to say?

ACTOR 2. I'm just saying that—

ACTOR 6. Ok.

ACTOR 2. That black people should know— Ok.
(Being more careful with his words than before:) Black people can understand what black people went through.

ACTOR 4. So basically, you're saying that I'm not [black]—

ACTOR 2. All I'm saying is we all should be thinking about being black right now.

ACTOR 6. OK guys,

ACTOR 5. What he means is—

ACTOR 6. What he's saying is that the whole point of this whole thing is that these people aren't so different from us.
Right? Right.
Like, for me the whole idea for this whole presentation started when I sat down
in my house, in my kitchen
and I opened a magazine
and I saw my Grandmother's face
in the middle of a page.
So I read the story around her face,
and the story was about people I'd never heard of,
in a place I'd never cared about.
An entire tribe of people nearly destroyed.
People who looked like my family.
And I thought about *my family.*
My father.
My grandmother—
a woman who died before I was born.
And I've missed her my whole life, and I always wondered what she would have sounded like,
and here she was,
speaking to me through the picture of this Herero woman. *That* was my way in.
It was like I was having a conversation with my Grandmother.

(ACTOR 5 *becomes Grandma. It's not ok.*)

ACTOR 5. Ooooh, chil'.

ACTOR 6. What are you—

ACTOR 5. Come on guys! Let's improv it!

ACTOR 2. Oh hell no.

ACTOR 4. Awesome.

ACTOR 6. Oh, I don't think we need to.

ACTOR 4. We should at least try it.

ACTOR 6. I don't think so.

ACTOR 5. Why not?

ACTOR 3. Because she wouldn't be in charge.

ACTOR 6. I'm not—

ACTOR 3. It's not supposed to be about leading or following.

ACTOR 4. *(Sung:)* We're all in this together.

ACTOR 6. I'm just trying to tell you that—

ACTOR 5. *(As Grandma:)* Whatchu think this is? Weez in it now. Can't just tell a talk no mo.

ACTOR 4. Come on, we'll support you. Just talk to her.

ACTOR 5. *(As Grandma:)* Talk to me girl.

ACTOR 2. Mmn-mm, we aren't doing this.

ACTOR 6. No. No—we can do this. But this is my Grandma, ok? I can't just—

(ACTOR 4 *becomes Grandma. Again, not ok.*)

ACTOR 4. *(As Grandma:)* Oooooh, chil'. Talk to me girl.

ACTOR 6. Uh-uh. We are exploring, but that is just too Tyler Perry for me.

(ACTOR 3 *becomes Grandma. Not Ok.*
But…pretty good?)

ACTOR 3. *(As Grandma:)* Ooooh, chil'.

ACTOR 6. Oh no—

ACTOR 3. Mmmmmmm-hmm. You can't play your own grandma, girl.

ACTOR 6. You're right, but my Grandma—

ACTOR 3. *(As Grandma:)* Don't 'My Grandma' me. You better let me talk when I am talking, girl.
There's Talking and then there's Listening

and when I'm around
you better just introduce yourself as Listening.

>*(Beat. ACTOR 5 jumps and claps.)*

ACTOR 5. Yay!

ACTOR 6. Ok. Fine.

ACTOR 3. *(As Grandma:)* Mmmm-hmmm.

ACTOR 6. So, my Grandma was full of folksy expressions, according to my Dad.
My Dad would say—

>*(ACTOR 4 becomes Dad.)*

ACTOR 4. *(As Dad:)* My mother had more folk in her than Woodstock.

ACTOR 6. Well—

ACTOR 2. That's not how black people talk.

ACTOR 4. That's how my dad talked.

ACTOR 2. Black people don't make jokes about Woodstock.

ACTOR 6. *(Pulling ACTOR 4 back into the improv:)* My Dad talked about my Grandma's cornbread.

ACTOR 3. *(In Grandma voice, to other ACTORS:)* Now, somebody better get me something to cook with. Grandma needs a prop.

ACTOR 6. *(Trying to get back to her story:)* Ok guys—

ACTOR 3. *(To ACTOR 4 as Dad, creating a scene:)* You touch that cornbread again, you'll be pulling back a stump, you hear me?

ACTOR 4. *(As Dad:)* Yeah.

ACTOR 3. *(As Grandma:)* Don't yeah me.

>*(ACTOR 3 hits ACTOR 4.)*

ACTOR 4. *(As Dad:)* Ow! Yes, mama.

ACTOR 6. That's interesting, because you couldn't sass my Grandma—

>*(ACTOR 3 hits ACTOR 4.)*

ACTOR 4. *(As Dad:)* Ow!

ACTOR 3. *(As Grandma:)* Don't sass me boy.

ACTOR 4. *(As Dad:)* Yes, Mama.

>*(ACTOR 3 smacks ACTOR 4 with his prop on each "Tell.")*

ACTOR 3. *(As Grandma:)* Tell me that you didn't eat that cornbread.
Tell me that you didn't hear me say don't you eat that cornbread.

ACTOR 3. Tell me that you didn't come in here, after I told you not to, and eat that cornbread.

ACTOR 6. So—

ACTOR 3. *(As Grandma:)* Tell me that corner piece isn't missing.

ACTOR 6. Ok—

ACTOR 3. *(As Grandma:)* Tell me that you didn't eat that corner piece of cornbread.
I don't need you to Tell me that you ate that corner piece of cornbread.
I can Tell the corner is missing so Tell me that you ate it.
Tell me.
Tell me.

ACTOR 6. He ate the cornbread.

ACTOR 3. *(As Grandma:)* I know he ate the cornbread.

ACTOR 6. Now, my Dad doesn't eat cornbread—

ACTOR 3. *(As Grandma:)* Not any more you don't.

ACTOR 6. —because of my Grandmother.
Who I never met.

ACTOR 3. *(As Grandma:)* I'm standin' right here girl.

ACTOR 6. Do you see what I'm saying, people?
The woman in that article looked just like my grandmother
and that doesn't happen to me—
I don't belong to a tribe
I don't know where my ancestors were from
I don't have a homeland where people look like me
I'm just American, African-American and
people tell me I look like other women all the time
but I never actually look like these other woman they say I look like
not really
because to some people
all black women look the same.

But the woman in this article.
She looked like my Grandmother.
And suddenly I felt like I have a lineage.
I felt like maybe
I could point to a place
a specific country
a specific homeland
and I could say
there.
My family is from there.

And I found that because my grandmother came to me and told me about a genocide, where eight out of every ten people in this tribe
my tribe had been murdered.

ACTOR 3. *(As Grandma:)* It's terrible what those people do to each other.

ACTOR 6. My Grandma wouldn't have said that.

ACTOR 3. *(As Grandma:)* You ain't ever met me girl.

ACTOR 6. She wouldn't say that.

ACTOR 3. *(As Grandma:)* You don't even know who I am.

ACTOR 6. I know it wasn't really my grandmother in that picture.
But the woman in that picture could have been my Grandma.

ACTOR 3. *(As Grandma:)* Have you gone crazy?
You can't be somebody when you're already somebody.

ACTOR 6. But if things had been different—

ACTOR 3. *(As Grandma:)* Then you would be different.

ACTOR 6. I know, but, just—

ACTOR 3. *(As Grandma:)* Just what?

ACTOR 6. Just taking a walk in someone else's shoes—

ACTOR 3. *(As Grandma:)* Ain't no puttin' on nobody else's shoes / and walkin' around—

ACTOR 6. Alright, that's enough.

ACTOR 3. *(As Grandma:)* —sayin' this is this and that is that—

ACTOR 6. I said that's enough.

ACTOR 3. *(As Grandma:)* You better shut your mouth and listen to me girl.
You can't take no walk in somebody else's shoes and know anything.
You ain't bought those shoes,
you ain't laced those shoes up,
you ain't put those shoes on day after day,
you ain't broken those shoes in.
Now, you can borrow somebody else's shoes, and
you can walk as long as you want,
they ain't your shoes.
You can go ahead and steal somebody else's shoes and guess what?
They ain't your shoes.

Scene: Presentation [1898]

WHITE MAN. Dear Sarah.
My shoes have finally worn completely through,
from all of our walking along the rails.
Sturdy old things,
they lasted far longer than they should have, I'm sure.

> (WHITE MAN *destroys this letter.*
> *He begins again.*)

WHITE MAN. Dear Sarah.
We have come across some problems
building this railway into the interior.
For one thing, it has been extremely dry—
tens, if not dozens of natives drop off
each and every day.
I fear for their morale,
and for, in turn, our safety.

> (WHITE MAN *destroys this letter.*
> *He begins again.*)

WHITE MAN. Dear Sarah.
The railway has been a great success.
The satisfaction in setting sturdy steel in straight lines toward the horizon,
Civilizing this wild landscape—it is a testament to German—

> (WHITE MAN *destroys this letter.*
> *He makes up a letter he doesn't write*
> *and would never send—a true letter.*)

WHITE MAN. Dear Sarah.
I've been meaning to thank you for your letters.
I would like to put each note
Back in its envelope,
Stack them in a stack
On my tongue and swallow the
Whole stack whole.

> (WHITE MAN *destroys this letter*—
> *The true letter.*
> *He writes the real letter.*)

WHITE MAN. Dear Sarah.
The weather has been more temperate of late.
But it has been dry here Sarah.
For all our sakes, I hope that soon it will
Rain.

Scene: Process

ACTOR 2. Dear Sarah, Let me tell you some boring shit.

ACTOR 6. Come on—

ACTOR 2. Dear Sarah, You thought that last shit was boring?
Well, you won't even believe how boring this new shit's gonna be.

ACTOR 6. Alright—

ACTOR 2. Dear Sarah, I'm killing black people every single day
but I'm not going to tell you about that
not when I can talk some more boring shit about your garden or your tree
to your boring skinny ass.

ACTOR 5. That's not fair—

ACTOR 2. You said we would get some Africa in here.

ACTOR 6. I know.

ACTOR 3. You know, I think—

ACTOR 2. And we're just reading these stupid letters.
We're never going to find out anything about the Africans in these letters.
Sarah doesn't care about black people.

ACTOR 3. Alright, Kanye.

ACTOR 2. You think you're cute, don't you.

ACTOR 6. Hold it hold it hold it.
You're right. You are. We need to see more of the Herero. We do.
And you know what? The letters aren't enough.

ACTOR 5. But they're so important.

ACTOR 6. I'm not saying they aren't important, but they aren't enough.

ACTOR 5. But—

ACTOR 1. So what do you want us to do?

ACTOR 6. I want us—

ACTOR 1. We can't just improvise the whole thing.

ACTOR 2.	**ACTOR 6.**
Why not?	I'm not saying that—
Because he's afraid of improv?	

ACTOR 1. I'm not afraid of improv.

ACTOR 3. You're kind of afraid of improv.

ACTOR 1. We shouldn't be pretending, we shouldn't be making things up,
we shouldn't be doing anything other than what's real.

ACTOR 6. I am agreeing with you—

ACTOR 2. What's real is that they don't even talk about Africans in those letters.

ACTOR 1. But these letters are the only thing we actually know.

ACTOR 6. That's not true—

ACTOR 1. They're the only personal, first person stories we have.

ACTOR 6. That is actually not the truth.

ACTOR 2. The letters don't have any evidence of anything happening to the Africans.
They don't mention one prison camp, one hanging, one incident of—

ACTOR 1. So how do we know what even happened to them? We—

ACTOR 2.	**ACTOR 4.**
So you're saying that we just Made up the genocide?	What do you mean how do we know?

ACTOR 1. I'm not saying the genocide was made up. I'm just saying we don't have physical evidence—

ACTOR 6. So where do you think all the people went?

ACTOR 1. I'm not saying it didn't happen—

ACTOR 4. Because we know that it happened.

ACTOR 6. We've done research—

ACTOR 3. But we haven't found anything about / the Herero.

ACTOR 2. We did all kinds of searches—

ACTOR 1. Yeah, on the internet.

ACTOR 6. Yes—

ACTOR 1. But these letters are the only *physical* evidence of—

ACTOR 5. He's just saying that it's not like the Holocaust.

(*Beat.*)

ACTOR 6. What?

ACTOR 5. No I don't mean—I just mean—

ACTOR 4. It is exactly like that.

ACTOR 5. I don't mean it like that—it's just like we know exactly what happened during the—that because of all the evidence.

ACTOR 4. So you're saying—

ACTOR 1. Right, she's saying—

ACTOR 5. I'm just saying we don't have the same kind of evidence for this. That's all.
You know? We just have the letters.

ACTOR 1. Exactly.

ACTOR 2. But we know—

ACTOR 1. With the Holocaust, we have documents, we have testimonials, we have pictures.

ACTOR 6. There are pictures of the Herero—

ACTOR 1. But not—

ACTOR 6. I showed you all the picture of that woman,

ACTOR 1. I know—

ACTOR 6. That old woman, who had been forced out into the desert, and barely made it, she was starved half to death, and she looked exactly like those pictures from—

ACTOR 1. But we don't know who she is. We have no idea who she is.

ACTOR 3. We don't even know her name.

ACTOR 1. Six Million People
and we know all of their names.
Every single one.
And—

ACTOR 4. We don't know the Herero names.

ACTOR 1. Exactly—

ACTOR 4. But that doesn't mean they weren't murdered.

ACTOR 1. That's not what I'm saying—

ACTOR 4. It's not like—

ACTOR 6. It's not like you can compare—

ACTOR 4. It's not like, oh, a tree falls in a forest, does it make a sound.
The tree fell. We know it fell.

ACTOR 6. It's—

ACTOR 4. It hasn't made a sound, it's not going to make a sound because it already fell.

ACTOR 5. I see what you're saying, but—

ACTOR 4. So what if we don't know their names. So what if we don't know exactly.

ACTOR 5. But—

ACTOR 4. We know enough.

ACTOR 5. Enough to *what*, though?

ACTOR 6. We know that it happened.

ACTOR 1. We are telling this story. This letter says—

ACTOR 6. We all keep saying the letter says, the letter says
But we don't need to follow exactly what they letters say.

ACTOR 1. So then what are we going to do.

ACTOR 6. I want you to make a letter up. [We need to clear the space people.]

ACTOR 1. Well I don't feel comfortable doing that.

ACTOR 6. I don't want you to feel comfortable. I want you to do it.

ACTOR 1. But it's—

ACTOR 6. What?

ACTOR 1. It's history, there's facts, there's truth. I have no idea what it's really like to be someone like him. And I'm trying to figure out what kind of—who does something like—how someone can—

ACTOR 6. So just be yourself, in his situation.

ACTOR 1. But I'm nothing like him.

ACTOR 6. You don't know that.

ACTOR 1. Yes I do.

ACTOR 5. Just talk to me.

ACTOR 6. All we're talking about is writing a letter home.

ACTOR 5. I'll support you.

ACTOR 1. Fine.

ACTOR 5. Great.

ACTOR 2. This is just going to be more white letters.

ACTOR 6. No, because I want you to own the letter he's writing.

ACTOR 2. What does that mean?

ACTOR 6. I just want to start with this, to build—

ACTOR 2. Start what?

ACTOR 6. Just to use his words to—

ACTOR 2. I have my own words.

ACTOR 6. I need you to trust me, Ok? Please.

ACTOR 2. Ok.

ACTOR 5. He needs a wife.

ACTOR 6. We're just developing—

ACTOR 5. He does.

ACTOR 3. She's right. If we're doing the whole love thing.

ACTOR 6. Fine, I'll do it.

ACTOR 3. But—

ACTOR 6. We're creating the Herero story, and for now, I'll be the Herero woman, the black woman, whatever,
Let's stop talking about it and just try it. Okay?

ACTOR 5. Ok.

ACTOR 6. And, the letter is just a starting point, ok people?
We all know that this ends in a genocide, so let's get there.
White Man, start us off.

Scene: Presentation [1899]

(At the start, WHITE MAN *&* SARAH *are foregrounded.*
BLACK MAN *builds a fire.)*

WHITE MAN. Dear Sarah.
I am hungry enough to eat something down to the bone.
As I write this I can hear you laugh—

*(*SARAH *&* BLACK WOMAN *laugh.)*

WHITE MAN. —and say—

SARAH. You are always hungry.

WHITE MAN. And I know it to be true.
The smell of meat over fire reminds me—

(During the following...)

SARAH. Reminds me of the time we ate off sticks round the fire. When we ate our sausages off sticks and hoped that they'd cooked all the way through.

*(*BLACK MAN *&* BLACK WOMAN *warm
themselves by the fire.)*

WHITE MAN. Reminds me of you—

SARAH. Until it began to rain—

*(*BLACK MAN *&* BLACK WOMAN *look
up at the rain.)*

WHITE MAN. It's raining here.
That reminds me—

SARAH. —until it began to rain and we had to duck in under that one tree in the field, in our field, and you told me we'd be struck by lighting—

> (BLACK MAN *runs under the tree.*
> BLACK WOMAN *is beautiful, enjoying the rain.)*

SARAH. —I wanted to run away from that tree as fast as I could but I wanted to stay as dry as I could and as warm as I could and so I ended up doing neither.

WHITE MAN. The rain reminds me of you too.

BLACK MAN. Dear Sarah.

WHITE MAN. Dear Sarah.

BLACK MAN. Dear, dear, Sarah.

WHITE MAN. Do you remember when it rained?

BLACK WOMAN. I love the rain.

WHITE MAN. We huddled under the tree.

BLACK MAN. You're shivering.

BLACK WOMAN. I'm warm enough.

SARAH. Trying to keep warm.

BLACK MAN. I could keep you warmer.

WHITE MAN. You looked so good wet
I told you if we stayed under the tree you'd get electrocuted.

BLACK MAN. You better come back under here.

WHITE MAN. It might have been true.

BLACK WOMAN. It's only water.

BLACK MAN. Look at you—

BLACK WOMAN. How do I look?

WHITE MAN. We ran out into the rain, and back under the tree—

BLACK MAN. Give me your hands.

BLACK WOMAN. Are you afraid of the rain?

WHITE MAN. —and out into the rain, and back under the tree—

BLACK MAN. I'm not afraid of anything.

WHITE MAN. You were soaked—

SARAH. Soaked down to the bone, my fingernails—

BLACK MAN. Your fingernails are blue.

SARAH. The tips were clear like I'd been in a bath.

WHITE MAN. And I held your hands and made them warm.

BLACK MAN. Come here and let me warm you up.

BLACK WOMAN. Thank you.

BLACK MAN. Look at you. Soaked right down to the hair on your arms.

BLACK WOMAN. I don't have hairy arms.

BLACK MAN. That's a shame. Since I like it so much.

BLACK WOMAN. Really.

BLACK MAN. Oh Sarah, the hair on your arms.

BLACK WOMAN. What about it?

BLACK MAN. I could write letters and letters about your arms.
Dear Sarah.
Do you remember the water, when we could go West to the Ocean?
And the rain—
do you remember swimming in the water while it rained?
Before the lightning struck?
We got out just before the lightning struck—
The sky and water were grey.
Your hair smells dirty when it's wet
and I told you so and you cried
and lightning struck the water
and the wet hair on our arms stood up.

And someday we will say
do you remember that tree?
When it rained?
When we leaned in close to the trunk?
And there was lightning
and thunder
and Sarah under that tree.
The hair on your arms slicked down.
Dear Sarah.
I think you should be my wife.
I think we should have children.
What do you think about that?

BLACK WOMAN. All you have to do is ask.

BLACK MAN. Will you be my wife?

BLACK WOMAN. Yes.

BLACK MAN. Will you have my children?

BLACK WOMAN. Yes.

BLACK MAN. You are my family.

>*(They kiss.)*

Scene: Process

>*(ACTOR 2 is kissing ACTOR 6.*
>*She stops kissing him.*
>*He doesn't stop kissing her.*
>*She struggles to get away.*
>
>*She starts arranging things, moving things.)*

ACTOR 2. What are you doing?

ACTOR 6. We're moving on.

ACTOR 3. Ok. What are we doing?

ACTOR 6. We need to do more Herero stuff, right?

ACTOR 4. Like a village?

ACTOR 6. Yes.

ACTOR 3. So we're just going to set one up?

ACTOR 6. Yes.

ACTOR 2. Do you have a better idea?

ACTOR 3. I have like seven better ideas.

ACTOR 4. Let's just try this, ok?

ACTOR 3. Let's just set up a village.

ACTOR 4. Yes.

ACTOR 3. I'm an actor not a stagehand.

ACTOR 4. Oh my god.

ACTOR 2. Why are you even here?

ACTOR 3. Me?

ACTOR 2. You clearly don't want to tell this story.

ACTOR 3. I've been trying to make this poignant—

ACTOR 2. Mmh-hhmn.

ACTOR 3. —and professional from the very beginning.

ACTOR 6. Guys.

ACTOR 3. You're the one that keeps stopping everything.

ACTOR 2. Because you all keep trying to pull some stupid shit.

ACTOR 3. If you think it's all so stupid, why don't you just leave?

ACTOR 6. No.

ACTOR 2. You'd like that wouldn't you.

ACTOR 6. Guys—

ACTOR 3. Yes, actually I think we all would.

ACTOR 6. No.

ACTOR 2. And leave you all to try and put this thing together?

ACTOR 3. I think we would be fine without—

ACTOR 2. Uh-uh, no way, what this thing needs is someone that is thinking about the Black experience.

ACTOR 3. Oh please.

ACTOR 4. We're all thinking about that.

ACTOR 2. You need me here.

ACTOR 6. Guys. I'm not saying this again.
No one is leaving, Ok?
We all said we wanted to do this.
All I want to do is tell this story.

ACTOR 2. So do I.

ACTOR 4. So do I.

ACTOR 5. So let's just do it.
What are we doing? Making the village.

ACTOR 6. Yes.

ACTOR 5. Ok.
We have huts over here.
And like the sacred fire—

ACTOR 4. Is right here.

ACTOR 5. Perfect.

ACTOR 6. Great.

ACTOR 4. And...

ACTOR 5. And there's cows, and the men watching cows
(To ACTOR 2 *&* ACTOR 4:*)* You guys watch cows, ok? Please?
(To ACTOR 1 *&* ACTOR 3:*)* And you guys watch them watch the cows.
(To ACTOR 6:*)* And whatever, we're here.
We're like—

(ACTOR 5 wraps something around her head—a scarf, a sweater.)

ACTOR 5. The Wives. We can be making a fire, or—

ACTOR 2. This is exactly what I'm talking about.

ACTOR 5. We can make a cooking fire—

ACTOR 2. *(To* ACTOR 6:*)* How can you stand there and let her do that?

ACTOR 6. I'm not—

ACTOR 1. Just let her make the stupid fire.

ACTOR 2. *(To* ACTOR 5:*)* You aren't a Herero wife, ok?

ACTOR 1. She can be whatever she wants.

ACTOR 5. We're finding the Herero in us.

ACTOR 2. No, we're finding the Herero in *us*—

ACTOR 6. We're all trying to find the Herero—

ACTOR 2. Y'alls finding Germans in you.

ACTOR 5. Well, I don't only want to be a German.

ACTOR 2. Too bad.

ACTOR 5. I want to have another part.

ACTOR 2. Well, you can't be an African.

ACTOR 5. I think I can—

ACTOR 2. You can't / it doesn't make any sense.

ACTOR 5. I just need / to get into my body.

ACTOR 4. What if you were a German sometimes?

ACTOR 2. That wouldn't make any sense either.

ACTOR 3. He couldn't play a German.

ACTOR 2. Oh, I could play a German.

ACTOR 6. Guys.

ACTOR 2. If we were doing some stupid-ass thing like that
I would be a better German than you / because I understand it
because I've been to Germany.

ACTOR 3. Oh, you think so, do you?

ACTOR 1. *(Response to* ACTOR 2's *"I've been to Germany":)* Oh, here we go.

ACTOR 2. What, I can't go to Germany?

ACTOR 6. That's not what he's—

ACTOR 2. I've been to Germany.

ACTOR 6. Ok.

ACTOR 2. I love Germany. I love German people.
And you know what?

ACTOR 6. Ok.

ACTOR 2. I was very successful in Germany, Ok? You know what I'm saying?

(He's saying that he had a lot of sex.)

ACTOR 6. Ok, guys.

ACTOR 2. That's not even bragging that's just the truth.

ACTOR 1. Well, have you ever been to Africa?

ACTOR 2. Have you ever been to Africa?

ACTOR 1. I'm not trying to play an African.

ACTOR 2. No you're not. Because you can't.

ACTOR 1. You know what?

ACTOR 2. What.

ACTOR 6. Guys.

ACTOR 1. I have had just about enough of your frickin' attitude.

ACTOR 2. Of my attitude?

ACTOR 1. First you're yelling at him for not getting it right, not being African right.

ACTOR 2. I'm not yelling at anybody.

ACTOR 6. Nobody's—

ACTOR 1. You're yelling at her, you're yelling at me,
but you don't know any more than any of us.

ACTOR 6. We're—

ACTOR 1. None of us has ever been to Africa.

ACTOR 2. Yeah, and I don't need to go to Africa to know what it's like to be black.

ACTOR 1. You're not supposed to be black, you're supposed to be African.

ACTOR 2. There's no difference between being black and being African / Africa is black.

ACTOR 1. Of course there is a difference. That is ridiculous.

ACTOR 2. You better get out of my face.

ACTOR 1. You don't know the difference between being black and being African?

ACTOR 2. I said you better get out of my face.

ACTOR 6. Guys guys guys.
Break it up.

(ACTOR 6 *separates the men.*)

ACTOR 5. Maybe we should take a break.

ACTOR 6. No. No more breaks, no more letters, no more bullshit, I've had enough.
You boys need to check your egos and put it into the work. Ok?

ACTOR 2. That's fine with me.

ACTOR 6. I said enough.
Sarah, when are we?

ACTOR 5. Um…

ACTOR 6. Where are we?

ACTOR 5. I don't know.

ACTOR 6. Oh come on.

ACTOR 5. We might have to go back a little.

ACTOR 6. To what?

ACTOR 5. To…1892.

ACTOR 6. Are you serious?

ACTOR 5. We haven't built the railroad, we haven't / changed the laws, we haven't executed anyone—

ACTOR 6. Ok I get it Ok.
We need to get it together people.
Let's go. 1892.

ACTOR 5. It's the Germans training the Herero and giving them the cows part.

ACTOR 6. So let's start training. Right now. Let's go people.

ACTOR 5. We should be like marching?

(ACTOR 5 *marches.*)

ACTOR 6. Yes. Hup two three four.
I am serious.
Hup two three four.

(ACTORS 1 & 3 & 4 *start marching.*)

ACTOR 6. Let's go two three four.
Move it two three four.
Hup two three four.

Scene: Presentation [1892]

*(*WHITE MAN *&* ANOTHER WHITE MAN *assume a soldierly stance.)*

ANOTHER WHITE MAN. Hup, two, three, four.

*(*BLACK MAN *&* ANOTHER BLACK MAN
SARAH *&* BLACK WOMAN *march.*
They might say Hups.
ANOTHER WHITE MAN *watches the training.*
WHITE MAN *writes a letter.)*

WHITE MAN. Dear Sarah.

ANOTHER WHITE MAN. Straighten the line.

WHITE MAN. I'm learning so much here—you will be proud of our work.

ANOTHER WHITE MAN. Stand up straight.

WHITE MAN. The General has picked out a tribe to be in charge of the others.
I am helping to train the leading tribe.

ANOTHER WHITE MAN. Straight back.

WHITE MAN. It is easier for them, as it is easier for us, to be led by one who resembles a better version of our own self.

ANOTHER WHITE MAN. Yes.

WHITE MAN. It is easier for us as well to simplify communications, logistics, organization, etc.

ANOTHER WHITE MAN. Straight arms.

WHITE MAN. In a group of natives—
—a soldier can walk up to the tallest one—

ANOTHER WHITE MAN. —Stand up straight—

WHITE MAN. —with the straightest teeth—

ANOTHER WHITE MAN. —Straighten the arms—

WHITE MAN. —and the fairest skin,
and without a doubt,
address him as Leader.

ANOTHER WHITE MAN. Yes.

WHITE MAN. Fair, of course, is a relative term.

ANOTHER WHITE MAN. Excellent.

WHITE MAN. The General is a wise man.

ANOTHER WHITE MAN. Yes.

WHITE MAN. He has worked with natives many times,
and treats them as family.

ANOTHER WHITE MAN. Good.

WHITE MAN. In this assignment,
I am learning how a father must be for his children.

ANOTHER WHITE MAN. Keep the pace.

WHITE MAN. Dear Sarah.
I am thinking of you.

ANOTHER WHITE MAN. Keep up the pace.

WHITE MAN. I am thinking of our future family.

(*ANOTHER WHITE MAN blows a whistle.*)

BLACK MAN. Dear Sarah.
I have been craving a fire.
But I don't want a fire that is just a fire.
I want my fire.
I want the fire that holds my ancestors. I want the fire that I believe in.
I want that fire that makes me believe I know who my ancestors are—know
that they are safe.
I want my belief—my belief that is so strong I search the desert for trees to
burn so that the fire of my ancestors will never go out.
I have spent my whole life coming home to that fire. And now.

(*ANOTHER WHITE MAN blows a whistle.*)

ANOTHER WHITE MAN. Rail Road Building.

> (*Rail Road Building:*
> BLACK MAN & ANOTHER BLACK MAN
> SARAH & BLACK WOMAN *lay tracks.*
> *A repetitive, exhausting, physical gesture.*
> *It is percussive in a count of 7:*
> *[1-2, 1-2, 1-2-3].*)

BLACK MAN. For months I have not built a fire.
For months I have been building
what the Germans call a railroad.
Two straight lines of metal.
The Germans love these straight lines,
Lines of metal, lines of wire, lines of men
Lines and lines and lines and
It seems as though they've always been here.

ANOTHER WHITE MAN. Keep up the pace.

Scene: Process [1904]

(The ACTORS *are stomp-clapping in the other count of 7: [1-2-3, 1-2-3, 1]
they have been doing it for a while.
Everyone is exhausted. Irritable.*
ACTOR 2 *breaks character.*
ACTOR 3 *is still fully engaged with the improv, addressing* ACTOR 2 *as*
BLACK MAN.*)*

ACTOR 2. *(To* ACTOR 6, *if it's to anyone:)* It feels like we've been doing this forever.

ANOTHER WHITE MAN. *(To* BLACK MAN:*)* Keep up the pace.

ACTOR 2. *(To* ACTOR 3:*)* I'm not talking to you.

ANOTHER WHITE MAN. Keep up the pace.

ACTOR 4/ANOTHER BLACK MAN. *(To* ACTOR 2/BLACK MAN:*)*
Just keep going.

ACTOR 2. Or what?

ACTOR 6. *(A growl at the* ACTORS:*)* Stay in it.

ACTOR 2. We're due for a break.

ACTOR 6. We are not taking a break until we are able to do this the way it needs to be done.
So stay in it.

ANOTHER WHITE MAN. *(To* BLACK MAN:*)* We will have a break at the designated time.
Get back into line.

ANOTHER BLACK MAN. *(To* ANOTHER WHITE MAN:*)* He's just thirsty.

ACTOR 2. *(To* ACTOR 6:*)* Why are we doing this?

ACTOR 6. For once, can't you just *shut up* and stay in line?

ACTOR 2. What?

ACTOR 6. Stay in line!

*(*ACTOR 2 *storms over to his water.*
ACTORS *gradually stop clapping/stomping as they notice* ACTOR 2 *&*
ACTOR 6.
ACTOR 2 *takes a long drink, a deep drink. Or two.
The other* ACTORS *watch him, catching their breath.*
ACTOR 2 *slams his water back down, or throws away his cup. He takes a breath.)*

ACTOR 2. Now I'll get back in line.

(Beat.)

ACTOR 6. *(Barely controlled:)* When you're trying to make something
Not everyone's going to be happy during every minute of it
But even though we're not comfortable or happy or—
We do stuff we don't want to do because it adds to the greater—
We—

ACTOR 2. I said I'll get back in line.

ACTOR 6. That's the thing! You can't just get back in line.

Scene: Presentation [1905]

(Chaos. Confusion.)

WHITE MAN. See you here those assembled.
Your grievances have been heard.
The General has issued a reply.

> *(*WHITE MAN *&* ANOTHER WHITE MAN *create a wall.*
> ACTORS *might be refugees gathering and fleeing.*
> *Everything that was in the space, gets built up so there is a barricade on one side of the space,*
> *and a barren, empty space on the other.)*

WHITE MAN. The letter says

ANOTHER WHITE MAN. Residents of Südwestafrika.

WHITE MAN. The letter says

ANOTHER WHITE MAN. Your permission to reside was at the pleasure of the German government.

WHITE MAN. The letter says

ANOTHER WHITE MAN. Your residence no longer pleases the German government.

WHITE MAN. The letter says

ANOTHER WHITE MAN. Your presence will no longer be tolerated.

WHITE MAN. The letter says

ANOTHER WHITE MAN. You have no one to blame but yourselves.

WHITE MAN. The letter says

ANOTHER WHITE MAN. We must set an example, as a father does for his children.

WHITE MAN. The letter says

ANOTHER WHITE MAN. If you are found within our border with guns, you will be shot.

WHITE MAN. The letter says

ANOTHER WHITE MAN. If you are found within our border without guns, you will be shot.

WHITE MAN. The letter says

ANOTHER WHITE MAN. If you are found within our border with cattle, you will be shot.

WHITE MAN. The letter says

ANOTHER WHITE MAN. If you are found within our border without cattle, you will be shot.

WHITE MAN. The letter says

ANOTHER WHITE MAN. We encourage you to move quickly and continuously, for your own safety.

> (WHITE MAN & ANOTHER WHITE MAN *salute.*
> ANOTHER WHITE MAN *marches off.*
> WHITE MAN *patrols the wall.*
> BLACK MAN *appears.)*

Scene: Process [1905]

(ACTOR 1 & ACTOR 2 *are thoroughly engaged in an improv, a good improv. A great improv. They are in this moment-to-moment, changing tactics, changing status, raising the stakes, keeping the ball in the air. The characters they play are equally matched—they each flip back and forth between being the aggressor and the victim.)*

ACTOR 1/WHITE MAN. You can't come this way.

Are you deaf? I said you can't come through this way.

Are you just going to stand there?

Hey, I said, you just gonna stand there?

Do you plan on answering me?

ACTOR 2/BLACK MAN. I don't want any trouble.

ACTOR 1/WHITE MAN. I didn't say you did.
You better listen to me.
I am saying this as an order.
An order came down that says that you can't come this way.

ACTOR 2/BLACK MAN. My home is that way.

ACTOR 1/WHITE MAN. Well, it says your home can't be this way.

ACTOR 2/BLACK MAN. But my home is that way.

ACTOR 1/WHITE MAN. If your home stays this way,

> *(He hold his fingers out in the shape of a gun.)*

ACTOR 1/WHITE MAN. I'll have to shoot you.

ACTOR 2/BLACK MAN. *(About the gun:)* I didn't know you had that.

ACTOR 1/WHITE MAN. Well, I do.
So.

> *(Beat.)*

ACTOR 2/BLACK MAN. I have a wife.
Do you have a wife?

ACTOR 1/WHITE MAN. Yeah.

ACTOR 2/BLACK MAN. I love my wife.
I don't want any trouble.

ACTOR 1/WHITE MAN. I didn't say you did.

ACTOR 2/BLACK MAN. My home is—

> *(A slight southern accent slowly starts to enter* ACTOR 1's *diction.)*

ACTOR 1/WHITE MAN. Your home is that way now.

ACTOR 2/BLACK MAN. There is nothing that way.

ACTOR 1/WHITE MAN. That's not true.
Your life is that way.

ACTOR 2/BLACK MAN. My wife—

ACTOR 1/WHITE MAN. Might just be over that way.

ACTOR 2/BLACK MAN. You know she's not.

ACTOR 1/WHITE MAN. You don't know that, and neither do I.
She could be—

ACTOR 2/BLACK MAN. You know she's not.

ACTOR 1/WHITE MAN. *(Using the gun again:)* I'll shoot you.

> *(A slight southern accent slowly, starts to enter* ACTOR 2's *diction.)*

ACTOR 2/BLACK MAN. Please. I don't want no trouble.

ACTOR 1/WHITE MAN. You keep saying that but—

ACTOR 2/BLACK MAN. *(Pacifying:)* Ok.

ACTOR 1/WHITE MAN. Your home is that way.

ACTOR 2/BLACK MAN. Alright.
I understand.
Just let me go and I'll come right back here—

ACTOR 1/WHITE MAN. No.

ACTOR 2/BLACK MAN. I say I'll come right back—

ACTOR 1/WHITE MAN. You won't.

ACTOR 2/BLACK MAN. You have my word.

ACTOR 1/WHITE MAN. You won't come back—

ACTOR 2/BLACK MAN. I will—

ACTOR 1/WHITE MAN. You won't. Because if you try to come in this direction
I will shoot you.

ACTOR 2/BLACK MAN. Why can't you let me go?
No one will know.

ACTOR 1/WHITE MAN. Might be true.

ACTOR 2/BLACK MAN. If I go off that way, I will die.

ACTOR 1/WHITE MAN. You might not.

ACTOR 2/BLACK MAN. What if I run.

ACTOR 1/WHITE MAN. I'm a good shot.

ACTOR 2/BLACK MAN. I'm a fast runner.

ACTOR 1/WHITE MAN. I'm a great shot.

ACTOR 2/BLACK MAN. I'm—

ACTOR 1/WHITE MAN. Don't make me shoot you.

ACTOR 2/BLACK MAN. I'm not making you do anything.

ACTOR 1/WHITE MAN. Do not even take a step over here.

ACTOR 2/BLACK MAN. You'll shoot me for a step?

ACTOR 1/WHITE MAN. I'll shoot you for breaking the law.

ACTOR 2/BLACK MAN. I ain't breaking no law—

ACTOR 1/WHITE MAN. Why can't you just respect that I'm telling you
the way it is.

ACTOR 2/BLACK MAN. I'm just tryin' to get home.

ACTOR 1/WHITE MAN. I am trying to help you.

ACTOR 2/BLACK MAN. You ain't helping no one but yourself.

ACTOR 1/WHITE MAN. Don't you talk to me that way—

ACTOR 2/BLACK MAN. If you was helping me—

ACTOR 1/WHITE MAN. Don't even know what's good for you—

ACTOR 2/BLACK MAN. I'd be halfway home by now.

ACTOR 1/WHITE MAN. Don't you take one step.

ACTOR 2/BLACK MAN. I'm going home.

ACTOR 1/WHITE MAN. Do not—

ACTOR 2/BLACK MAN. You can't stop me—

ACTOR 1/WHITE MAN. take one step—

ACTOR 2/BLACK MAN. From going home—

ACTOR 1/WHITE MAN. Don't—

ACTOR 2/BLACK MAN. You can't stop me—

ACTOR 1/WHITE MAN. Not one step—
Don't—

> (ACTOR 2/BLACK MAN *takes a step.*
> ACTOR 1/WHITE MAN *immediately shoots him.*
> *We hear a LOUD shot.)*

Scene: Presentation [1906]

> (BLACK MAN *immediately falls.*
> BLACK MAN *is still alive.*
> BLACK MAN *is breathing.*
> *So,* WHITE MAN *shoots him again.*
> BLACK MAN *is still alive.*
> BLACK MAN *is breathing—gasping.*
> BLACK MAN *&* WHITE MAN *get into a pattern:*
> *Breath in.*
> *Click.*
> *Shot.)*

WHITE MAN. Dear Sarah.

BLACK MAN. *(Breath in.)*

WHITE MAN. *(Click.)*

> *(Shot.)*

WHITE MAN. Dear Sarah.

BLACK MAN. *(Breath in.)*

WHITE MAN. *(Click.)*
I'm writing to you today.
Today is a day

> *(Shot.)*

Just a day.
Like any day.

BLACK MAN. *(Breath in.)*

WHITE MAN. Dear Sarah.

> *(Click.)*

I'm writing to you today
Today I'm wondering,
Like I've been wondering.
When it's gonna rain.

> *(Shot.)*

Dear Sarah
People here could use some rain.

ACTOR 1. Can I have a minute?

Scene: Process

ACTOR 6. Fine. Take a minute.

> *(ACTOR 1 takes a few seconds.)*

ACTOR 1. I can't do this.

ACTOR 6. You just did.

ACTOR 1. I can't—I'm not that person.

ACTOR 2. Neither am I.

ACTOR 6. Can we help Black Man up people?

> *(ACTORS 4 & 5 help ACTOR 2 up.)*

ACTOR 6. You guys just did some amazing work.
Really great.
But we can't keep stopping like this.
We need to stay in it and move
Or we're never going to figure out this whole genocide thing.

ACTOR 1. No. I can't do this.

ACTOR 6. Yes you can.

ACTOR 1. I'm not—I'm not the kind of person who could have done that—

ACTOR 2. I'm the one that got shot.

ACTOR 1. But I wouldn't have done that if—

ACTOR 6. We all know that.
It's just, White Man—

ACTOR 1. Can you stop calling me White Man?!

ACTOR 6. No.

ACTOR 1. I've got a name.

ACTOR 6. I know.

ACTOR 1. And if it was me in that situation,
if it was me,
I would have let him go.
I would have.
I wanted to.

ACTOR 6. So why didn't you.

ACTOR 1. Because—because that wasn't what happened.
That wasn't what he could have done.

ACTOR 6. That's right.

ACTOR 1. And who is that? Who is that person?

ACTOR 6. That's what we're talking about—

ACTOR 3. Can I jump in here?
Because, it's like,
I know about this.

ACTOR 1. Who is that person?

ACTOR 3. I know about the feelings this character is feeling.
Because, it's like
Ok. So, I'm from Pennsylvania.

ACTOR 6. We don't have time for this.

ACTOR 3. Hear me out.
I am from Pennsylvania and so was my father. And his father. And his.
And my great-grandfather fought for the Union Army in the Civil War,
And my great-grandfather was in a company from Pennsylvania
that was made up entirely of coal miners.
Now, I am not a coal miner. I have never been in anything resembling what
you would call a mine, but great-grandfather *was* a coal miner. To the core.
Ha.
Anyway, seriously, listen listen, ok—
So during this one battle, the Unions and the Confederates were in a total
deadlock for days and days and days, and no one was gaining any ground,
so finally
The Pennsylvania miners were like: um, hello? We're miners.
So they *mined* underneath the Confederate front line,
and they packed their mine with gunpowder,
and when the time seemed right,
they blew everything up.

ACTOR 6. How does this have anything to do with—

ACTOR 3. I'm getting there.
So the idea had been to blow up the Confederate troops
but as they were mining they got lost somehow
got turned around
and instead
they ended up imploding the front lines of their side
the Union army.
Half of the divisions that made up the Union Front fell through the ground
into this Crater.
And The Confederate Troops charged and broke the Union line—because
the line wasn't a line anymore and
Through the smoke of the molten explosion and the mud of men and soil
and confusion, the Confederate Troops got close enough to see
for the first time
the individual men they had been deadlocked with for days.
An entire division of black men
trained by the Union Army
fighting in their first battle.
Black men fighting in uniform, as equals.
And to the Confederate soldiers, this was like the most offensive—
And my great-grandfather saw his fellow soldiers not just being shot,
He saw them being ripped apart in fury.
And my great-grandfather got pinned in a ditch with a blac—African-
American Union soldier, and
As the Confederates got closer and closer,
And my great-grandfather saw the rage in their faces, the confusion,
So my great-grandfather looked that Union soldier in the eye
and said "I'm Sorry." And shot him.
And my great-grandfather saw that that Union soldier was still alive.
So my great-grandfather shot him again.
And he shot that soldier again,
And again, and
my great-grandfather shot him in fear—out of fear for his own life and
he shot him so that they would see him shooting him and
he shot him so that he would be captured and kept alive.
He shot him to save his own life.

And he did.
My great-grandfather was captured
and kept alive until the war ended, and
my great-grandfather headed back to the mine to
mine and raise my grandfather to
mine and raise my father to
mine and raise me.

      (Beat.)

ACTOR 2. Are you finished?

ACTOR 3. *(Furious:)* Excuse me?

ACTOR 2. That story doesn't have anything to do with Africa.

ACTOR 3. It's the same thing—

ACTOR 4. It's not the same—

ACTOR 6.	**ACTOR 5.**
This isn't—	He's just trying to.

ACTOR 3. It's the same dynamic—

ACTOR 6. This isn't what we should be focusing on—

ACTOR 4. It's a white man and a black man in America, not—

ACTOR 2. It's about you instead of us—

ACTOR 3. My great-grandfather—

ACTOR 2. Again.

ACTOR 4. There is a difference between here and—

ACTOR 2. That's your story that's not my story.

ACTOR 3. I told this deeply personal story because—

ACTOR 2. All we are doing is hearing the white version of the story / over and over—

ACTOR 3. The white version?!

ACTOR 4. He's just saying that you could tell that story / because your grandfather told it to you—

ACTOR 1. He's never done anything to you.

ACTOR 6. We're never going to get this done if we keep—

ACTOR 4. No one is even listening to me.

ACTOR 5. I am. / I'm listening.

ACTOR 3. I told that story because we're all trying to understand how someone could do something horrible—

ACTOR 6. Yes.

ACTOR 4. And I'm saying that—

ACTOR 2. I don't want to hear another story about how hard it is to be a white man—

ACTOR 3.	**ACTOR 5.**
That isn't what I am saying—	Wait, you guys, listen to—

ACTOR 2. I don't want to hear anything more from any of you—

ACTOR 1. You keep putting words in his mouth—

ACTOR 2. All we do is listen to your version of things over and over and—

ACTOR 3. Well, [sorry,] but you don't get to tell me what I say / and when I say it—

ACTOR 2. And I especially don't want to hear you tell some story you just made up—

ACTOR 3. I didn't make it up.

ACTOR 2. —so that you can make this all about you—

ACTOR 3.	**ACTOR 5.**
I didn't make it up.	Are you even listening to yourself?

ACTOR 2. —and tell us your version / of everything when it isn't even about you.

ACTOR 3.	**ACTOR 5.**
That really happened.	Why would he make that up?

ACTOR 6. We all know it did—

ACTOR 3. That really happened. I didn't make it up—it's true.

ACTOR 2. It doesn't matter if it's true or not—

ACTOR 3. It's not just some story.

ACTOR 4. None of this is. All of this really happened.

ACTOR 2. In Africa.

ACTOR 3. You don't understand.

ACTOR 2. I'm done with this.

ACTOR 3. That happened to my family.

ACTOR 2. I'm done with you.

ACTOR 3. Actually happened in my family.

ACTOR 4. And everything we're talking about happed to real people, a whole people, not just one family, thousands of families.

ACTOR 6. Right—we're talking about something really big here—

ACTOR 4. An entire tribe of people—

ACTOR 3. I know I was just—

ACTOR 1. He knows that we're talking about a Genocide.

ACTOR 6. Tortured, experimented on, enslaved—

ACTOR 1. Yes a German genocide. A rehearsal Holocaust.

ACTOR 4. It wasn't a rehearsal.

ACTOR 1. I know.

ACTOR 6. It was—

ACTOR 4. It was real people, in a real place.
It's not a rehearsal if you're actually doing it.

ACTOR 1.	**ACTOR 5.**
I know that.	Of course, but—

ACTOR 4. And you know what? Not all of the Herero died. Some of them survived.

ACTOR 1. I didn't mean rehearsal—

ACTOR 4. Some of them survived their / expulsion into the desert.

ACTOR 5. *(To* ACTOR 1:*)* I know.

ACTOR 4. There are still Herero in the world.

ACTOR 1. And don't you think it's—
Don't you think it would be offensive to them to have us like
Make up their story for them?

ACTOR 6. No. I don't think so.

ACTOR 5. We're just trying to—

ACTOR 3. We don't have to make it up—we can use our own stories to—

ACTOR 5. It can't be offensive if we're all, if we're all just trying to—

ACTOR 1. But we didn't find anything about them. Their stories are gone.

ACTOR 4. Right. We can use our stories but—

ACTOR 5. But we're all just trying really hard to understand—

ACTOR 3. Like some German man has a story just like mine.

ACTOR 4. Well, we have to be careful—

ACTOR 3. Right—

ACTOR 4. Because it's not just—
I mean we could say that there is a *Herero* person somewhere
that had a story exactly like yours.

ACTOR 3.	**ACTOR 5.**
That's what I'm saying—	And we're trying to—

ACTOR 4. Where he knows exactly where he's from, and it's where his father is from, and it's where his grandfather is from—

ACTOR 3. That is what I'm saying—

ACTOR 4. But the difference is the Herero man isn't allowed to go back to his home.

ACTOR 6. Right.

ACTOR 4. You can go to Pennsylvania whenever you want
but that Herero man was never able to go back home.
That man knew all of the names of the people who were killed
and not only that
he knew all of the names of everyone
all of his ancestors
because he believed that they were contained in a sacred fire.

ACTOR 6. Yes, we know this—

ACTOR 4. But that fire went out when his grandfather was forced out of
his home,
And when that fire went out his ancestors died.
He believed that his ancestors, all of them,
were murdered because the fire went out.
Can you imagine that?
His entire lineage, all of that history
that was remembered and remembered and remembered
until it was killed
and then it was forgotten.
And I'm not African.
I can't be.
But I know what that is to know that you've lost your heritage,
you've lost the names of your ancestors.

ACTOR 6. *(Fiercely:)* And that is why we need to figure out what it was like
for them.
That is exactly what I have been trying to do since the very beginning.

ACTOR 4. But I'm saying that, as Americans—

ACTOR 5. As Americans, we should try to—

ACTOR 6. No. We keep stopping and we keep talking and we just need to
do it.
So I'm gonna push you to do it so Everyone is going Keep Going
And no one is stopping, no one is done nothing is over because
we're going to stay in it until I say stop.
OK?
We are going to Stay In It until I Say Stop.
So let's go.
Let's go.
1905.
The wall has been erected.
One hundred and fifty miles wide.
On one side, there is home. On the other side, there is desert.
Black Man, you've been in the desert for days without anything to drink.
Go.

Scene: Processtation

ACTOR 2. There must be some water somewhere.

(Beat.)

ACTOR 4. *(Jumping in, eventually:)* The Germans have poisoned the watering holes.

ACTOR 6. Yes, the Guards made to stand the line were ordered to shoot on sight.

ACTOR 2. So, get down.

ACTOR 4. Oh I didn't realize—

ACTOR 2. Get down.

(They're on the ground.)

ACTOR 4/ANOTHER BLACK MAN. I'm thirsty.
Maybe it will rain soon?

ACTOR 2. In the middle of the desert?

ACTOR 4/ANOTHER BLACK MAN. Yeah.

ACTOR 2. I don't think so.

(Beat.)

ACTOR 4/ANOTHER BLACK MAN. Did you feel that?

ACTOR 2. What?

ACTOR 4/ANOTHER BLACK MAN. I think I felt a drop of rain.

ACTOR 2. You didn't feel anything.

ACTOR 4/ANOTHER BLACK MAN. You know what? I just felt another drop.

ACTOR 2. Stop it.

ACTOR 6. [No, keep going.]

ACTOR 4/ANOTHER BLACK MAN. I felt it! A drop of rain.

ACTOR 2/BLACK MAN. Ok.

ACTOR 4/ANOTHER BLACK MAN. Did you feel it? I felt it, so you must have felt it.

ACTOR 2/BLACK MAN. You're hallucinating.

ANOTHER BLACK MAN. No. You can feel it.
Cool clear water, pouring down from the sky.

ACTOR 2/BLACK MAN. I think I heard thunder.

ANOTHER BLACK MAN. A roar of thunder. A clap of lighting.

BLACK MAN. I can't even hear you over the storm.

ANOTHER BLACK MAN. I'm soaked right down to the bone.
I can feel the rain on my tongue.

BLACK MAN. Dear Sarah.
I have been waiting for you to arrive.

BLACK WOMAN/ACTOR 6. I will arrive and it will rain.
We will collect the rain in our clothes,

BLACK MAN. and skin and hair,

BLACK WOMAN/ACTOR 6. and we will walk across the desert

BLACK MAN. and when we get thirsty

BLACK WOMAN/ACTOR 6. we will hold our clothes and skin and hair
to our mouths and be refreshed.

BLACK MAN. Dear dear Sarah. She's so right.

ACTOR 6. You can see them

WHITE MAN/ACTOR 1. Yes.

ACTOR 6. You can see them. And you know it's not raining.

WHITE MAN/ACTOR 1. Yes.

ACTOR 6. You can see them. And what did the General say?
You know what the general said.

WHITE MAN, ANOTHER WHITE MAN, & SARAH.
The General Said.
Within the German Borders,
Every Herero,
Whether armed or unarmed,
With or without cattle,
Will be shot.

ACTOR 6. And where are we.

WHITE MAN, ANOTHER WHITE MAN, & SARAH.
Südwestafrika.

ACTOR 6. This is Germany.
The General has made this Germany.
And they are rebels.
They have started a rebellion that has raged on for years.
They have forced you to be here for years.
You have been standing on this wall for years.
They have threatened your lives.
Now you have orders.
You have new orders.
What are your orders.

WHITE MAN, ANOTHER WHITE MAN, & SARAH.
We are to round them up.
We are to chain them up.
We are to lead them up to the camp.
We are to imprison them there.
We are to keep our country safe for our countrymen.
We are to control them to keep the safety.

ACTOR 6.
Round them up.
Chain them up.
Lead them up.
Lock them up.

> *(*WHITE MAN, ANOTHER WHITE MAN, *&* SARAH *pick up and continue* ACTOR 6's *chant.*
> WHITE MAN *&* ANOTHER WHITE MAN *are leading* BLACK MAN *&* ANOTHER BLACK MAN *to begin hard labor. It turns into a song. A work song. A slave song.*
> *Southern accents creep in as the song is sung and the chant is chanted.)*

WHITE MAN, **ANOTHER WHITE MAN,** **[SARAH].**	**BLACK MAN,** **ANOTHER BLACK MAN,** **[BLACK WOMAN].**
Round 'em up.	*Take me to my home*
Chain 'em up.	*Take me to that place*
Lead 'em up.	*Place that I am from*
Lock 'em up.	*Take me to my home*
(repeat)	*Home that ain't my home*
	Where do I belong
	Took me from my home
	Place where I belong
	Place that's now your home
	Where I don't belong—

BLACK MAN. I don't belong here.

ANOTHER WHITE MAN. You can't just stop.

BLACK MAN. I ain't supposed to be here.

ANOTHER WHITE MAN. *(Referring to* ANOTHER BLACK MAN:*)*
You got that one?

WHITE MAN. Yeah. You better not give me no trouble.

ANOTHER WHITE MAN. Now where you think you going to run to?

BLACK MAN. I ain't supposed to be here.

ANOTHER WHITE MAN. I ain't supposed to be here either.

BLACK MAN. You bessa let me go.

ANOTHER WHITE MAN. That ain't how this works, boy.

    (BLACK MAN pushes ANOTHER WHITE MAN aside, and goes toward exit.)

ANOTHER WHITE MAN. You better / come back here.
You better get right back here.
You are breaking the law right now.

WHITE MAN. You move and I'll shoot you, you hear me?
I will shoot you and you better believe I won't blink an eye.

    (WHITE MAN & ANOTHER WHITE MAN catch BLACK MAN.)

BLACK MAN. You bessa take your hand off me.

ANOTHER WHITE MAN. You shut the fuck up.
Sit down.

WHITE MAN. Sit down.
Sit your ass down, you do what I tell you.

    (ACTOR 2/BLACK MAN goes to hit WHITE MAN.)

WHITE MAN. You gonna hit me, or you gonna sit?

    (The Scene Continues.)

WHITE MAN. Now answer me this.
You know what you done?

ANOTHER WHITE MAN. What are you asking him for?
I know what he done.
He trespassed, he stole from the government.
He assaulted me.

WHITE MAN. You know what that means?
That means you broke the law.

BLACK MAN. I ain't broke no law.

WHITE MAN. You don't talk back to me boy.

BLACK MAN. I said—

ANOTHER WHITE MAN. Don't you lie, boy. You lie again, I'll cut your tongue you son of a bitch.
You broke the law.
Say it.

    (ANOTHER WHITE MAN lands blows on BLACK MAN on each Tell.)

ANOTHER WHITE MAN. Tell the man you broke the law.
Tell the man you tried put your hands on me.
Tell the man before I Tell him for you.

Tell the man you tried to kill me.
Tell the man you were gonna kill me.
I don't need you to Tell me that you were gonna kill me.
I can Tell you wanted to kill me so Tell the man.
Tell him.
Tell him.

> (BLACK MAN *pushes back. A struggle.*
> BLACK MAN *knocks* WHITE MAN *down.*)

WHITE MAN. You better run nigger.
I said run.
Run nigger.

> (BLACK MAN *runs.*)

BLACK MAN / ENSEMBLE. *(Under his breath, in a rhythm of 7: 1-2-3, 1-2-3, 1:)*
Running. Running. Run Running. Running. Run

> (BLACK MAN *runs. The Ensemble blocks him.*
> WHITE MAN *&* ANOTHER WHITE MAN *chase.*
> WHITE MAN *&* ANOTHER WHITE MAN *catch him.*)

ANOTHER WHITE MAN. What do you want to do with him?

WHITE MAN. I got to think.

> (WHITE MAN *&* ANOTHER WHITE MAN *bind him.*
> *A beat of 7 continues—a stomp/clap—stomps*
> *on the down beats claps in between.*
> *The women are the source.*
> *1-2, 1-2, 1-2-3.*)

ANOTHER WHITE MAN. We got to do our order.

WHITE MAN. Let's see it.

> (*A letter is handed to* WHITE MAN.
> *He shows it to* BLACK MAN.)

WHITE MAN. You know what this means?
Do you know what this means?
I'll show you what this means.

> (WHITE MAN *rips the letter.*
> *He rips holes for eyes.*
> *He rips a hole for a mouth.*
> *He has made a crude mask.*
> *He holds it in front of* BLACK MAN's *face.*
> *A Show for a Crowd of 1,000.*
> *The Audience is Part of the Crowd.*)

WHITE MAN. You understand what this is now?

> (WHITE MAN *sticks the mask onto* BLACK MAN's *face.*)

WHITE MAN. You understand what this is now?

(WHITE MAN pretends his arms are BLACK MAN's arms. WHITE MAN pretends to be BLACK MAN)

WHITE MAN. *(As BLACK MAN:)*
Oh I understands!
You is gonna kill me.
But you bessa be careful white man.
Cause Lawd knows I is gonna haunt you.
I's gonna be a ghost prince of Africa!
I's gonna scream like my Brother Jungle Apes!
Oooga Booga!

ANOTHER WHITE MAN. Oooh, I am terrified!

WHITE MAN. Oooga Booga!

ANOTHER WHITE MAN. Oooga Booga!

WHITE MAN. Oooga Booga Boo!

(The beat of 7 grows even louder.
Their words become chants or song.
Eventually their movements become dance.
Eventually the entire ensemble share
the chants / song / dance.
A Production Number for a Crowd of 1,000.
They feel the rhythm for dance and speech/song in measures of 7.
7a: 1-2, 1-2, 1-2-3.)

ANOTHER WHITE MAN.
Ooogaaa Booga
Ooogaaa Booga
Ooogaaa Booga

ANOTHER WHITE MAN.	**WHITE MAN.**
Ooogaaa Booga	I black man
Ooogaaa Booga	I black man
Ooogaaa Booga	Remember
Ooogaaa Booga	Africa

ANOTHER WHITE MAN.	**WHITE MAN.**	**BLACK MAN.**
Ooogaaa Booga	I am man from	I am a black man I have
Ooogaaa Booga	Africa and	been a black man always I
Ooogaaa Booga	I alone can	remember what it was to
Ooogaaa Booga	Remember the	be a man alone I am
Ooogaaa Booga	Africa that	a black man I have been a
Ooogaaa Booga	I was from	black man always black
		always

(7b: 1-2-3, 1-2-3, 1.)

ALL. Running. Running. Run Running. Running. Run.
Running. Running. Run Running. Running. Run.

(7a: 1-2, 1-2, 1-2-3.)

ANOTHER BLACK MAN.	SARAHS.	WHITE MEN.
When they first came		
they called me prince		
called me leader	They	
of all people.	They	
They called me straight	They	Straight
straightest, straight back	They	Straight straight
straight teeth. Straight was	They	Straight
the best to them:	They	Straight straight
straight lines, straight	They	Straight
seams,		
straight gaze ahead,	They	Straight straight
straight heads of hair.	They	Straight

(7b: 1-2-3, 1-2-3, 1.)

BLACK MAN.	ALL OTHERS.
I have been black all my life	Running. Running. Run
I have been black all my life	running. Running. Run
I have been black all my life	running. Running. Run
I have been black all my life	running. Running. Run

(Cheers from the Crowd.)

(7a: 1-2, 1-2, 1-2-3.)

ANOTHER WHITE MAN.
I heard a joke once.
How come all the damn
Niggers that we see
Can run so damn fast?

Cause the slow niggers
Are locked up in Jail.

(7b: 1-2-3, 1-2-3, 1.)

BLACK MAN.	ALL OTHERS.
I have been black all my life	Running. Running. Run
I have been black all my life	running. Running. Run

(Cheers from the Crowd.)

(7a: 1-2, 1-2, 1-2-3.)

WHITE MAN.
I heard a joke once.
How do you stop a
Nigger from going out?

Pour more gas on him.

(7b: 1-2-3, 1-2-3, 1.)

BLACK MAN.	**ALL OTHERS.**
I have been black all my life	Running. Running. Run
I have been black all my life	running. Running. Run

(7a: 1-2, 1-2, 1-2-3.)

ANOTHER WHITE MAN.
I heard a joke once.
If you throw a nigger
And a kike
Off a roof
Which one is going to land first?

The nigger lands first

Because shit falls faster than ashes.

(7b: 1-2-3, 1-2-3, 1.)

BLACK MAN.	**ALL OTHERS.**
I have been black all my life	Running. Running. Run
I have been black all my life	running. Running. Run

(7a: 1-2, 1-2, 1-2-3.)

(WHITE MAN tops ANOTHER WHITE MAN's joke.)

WHITE MAN. I heard a joke once—

(Punch line: WHITE MAN shows off a noose.)

(7b: 1-2-3, 1-2-3, 1.)

ALL OTHERS.
Running. Running. Run
running. Running. Run
running. Running. Run
running. Running. Run
(cont.)

*(WHITE MAN & ANOTHER WHITE MAN
put the noose around BLACK MAN's neck and throw it over a beam or
branch.
They threaten and terrify him, and enjoy his fear.
BLACK MAN breaks character.)*

ACTOR 2. Help me.
Seriously.
Help me.
Get this fucking thing off me.

> *(ACTOR 6 eventually helps ACTOR 2.)*

ACTOR 2. Get this thing off me.
Get this fucking thing off me.
Get this thing off me.
Get this thing off me.

ACTOR 6. You're ok. It's off. You're ok.

> *(A Silence.*
>
> *ACTOR 2 leaves the stage.*
>
> *ACTOR 6 leaves after him.*
>
> *Silence.*
>
> *And in that silence something starts to happen. The actors start to process what just happened.*
> *And there is something…*
> *Discomfort. Frustration. Awkwardness.*
> *Nerves. Adrenaline. Uncertainty. Buzzing. Embarrassment. Guilt. Shame. Anger. Excitement.*
> *Something…*
> *Which might lead to a smile.*
> *Which might lead to laughter.*
> *If it does, ACTORS 5 and 3 and 1 find laughter.*
>
> *The laughter starts and stops.*
> *There might be failed attempts to shake off the moment in the laughter. There might be failed attempts to congratulate each other in the laughter. There might be failed imitations of the performance in the laughter. There might be failed explanations in the laughter. There might be failed attempts to stop laughing in the laughter. They might laugh and cry, they might laugh and scream, they might laugh and be silent, they might laugh and rip things apart. They might laugh and break. The actors might break, the moment might break, the momentum might break, the play might lose control, but the performers cannot stop until there is laughter, and it is genuine. The performers say and do whatever is in their minds.*
>
> *But ACTOR 4 is not laughing.*
>
> *He might try. But he cannot laugh.*
> *He cannot leave. As the other ACTORS have their reaction, ACTOR 4 eventually notices the audience. And then…*
>
> *ACTOR 4 cleans up the space.*
>
> *ACTORS 5 & 3 & 1 see ACTOR 4.*

It jolts them out of whatever they were in.
They watch him clean up the space.
He picks up objects that have come to hold significance:
Bottles of water, the bits of the mask, etc.
And places them in the box of letters.

ACTORS 5 *&* 3 *&* 1 *eventually remember the audience, and take them in, or they just remember* ACTOR 4, *or they remember themselves. In this remembering, they might be forced to leave the space.*

ACTOR 4 *takes down the noose. It is the last object to be dealt with. He puts it in or on the box of letters, the archive. He closes the box.*

ACTOR 4 *looks to the audience.*

He tries to say something to the audience but...
He might produce the air of a word beginning with the letter "w" like
We or Why or What.
He tries to speak, but he fails.)

End of Play

Addendum

Felt in 7a: 1-2, 1-2, 1-2-3

Beats / Parts	1	2	3	4	5	6	7
AWM		Ooo		Gaaa		Boo	Ga
WM	I		Black		Man		
			Black		Man		
	Re		mem		ber		
	Af		ri		Ca		
	I		am		man		from
	Af		ri		ca		and
	I		a		lone		can
	Re		mem		ber		The
	Af		ri		ça		that
	I		was		from		
BM	I	am	a	black	man	I	Have
	Been	a	black	man	al	ways	I
	Re	mem	ber	what	it	was	To
	Be	a	man	a	lone	I	Am
	A	black	man	I	have	been	A
	Black	man	al	ways	black	al	Ways

Felt in 7b: 1-2-3, 1-2-3, 1

Beats / Parts	1	2	3	4	5	6	7
En-semble	**Run-**	-ing		**Run-**	ing		**Run**
	I	have	been	**black**	all	my	**life**

Felt in 7a: 1-2, 1-2, 1-2-3

Beats / Parts	1	2	3	4	5	6	7
ABM		When	they			first	came
		they	called			me	prince
		Called	me			lead	er
		of	all			peo	ple
		They	called			me	straight
		straight	est			Straight	back
		straight	teeth			straight	was
		the	best			to	them
		Straight	lines			straight	seams
		Straight	gaze			a	head
		Straight	heads			of	hair
En-semble					They		
En-semble							Straight
		straight					Straight

Felt in 7b: 1-2-3, 1-2-3, 1

Beats/ Parts	1	2	3	4	5	6	7
E n - semble	**Run-**	-ing		**Run-**	ing		**Run**
	I	have	been	**black**	all	my	**life**

TREVOR

Nick Jones

About the Collaboration
Taking Risks to Reward the Audience

Lesser America was founded in 2010 by Daniel Abeles, Nate Miller, and Laura Ramadei, who continue to share creative and productive responsibilities. The company is designed to bridge the gap between safe, institutional theater and often inaccessible, experimental work. The Lesser Americans seek to produce new plays that tell uncommon stories but stories still relevant to a young, modern audience. The work is of high entertainment value, but comes at a low cost to the viewer. Simply, Lesser America puts on good new plays for less money and they're damn proud of that.

§

Trevor was a big moment for Lesser America. Not only because it sold out and gained us unprecedented critical praise, but because we so successfully executed our company mission. Before we got our hands on it, Nick's play made the rounds at several major theatrical institutions. None of them jumped at the opportunity to produce it presumably because it was too edgy or risky, or directors feared it wouldn't resonate with an older, subscriber-based audience. We took a chance that more seasoned producers might have shied away from, and the result was incredible and deeply gratifying. The show was a hit, and the tickets cost less than a third what anything else of its quality would have. We're honored to have given this play a life, and hope to continue providing a platform to similarly daring, effective writers.

—Laura Ramadei, Founding Member of Lesser America

Mission Statement: Lesser America

Lesser America is pop theater. They are an ensemble of renegade artists dedicated to smart, quality entertainment that puts the audience first, fulfilling the promise of affordable, accessible theater for the 21st century.

About the Author

Nick Jones is a performer and writer for theater, television and film. His most recent play was the critically-acclaimed *Trevor,* starring Steven Boyer as a has-been show biz chimp. His previous play *The Coward* was produced at Lincoln Center Theater/LTC3, where it was nominated for four Lortel Awards (winning two) and is now being made into a motion picture. His show *Jollyship the Whiz-Bang* at Ars Nova, a puppet rock musical about pirates, also received an extended critically-acclaimed run, and was subsequently revived for the Under the Radar Festival at The Public Theater.

Other plays include: *Salomé of the Moon* (PPAS Performing Arts High School), *The Wundelsteipen* (The Flea), *Little Building* (Galapagos Art Space), *Straight Up Vampire: A History of Vampires in Colonial Pennsylvania as Performed to the Music of Paula Abdul* (Philadelphia Fringe Festival, Joe's Pub), *The Nosemaker's Apprentice* (The Brick Theater, with Rachel Shukert), *The Sporting Life* (Studio 42 at Vineyard Theatre, also with Shukert), and *The Colonists,* a puppet work for children. Upcoming premieres in 2015 include: *Verité,* at LTC3, and *Important Hats of the Twentieth Century,* at Manhattan Theatre Club.

Mr. Jones was born and raised in Anchorage, Alaska. He earned his Literature/Creative Writing BA from Bard College and a Lila Acheson Wallace Playwriting degree from Juilliard, where he was a two-time winner of the Lecomte du Nouy Prize. He has received theater commissions from Lincoln Center Theater, Ars Nova, The Old Globe, Manhattan Theatre Club, The Huntington Theatre Company, Center Theater Group, and South Coast Repertory.

Mr. Jones currently lives in Los Angeles, where he is a writer and co-producer for the critically-acclaimed Netflix series *Orange is the New Black,* which has garnered numerous accolades, including Writer's Guild Award, Golden Globe, and Emmy nominations.

More at nickjonesland.com.

Cast of Characters

TREVOR, a 200 pound, 11-year-old chimpanzee.

SANDRA MORRIS, a 56-year-old widow, and Trevor's "mom."

ASHLEY, 33, the next door neighbor.

JIM, the county sheriff. 40s.

OLIVER, another chimp, known to be quite successful, and often well dressed. He is first seen wearing a white tuxedo.

P.A./JERRY, a young man, 20s or 30s. The doubling is not simply for convenience, but serves to illustrate how these characters are interchangeable in Trevor's mind. Non-white.

MORGAN FAIRCHILD, 50s, a blonde starlet. Likes to laugh.

Production Notes

This play is divided into 2 acts, with an intermission intended between Act 1 and 2 (if necessary).

/ indicates overlap (the point where the next line of dialogue should begin).

The actor playing Trevor should be dressed simply (not in fake fur, etc). He wears a diaper but this may not be visible underneath his clothes.

All scenes take place in or around the house, except for daydreams in which Trevor is transported in his mind to other realms. Generally, other characters cannot understand Trevor as he speaks, but through physical communication, and sign language. This convention is broken in scenes with Oliver and in some imagined scenes with Morgan Fairchild.

Feel free to add additional sign language, besides that which is indicated.

Occasionally, the characters will speak in a gibberish talk, consisting of variations of "kai-kai-ta-chai-chai." This represents human language from Trevor's point of view, when he's not understanding. Actors can feel free to improvise with the gibberish and need not bother trying to memorize "to the letter." However, to operate as a sort of bed of incomprehensible static, in which understandable English clearly stands apart, the language should not stray far from the baseline of "kai-ta-chai-chai" type sounds.

Because many scenes involve multiple characters talking at once (without hearing each other) there is some overlap. The actors playing Sandra and Trevor must often maintain the appearance of continuous speech, while actually allowing pauses for the other character to get their lines in. There are plenty of comic and absurd elements in this piece (starting with the premise) but ultimately, it is quite sad. Explore the comedy. Own the tragedy.

Acknowledgments

Trevor was first produced by Lesser America at Theater for the New City on February 28th, 2013. It was directed by Moritz von Stuelpnagel with the following cast and crew:

TREVOR	Steven Boyer
SANDRA MORRIS	Colleen Werthmann
MORGAN FAIRCHILD	Geneva Carr
OLIVER	Nathaniel Kent
JIM	Andy Nogasky
ASHLEY	Amy Staats
JERRY/PA	Shawn Randall

Set Design	Andrew Boyce
Costume Design	Elizabeth Barrett Groth
Lighting Design	Mike Inwood
Sound Design	Chris Barlow
Props	Sarah Dowling
Stage Manager	Kelly Burns
Fight Direction	Robert Westley
Technical Direction	Sean Gorski
Crew Master	Brendan Spieth
Press	Emily Owens
Producers	Daniel Abeles, Nate Miller and Laura Ramadei

Geneva Carr (in cardboard cutout), Steven Boyer, and Colleen Werthmann in *Trevor,* Theater for the New City, New York, New York (2013). Photo: Hunter Canning.

TREVOR
by Nick Jones

ACT I

(A middle class home in rural America. 2009.

A kitchen stage right is open to the living room, where there is a couch, a computer, and a large screen television. A screen door from the kitchen leads down some steps to a gravel parking lot. From the living room, a sliding door leads to a sundeck stage left, and a chain link animal enclosure in the yard. It is a large house, capable of housing a large family, now overrun with clutter. There is a sense that nothing is ever thrown away: books and toys and magazines and DVDs are piled on all available surfaces. There are several ribbons or other homemade awards visible, as well as drawings hung on the fridge.

Before lights rise, the sound of a car pulling up the gravel drive. On the car stereo, "Nobody's Fool" by Cinderella, can be heard, before the engine is shut off.

TREVOR, a 200 pound chimpanzee, enters the house through the kitchen. He tosses the car keys on the kitchen table, and heads for the living area.)

TREVOR. Sandra! I'm home!

SANDRA. *(Offstage:)* Trevor?

TREVOR. No go on that Dunkin' Donuts job. I went down there myself. Idiots had no idea what I was talking about…

SANDRA. *(Offstage:)* Trevor, did you take the car again?

TREVOR. …I mean maybe the spot was already taken, though I can't think who'd it have gone to, I mean there's not a huge pool of actors in the area.

(He sits down and turns on the TV with the remote as SANDRA enters. She picks up the keys and shakes them in his face.)

SANDRA. Trevor? Look at me. This is BAD. You are not to take mommy's keys. It isn't SAFE.

TREVOR. What? What are you saying? Oh the Corvette? Yeah I might have dinged it up a little. It isn't handling as well as it used to. You should tell Jerome.

(SANDRA grabs the remote and turns off the TV.)

TREVOR. Hey!

SANDRA. Trevor, BAD! BAD, Trevor…

TREVOR. Okay okay…I'm sorry. I'll be more careful.

SANDRA. You won't take mommy's keys without asking?

TREVOR. I'm not sure what you're saying. You want me to take it in for an inspection?

SANDRA. It isn't SAFE.

TREVOR. Okay. I'll do that tomorrow. But first, I just need to rest. I'm really frustrated by this work situation.

SANDRA. It's alright Trevor. Now give me a hug.

(Holding out her arms for a hug…)

TREVOR. I mean, it's not that big a deal. Well, okay…

(TREVOR hugs her.)

SANDRA. There you go.

TREVOR. Thanks Sandra. It's just really confusing. I mean, I've been watching their commercials and they have not once used a primate. Not once. I really think they're losing a big sector of the market this way. I tried to explain that to them, but they just, they just looked at me.

(There is someone walking up the steps of the porch outside: ASHLEY.)

SANDRA. Oh who is that?

(She goes to the door to see who it is, then continues outside.)

TREVOR. I don't know what it is. People just don't take to me, the way they take to some actors.

SANDRA. *(Stepping outside/offstage:)* Hiii.

TREVOR. I think it's because I don't have an easily definable look; I mean I don't fall into a type like some chimpanzees. I'm not always silly and I'm not always brooding, I have a full palette of emotions. You'd think people would be looking for someone with that kind of depth, of complexity, but nooo, not on television.

(SANDRA and ASHLEY have a conversation outside, heard faintly.)

ASHLEY. …Sandra, you can't let him DRIVE YOUR CAR…

SANDRA. …I know, I know…

TREVOR. You know, you'd think the phone would be ringing off the hook. I mean, I have a proven track record. I've already appeared with Dave the Weatherman; I've held the sign at the fruit stand—many times. I've been on a national television show. I mean, what other animal around here has been to Hollywood? Not the cat who lives by the intersection. Not the chimps in the zoo. They never leave the zoo. I don't get it.

ASHLEY. *(Offstage:)* Well are you going to do something?

(SANDRA comes back inside and ASHLEY follows her in. SANDRA looks for her phone, while demonstrating her willingness to discipline.)

SANDRA. Yes. Look, it's fine, I'll take care of it. I just need to hide the keys better—sorry it's such a mess. BAD, TREVOR, BAD.

TREVOR. I know it's bad. It's a very, very bad situation. That's what I've been saying.

SANDRA. Was he driving well?

TREVOR. ...There must be a way to get back on top.

SANDRA. Ashley?

ASHLEY. Your car is in my lawn!

SANDRA. I know. But, I mean, before then.

ASHLEY. I don't know. Sure. For an animal. / Sandra.

SANDRA. Shh— *(On phone:)* Oh hi, Ronnie, it's me. Can you send a tow truck to my house?

(As SANDRA is preoccupied on the phone, TREVOR investigates their new guest, who feels uncomfortable with the attention.)

TREVOR. *(To ASHLEY:)* Who's this? Hey. / Who are you?

SANDRA. Yeah...

TREVOR. Sandra?

SANDRA. I accidentally uh parked my car up on an embankment. Better bring the belt lift.

TREVOR. Wait, I know you.

SANDRA. Alright, thanks Ronnie...

TREVOR. You're the lady from next door. The new lady.

SANDRA. Anytime today...

TREVOR. I hear weird sounds coming from that house.

SANDRA. But the sooner the better...

TREVOR. You better not be doing any freaky stuff over there. This is a nice neighborhood.

SANDRA. Thanks, Ronnie. *(She hangs up.)* There. No problem. And I'll pay for the landscaping damage, or do it myself.

ASHLEY. No. That won't be necessary. Just, please, try to keep him under control.

SANDRA. I will, I will.

(TREVOR *goes and takes down a stack of headshots which he brings to* ASHLEY.)

ASHLEY. Maybe you should keep him in the kennel?

SANDRA. No. I don't like putting them in there.

ASHLEY. Well…

SANDRA. I'll hide the keys better. It's just he's a very clever boy. / Very clever.

ASHLEY. It's not just about the car, / Sandra.

TREVOR. *(Handing her a headshot:)* Here.

SANDRA. Oh look he wants to show you something.

TREVOR. Little souvenir. This is my headshot. You should take one, in case you're someone important.

ASHLEY. Thanks. I have one. He's been throwing these into our yard.

TREVOR. Or you might become someone important. You never know. Take several. Remember this face. I'm going to take back Hollywood. Mark my words.

ASHLEY. It's not just about the car. He is, in general, getting out of hand. I have a baby over there.

TREVOR. This is just one look. You know, I can play a nerd. Or a fireman. Or the devil.

SANDRA. No, no. He's just—he's been a little rambunctious, but I'm dealing with it.

ASHLEY. Are you? It doesn't seem like it.

SANDRA. Yes. I am. I am. It's just…

TREVOR. Special skills: roller skates, catching balls, dramatic costume wearing.

SANDRA. …it makes him very upset to be locked in a cage. He takes it personally.

ASHLEY. Personally?

SANDRA. Like, well, he knows that people don't go in cages, and I think it makes him feel like…he's…

ASHLEY. Like what? Like he's an *animal?*

SANDRA. Shhh—Don't!

(TREVOR *looks in their direction.* SANDRA *tries to play it off.)*

TREVOR. Hm?

SANDRA. Don't call him that. *(Low:)* He doesn't like that.

ASHLEY. It's not meant as an accusation.

SANDRA. Well, he's sensitive. / Besides…

TREVOR. Just because I don't always know what you're saying doesn't mean I don't know when you're talking about me.

SANDRA. …I wouldn't want him to feel like he has barriers.

ASHLEY. Oh, well you see, I would. I would like that more than anything in the world. Barriers. Fences. Cages. You have a kennel, / why don't you keep him in the kennel?

SANDRA. No no no no, you know what the problem is?

ASHLEY. …

SANDRA. He misses acting. And that's just killing him. He needs to act.

ASHLEY. *("Give me a break")* I don't know, if…okay…

SANDRA. No it's true. He's not used to not performing. It's what he's always done.

ASHLEY. Yeah…

SANDRA. …It's how he channels his emotion…

ASHLEY. I'm going to go.

SANDRA. What? Ashley. Don't be like that.

ASHLEY. No, I just should get back. My mother is watching Teddy…

SANDRA. Your mother?

ASHLEY. *(Continuous:)* …I just wanted to tell you your chimp was joyriding again.

SANDRA. Your mother's here? Where's uh…your husband?

ASHLEY. Doug's looking for work. My mother's just visiting.

SANDRA. Well let her spend some time with the baby. We need to talk. I take this seriously, Ashley, really freaking seriously. But I don't know if you understand, I've been going through a hard time lately.

ASHLEY. I know.

SANDRA. And I see things from your point of view, but what you don't understand is everyone who moves into that house, they all go through this period where they're like, oh there's a chimpanzee next door, that's unusual. But then they get to know Trevor. And then everything's fine.

> *(A beat.)*

ASHLEY. They really come and go, don't they?

SANDRA. What?

ASHLEY. Nothing.

SANDRA. I'm just saying, maybe if you took the time to get to know us better, you'd feel better about the situation.

ASHLEY. I guess that's probably true.

SANDRA. We're neighbors and I want you to feel good about all this, so… let's talk. You want some coffee?

ASHLEY. …

SANDRA. Come on.

(SANDRA *goes to make coffee.*)

ASHLEY. Okay. Okay, sure.

(ASHLEY *sits down.* TREVOR *approaches her wearing sunglasses.*)

TREVOR. Look. Cool Trevor.

SANDRA. What's that, Trevor, you got Jerome's glasses? Oh look at that. What a ham.

ASHLEY. Yeah.

TREVOR. Do we have a leather jacket? Sandra?

SANDRA. You've met people in town? They tell you about him?

TREVOR. Okay, I'll go look. *(He wanders off.)*

SANDRA. I mean, have you told people you live by Trevor's house?

ASHLEY. A few people.

SANDRA. Everyone knows Trevor. They named a sandwich after him at Tom's Deli.

ASHLEY. I know. And I feel bad, even asking you to… I know you're going through a tough time. But. It just, it reaches a point where…well the reason we even moved out of the city is because we wanted to live somewhere safe.

SANDRA. For the baby.

ASHLEY. Exactly.

SANDRA. And it is safe. And you are so lucky, because Trevor loves babies. I mean, that's how we got into show business. We'd visit schools and camps, and then eventually someone said, you ought to think about taking him out for film shoots. And you know, I was skeptical at first, but he just took to it, you know. He's a born thespian. And that's what's going to get us through this. Getting him back acting again.

ASHLEY. You ever hear that expression, treat the symptom not the problem?

SANDRA. *(Angrily:)* The problem is complicated because nobody understands what they're talking about.

ASHLEY. *He was driving your car on the highway!*

TREVOR. What are you saying?

(TREVOR *approaches to investigate once more.*)

SANDRA. Look, lower your voice. Please. He doesn't like hearing people get upset. It agitates him.

ASHLEY. Okay, I'm sorry.

SANDRA. Please, try to be understanding. This is not normal. We're just going through a rough spot.

ASHLEY. I know.

TREVOR. You making coffee? Is it coffee time?

SANDRA. Hello Trevor.

TREVOR. I want some. Make me some.

SANDRA. I bet I know what you want…

TREVOR. Yes. That.

SANDRA. But you can't have it, because the doctor says it's bad for you. Only herbal tea now. You want some tea?

(*Taking a box of tea from the cupboard and showing it to him, signing for "drinking."*)

TREVOR. What? No, come on. Fuck that.

(*He knocks the box from her hand.*)

SANDRA. Trevor. Bad. BAD. Apologize.

(TREVOR *goes and picks up the box and hands it back to her.*)

TREVOR. Sorry.

(*He touches her, in apology.*)

ASHLEY. So he does at least have a doctor you / take him to?

SANDRA. Now apologize to Ashley.

TREVOR. What?

SANDRA. To Ashley too.

ASHLEY. It's really alright.

TREVOR. I don't feel like apologizing to her. I do what I want in my house. Though I like your haircut.

(*He touches* ASHLEY's *hair.* ASHLEY *tenses, but* TREVOR's *interest is short-lived. He walks to the living room.*)

TREVOR. Let me know when the coffee's ready.

SANDRA. You see, he's very good. He's just a big sweetheart.

ASHLEY. Yeah…

TREVOR. I want to use the computer. *(He goes over to use the computer, bangs on the keyboard.)*

ASHLEY. How about at night? Can you at least lock him up at night? So I can sleep?

TREVOR. Sandra! This isn't working!

SANDRA. Hold on. Trevor, what are you trying to do honey?

TREVOR. I'm sending emails, to important people, in business. To get work. Have we renewed my membership to SAG yet?

SANDRA. You want to say hi to your friends on the computer? Is that what you want?

TREVOR. Yeah. Come here.

SANDRA. *(To* ASHLEY*:)* Hold on, one sec.

TREVOR. It's not working. Might need to shake it.

SANDRA. No. Use the mouse, honey. The mouse, remember?

TREVOR. Oh right…

> *(She goes to click on large icons created for links. When the image of a familiar face appears on the screen,* TREVOR *lights up.)*

SANDRA. Remember, just click over here.

TREVOR. Oh, what—Oliver!

SANDRA. That's right, Trevor. It's Oliver. Your friend. Okay?

TREVOR. Oliver…

> *(She goes back to* ASHLEY *and goes to pour the coffee.)*

SANDRA. Oliver's a chimp we met in Hollywood.

TREVOR. Hollywood? What? You said Hollywood.

SANDRA. *(Pointing to screen:)* Oliver. Your friend.

TREVOR. *(Rediscovering:)* Oliver! Oliver, oh man, look at him. Every day a different outfit.

SANDRA. *(Returning to kitchen:)* You take cream or sugar?

ASHLEY. Just cream.

TREVOR. There's someone who really made something of themselves. He's been a movie star, an astronaut, a scientist…

SANDRA. Listen Ashley, you don't have to worry. Really.

ASHLEY. Sandra, I really don't want to get off on the wrong foot…

TREVOR. He has a great career.

ASHLEY. I'm sure Trevor's very talented.

TREVOR. …A great family.

ASHLEY. I mean he's obviously / very talented…

TREVOR. You can do so much in a lifetime…

ASHLEY. But that's not the issue here. / What if he decides he wants to—

TREVOR. …or you can waste it on the computer AAAAAAAAAH, WHAT AM I DOING?!

(TREVOR suddenly breaks from the computer and starts pacing the room.)

SANDRA. Trevor! Oh freaking hell…

TREVOR. I need to work! I feel so cramped up in this house!

SANDRA. He's all wound up.

TREVOR. You can't just live cramped up inside all the time. You've got to do things!

SANDRA. You see, how frustrated he is? He needs a creative outlet.

(She goes and gets some crayons and paper.)

TREVOR. …I mean, I know I'm not as young as I used to be, but I can still make an impression. I mean back in the day…they used to love me. Morgan Fairchild brought me out to Hollywood for Chrisssake…MORGAN FAIRCHILD!

(He brings out a cardboard cutout of Morgan Fairchild as SANDRA tries to calm him.)

SANDRA. Trevor…

TREVOR. And now what? Where is the work? WHERE. IS. THE WORK.

SANDRA. Trevor…

TREVOR. Wait. That's what I ought to do. Call Morgan…

(He picks up the phone.)

SANDRA. Trevor, you want to do a picture for mommy?

TREVOR. Hello, operator? Get me Morgan Fairchild.

SANDRA. Trevor?

TREVOR. Hello? Hello? Broken. Every damn thing in this house, broken!

(Hangs up.)

SANDRA. TREVOR!!

(He looks at her, forgetting what he's doing for a moment.)

TREVOR. What?

SANDRA. *(Gently:)* Trevor. Okay. Now why don't we go outside now, honey… You want to draw a picture out on the deck?

(She hands him a piece of paper.)

TREVOR. I need your help here. We need to work together.

(She hands him the crayons, and points toward the door.)

SANDRA. Do a nice picture for mommy?

TREVOR. Do I look like I'm in the mood for drawing pictures??

(He looks at it, forgets what he was doing.)

TREVOR. I mean…I guess that does sound kind of nice.

(He takes the paper.)

SANDRA. Alright, good boy. We can take Morgan too if you want.

(SANDRA leads him outside to the deck stage left, taking the cardboard cut out with her. TREVOR looks back at ASHLEY.)

TREVOR. …Morgan. Morgan's my friend. We did the commercial, and we did the show. We're practically partners. We need to get in touch with Morgan. She'll know what to do. She's very powerful.

(SANDRA lays paper and crayons on the deck, and TREVOR begins scribbling. SANDRA returns inside.)

SANDRA. Sorry about that. I don't know what his problem is / today…

ASHLEY. He's an animal. That's his problem.

SANDRA. …I think he may have attention deficit disorder.

ASHLEY. He's an animal and he's very strong. And he frightens people. He frightens me.

SANDRA. That's a problem you have with yourself.

ASHLEY. Yeah. Alright, I'm going to go.

SANDRA. He's intelligent.

ASHLEY. This is not productive. I'm going to go.

SANDRA. But just I'm trying to tell you, it's not like we're talking about a dog here.

ASHLEY. No. Dogs don't drive cars. Dogs are kept in their kennels. I mean why even bother / to have one? Is that thing just for show?

SANDRA. I thought we were going to have a conversation.

ASHLEY. What's the point? There's no point. You're not listening!

SANDRA. You're not listening!

ASHLEY. Yeah…I need to get back.

(ASHLEY goes. SANDRA follows her out.)

SANDRA. Wait, just wait one minute…Ashley…

(Out on the deck, TREVOR is drawing a picture…)

TREVOR. It's important to have a hobby, between jobs. You need to have a hobby in this business. Otherwise it's just waiting. The waiting is what will kill you. So I practice my autograph.

I like to do a big scribble. I start from the middle, then I scribble all the way around, and then I pound it pound it pound it. That's my signature.

Oh they used to get such a kick out of this. The way they smiled. 'Oh Trevor,' they'd say. 'Bravo, Trevor. Trevor, one more?'

(Scribbling again.)

And after I'd sign a few I'd shake my hands like my hands were getting too tired, and then I'd switch to clutching the pen with my feet. Ah the people loved that trick…

(He smiles, wistfully.)

Had a job once, a commercial gig, with Morgan Fairchild. We really hit it off. She's one of the few actresses I feel comfortable calling a peer. Which is not to say I don't think there are many excellent actors working in the field. But Morgan Fairchild is exceptional.

(The scene becomes a TV shoot. P.A. enters with a chair, followed by MORGAN FAIRCHILD, a blonde in her 50s. The P.A. and MORGAN speak in a form of gibberish, as human speech would be heard by TREVOR, except for certain words he's learned. He speaks out to the audience.)

TREVOR. You have to pay attention on the set. Things move very fast, and not everyone knows sign language.

P.A. Chai-ta-kai-kai.

MORGAN. Kai-ta-chai-ta-chai.

TREVOR. You don't need to know the names for all things, but you should learn the important words if you want to work in the business.

P.A. Chai-ta-chai-chai-kai AGENT.

MORGAN. Chai-ta-kai HOLLYWOOD. Kai-chai-chai-ta-chai SERIES REGULAR.

TREVOR. You have to know when they're saying your name.

MORGAN. Chai-ta-kai kai TREVOR?

TREVOR. And you need to do what they tell you. Especially when 'they' is Morgan Fairchild.

MORGAN. Chai-ta-kai I'M MORGAN FAIRCHILD.

(The P.A. *walks off, calling off to someone.)*

P.A. Kai-kai-chai-chai ANOTHER APPLE BOX.

MORGAN. Kai-ta-chai-kai HELLO, TREVOR.

*(*TREVOR *takes her hand and shakes it.)*

TREVOR. If you shake their hand like a normal man, they will smile at you.

MORGAN. *(Delighted:)* Kai-ta-chai-ta-chai.

TREVOR. I've been doing normal man things like this my whole life.

MORGAN. Kai-ta-chai GOOD. Kai chai GOOD BOY.

TREVOR. Just doing my job, Morgan Fairchild.

(The P.A. *brings some water.)*

P.A. Kai-ta-chai MORGAN FAIRCHILD.

MORGAN. Chai-chai-ka-chai THANK YOU.

TREVOR. Please, allow me.

(He takes the bottle and opens it for her.)

MORGAN. Chai-chai-chai TREVOR. *(To someone unseen offstage:)* Chai-ta-chai-kai. *(Laughs.)*

TREVOR. It's nothing. I open bottles all the time. Oh you have a little thing. *(He picks off some lint and eats it.)*

MORGAN. *(In deep actorly voice:)* Kai-chai-ta-chai-ta-chai-ta-chai.

TREVOR. Oh you changed your voice.

MORGAN. Chai-chai-ta-chai. *(She begins doing a monkey routine.)*

TREVOR. That's amazing, the way you can make your voice high and then low. You see? You see that's why you're… And that's a…is that a chimp? Okay, that's borderline offensive, but good. You're good. *(Speaking out:)* Morgan Fairchild has a natural charisma, and her hair is the color of pee. That's why she works so much. Good, Morgan, good, but here, try it like this.

*(*TREVOR *begins to act up in a monkeyish way, alongside* MORGAN.*)*

You've got to go bigger than feels natural. And they like it when you bear your gums so it looks like you're smiling. Not sure why. Also, if there's anything around to dump on your head that's usually appreciated.

MORGAN. *(Impressed:)* Chai chai-ta-chai.

TREVOR. Yeah, I know. I feel like we have a lot we could learn from each other.

MORGAN. Chai-ta-chai chai TREVOR. AGAIN?

TREVOR. Again? The uh…well, I mean I'd rather not. Truth is, I don't really go in…

MORGAN. AGAIN!

TREVOR. …for the monkey stuff anymore. I'm trying to branch out…

MORGAN. AGAIN!

TREVOR. But, if the lady insists.

> *(TREVOR begins to jump around and do a ridiculous stupid monkey routine. The P.A. comes in to give him paper to tear up, and things to dump on his head.)*

TREVOR. How was that? Was that sort of what you were…

> *(…he trails off as he and MORGAN lock eyes. He breaks away, speaks out.)*

TREVOR. It's easy to get caught up in the glamour of the set. All the eyes are on you, and they give you your own place to sit. But you have to remember that in the end, you got a job to do.

P.A. Chai-ta-chai chai LOCKING DOWN THE SET.

TREVOR. You see these other chimps on the nature channel. They just sit around. They have no costumes. And there are snakes and things, it's depressing. I feel incredibly lucky to be working in this industry, alongside so many talented artists. I don't take this job lightly.

P.A. Chai-chai-kai-LAST LOOKS.

TREVOR. So when the lady says dance, you better cut a rug, fella.

P.A. Kai-kai-chai.

TREVOR. And if the man wants you to dump stuff on your head, you better make sure that bowl is empty.

P.A. Chai-ta-kaaaaiii…ACTION!

> *(A change, in which we see the actual commercial objectively. It is for accounting software. MORGAN FAIRCHILD is overwhelmed with receipts. TREVOR is dressed as an accountant, with a green visor and a calculator, perhaps…)*

MORGAN. Hi, I'm Morgan Fairchild and I hate tax season. Papers and receipts, how do I keep it all organized? Well with the new Tax Wiz Pro I don't have to. I just type in my deductions, and Tax Wiz does the rest. It's so easy even a monkey can do it. Right, Trevor?

TREVOR. That's right, Morgan. I can open water bottles. And so can you. Follow your dreams and anything is possible.

P.A. CUT!

> *(MORGAN and the commercial film crew disappear.)*

TREVOR. Yeah, you got what you needed? You want one more? One more for safety?

§

(Sheriff JIM BABBETT *is inside, holding a cup of Dunkin' Donuts coffee.)*

SANDRA. Dunkin' Donuts, that's so far. That's like a mile away. He drove that far? That's incredible. Jim, isn't that incredible?

JIM. Sandy, this is serious.

SANDRA. I know.

JIM. Someone could have been killed.

SANDRA. I know. I know! And I told him, it's BAD. It won't happen again.

JIM. You always say that…

SANDRA. I know, but / this is different.

JIM. …and then something happens.

SANDRA. I'm serious. I am freaking furious. I am going to be strict as hell with him from now on.

JIM. Sandy…

SANDRA. It was a mistake. It's my fault.

JIM. It's time to do something.

SANDRA. It's my fault.

JIM. This is a public risk.

SANDRA. But Jim. Jim, come on. You know he didn't mean anything.

JIM. That's not the point—

SANDRA. You know he'd never hurt anyone—on purpose. You know how gentle he is. He was at your daughter's baptism…

JIM. I know—

SANDRA. …He officiated the ceremony.

JIM. He did not officiate the ceremony. We dressed him up as a priest for pictures. For a laugh. And that was when he was a little. He's big now.

SANDRA. He's only eleven.

JIM. And strong. And he's getting to be more than you can handle.

(ASHLEY knocks on the door outside.)

SANDRA. Did cuntface call you?

JIM. He was driving your car on the highway, Sandy. *Everyone* called me. I don't know why you're so resistant. I mean it'll be good for him too. To go somewhere where he can be with other chimps.

SANDRA. No, I won't put him in one of those places. They're dirty. It will be too traumatic for him, he wants to be here with me.

JIM. I know, but…this is…I mean, look at this from my position.

(ASHLEY *enters.*)

ASHLEY. I'm sorry to interrupt, but I just wanted to say, if you need a statement, I also saw him.

SANDRA. Oh that's great, that's just great, / real nice, real neighborly…

(TREVOR *enters.*)

ASHLEY. *(Overlapping:)* I'm sorry, but I have a baby.

SANDRA. So do I.

TREVOR. Hey, / what's going on?

ASHLEY. *(Overlapping:)* Except that I'm talking about a human being.

SANDRA. *(Overlapping:)* And you know I hear your baby crying. It keeps me up all freaking night. / Do I say anything? No.

ASHLEY. *(Overlapping:)* It's the Ferber method!

JIM. *(Overlapping:)* Alright, / hey!

TREVOR. *(Overlapping:)* Hey. Yeah. Hey. Everybody calm down! Why are there so many people talking at once?

JIM. Hello Trevor.

TREVOR. …It's very confusing. Hi, Cop.

JIM. Everybody calm down. We're going to figure this out.

SANDRA. It's going to be okay. I'll put him in his kennel at night. And I'll hide the keys.

TREVOR. I like cops.

ASHLEY. I don't believe her.

SANDRA. You don't believe me?

ASHLEY. I'm sorry I just don't.

TREVOR. Beautiful costume. Beautiful.

JIM. Okay, okay. Well, look, what would make you feel better?

ASHLEY. Honestly, I don't think I'll ever feel safe with him here.

TREVOR. Oliver was a cop once.

SANDRA. What do you want? You want me to just throw him away, to some roadside zoo somewhere?

ASHLEY. *(Overlapping:)* It is just common sense, you don't let animals drive cars.

SANDRA. No one's letting him drive cars. / It's an accident.

JIM. *(Overlapping:)* I know, I know, but, hey, listen…

SANDRA. *(Overlapping:)* What you've / never made a mistake before?

TREVOR. Oliver's costume wasn't as fancy as this.

JIM. Ladies…

TREVOR. It didn't have so many shiny things.

> *(He reaches for Jim's gun, takes it.)*

JIM. HEY!!!

TREVOR. Hey!

SANDRA. TREVOR!

> *(JIM has startled TREVOR with his shout. TREVOR looks around for the source of the disturbance, confused and on guard, gun in hand.)*

JIM. *(Carefully:)* What do you think you're doing?

TREVOR. What's the problem? What's going on?

> *(JIM moves slowly towards TREVOR. Gently:)*

JIM. Hey.

TREVOR. *(Confused:)* Hey.

JIM. Heyyy… *(JIM grabs the gun back, then becomes strict as TREVOR tries to retrieve it.)* NO! NO! Goddamn it. Sandy?

> *(TREVOR stops his approach.)*

SANDRA. NO! NO! BAD!

TREVOR. *(Stepping back slowly:)* Okay okay… Everybody calm down. Party's over.

JIM. Keep him away from me.

SANDRA. I'm sorry, he's just grabby.

JIM. Grabby?

ASHLEY. You see? You see? This is out of control.

TREVOR. Sandra, does Jerome know all these people are over?

JIM. Sandy! Put him in the kennel. Now!

TREVOR. Cop. Stop yelling. / You've had too much coffee.

SANDRA. Okay. Okay. Trevor.

TREVOR. What? Why are you looking at me?

SANDRA. *(Trying to take TREVOR by the hand:)* Trevor, come with me.

(He shakes off her hand.)

TREVOR. What?! He's the one yelling!

SANDRA. It's time to go outside...

(She takes him more forcefully by the hand, but he again shakes her off.)

TREVOR. He's the one yelling. He's the one who's drinking coffee!

SANDRA. *(Looking into his eyes, pleading:)* Trevor, PLEASE. Just come with me.

TREVOR. *(Obeying, with difficulty:)* Alright. Fine.

(He follows SANDRA out onto the deck. Just before leaving, he looks back at ASHLEY and JIM. He calmly knocks over a plastic cup.)

SANDRA. TREVOR!!

TREVOR. *(Not sorry:)* Oops.

(He then lets himself be led out onto the deck, and then from there, down some steps into the yard, and his backyard enclosure. JIM and ASHLEY are alone in the house.

Outside, SANDRA lets TREVOR into his enclosure.)

SANDRA. Trevor, you have to learn to control yourself. It's very important.

TREVOR. Oh it's like that, huh? I know, I was bad. But it's not fair.

SANDRA. Now you just stay here. I'll be right back, okay?

TREVOR. They were shouting. I got confused.

SANDRA. I'll be right back. Then we'll go for a walk or something.

TREVOR. Sandra, don't leave me in here for long, okay?

SANDRA. I'll be right back.

(SANDRA returns to the house.)

TREVOR. Sandra, I'm sorry, I'm sorry...I don't know why I do these things sometimes...

(From somewhere in the distance, a strange lilting music is heard...)

OLIVER. *(Offstage:)* No one ever said it was easy.

(OLIVER, a chimpanzee in a white tuxedo, enters and addresses TREVOR from the other side of the enclosure. He walks upright and has a regal air about him.)

TREVOR. Oliver? What are you doing here?

OLIVER. Well, I was in town for a conference and thought I'd pay you a visit. How are you my friend?

TREVOR. I don't know. I feel cooped up in this house. I need to work.

OLIVER. Well, it's a bad economy.

TREVOR. I know. But you're still doing great.

OLIVER. Sure, I do swell. I live down in Florida now, with my human wife and our three half-human children. Oh and did I tell you—a three-quarter human grandchild on the way.

TREVOR. Oh why that's tremendous. Just tremendous.

OLIVER. Yes sir. Seems little Timo took quite a liking to his human handler down in Cape Canaveral. They were spending a lot of time together in the science lab and I guess they really hit it off. He mounted her.

TREVOR. Tremendous. I didn't know the kids were already out there, uh…

OLIVER. Working as scientists? Yes they all are. Being half human, the science community took a keen interest in them. All the exciting jobs go to the young ones. Plus, they prefer to work with chimps before their genitals become engorged.

TREVOR. I know, I know. Then how do you do it then? How do you stay relevant after puberty? I mean, you still have a great career. I see all the costumes you get to wear.

OLIVER. Truthfully, it takes everything I got. To behave. At this age. But you've got to behave. You've got to.

TREVOR. I know. Sometimes I…I do things I'm not proud of. I knocked a cup over.

OLIVER. You shouldn't knock cups over. You'll never get ahead that way. You have to fight those urges.

TREVOR. It just seemed fun.

OLIVER. Of course it's fun. You think I don't know it's fun? You think most days I wouldn't rather just be going berserk, smashing watermelons and hurling clods of my own feces? Oh my god what a release that would be. But you'll never get work that way. I knew a guy, worked in the Barnum Circus all-chimp production of *Hamlet,* started beating his trainer with a prop skull. You won't be seeing him on stage again. People don't understand that kind of humor. You've got to be able to sit still, and follow instructions.

TREVOR. I try. Sometimes I don't understand the instructions.

OLIVER. Well if you can't understand instructions, then just sit still and bear your gums so it looks like you're smiling. Believe me, if you can just do that—if you can just behave—the world will open for you. Just look at me. I live in Florida, with a human wife and three half-human children…
And I wear a white tuxedo.

    (He starts to exit.)

TREVOR. How did you do it, Oliver? Where'd you get the white tuxedo?

OLIVER. *(Wistfully:)* I don't know. They just dressed me up in it one day.

(He vanishes. Back in the house, SANDRA, ASHLEY, *and* JIM *are talking.)*

JIM. I remember when you got him. And I know it was never meant to be forever. Jerome never planned… It was just going to be for a little while.

SANDRA. He won't like living with other chimps. He doesn't relate to them anymore. And this is not some dog we're talking about. It's Trevor. He's part of what makes this town unique. They named a sandwich after him. And look…

(She goes and finds a pamphlet.)

JIM. *(Overlapping:)* Sandy, you don't need to do / that, I know, that…

SANDRA. *(Continuous:)* …He's on the brochure. He's on the brochure for the town. You see? That's his picture. He's the symbol of the town. The face of the town.

JIM. I know that, Sandy. But the thing is, that's just a picture. It doesn't mean anything. This is an issue of safety.

SANDRA. He's never hurt anyone.

JIM. Not yet.

SANDRA. So what then? Because he might hurt someone, you're going to take him away…?

JIM. I didn't say that.

SANDRA. You're going to take him and put him down like a dog? The chimp who baptized your daughter!

JIM. I didn't say that.

SANDRA. Then what?? What are you saying??

JIM. I'm saying…if we're going to be serious about this—okay, look—I know a guy. He works in Animal Control in the next / county over.

SANDRA. No, no, / no no.

JIM. I could ask him / his opinion.

SANDRA. That's a bad idea.

JIM. He knows about animals.

SANDRA. But he doesn't know Trevor. This is a special case…

JIM. Sandy…Sandy…

SANDRA. *(Continuous:)* …You ask someone like that, you know what they're going to say, it's their business to put away animals. But you can't just have someone make a judgment like that, someone who doesn't know him personally…

JIM. Sandy…

SANDRA. …He's a special case. You need to consider his history, you know, his / accomplishments.

JIM. Sandy, will you just listen to me! You can tell him all of that. It will be off the record. Jerry's a friend. It would just make me feel better to have a professional assess the situation.

ASHLEY. What is it you need to know?

(JIM *motions for her to hold off talking.*)

JIM. I think that's only fair. Nobody here is trying to hurt you, Sandra. We all love Trevor. This town remembers when he was little, and cute, and he gave us a lot of joy. And we're not going to send him anywhere / that won't be for his own good.

SANDRA. No, don't send him anywhere.

JIM. But I have to make sure this is a safe situation. Right? You must agree we have to have a safe situation. Right?

SANDRA. Yes, I know, but—

JIM. So this is what we have to do. To make sure. I'm going to call Jerry and see if he'll come by.

SANDRA. Well he can't come by today.

JIM. Not today, tomorrow is fine. We could see about tomorrow.

ASHLEY. (*About to ask a question:*) Um…

(JIM *motions for her to hold off.*)

JIM. Sandy? Tomorrow good for you?

SANDRA. I don't know, I was going to go by the garage and check up on things.

JIM. You don't need to do that. The garage will be fine. This is what you need to do tomorrow. Meet Jerry. And that's final. Okay?

SANDRA. …

JIM. Okay?

SANDRA. Fine.

JIM. Great. That's great. Look, and this doesn't mean…this doesn't mean he has to go away, it just means we need to get all our facts straight, you know, take a hard look and…we'll make the decision all together, okay? Okay?

SANDRA. …

JIM. …Alright.

(JIM *and* ASHLEY *start to leave.*)

SANDRA. You think Jerome ever lifted a finger?

(JIM turns.)

SANDRA. You think I can't handle him by myself? Why, because Jerome is gone? Because Jerome helped out so much? Jerome never lifted a finger. Hiding out in the garage or out with you and the others drinking beer or whatever the fuck you did.

JIM. Well, look, I / don't know what you—

SANDRA. So don't you talk to me about how Jerome never planned on keeping him, because that is NOT HOW THIS WORKS. You don't adopt an animal and throw it away like a piece of garbage just because it stops being cute. What YOU think is cute.

JIM. We're not.

SANDRA. You are. YOU ARE. And in the name of my husband. How dare you. This has nothing to do with Jerome. This is about Trevor. About what Trevor needs.

JIM. About what Trevor needs or what you need?

SANDRA. WHAT I NEED IS WHAT TREVOR NEEDS. He never turned his back on me. He's the ONLY ONE never turned his back on me. And I have a responsibility to him, you understand?

JIM. Yeah, Sandy. I understand.

(He exits.)

§

(SANDRA goes down to the kennel.)

TREVOR. Hey, Sandra, look I've been thinking. You were right. I shouldn't have knocked the cup over. It was wrong. I see that now.

SANDRA. *(Letting loose:)* Goddamn FUCKING BITCH!

TREVOR. Whoa. Sandra.

(She begins to cry.)

TREVOR. Sandra. Sandra. Hey. Don't cry. What's going on?

SANDRA. I won't let them. I won't let them take you.

TREVOR. What is it? What did they say to you? Who was bad? WHO WAS BAD? Oh, it was that cop wasn't it? Oh, I knew there was something wrong. I never should have left you alone with him. Where is he? Where is he? One phone call, cop! One phone call and you'll never wear a cop costume again! I know Morgan Fairchild! Morgan Fairchild will eat you for breakfast!

(SANDRA sobs.)

TREVOR. Hey, don't cry. Don't cry.

(He raises his hand up. SANDRA looks at it.)

TREVOR. I'm sorry.

SANDRA. Oh Trevor.

(They touch through the chain link fence.)

What are we going to do with you?

TREVOR. Hey, hey. Trevor's going to take care of you now. Open the gate.

(SANDRA opens the gate.)

That's right.

(They hug.)

TREVOR. Now you don't worry. I'm never going to let anything happen to you. You, and Jerome. You're my family, and I won't let anything happen to my family.

SANDRA. Come on inside, sweetheart.

(She takes him by the hand and leads him up the stairs and into the house.)

TREVOR. But look, let's face some facts, you're getting older, Sandra. I don't know if you can fight off an enemy the way Jerome and I can. That's why I think it's better for you to never put me in the cage again. At least until Jerome gets home.

SANDRA. Don't worry, Trevor, those nasty people are all gone now. Are you hungry, sweetheart?

TREVOR. Do you understand?

SANDRA. How about some pot pie? You want some pot pie for lunch?

TREVOR. What?

(SANDRA takes some pot pie from the freezer, shows it to TREVOR.)

TREVOR. Oh sure, that's great. And maybe some… *(Points to wine bottles.)*

SANDRA. Wine?

TREVOR. Just to take the edge off.

SANDRA. Well, Trevor, I don't know if you should…

TREVOR. I'm really stressed out.

SANDRA. You've been bad.

TREVOR. *(Signing:)* I love you.

SANDRA. Oh, honey…

(TREVOR tries to look cute and pathetic. He knows how to play her.)

SANDRA. Well, you have had a rough day. And that does sound nice. For mommy too. Okay. Some nice red wine and pot pie for mommy and her little man.

> *(She opens the bottle, while he takes two long stemmed glasses from the cabinet and places them on the counter. They cooperate marvelously.)*

> *(There is a sound of a baby crying next door.)*

TREVOR. Listen, Sandy, about that neighbor woman…

SANDRA. *(Pouring:)* And now just a little bit…

TREVOR. I don't trust her. I don't think you should let her in here.

SANDRA. But we have to let / it breathe first.

TREVOR. I hear screaming sounds coming from her house. There's something up with her. *(He drinks his wine.)* I think she might be a monster. We don't want to get involved with people like that. / Things are hard enough as it is.

SANDRA. Wait Trevor you have to let it breathe first. Oh what's the difference… *(She drinks her wine as well.)*

TREVOR. By the way, did anyone call? Sandra? Maybe… *(He points to Morgan.)*

SANDRA. You want Morgan to come to dinner, honey? Alright…

TREVOR. But did she call?

SANDRA. She's your friend, isn't she? Your friend. *(Signs.)*

TREVOR. My personal friend, yes. We did a commercial for water bottles, or possibly paper.

SANDRA. *(Signs.)* She loved you.

TREVOR. *(Signing:)* She loves *me??* I love *her.*

SANDRA. You did so good on that commercial, Trevor. You did so good.

TREVOR. What did she say?

SANDRA. …That's why Morgan invited you to be on her show. Remember when you were on the show, honey?

TREVOR. The show? Yes, yes! What about it?

SANDRA. That could have been a great show. But oh well…

TREVOR. What?

SANDRA. TV's for the freaking birds, right Trevor? It's the live show that matters…

TREVOR. What did she say? About the show?

SANDRA. Wait a minute, that's what we ought to do…

TREVOR. What?

(*As* SANDRA *comes up with her plan her voice becomes slower and deliberate, which* TREVOR *notices and emulates, as he tries to understand.*)

SANDRA. Do the show…right here.

TREVOR. I like…the tone of your voice…

SANDRA. They want you to go to a sanctuary, we'll make *this* the sanctuary.

TREVOR. Something…is happening.

SANDRA. Sanctuary of the stars!

TREVOR. Are we going back to Hollywood?

SANDRA. I'll have Ronnie build us a stage in the back.

TREVOR. Did they pick up the pilot?

SANDRA. We'll put a sign out on the highway: Trevor: World Renowned Star of Stage and Screen.

TREVOR. Yes!

SANDRA. We'll see how that smug bitch likes it when you become a tourist attraction.

TREVOR. Ahh, I can't believe it!

SANDRA. I'll make this place into, like, a museum. We'll put all your stuff on display. And do your old act!

TREVOR. Yeah!!

SANDRA. Put a cage around the stage if we have to but we'll do right here. You are not going anywhere, buddy, you are staying right here!

TREVOR. We're going to Hollywood!

(SANDRA *goes to turn on some music.*)

TREVOR. Oh, man I can't wait. Ah man, I knew they'd go for it. America loves an animal variety show. I mean, I always said, that's where everything is headed. What is it, a mid-season replacement? Ah man, yeah, and why not? It was a great show Morgan put together. Great acts all around. Except for that seal.

(SANDRA *puts on some music. It's an eighties hard rock song like "Dr. Feelgood" by Mötley Crüe.*)

TREVOR. What's that?

SANDRA. Trevvvooor…

TREVOR. My song.

SANDRA. It's your song!

TREVOR. My song from the old act!

SANDRA. You remember?

TREVOR. Where's my guitar? Give me my guitar.

SANDRA. Of course you do...you're so smart.

(*He looks for his toy guitar. SANDRA gets it for him.*)

TREVOR. I gotta get back in shape. I gotta practice my moves.

SANDRA. Here you are, sweetheart.

TREVOR. Give me that. Yeah. Yeah, my old axe. Is this thing tuned?

(*TREVOR takes the guitar and moves from side to side with the guitar, making guitar rocker approximations. SANDRA laughs in delight.*)

TREVOR. Like this, right?

SANDRA. That's right. Yes, that's wonderful. It's hilarious! Oh my god, it's genius. Genius!

(*She goes and gets some juggling balls.*)

TREVOR. Yes, this is it. I've got it. I've still got it!

SANDRA. Now wait, this is the part, where you stopped to juggle, remember, Trevor?

TREVOR. (*Still caught up in the guitar part of act:*) I'm playing guitar!

SANDRA. Okay, now I throw you the ball, right?

TREVOR. What?

(*SANDRA throws him the first ball. It hits his chest, and falls to the ground.*)

SANDRA. No, Trevor. You have to pick up the ball, remember?

TREVOR. But I'm playing guitar.

SANDRA. No but that's just the first part, Trevor. You have to juggle the balls now. Don't you remember?

TREVOR. Oh. What? I don't know...

SANDRA. Well, we'll get to it later. I forgot to put the pie in...

(*She stops the song, then goes and begins preparing the meal in the microwave, and setting the table.*)

TREVOR. It's alright, I just need to practice. I have the talent. Of course I have the talent. I was on a commercial with Morgan Fairchild, I appeared with Dave the Weatherman, and...I have all these awards. I have the talent. And anyone with talent eventually is recognized. Sometimes it just takes a long time. Sometimes it just takes a very long time.

(*The lilting music returns. OLIVER enters.*)

OLIVER. How long has it been, Trevor? Since you were in Hollywood?

TREVOR. I don't know. I don't have a watch.

OLIVER. Ahhh yes. I used to have one. But it was just a toy.

TREVOR. Oliver, what are you doing here? Another conference?

OLIVER. Conference, no. I just came to congratulate you on the show getting picked up.

TREVOR. Oh is it in the trades already? Yes, it's very exciting.

OLIVER. You must have done a great job the first time around.

TREVOR. Yes, I guess I did. Morgan loves me.

OLIVER. I'm not surprised. There's a lot she could learn from you. There's a lot we all could learn from you. You have such depth as a performer.

TREVOR. I'm just happy to be working…

OLIVER. Ah. Trevor, I hate to ask you this, but do you suppose you could put in a word for me with Morgan?

TREVOR. Me? Put a word in for you? But you're Oliver. I thought you were doing so well.

OLIVER. I was. I'm afraid my fortune has turned.

TREVOR. What? But you have a great career, and a wife, and…

OLIVER. The half-human children, I know…but they're gone now.

TREVOR. I was just talking to you.

OLIVER. They were chased out of Florida.

TREVOR. But I thought they were scientists.

OLIVER. It was a misunderstanding. They were just wearing lab coats. Turns out they were never appreciated for their human qualities. They just wanted some primates to strap to rocket sleds for impact tests. Well when we found that out, my wife and I were incensed. We protested, we wrote letters to Congress—or she wrote letters—but I took night classes to learn to write—or at least I was going to—she drove me to the enrollment office to sign up—and, and, that's where she met Frank.

TREVOR. Frank?

OLIVER. A full human. And now she's gone. And my children were shot trying to escape and sold for bush meat to the Floridians. I've lost everything, Trevor. I'm washed up.

TREVOR. Oh my god, Oliver!

OLIVER. …And now I've got all this alimony to pay. And I don't know where I'm going to get the money. I can't even get a callback!

TREVOR. I don't understand. How could this have happened?

OLIVER. I don't know. I did everything they asked of me. I did everything they asked of me.

TREVOR. Hey buddy don't worry. Of course I'll put in a word for you. You were a big inspiration to me when I was coming up, and I really feel like I owe you one.

OLIVER. Thank you, Trevor. You are a great friend. And a fantastic actor.

(*The microwave beeps.*)

SANDRA. Okay, lunch's almost ready. Trevor, you want to set the table? Trevor? What are you looking at, honey?

TREVOR. You better go, it's dinner time.

OLIVER. Yes, well that's the other thing. I hate to ask you for anything more, but would you mind if I stayed with you for a little while? Just while I got back on my feet.

(TREVOR *goes to the kitchen and takes knives and forks from out of the drawer and begins setting the table, while* SANDRA *prepares plates.*)

TREVOR. Stay, here? / Ehnnnnnn…

OLIVER. I promise I'll stay out of the way.

TREVOR. Well, I don't have a problem with it, but…

OLIVER. You've seen the nature shows. There's snakes out there. And monsters.

TREVOR. I know.

OLIVER. (*Overlapping:*) I'll groom you.

TREVOR. I appreciate that. But it's Jerome you should groom. This is his house.

OLIVER. Jerome?

TREVOR. My dad. (*He picks up a picture of Jerome.*)

OLIVER. Oh. Where is he?

TREVOR. I'm not sure. He's been gone a while.

OLIVER. Maybe he's hiding.

TREVOR. No, he's not hiding. I've looked everywhere.

(*Beat.*)

SANDRA. Alright very good Trevor…

(*She sees* TREVOR *holding the picture of Jerome.*)

Come sit down now.

(They sit at the table. TREVOR *still holds the picture.)*

SANDRA. Okay Trevor, let's put that down now.

(She tries to take the picture but he holds onto it.)

SANDRA. Oh honey. You miss Jerome, don't you?

TREVOR. We used to wait for him before eating.

SANDRA. I miss him too.

(They look at each other. She puts her hand upon his. A pause.)

TREVOR. Sandra. Did Jerome run away? *(Gesturing.)*

SANDRA. Jerome is gone, honey. He went to the hospital and he's not coming back.

(Beat.)

TREVOR. Did you forget to feed him?

SANDRA. But it's not your fault.

TREVOR. He ran away didn't he?

SANDRA. And we still have each other. *(She begins to eat.)* And pot pie. Yum.

TREVOR. He ran away…

*(*TREVOR *looks at* OLIVER.*)*

TREVOR. I guess that means I'm the dominant male now.

(From Ashley's house, a baby can be heard crying. TREVOR *perks up, turns toward the sound.)*

SANDRA. Nevermind that Trevor. Nevermind.

(He lifts his fork, still listening.)

SANDRA. Look at you Trevor. So sophisticated. With your fork.

(Lilting music. The baby continues to cry. Lights fade.)

End of Act I

ACT II

(The next day. TREVOR *is flipping through the television, as* SANDRA *nervously tries to straighten up the house.)*

TV. *("Wheel of Fortune":)*
"Is there an E…?"
"Is there an E? Yes there are two Es…Spin again…okay…"
"J?"
"No there is not a J…, and we're on to George's turn. George, you want to spin?"
"No Pat, I'd like to try to solve the puzzle. Is it 'Frequent Flyer Miles?'"
"…No…."

SANDRA. Trevor, change the channel please.

(He changes it.)

TV. *(From the VH1 "Behind the Music" special…)* "…In the 1980s, Judas Priest were the apostles of the new wave of British Metal; a fiery band of headbangers, led by chief preacher, Rob Halford…"

SANDRA. No. Change it.

TV. *(Dating show:)* "I think Angela's a really nice girl, but she has some issues she needs to work through, and I just think…I'm not the guy / she's waiting for…"

SANDRA. Change it.

TV. "…but few of the Priest disciples knew that Rob was / imprisoned in a self-imposed hell, living a secret life as a gay man…"

SANDRA. No! The other way. I don't want you watching TV if it's just crap. Trevor can you get up please?

TV. *("Jerry Springer":)* "…My name is Becky and when my mom tries to control me, I just punch her in the face. Nobody tells me what to do. I'll have as much sex as I want. I had sex with three guys in / one night the other day, cuz I got it like that…"

SANDRA. Trevor, can you please get up?

(He ignores her. SANDRA *walks in front of the TV and clicks it off.)*

TREVOR. *(Getting off the couch:)* Hey! I was watching that. Why'd you do that? What are you doing?

*(*SANDRA *lifts up one of the couch cushions. Underneath there are all kinds of hidden food items from the kitchen.)*

SANDRA. *(Holding up a mustard jar:)* Oh Trevor, I was looking for this!

TREVOR. Sandy you need to relax. What's going on?

SANDRA. I just can't…

TREVOR. What? Let me help. What are you trying to do? *(Taking an open package of hot dogs:)* You want me to hide these somewhere else?

SANDRA. No, give me that.

(He takes it and puts it on the coffee table, then takes the other couch cushions up.)

TREVOR. Oh I see. *(He takes the cushions and begins arranging them.)* You want to make a fort…

SANDRA. No Trevor, just—don't touch anything!

TREVOR. For Chrissake woman, what do you want??

SANDRA. I need to try to make things nice… We want to make a nice impression today. It's very important.

TREVOR. What is it? What's happening?

(A car is heard coming up the drive.)

SANDRA. Oh no. He's here.

(SANDRA puts the cushions back, then takes the other food items into the kitchen for disposal, save the hot dogs on the coffee table.)

TREVOR. What's happening? Who is that?

SANDRA. He's here early.

TREVOR. Is it Morgan? Did she send a car?

(She makes a last ditch effort to make things presentable. She takes a wilted plant and throws it in the trash, and throws a blanket over a desk overflowing with mess.)

(TREVOR looks out the window.)

TREVOR. Ahhh I forgot! Or never knew! Oh my god, what am I wearing? I'm not wearing anything! Where's my fireman hat? I want to wear my fireman hat!

(TREVOR too, crosses the room frantically, looking for his hat. JERRY, 30s, from animal control, approaches the front door, holding a supply bag. TREVOR tears the sheet off the desk, knocking items to the floor.)

SANDRA. No, Trevor, don't touch that! What are you doing?

TREVOR. I'm looking for my hat, woman!

SANDRA. No no…

(JERRY knocks on the front door. SANDRA gives up, goes to answer it. TREVOR ends up wrapping the sheet around his body like a shawl, and turning to receive their visitor.)

SANDRA. Hello. You must be Jerry…

JERRY. Hi. Yeah. Hi.

SANDRA. Come on in.

TREVOR. Hello, welcome to my home.

JERRY. Ah here's the famous Trevor.

SANDRA. Yeah, that's him. Trevor, / say hello.

TREVOR. It's so nice to meet you. You're one of the producers?

(*TREVOR goes and touches him in greeting.*)

TREVOR. You look familiar.

JERRY. Hey there / big guy.

TREVOR. Though I have trouble with faces.

SANDRA. Oh look at that…

TREVOR. Especially with hu / mans.

SANDRA. …He likes you. Please Jerry, have a seat. Can I get you anything?

JERRY. I'm fine.

(*TREVOR leads him to the couch.*)

TREVOR. Here. Sit here. This is where we sit.

SANDRA. I'm sorry about the mess…

JERRY. This is nothing. You should have seen the place I visited last week. A woman was keeping 30 cats.

SANDRA. Oh.

JERRY. Carcasses she didn't notice, urine on everything, rotting the wood, toxifying the air.

SANDRA. Oh no.

JERRY. A real bad scene. Might have to raze the house.

SANDRA. Oh my. Some people, they are just…

TREVOR. Are you sure we can't get you anything? Some coffee? Or a hot dog?

(*TREVOR offers him a hot dog.*)

JERRY. Oh…

TREVOR. Take it.

SANDRA. Oh Trevor get that away from him. I'm sorry…

(*She takes the hot dogs from him…*)

TREVOR. Hey!

(*…and goes to the kitchen to dispose of them.*)

TREVOR. Well that was rude. I apologize for my mom—she gets a little over-agitated sometimes. I'm so excited to be going back on the show. I really got a kick out of it the first time around.

SANDRA. So. Jerry. What do you need from us?

JERRY. Well mostly just, I want to get to know you both. I can't really make any assessment 'til—Oh!

TREVOR. Here let me groom you. *(TREVOR begins grooming him.)*

SANDRA. Trevor, leave him alone. It's just his way of saying hello. He likes you.

JERRY. It's fine. As long as he's gentle.

SANDRA. He's always gentle. He always has been. He's very good, very good.

TREVOR. I'm a very good boy. I don't even need to wear a diaper. I just wear this just in case. You know. Better safe than sorry.

JERRY. You know I saw Trevor perform once. At the zoo. I sort of figured he lived there.

SANDRA. No, just came as a special guest. I remember that show.

JERRY. Does he still roller skate?

SANDRA. Oh yes. I mean, we're getting there. He's a little out of shape.

JERRY. Aren't we all.

SANDRA. *(Laughs too loud, too enthusiastically:)* Ha ha ha ha ha ha... "Aren't we all."

JERRY. Where did you get him?

SANDRA. My husband got him for me, as a gift. He bought him out of a van in a Wal-Mart parking lot.

JERRY. Hmm.

SANDRA. But he's been tested. He's had all his shots. And I've had him since he was a baby so I know he hasn't been abused. I mean, I know sometimes with chimps if they're abused, they develop behavioral problems.

JERRY. That's true. And there's been no abuse, in this house? / From you, or anyone else?

SANDRA. No. Never. No way.

JERRY. Good.

TREVOR. Alright, I'm all done grooming. You're good. No nits.

JERRY. What about with his training? For the acts? You...ever hit him?

SANDRA. No. Absolutely not. I would never hit him. / Never!

JERRY. Well it is important to discipline.

SANDRA. Well of course. I didn't say I...of course I *discipline,* but not... I believe in positive reinforcement. Isn't that right, Trevor? *(Touching him.)*

TREVOR. Get off me! Oh, what?

SANDRA. Isn't that right, Trevor?

TREVOR. What?

SANDRA. *(Signing:)* I love you.

TREVOR. *(Gets it:)* Oh. I love you too.

JERRY. I was hoping to do a quick physical.

TREVOR. What are you talking about? / Contract stuff?

SANDRA. Of course. Trevor.

TREVOR. That's between you and Sandra. She's the manager. I just do my thing.

SANDRA. Trevor, come here, honey.

TREVOR. Worth the money. Trust me...

SANDRA. Trevor.

TREVOR. Oh hey, I'm trying out some new looks. You know, cuz if I do the same act every week, people will get bored, so picture this... *(Holding up the DVD case picturing Morgan and Trevor.)* But with me wearing sunglasses.

> *(A DVD falls out of the case.)*

SANDRA. Trevor, come here, honey.

TREVOR. What's this? I didn't know there was a disc thing in here. I thought it was just a picture.

SANDRA. Come here, honey.

TREVOR. Is this my reel? Did you make an actor's reel and never show it to me?

JERRY. What is that?

SANDRA. That's the show we did with Morgan Fairchild.

TREVOR. Put this on. Put this on now.

SANDRA. We'll watch that later honey. As a treat. You have to be very calm now sweetie, so Jerry can do his check up.

TREVOR. We're not going to watch it?

SANDRA. *(Soothing:)* Later.

> *(JERRY opens his bag and takes out a stethoscope. SANDRA pets him to calm him.)*

SANDRA. Just sit still.

TREVOR. *(SANDRA petting him.)* Oh are you going to groom me now?

JERRY. Okay big guy, this is going to be really easy. Nice and easy.

(Checks his heart.)

TREVOR. Oh you're both grooming me now. I like this. This feels good. Wait a minute. I know where I remember you from. You're from the commercial, with Morgan! You're the P.A. Or the A.D. Or the D.P? E.P? Key grip? Best boy?

SANDRA. Trevor, relax.

(JERRY checks his blood pressure.)

TREVOR. Stylist! Stylist! You're taking my measurements, I get it now. That's great. Wardrobe is essential. Ah, measuring the biceps. I think you'll be pleasantly surprised. I have been getting stronger. And fatter.

JERRY. Blood pressure's a little high.

TREVOR. I don't think we should be afraid to get dark with this show either.

SANDRA. Well I think he's excited. We don't have many guests.

TREVOR. I mean, it should be family friendly, but have an edge. For edgy families. Or, well, I guess I actually want as many people to like it as possible. But, I mean, you have Morgan Fairchild so it's gonna be a hit no matter what, so why not take some chances? Push some envelopes. I am comfortable with nudity. I trust you to be tasteful, so I'm just putting that out there. If it makes sense for the story. If there's a story. Even if there isn't…

(JERRY looks in TREVOR's ears.)

TREVOR. Hey! What are you doing?

SANDRA. Now Trevor calm down. He's just checking your ears.

JERRY. Okay, all done. We should talk about the hard part now.

TREVOR. I wonder if this time Morgan'll let me visit her house. I bet she lives in a castle.

(JERRY mimes drawing blood.)

SANDRA. Oh, right. He doesn't like shots.

JERRY. It's pretty quick. Unless you think he'll get aggressive?

SANDRA. No. He never gets aggressive… He just gets…he just doesn't like shots.

JERRY. Okay, well…

SANDRA. Maybe if I give him something to settle him.

JERRY. Give him something? You mean like / prescriptions?

SANDRA. No! No! Just tea, I mean.

TREVOR. *(Whispering to SANDRA:)* What are you saying? Don't get greedy. We need this.

JERRY. That might be a good idea.

SANDRA. Okay.

(SANDRA gets up to put some water on to boil.)

TREVOR. Is Morgan coming here? God, I hope not. This place is a mess.

JERRY. He seems a bit jumpy.

TREVOR. God Sandra would it kill you to pick up the place sometimes…

JERRY. Hello there, big guy.

TREVOR. What? Hello.

JERRY. *(Stroking him:)* How are you feeling?

TREVOR. *(No idea:)* Hey, yeah, I, uh…I…

JERRY. You like it here?

TREVOR. *(Doesn't understand, leaving:)* Saaaandra…

(TREVOR joins SANDRA in the kitchen, where she is preparing the tea.)

TREVOR. What are you doing? Making coffee for our guest?

SANDRA. Trevor, I'm making you some tea. Just relax. / Please.

TREVOR. Tea? Are you crazy? This is an important man!

SANDRA. *(Whispering:)* Trevor, please. Just go sit down and relax. Here, take your Boo Boo doll.

TREVOR. Why do you keep buying tea anyway? Nobody likes tea around here!

SANDRA. Trevor, sit down! Behave!

TREVOR. No you behave! I told you to stop buying tea. You need to trust me. I know what I'm talking about. Besides, I'm the dominant male in this house, and… *(Whispering:)* I don't appreciate you undermining my authority in front of guests.

SANDRA. Trevor…

TREVOR. Bottom line: we need to communicate better, and you need to listen better. And you need to tell me things better, so I understand better. I didn't even know this was happening today. I had no notice. I could have worn my fireman hat…but…we'll talk about this later. Just try to behave, okay?

(He walks back over to where JERRY *has taken a needle out to draw blood with. He stops in his tracks.)*

TREVOR. Whoa, what's that for?

JERRY. Oops.

TREVOR. Hey! Hey! What the hell kind of stylist are you?

SANDRA. Trevor, it's just a little prick. You have to be brave, okay?

TREVOR. What is this? Some kind of trap? Is this some kind of trap?? Ahhh it's a trap! It's a trap! / It's a trap!

*(*OLIVER *re-emerges.)*

OLIVER. Trevor, what's going on?

TREVOR. They're going poke me with that stabby thing.

SANDRA. Trevor, It's just a little prick. You've done this before.

TREVOR. No, you don't understand, I've done this before. And it hurts!

OLIVER. Listen Trevor. You've got to behave. Especially before any contracts have been signed.

TREVOR. But it will hurt. Why do they want to hurt me?

OLIVER. I'm sure there's a good reason. Sometimes they give you shots to knock you out before they put on the plane. As a courtesy, so you don't have to deal with all the hassle at the airport.

TREVOR. Oh, but, but that doesn't seem necessary though. Why—why—

OLIVER. Trevor! Don't ask questions, it's unprofessional.

TREVOR. But it will hurt!

OLIVER. *(Becoming more stern:)* So?? I thought you were you the dominant male around here…

TREVOR. I am.

OLIVER. Well then start acting like one! You want to end up like those chimps at the zoo. Or those chimps on the nature shows. Naked. Lawless. With nobody to applaud their tricks, and nobody to remember them.

TREVOR. No.

OLIVER. Then get it together. *(Signing:)* Behave.

TREVOR. *(Signing:)* Behave.

OLIVER. Behave, and the whole world will open up to you.

*(*MORGAN *enters. With her comes the din of a crowd, as would be heard from a backstage area, and sounds of crew members preparing for a show. Strange music plays.)*

MORGAN. Well Trevor, are you ready? I'm waiting.

(He steps forward to take his shot, bravely. SANDRA *comes forward with tea.)*

SANDRA. Kai-ta-chai-chai. Chai-ta-chai TEA, Trevor?

TREVOR. Nevermind the tea. You and your fucking tea. *(He extends his arm for an injection.)* Just do it. Drug me and take me to Hollywood. Whatever it takes.

JERRY. Chai-ta-kai, Trevor, Chai-ta-kai.

SANDRA. Chai-ta-kai. Chai-ta-kai. Good boy. Good boy!

MORGAN. Good boy, Trevor. Good boy. Trevor, where have you been?

TREVOR. I've been right here. I've been right here waiting. I didn't know how to get hold of you.

MORGAN. I didn't know how to get hold of you.

TREVOR. We need better handlers.

JERRY. Kai-ta-chai-chai. Trevor?

TREVOR. What?

MORGAN. Oh I can never understand what he's saying, can you?

(JERRY gives him the shot.)

TREVOR. AHHHHHHHHHH!!!

SANDRA. Chai-ta-kai. Chai-ta-kai.

JERRY. Chai-ta-kai. Chai-ta-kai.

MORGAN. Are you alright?

TREVOR. It's alright. I'm fine. I can take it. I can take it.

MORGAN. You see that's what I like about you, Trevor. You're a professional. I could see that from the moment I met you, when we were doing that commercial for water bottles or possibly paper.

TREVOR. You don't think I'm too old, for prime time?

MORGAN. Who said it's prime time?

TREVOR. Oh…

MORGAN. I'm just kidding, of course it's prime time. I'm Morgan Fairchild. Oh Trevor, I'm sorry it's taken so long to get this show on the air, but these things just take a long time sometimes. And I couldn't imagine doing it without you.

TREVOR. Really?

MORGAN. *(With a serious tone:)* Yes, now I'm not joking. I'm serious. You see? You see how my voice just changed to serious voice.

JERRY. Kai-ta-chai chai?

TREVOR. What?

JERRY. Kai-ta-kai-ta-chai chai chai? Trevor? ...You're on in five.

> *(*JERRY *opens the sliding door. Outside we hear the sound of a huge audience.*
> JERRY *goes out and* SANDRA *follows him.)*

SANDRA. Chai-ta-kai-kai.

MORGAN. Are you ready, Trevor? To be a good boy? To make me proud?

TREVOR. I was born ready, Miss Fairchild.

MORGAN. Well...break a leg.

> *(She exits.)*

TREVOR. When you do live television, there are a few rules you need to remember. Rule number one: don't look into the camera. Rule number two: do not, under any circumstances, break the camera. Rule number three, do not poop, no matter how intense things get out there. That will be un-usable footage. It's actually a good idea to not eat a few hours before going onstage. Because they might give you reward snacks during the show. And you don't want to look bloated.

> *(*MORGAN *reappears, and addresses the invisible audience.*
> *Huge applause.* TREVOR *prepares for his act, puts on his roller skates.)*

TREVOR. With some animals, like tigers, they will eat right before going onstage, because they don't have any self control—they're animals. You don't want to fraternize with tigers. They're basically a type of monster. You can play with little kitty cats, and seals, because they're small, and you can CRUSH THEM, but you shouldn't, because that would disqualify you in a competition. And it might not even be funny. It might be funny, but it's not worth the risk. Anyhow, as an artist, my goal isn't just to make people laugh. I want to make them think.

> *(*TREVOR *enters on roller skates, and begins his act. [or a bicycle, or*
> *something else appropriately impressive/ridiculous.])*

MORGAN. *(Offstage:)* And now welcome, my personal friend...Trevor the Chimp.

> *(Applause.)*

TREVOR. The lights onstage can be bright, but you have to focus. You will also notice a lot of interesting smells. Save investigating them for later. You have a job to do.

> *(*JERRY *comes out to throw* TREVOR *a ball as he roller skates around.*
> *Applause as he catches it.)*

TREVOR. Hit your marks. Do your tricks.

> *(He throws the ball at a basketball hoop.)*

TREVOR. It's alright if you don't do everything perfectly. The important thing is that you are doing things that a real man would do. America loves an underdog. Someone who defied the odds, and did something incredible. Like play basketball. Like smoke a cigarette. Who pulled themselves up by their bootstraps and smoked a cigarette.

(TREVOR *smokes a cigarette. The crowd goes wild.*)

I'd like to see a tiger do this. With its stupid fucking paws.

(MORGAN *returns.*)

MORGAN. Trevor...

TREVOR. Morgan? You changed dresses.

MORGAN. Oh yes. I change costumes all the time. Trevor, you were... that was...you were just magnificent out there. I'm speechless. See, how speechless I am.

TREVOR. Really, it was alright?

MORGAN. Oh yes. America's going to love you, Trevor. We're going to make a great team.

TREVOR. Team?

MORGAN. Oh Trevor, why do you think I called you back to Hollywood?

TREVOR. To do the show, I thought.

MORGAN. Oh sure, the show, the show, I have a thousand shows. They're all successful. I'm sure this will be no exception. I mean, with your talent. But I'm not just looking for some animal to do tricks for me. I'm looking for an animal to spend my life with.

TREVOR. You mean, this is just a...

MORGAN. Yes, a competition. To see who is the most talented animal in the world. To see which animal can most act like a man. And it's you, Trevor. You look just like a man. Especially with those cool sunglasses.

TREVOR. And you don't think I'm too old?

MORGAN. You're experienced.

TREVOR. I have bulbous pink genitals.

MORGAN. That doesn't frighten me. What's the matter, Trevor? Don't you want me?

TREVOR. No, I do, I do. I want to marry you. I want to have half-human children with you.

MORGAN. Well then take me. Come and take what you want.

TREVOR. Morgan, but we're still on stage. Aren't we?

MORGAN. Are we? What if we are...

TREVOR. On stage, I'm supposed to behave.

MORGAN. Til when?

TREVOR. Til I get what I want.

MORGAN. Well I'm what you want, aren't I?

TREVOR. Yes but…

MORGAN. So you're supposed to behave to get what you want. But you can't get what you want while you're behaving, is that it?

TREVOR. Yes. No. Now you're confusing me.

MORGAN. Oh Trevor, you're so silly. You're a silly billy.

TREVOR. Morgan, where are you going?

MORGAN. You're a silly silly billy. See you at the castle.

> *(She backs away, into the darkness.)*

TREVOR. Morgan? Morgan!

> *(Her laughter trails off as* TREVOR *again tries to open the door and the lights rise on the normal living area.* JERRY *is preparing to leave.)*

SANDRA. Trevor. Trevor, come here honey.

> *(*SANDRA *comes in from the sun deck.)*

SANDRA. Trevor! Trevor what are you doing?

TREVOR. What? What's going on?

SANDRA. Come sit down, Trevor. Please. Here. Take Boo Boo.

TREVOR. Boo Boo? Where is Morgan's friend? Where did he go? Where did the man go?

SANDRA. Jerry's outside. He's looking at your kennel. Look, I put on your DVD.

TREVOR. Why aren't we in Hollywood? I thought I was supposed to get knocked out.

SANDRA. You wanted to watch your DVD, remember?

TREVOR. What? My reel? My actor's reel. Oh good. Good Sandra.

> *(*JERRY *enters.)*

TREVOR. Come on over. Watch this.

JERRY. Well, the enclosure seems okay.

TREVOR. Sit down.

> *(The DVD begins on the television. Familiar music is heard.)*

JERRY. Of course it would only work if you kept him inside it.

SANDRA. *(Cheerful:)* Oh, I know…

MORGAN. Hello, I'm Morgan Fairchild. And welcome to AMAZING ANIMALS.

TREVOR. Hey, Morgan!

JERRY. Look, I know Jim's a friend and… / I'd really like to try to make this work…

TREVOR. Look at her, so beautiful. That hair, so yellow.

> *(Morgan's show plays in the background as* JERRY *and* SANDRA *talk over it.*
>
> MORGAN* *is heard only from the TV now.)*

MORGAN.* This is a show I've been dreaming about since I was a little girl. A show to celebrate all things furry…friendly…and FUNNY.

> *(Applause.)*

SANDRA. I'm willing to cooperate. I think we can make this safe. I mean, really I'm interested in doing what's best for Trevor. Jim thinks we can just dump him in some sanctuary, but it's not that simple.

TREVOR. Quiet! Morgan's on TV. Show some respect.

MORGAN.* Some of the animals on this show are in a tough spot. Many are facing extinction.

JERRY. I know. I'd be worried that a chimp like Trevor / wouldn't socialize well with other chimps.

MORGAN.* Our hope with this show is to help raise awareness of their plight.

TREVOR. SHHHH!

MORGAN.* …and show you why you should care about them.

JERRY. What's this?

MORGAN.* And believe me, you ARE going to care about them, as soon as you SEE HOW FUNNY THEY ARE.

> *(Applause.)*

SANDRA. Oh, this is the show Trevor was on.

JERRY. Oh.

MORGAN.* Let me introduce you to the stars.

SANDRA. Sit down. You have to see this.

MORGAN.* Our first contestant was born in Bengal, India, but now lights up the stage 7 nights a week in Las Vegas. Please welcome Sonny the Tiger…

TREVOR. Don't tell me he's coming back. Disqualified! Ha ha ha.

(He laughs. Bares his teeth.)

JERRY. Is he baring his teeth?

SANDRA. No, that's Trevor's smiley face.

JERRY. Oh. *(He sits down.)*

MORGAN.* Next up, all the way from SeaWorld, he's a little guy with a lot of hot moves, it's Billy the Seal…

TREVOR. Piece of shit. Can't wear clothes. No contest. I'm going to mop the floor with him.

SANDRA. He's excited because he sees his friends.

MORGAN.* And now, I'd like to introduce you to a very special friend.

SANDRA. Oh Trevor, look, this is you, honey.

MORGAN.* Please welcome…TREVOR THE CHIMP.

　　　　*(*TREVOR *doesn't recognize himself at first.)*

TREVOR. Who is that? Who is that?

SANDRA. That's right. That's you, sweetheart. That's Trevor.

TREVOR. Trevor? But I'm so…do I really…? *(Looking at himself.)*

JERRY. It's incredible, the way he recognizes himself.

TREVOR. Is that really what I look like?

SANDRA. He's very smart.

TREVOR. No, this is…this is…

JERRY. When was this on?

SANDRA. It wasn't. It didn't get picked up. Haven't watched this in years.

JERRY. Is that Morgan Fairchild?

SANDRA. Morgan Fairchild.

TREVOR. Morgan Fairchild! Look, I have some ideas about how to update the act. This is not where I'm at as a performer.

SANDRA. Trevor. Sit down.

TREVOR. Personality, that's the key. And physical strength. TV audiences want to know that Morgan's being protected.

SANDRA. Trevor.

TREVOR. Look at this. Look at this.

　　　　(He throws something across the room. JERRY *backs away.)*

JERRY. Ohhh shit…okay.

SANDRA. Trevor! BAD!

TREVOR. What? No, I'm explaining something.

SANDRA. Trevor, you silly billy. Come sit / with us.

TREVOR. Get off!

(TREVOR *pushes her off, powerfully. She staggers back.*)

SANDRA. Oh!

JERRY. Are you alright?

SANDRA. I'm fine.

TREVOR. It's fine. She's fine. Listen, I'm just saying, I'm not a kid anymore. I'm ready for serious roles. The only question is, is America ready for me?

(*Laughs, smiles/bares teeth.*)

JERRY. I think he's getting aggressive.

SANDRA. No. No. Trevor!

TREVOR. What? What's wrong?

(*He becomes soothing to assuage* JERRY.)

TREVOR. It's fine. See? It's fine. Everything's fine.

SANDRA. Oh good, good. See? He's calm.

TREVOR. Yeah, look, I'm behaving. Hey let's just forget about the tape. That wasn't me. I mean, I think that literally wasn't me. I think that was the wrong tape. It was a misunderstanding.

SANDRA. You see? He's calm.

TREVOR. Sandra, I forgive you, because it was just a mistake, but you put in the wrong tape.

SANDRA. Good boy.

JERRY. Yeah, yeah. Well I'll let you know when I get the lab results.

(JERRY *starts to leave.*)

TREVOR. Okay, I don't know what you're saying. Sandra, did you tell him about the live act?

SANDRA. But you agree, that if everything is fine and he doesn't have rabies or something, then why not just let him stay here, if I keep him contained?

JERRY. Well, there are a lot of factors, but…we'll be in touch.

SANDRA. Jerry…

TREVOR. What? What did he say? Hey. Wait. Wait. You need to see me perform live.

SANDRA. (*Tries to stop him:*) Trevor! Get away from Jerry.

TREVOR. Sandra get my guitar. You like music? I'm a musician.

SANDRA. Trevor.

TREVOR. *(Throws her off:)* Get off!

> *(JERRY exits.)*

SANDRA. TREVOR! BAD! BAD!

TREVOR. Hey! Don't yell at me!

SANDRA. Trevor—

TREVOR. You're the one who put in the wrong tape. Oh no. Oh no, he's getting away. You've got to stop him. You've got to fix this!

SANDRA. Trevor…

TREVOR. Is he coming back? He's coming back, right? Sandra? Sandra? Sandra?

SANDRA. We need to go in the shower.

TREVOR. What?

SANDRA. We need to go in the shower right now.

TREVOR. What? Oh no.

> *(He reaches in his pants…)*

SANDRA. No, Trevor don't do that. TREVOR!

> *(…and comes out with shit on his hands.)*

TREVOR. How long has this been in there? No, no, w-what is this? This isn't mine.

> *(JERRY comes back in, with a tranquilizer gun.)*

TREVOR. No no, it's not how it looks.

SANDRA. No!

JERRY. Sandra, get back.

TREVOR. I wouldn't do this. I was framed!

SANDRA. No, but you can't shoot him. You can't!

> *(She rushes to try to stop him.)*

JERRY. Sandra, relax, it's just a tranquilizer.

TREVOR. This is not my shit.

SANDRA. *(To JERRY, about to shoot:)* No!

> *(JERRY shoots a tranquilizer into TREVOR.)*

TREVOR. AHHHHHHHHHH!!!!

(TREVOR recoils in pain.)

TREVOR. What are you doing???

JERRY. Come on, get outside.

TREVOR. WHY DID YOU DO THAT TO ME!?

(JERRY pulls SANDRA outside on the deck and closes the door and TREVOR comes charging forward)

TREVOR. YOU CAN'T DO THAT TO ME!!

(He charges through the door.)

JERRY. Get back get back!

TREVOR. I AM THE TALENT! I'm the talent…

SANDRA. Trevor, stop!

(Outside now, TREVOR begins to stagger, and lose consciousness.)

TREVOR. …Listen, you've made a huge mistake… This isn't my shit. I was set up. It must have been that seal. Because he was jealous of my relationship with Morgan… I need some coffee… Someone make me coffee. *(He loses consciousness.)*

JERRY. Oh my god. Oh my god.

SANDRA. Trevor.

JERRY. Don't get near him. Let's go inside. Go this way.

(They go back inside the house.)

SANDRA. Jerry, this is not normal. This is not normal.

(He gets out his cellphone.)

SANDRA. What are you doing?

JERRY. …

SANDRA. Jerry? What are you / doing?

JERRY. I'm calling for a truck.

SANDRA. A truck? A truck??

JERRY. Sandra, I'm sorry but this is…this can't go on.

SANDRA. But if I put him in his kennel. If I put him in his kennel! This was an isolated incident.

JERRY. I… Hello? Hello? Nick? Nick?

(JERRY's call is dropped. Bad reception.)

SANDRA. Aren't you going to talk to me?

JERRY. I'm sorry.

(SANDRA takes the tranquilizer gun and points it at JERRY.)

SANDRA. Jerry? Jerry?

JERRY. Hold on.

SANDRA. JERRY!

(He looks at her, sees the gun.)

JERRY. Hey. Hey, put that down. Sandra.

SANDRA. You won't even talk to me? You don't get to make decisions like this, without even talking to me ABOUT MY CHIMP!

JERRY. Sandra, put that down.

SANDRA. He's not always like this. This is not normal. He's riled up.

JERRY. He's aggressive.

SANDRA. He's having a bad day! Haven't you ever had a bad day, Jerry? Haven't you ever had a bad day and yelled at your wife or something? What if you yelled at your wife and then your wife called some men in a truck and they came and took you away?

JERRY. He's an animal.

SANDRA. He's an animal. I know that. I know that! I'm not crazy. But we give ourselves second chances, why don't animals get any? Huh? Jerry?

JERRY. Okay, Sandra…

(JERRY approaches.)

SANDRA. Don't come near me. Jerry! Jerry! Don't come near me.

(She shoots him with a dart. It hurts.)

JERRY. OW! GODDAMN IT.

SANDRA. Jerry, I'm sorry—

JERRY. You crazy fucking bitch!

SANDRA. That's not nice.

JERRY. Crazy fucking bitch.

SANDRA. I…look, I…I won't be rushed into a decision. If he goes to a sanctuary it will be one that I decide. Or one that we choose together.

JERRY. Oh fuck. Fuck…

SANDRA. You should lie down.

JERRY. You can't… Fuck—you can't…

(He tries to leave, but staggers.)

SANDRA. Jerry, I'm sorry. I have nothing against you personally. I want you to know that.

(JERRY *collapses, unconscious.*)

§

(*Several hours later. Night has fallen.*

Outside, TREVOR *comes to.* OLIVER *is sitting nearby, smoking a pipe. Inside,* SANDRA *is hurriedly packing bags to leave.* JERRY *is tied up somewhere offstage.*)

OLIVER. Well hello, sleepy head.

TREVOR. Oliver, what happened?

OLIVER. Seems like you had some trouble. It's alright, it happens to the best of us. Good thing you weren't wearing white.

TREVOR. I blew it.

OLIVER. Nooo.

TREVOR. I pooped my pants in the middle of an audition.

OLIVER. You don't know it was an audition.

TREVOR. You're right. I don't know. I don't know anything.

OLIVER. But look, there's always next time. So you pooped your pants. You showed them you could play guitar and zip around with rolley things on your feet. You should feel good about that.

TREVOR. Why? What does that get me? What has any of this gotten me?

SANDRA. Trevor? Oh good you're awake. Alright, take off your clothes, honey.

TREVOR. What?

SANDRA. Take off your clothes. You need to get in the shower.

OLIVER. Seems like she wants you to go with her.

TREVOR. She doesn't know what she wants.

SANDRA. Trevor? Time to wake up, honey. Come inside.

OLIVER. Speaking of leaving… It's time for me to take my leave as well.

TREVOR. You? You too? Where are you going?

OLIVER. Well, I got a job. There was an opening on um…

TREVOR. On what?

OLIVER. …

TREVOR. On *what?*

OLIVER. It's just one of those things.

TREVOR. You took my spot. I take you in my house. And you take. My spot!

(He doesn't have the strength to care anymore.)

OLIVER. Sometimes you groom, sometimes you are groomed. It's just the business, Trevor.

TREVOR. The business…

OLIVER. Just one of those things.

TREVOR. Sure, sure.

OLIVER. But I would like to introduce you to an agent I know, Trevor.

TREVOR. Get away from me.

OLIVER. But Trevor, friend—

TREVOR. I should bite you in the face, you know that?

OLIVER. That would be a huge career mistake.

TREVOR. So what? I don't have a career. It's over. I never had one to begin with. It's all a sham.

OLIVER. Morgan believes you have a rare talent.

TREVOR. Morgan? MORGAN?

OLIVER. My personal friend.

TREVOR. Morgan is not your personal friend. Morgan isn't any of our personal friends.

OLIVER. That's not true.

TREVOR. …We're just animals they dressed up for a laugh. We're just PROPS. You hear me? PROPS!

SANDRA. Trevor, we're going to go for a ride, honey. You want to go for a ride in the car?

TREVOR. Shut up. Chai-ta-kai-chai-chai that's all I ever hear from you. You don't even make sense.

SANDRA. You still woozy, honey? You want me to make some coffee? We have to go, honey.

TREVOR. Oh, coffee? NOW she makes coffee. WHY? WHY NOW? Because you think it will LOOK CUTE? To see me hold a goddamn coffee cup? My whole life I've been holding coffee cups with NOTHING INSIDE.

SANDRA. Trevor…

(The phone rings.)

TREVOR. Well, go ahead. Answer it. I'm not going anywhere.

(SANDRA looks at it and sees it's Jim. She takes the call and goes into the other room.)

SANDRA. *(Bright:)* Jim, hello!

(TREVOR *goes and pours himself some coffee.)*

SANDRA. Yes, well I thought it went very well. Very well… *(Exiting.)*

(OLIVER *returns.)*

OLIVER. Trevor, look, pal, great news. Morgan is offering you a spot on her new show.

TREVOR. Suck it, Oliver.

OLIVER. It's not a variety show, it's a sitcom. With lines. Don't turn your nose up at comedy, pal. It might feel a little light and silly but it can lead to big things.

TREVOR. Oliver, do you how to use a doorknob?

OLIVER. Yes, I do. I learned it doing research for a role.

TREVOR. Then why don't you reprise that role, open the door and GET THE HELL OUT.

(*The baby is heard crying next door.* TREVOR *perks up.)*

TREVOR. What the hell is that?

OLIVER. Oh Trevor, don't pay attention to that. You need to focus.

TREVOR. What did I just tell you? You want me to sign it?

OLIVER. But Trevor, you can't give up. You could really be successful.

TREVOR. What is that?

OLIVER. Just look at me. I live in Florida, with a human wife.

TREVOR. What?

OLIVER. I mean, I have a new one.

TREVOR. I'm sick of listening to you.

OLIVER. Leave that alone, Trevor.

TREVOR. Florida doesn't exist. Hollywood doesn't exist. It's all a sham, and I'm sick of it. It's time I trusted my instincts…

(*He heads off stage left toward Ashley's house.)*

OLIVER. No, Trevor. You can't go alone. Not at night. There could be snakes out there. And tigers. And paparazzi. And don't you want to wear a white tuxedo? You can wear a white tuxedo, Trevor. Trevor? …Oh dear.

(OLIVER *makes his exit.)*

(SANDRA *returns with the phone, also hurriedly packing at the same time.)*

SANDRA. …Well he said he needed to wait for the blood test results but he was very optimistic… Oh, well, that's strange…well if he said he'd call you I'm sure he'll call you, maybe he's just in one of those reception blackout areas...why don't you come by tomorrow and we'll do some follow-up. Thank you, Jim, thank you. I hope everything works out, but I know you have to do what you have to do. Okay, you tell Angie hi okay? Okay...okay, talk soon. Bye, hon.

(She hangs up.)

SANDRA. Trevor? *(She sees the sundeck door is open.)* Trevor?

(TREVOR comes back onstage with a baby swaddled gently in his arms.)

TREVOR. Look at this. Look at this.

SANDRA. *(In horror:)* Trevor, no...

TREVOR. He was just lying in his crib. She was just letting him cry and cry.

SANDRA. Trevor, no. Give me that Trevor.

(ASHLEY bursts in the front door.)

ASHLEY. NO! NO! SANDRA!

SANDRA. SHHH!

TREVOR. This is how you raise a child? You people are crazy. All of you, crazy.

ASHLEY. Sandra! STOP HIM!

SANDRA. SHHH! Don't make him agitated.

TREVOR. If he was my son, I'd never let him cry like that.

ASHLEY. Please, make him give him back. SANDRA!

SANDRA. Shhhh!

TREVOR. If he was my son I'd take him a million miles from here.

ASHLEY. Make him give him back. Make him give him back.

(She motions to be calm so that TREVOR also remains calm.)

TREVOR. Into the wild.

SANDRA. Trevor! What are you doing?

TREVOR. Raise him in the wild.

SANDRA. That's not yours.

TREVOR. Without a name...

SANDRA. Trevor.

TREVOR. Without a handler.

SANDRA. Gentle.

TREVOR. Free. The way I should have been raised.

SANDRA. That's Ashley's. Put that down, Trevor.

TREVOR. Where are the keys?

> (TREVOR *goes up the deck steps and into the house.*
>
> *He goes inside to look for the keys.* SANDRA *and* ASHLEY *follow him in.*)

ASHLEY. What is he doing?!

SANDRA. I don't know. Please! We have to keep calm…

ASHLEY. Oh my god.

> (TREVOR *rummages through drawers, potted plants, any possible hiding place…*)

TREVOR. Now where are they?! I know they're here somewhere…

> (*The baby starts to cry.*)

Shhhhh, it's okay, baby. It's just me.

> (*The baby continues to cry.*)

I need you ladies to back off, okay? You're scaring the baby.

SANDRA. What are you doing?

TREVOR. I said BACK OFF!

SANDRA. Trevor…

ASHLEY. Oh my god oh my god.

TREVOR. NO! I won't let you do this again. I won't let you do this to him.

SANDRA. (*Realizing what he's looking for:*) Oh, no, Trevor…

TREVOR. I won't let you do to him what you DID TO ME! NOW WHERE ARE THE FUCKING KEYS!?

> (SANDRA *gets the Boo Boo doll and threatens it again.*)

SANDRA. Trevor, don't make me throw this away. You want me to throw this away?

ASHLEY. Sandra…

SANDRA. Shh! I'll handle it.

TREVOR. What's that? You're threatening me now? Go ahead, throw away the rabbit. I KNOW IT'S NOT A REAL RABBIT! You think I'm an idiot!

SANDRA. Trevor, put down the baby. Gentle, honey.

TREVOR. Lies! It's all lies. No wonder Jerome ran away! Because he wised up! And I'm wising up too, Sandra!

> (ASHLEY *rushes to take her baby back.* SANDRA *tries to stop her.*)

ASHLEY. Oh no, NO!

SANDRA. Don't go near him. Ashley!

ASHLEY. Get out / of my way!

SANDRA. *(Simultaneous:)* But you shouldn't go near him like this.

ASHLEY. Teddy!

SANDRA. *(Simultaneous:)* I'll talk to him.

ASHLEY. NO.

> (ASHLEY *screams at* TREVOR, *making herself big and loud, in a monster voice.*)

ASHLEY. TREVOR!

SANDRA. No. Don't. He doesn't react / well to that.

ASHLEY. Shut up—TREVOR!

> (*She bangs something to get his attention, maybe gets up on the couch.*)

YOU! PUT THAT! DOWN!

> (TREVOR *stops, a bit startled.*)

TREVOR. What the hell is this?

ASHLEY. YOU. PUT. THAT. DOWN!

SANDRA. No Ashley, be careful, you might provoke him.

TREVOR. What's that, some monster voice?

ASHLEY. TREVOR! I AM BIGGER THAN YOU.

SANDRA. He doesn't react well to that.

ASHLEY. TREVOR. YOU GIVE ME THAT. NOW!

> (ASHLEY *starts stomping around, making aggressive displays.*)
>
> (TREVOR *breaks something.*)

TREVOR. You think you can come in here and try to intimidate me? Like I'm some chump, with some two bit monster voice??

> (*He puts down the baby.*)

ASHLEY. TREVOR! YOU DO WHAT I SAY!

TREVOR. I DON'T THINK SO!

SANDRA. Trevor, STOP!

TREVOR. Oh what, you don't like this? Am I misbehaving? SO WHAT?

SANDRA. TREVOR!

TREVOR. No one's watching. NO ONE WAS EVER WATCHING!

> (*He moves aggressively towards* ASHLEY, *while breaking things.*)

TREVOR. I put my heart and soul into this business. MY HEART AND SOUL!

SANDRA. *(Simultaneous:)* Trevor, YOU NEED TO STOP IT. RIGHT NOW!

TREVOR. And WHY? FOR WHAT? Because I believed that somehow there'd be a treat for me in the end. Well WHERE'S MY TREAT, Sandy!!? WHERE'S MY TREAT!??

(He corners ASHLEY.)

ASHLEY. Oh no. Trevor, nice, Trevor…

SANDRA. BAD! BAD! BAD!

TREVOR. What? You don't like this? You don't think this is FUNNY? Well too bad. I'm doing it for ME NOW. Because I think it's funny! I THINK IT'S HILARIOUS!!

(Before he can hurt ASHLEY, SANDRA takes a knife from the kitchen drawer and stabs TREVOR.

TREVOR *is stunned.*

ASHLEY *grabs the baby and runs out the door.*

TREVOR *turns to* SANDRA.)

SANDRA. Oh Trevor…I'm sorry…

TREVOR. Mom?

SANDRA. *(Signing:)* I'm so so sorry.

TREVOR. …

SANDRA. I'm so sorry.

(TREVOR goes out the back door.)

TREVOR. …

SANDRA. I'm sorry, Trevor.

TREVOR. …

(He takes Boo Boo and gets in the kennel. SANDRA tries to follow but he closes the door behind him, locking it automatically.)

SANDRA. Trevor, I'm sorry. Please, please forgive me. Trevor…

(She signs "I love you.")

I love you, Trevor.

(She signs "Family.")

Family. I love you. Family.

(She keeps signing, desperately. TREVOR looks at her.)

TREVOR. Family.

(He allows her to approach.)

(SANDRA takes out her keys and opens the gate to the enclosure. She embraces TREVOR.)

SANDRA. I love you.

(TREVOR nimbly takes her keys and darts out of the kennel, closing the door behind him.)

SANDRA. Trevor? Trevor, what are you doing? Open the door, Trevor. Open the door.

TREVOR. I'm going for a little drive.

SANDRA. You can't go. You're hurt. Trevor!

TREVOR. I'm going to the wild. I'm going where Jerome went.

SANDRA. Trevor, I'm sorry…

TREVOR. In the wild they don't wear costumes…

SANDRA. It was a mistake. Please.

TREVOR. If I had my fireman hat, I bet they'd worship me as a god.

SANDRA. Don't leave me.

TREVOR. But there's no time for that now.

SANDRA. Trevor…

TREVOR. And who really wants to be a fireman anyway.

SANDRA. Trevor…Trevor…TREVOR!

(He exits stage right. The sound of the Corvette engine turning. Headlights illuminate SANDRA in the animal enclosure. Cinderella's "Nobody's Fool" resumes, just where it left off, at the beginning of the play. The volume is cranked up, and the car is heard speeding away…)

§

(ASHLEY is doing yard work. JIM approaches her, holding a cardboard box full of pictures and other mementos from Sandra's house. She doesn't see him approach.)

JIM. Hey Ashley.

ASHLEY. *(Startled:)* Oh!

JIM. I'm sorry. I didn't mean to startle you.

ASHLEY. How long have you been standing there?

JIM. About fifteen minutes. I've just been standing here ogling you.

ASHLEY. What??

JIM. I'm just kidding.

> *(As it sinks in, with self-disgust:)*

…ah dang it. That's not a very funny joke, is it?

ASHLEY. No.

JIM. You see, this is why I never should have been given a position of authority.

ASHLEY. I didn't say that—

JIM. I did…I want to apologize. For what happened. I never should have let it all go on so long.

ASHLEY. No—

JIM. I put you at risk. I put everyone at risk. I let my emotions get the better of me. I feel like a pudding head. A grade A pudding head.

ASHLEY. No one thinks you're a pudding head.

JIM. Well, that's kind of you to say.

> *(ASHLEY indicates the box.)*

ASHLEY. What's that?

JIM. Oh, I was just picking up some things from Sandy's.

ASHLEY. How is she?

> *(JIM shrugs.)*

JIM. I don't know. She's not seeing visitors…

ASHLEY. Have they set a trial date—?

JIM. …I hear she's not eating.

> *(ASHLEY processes this.)*

ASHLEY. None of it seems very fair. She's a good person.

JIM. Yeah well, we're all good people, Ashley. That doesn't mean we're not dangerous to each other. Trevor was a good person, too.

ASHLEY. It wasn't just her. You really cared about him, didn't you?

JIM. Yeah. Yeah, I did. Here, take a look.

> *(He takes out a photograph of Trevor from the box.)*

ASHLEY. Oh. It's…he's…

JIM. Dressed as a priest. I couldn't let this one go.

ASHLEY. It sounds like he really was amazing when he was young.

JIM. Not just when he was young. He drove a car. That's the thing that people forget. It wasn't like he was going berserk all the time. He stole a baby, he stole a car, sure—but what about all the years he *didn't* do any of that. That he lived like you and me. *That* should be the story.

ASHLEY. He wasn't like you and me.

JIM. Well, he sure looked like it, when you dressed him up. Maybe that was the problem. He didn't just fool us. He fooled himself.

ASHLEY. I don't know if it's a good idea to try to understand what he did, in human terms.

JIM. Sure. I know. You're right. I'm just saying, I think I know what he was going through.

ASHLEY. Who knows.

(*A beat.* JIM *starts to leave, stops.*)

JIM. I just think it's important to recognize that…they found the wreck 4 miles away. That means he drove that car for 4 miles…That's far, don't you think?

ASHLEY. You're right, Jim. You're right. For an animal, that's far. That's really pretty far.

End of Play

THE LILY'S REVENGE

Taylor
Mac

About the Collaboration
Investing in the Experimental Artist

Founded in 1993, the award-winning HERE Arts Center has spent the last two decades solidifying itself as a hub for experimental artists working in a vast array of forms. Puppeteers, media artists, composers, and choreographers as well as theatre makers with non-traditional leanings can find their home at HERE. With their specific experimental and hybrid lens, Kristin Marting, Artistic Director and co-founder, and Kim Whitener, Producing Director, have successfully designed and built programs that help artists at all stages in their careers navigate their way from early workshops to final productions and on to rich touring lives. Over 12,000 artists have been supported by HERE (that's over 500 per year!) and in fact, Basil Twist, Joey Arias, Eve Ensler, Young Jean Lee, Faye Driscoll, and, of course, Taylor Mac, have all developed work there, proving that HERE does indeed celebrate "the independent, the innovative, and the experimental."

HERE is unique in the downtown theatre in part because a true "Arts Center" is hard to come by in lower Manhattan, and HERE embodies this vision literally and spiritually. At any given moment on any given day, artists are hanging in the lounge / lobby, loading into the intimate downstairs theater, rehearsing in the larger upstairs Mainstage, or chatting in the offices with HERE's incredibly skilled and whip-smart staff. This sense of community is at the center of HERE's institutional genius, and a large part of the reason they can dream so big and accomplish so much. It's no surprise that nearly a million audience members have attended a show at HERE in its 21-year tenure. There's nowhere else to find their particular brand of collaborative hybrid work. From 90-minute puppet operas, to six-hour performance art epics, to multimedia interactive events, HERE never shies away from the magical, the outlandish, the difficult or the fiercely original and inventive.

§

In 2005, I applied to the HERE Arts Center Residency Program (HARP) with a little show about nostalgia, got accepted, and started making what I thought would be a play with a cast of five performers and last around ninety minutes. About a year into my development, I went to Kristin Marting (HERE's Artistic Director) and said, "I think the play is going to be five-hours and have a cast of forty." Kristin's response was, "Great." To which I replied, "I don't have any money." To which she replied (and I'm paraphrasing), "Let's teach you how to fundraise." I did in fact raise the money for the production because HERE taught me how and because they also put their backs into the fundraising; we premiered it in 2009 to great success because of multiple workshops at HERE; it made budget because HERE showed me how to create one; and The Lily's Revenge has now gone on to be seen throughout the United States because HERE committed to the art, the relationship with the artist, and the artist's development, which was a necessity in proving this play could be done. I love them oh so very much.

—Taylor Mac, Playwright

Mission Statement: HERE Arts Center

HERE builds a community that nurtures career artists as they create innovative hybrid live performance in theatre, dance, music, puppetry, media and visual art. Their artist residencies support the singular vision of the lead artist through commissions, long-term development, and production support. HERE's programs and performances promote relationships among local, national, and international artists. Their space is a destination for audiences who are passionate about ground-breaking contemporary work and the creative process behind it.

About the Author

Taylor Mac has been named one of New York and the country's best theater artists by the *New York Times, American Theatre* magazine, the *Village Voice* (also naming Mr. Mac Best Theater Actor in New York, 2013), *Time Out New York* (also naming him New York's best cabaret performer of 2012 and a future legend of New York City), and the *New Yorker.* A playwright, actor, and singer-songwriter, Mr. Mac's work has been performed at New York City's Lincoln Center and The Public Theater, the Sydney Opera House, American Repertory Theater (A.R.T.), Stockholm's Sodra Teatern, the Spoleto Festival USA, Dublin's Project Arts Centre, London's Soho Theatre, and literally hundreds of other theatres, museums, music halls, cabarets, and festivals around the globe. Mr. Mac is the author of sixteen full-length plays and performance pieces including *The Lily's Revenge* (Obie Award), *The Walk Across America for Mother Earth* (named one of the Best Plays of 2011 by the *New York Times*), *The Young Ladies Of* (Chicago's Jeff Award nomination for best solo), *Hir* (premiering at Magic Theatre, starring Nancy Opel, in February 2014), *The Fre* (premiering at the Children's Theatre Company in Minneapolis in 2016/17), *Red Tide Blooming* (Ethyl Eichelberger Award) and *The Be(a)st of Taylor Mac* (Edinburgh Festival Fringe's Herald Angel Award). Mr. Mac's plays have been published by Playscripts, Inc., Vintage Press, New York Theatre Review, and New York Theatre Experience and been the recipient of two Sundance Institute Theatre Lab residencies, three MAP Grants, a Creative Capital grant, The James Hammerstein Award for playwriting, three GLAAD Media Award nominations, two New York State Council on the Arts grants, a Massachusetts Cultural Council grant, an Edward F. Albee Foundation residency, a Franklin Furnace grant, a Peter S. Reed Foundation grant, and Ensemble Studio Theatre's New Voices Fellowship in playwriting. Mr. Mac is a graduate of both the HERE Artist Residency Program, New Dramatists, and is a New York Theatre Workshop Usual Suspect.

Cast of Characters

WHITE ROSE, our host

MARY PRIME DEITY, a flower girl referred to as Prime

MARY SUBPRIME DEITY, a flower girl referred to as Subprime

THE MARYS DEITY #1, a flower girl

THE MARYS DEITY #2, a flower girl

SUSAN STEWART, a flower girl and a philosopher

TIME / WIND / STEPMOTHER, all the same character

LILY, a five petaled flower

THE GREAT LONGING, a talking curtain. Child of Time and sibling of Dirt. Also plays Diane, Ron, and John Paul in film.

BRIDE DEITY, the bride hopeful as an adult human

DAISY 1, also plays piano in band

DAISY 2, also plays bass in band

DAISY 3, also plays reeds / brass in band

TICK, also plays drums in band

GROOM DEITY, a regular guy

MASTER SUNFLOWER, a sunflower and leader of the garden

BABY'S BREATH

TULIP

POPPY

RED ROSE

PANSY

LILAC

PINK LADY SLIPPER*

BRIDE LOVE

GROOM LOVE

MARY PRIME LOVE, a flower girl called Prime Love

MARY SUBPRIME LOVE, a flower girl called Subprime Love

THE MARYS LOVE # 1, a flower girl

THE MARYS LOVE #2, a flower girl

DIRT, The God of Here and Now (sibling to Great Longing and child of Time)

INCURABLE DISEASE

THE POPE

A deaf actor originally played the role of Pink Lady Slipper. It would be great if future productions continued this practice. If so, the line "You're the one who's so proud of their manhood" should be signed and not spoken and the line "Act like a man" should be spoken. Also the actor should use sign language to interpret the last song of the play. Have them start with the lyric, "And I would rather end my life" and continue interpreting to the end of the play, while excluding dialogue (unless the play is being performed for a deaf or partially deaf audience).

Production Notes

The Lily's Revenge can be done with more performers by adding as many Flowers, Flower Girls or band members (all to be dressed as Daisies) as you like. Extra Flowers should say all group Garden/Flowers lines. Extra Flower Girls should say all group Flower Girl lines.

All cast members perform during the intermissions. Cast members who have smaller roles in the play should take on larger roles during the intermissions (example: the actors playing the Incurable Disease and The Pope should be featured, not wearing their Incurable Disease and Pope costumes, in all of the intermissions in a major way).

Settings and Styles

The Deity (Act I): A Princess Musical

In the proscenium. A stage on a stage. A play within a play. The home of the Bride. An eclectic mish-mash of nostalgia. A 1950s *Home and Garden* photo display. A vaudevillian theatrical. A Victorian picture book. A movable window. A brief moment happens where the Bride goes into the garden. The garden in Act I is where the band plays.

The Ghost Warrior (Act II): An Act in Iambic, Song, and Haiku

In the round. The Garden that is really a revolutionary meeting place. Dewey. Mysterious. Wild. Not a manicured controlled garden. A fecund one.

The Love Act (Act III): A Dream Ballet

A bare church/apartment. An aisle. The audience sits in two distinct sections: The Bride's side and The Groom's side. Taped outlines suggest furniture. They are given their sides when they come in.

The Living Person (Act IV): A Silent Film

Screens surround all four sides of the audience. A cave of technology. Audience members watch the act with their backs to each other.

The Mad Demon (Act V): A Pastiche

Back in the proscenium only much larger. Now there is no longer a stage on a stage. The audience sits where the performance was in the first act and the players primarily play where the audience initially sat in the first act. Essentially everything has been flipped. Action can happen in the audience or on the stage.

A Note About Susan Stewart

When my dramaturge, Nina Mankin, found out I was writing a play about nostalgia, she suggested I read the quintessential text on the subject, *On Longing* by Susan Stewart. I fell in love with the poetry, ideas, and dissection in the book and decided its author needed to be a character in the play. I've never met Susan Stewart but I did send her an email, asking her permission to use her name and the quotes from her book. She was gracious enough to give me her blessing (otherwise I would have had to make up my own academic language about Nostalgia and Time would have to fall in love with a character named The Mary Deity #3—perhaps making their relationship more profound but ultimately not what I wanted). It is important to point out that the only similarities (that I know of) between the Susan I created and the actual Susan Stewart are: both are poets, both are critical theorists, and both have been influenced in some way by the topic of nostalgia. To my knowledge all the other details about her, found in my text, have nothing to do with the actual Susan Stewart. I thank her again for the inspiration and generosity. And now, I humbly ask that we leave Susan alone. My nightmare is that somehow she is mined for her personal attributes by all the research-obsessed actors (trying so hard to get it right) destined to play the role of her. I encourage you to make up your own Susan Stewart, free from restraining reality, just as I imagine the actual Susan Stewart does on a daily basis. There is no getting Susan right. For my Susan Stewart is not a mirror but a product of oppression, action, and liberation. My Susan Stewart is an ellipsis that asks you to confer with the implied rather than the facts. My fantasy is that one day, in twenty years perhaps, there will be so many actors who have played the Susan Stewart found in these pages that we can all come together for a party called: Night of a Thousand Susan Stewarts.

Acknowledgments

The Lily's Revenge was created as part of the HERE Arts Center resident artists program (HARP) and could not have manifested if it weren't for their support, encouragement, and vision. It premiered in the fall of 2009 at the HERE Arts Center in New York and was a co-production between Taylor Mac and HERE Arts Center with the following cast and crew:

THE LILY . . . . .Taylor Mac
THE GREAT
LONGING DEITY. . . . . James Tigger! Ferguson
TIME / WIND . . . . Bianca Leigh
CARDGIRL
(THE WHITE ROSE). . . . . .The World Famous Bob
BRIDE DEITY . . . . .Amelia Zirin-Brown
(aka Lady Rizo)
SUSAN STEWART . . . . .Heather Christian
PRIME DEITY . . . . .Tina Shepard
SUBPRIME DEITY . . . . .Ellen Maddow
THE MARYS DEITY #1 . . . . Rae C. Wright
THE MARYS DEITY #2. . . . . .Muriel Mugel
GROOM DEITY. . . . . Frank Paiva
HOT GUY / WHITE ROSE PUPPETEER /
BRIDE PUPPETEER. Kristine Lee
MASTER SUNFLOWER. . . . . .Daphne Gaines
BABY'S BREATH. . . . . Barb Lanciers
AUDIENCE MEMBER/POPPY . . . . Glenn Marla
TULIP. . . . . Ikuko Ikari
RED ROSE. . . . . Kim Rosen
THE TICK . . . . .Salty Brine
BRIDE LOVE . . . . .Darlinda Just Darlinda
GROOM LOVE. . . . . Phillip Taratula
PRIME LOVE . . . . Vanessa Anspaugh
SUBPRIME LOVE . . . . Nikki Zialcita
THE MARYS LOVE #1 . . . . .Jonathan Bastinan
THE MARYS LOVE #2. . . . . .Saeed Siamac
DAISY / BEE . . . . Kayla Asbell
DAISY / QUEEN BEE . . . . Machine Dazzle
DAISY / INCURABLE DISEASE /
BEE. . . . . Matthew Crosland
BEE. . . . . Una Aya Osato
PONY / BEE / THE POPE . . . . .Edith Raw
THE DIRT . . . . .Justin Vivian Bond

Composer .... Rachelle Garniez
Dramaturge............................Nina Mankin
Directors .... Paul Zimet, Rachel Chavkin,
                                      Faye Driscoll, Aaron Rhyne,
                           David Drake, and Kristin Marting
Production Stage Manager.................... Julia Funk
Musical Direction and Arrangements .... Matt Ray
Costumes......................... Machine Dazzle
Makeup .... Derrick Little
Set Design.............................. Nick Vaughn
Lighting Design ....Seth Reiser
Puppet Design......................... Emily DeCola
Part I Choreography.................... Julie Atlas Muz
Photographer................................Karl Giant

Piano, Guitar............................. Matt Ray
Upright Bass ....Derek Nievergelt
Drums................................Stefan Schatz
Sax, Trumpet, Clarinet, Ukulele ....Jon Natchez

Additional filmed performances were by Cary Curran, David Drake, Bridget Everett, Matt Fraser, Tracey Gilbert, Karen Hartman, Morgan Jenness, Karen Kohlhaas, Lisa Kron, Nina Mankin, Dirty Martini, Julie Atlas Muz, Our Lady J, James Scruggs, Lucy Thurber.

The role of Pink Lady Slipper was added to the script for the American Repertory Theater production and was originated by Elbert Joseph.

The live-actor version of the role The Dirt was premiered at Magic Theater and originated by Monique Jenkinson.

The roles of Pansy and Lilac were added to the script for the Magic Theater production and were originated by Miss Trixxie Carr (Lilac) and Chris Quintos (Pansy).

Acknowledgments (continued)

All production groups performing this play are required to include the following credits on the title page of every program:

The Lily's Revenge

Written and Conceived by Taylor Mac

Composed by Rachelle Garniez

Dramaturgy by Nina Mankin

The Lily's Revenge was developed at HERE Arts Center through the HERE Artist Residency Program (HARP); with the assistance of the Sundance Institute Theatre Program; and at New Dramatists as part of the Working Sessions Program and with support from the Creativity Fund. *The Lily's Revenge* is a project of Creative Capital [which currently receives support from The Andy Warhol Foundation for the Visual Arts, Doris Duke Charitable Foundation, Ford Foundation, The William and Flora Hewlett Foundation, The TOBY Fund, The James Irvine Foundation, The Nathan Cummings Foundation, and more than 150 other individuals and institutional donors]; and was made possible in part by The MAP Fund, a program of Creative Capital supported by the Doris Duke Charitable Foundation and the Rockefeller Foundation; the Franklin Furnace Fund for Performance Art, supported by Jerome Foundation and the New York State Council on the Arts, a state agency; Ars Nova; the New York State Council on the Arts Individual Artists Program; The JB Harter Charitable Trust; and The Visionary Trust.

The Lily's Revenge was further developed and had its rolling world premiere launch at Magic Theatre, San Francisco, California. Loretta Greco, Producing Artistic Director.

The Lily's Revenge *is dedicated to the memory of
director, teacher, and friend Tracy Trevett.*

*The play is also dedicated to Kristin Marting
for her dedication to the artists of New York City as well as all the
company members of the New York, San Francisco, and Cambridge
productions. Your talent and verve are what made this text possible.*

*Thank you to Patt Scarlett, Morgan Jenness, Nina Mankin,
Kim Whitener, Phillip Himberg, Loretta Greco,
And the members of the Theater of the Ridiculous.*

The Lily's Revenge, HERE Arts Center, New York, New York (2009). Photo: Ves Pitts.

THE LILY'S REVENGE

A FLOWERGORY MANIFOLD

book, lyrics, and concept by Taylor Mac
music by Rachelle Garniez

THE DIETY
Act I: A Princess Musical

"Find out who you are, without praise or blame, and be it."

—Quentin Crisp

(On stage, in front of a closed red stage curtain, are five FLOWER GIRLS who lay about in reverie coma. They are wrinkled crones, centuries old, and look like crack addicts in the midst of a waning fix. A person, whose head is trapped in a cuckoo clock, which is affixed to the wall, is asleep while standing. The person has an hourglass figure and wears a dress that is an hourglass. The sand in the hourglass dress covers the person's breasts but is slowly dripping down, creating a reveal. Perhaps other instruments of time [digital watches, alarm clocks, cellphones] are attached to the outfit. A human-size flower, in a pot, enters. It is late.)

(The LILY finds its seat with great disturbance and blocks the person behind with its enormous petals.)

LILY. *(To person behind it:)* Sorry.

(The house lights dim. A cuckoo is heard. The cuckoo clock doors open. Other alarms go off [ring tones, beeps, the radio, etc.]. TIME wakes up as if from a fever dream.)

TIME. *(A gasp of air and then:)* THIS! PLAY! IS! LONG!

(She looks at the audience and speaks a dire warning.)

No, really. LONG. In fact this play will be much longer than ADVERTISED. It is so long you may actually FORGET YOUR NAME. My name is Time. So trust when I say, this play could very well last the REST OF YOUR LIFE! You don't believe me? These Flower Girls, that lay about the stage in drool, were once AUDIENCE MEMBERS!

FLOWER GIRLS DEITY. *(Stirring at the mention of their name:)* Errrrrr.

LILY. *(To its fellow audience members:)* I didn't know just by coming to a play you could be in it. I thought you had to audition.

TIME. My eldest child, the malicious Great Longing Deity, God of Nostalgia, has trapped them in this cock-and-bull story with institutionalized narrative. INSTITUTIONALIZED NARRATIVE! Little by little they have turned from lively questioning individuals, like you, to cliché crones of mediocrity. Woolgathering junkies of wistfulness. Escape now or the telling of this tale will reduce *you,* like these Flower Girls, to an addicted coagulation of nostalgia and hope.

FLOWER GIRLS DEITY. *(Stirring at the mention of their name:)* Errrrrr.

TIME. When the play starts, The Great Longing will use the promise of a climax. A climax in the shape of the most banal and contemptible contrivance of all: The Wedding.

LILY. THERE'S GONNA BE A WEDDING!

FLOWER GIRLS DEITY. *(Stirring at the mention of their name:)* Errrrrr.

TIME. *(Shushing the LILY so as not to wake the FLOWER GIRLS:)* Shhhhh! *(Sotto Voce:)* It will use a wedding to nail you to this benighted narrative. Flee. I beg you. Make your escape now, in this moment, or this moment will be no more. No. Really. THE EXITS ARE WHERE YOU ENTERED! Any takers? I BEG YOU!

LILY. Could it really last my whole life?

TIME. YES!

LILY. And you get to be in it?

TIME. Yes.

LILY. Fun.

TIME. *Fun!*

LILY. I've never been to a play before.

TIME. *(A warning to both the LILY and the audience:)* This is not *fun.* This is not something to enjoy. It is ugly. Plastic. Is a plastic deck chair fun? No. It is tacky! This is the most base, poorly crafted, pulled together at the last minute, ready for mass consumption, demonstrative, manipulative, repetitive, oversexed, histrionic, reductive piece of…crap known to mankind. It is so cheap. Not cheap *(Indicating stingy).* But cheap *(Indicating slutty).* So cheap that as an incentive to stay 'til journey's end, The Great Longing has forced me into this hourglass dress. When the play has run its course, my breasts will be exposed!

(The LILY laughs and claps [and hopefully other audience members as well].)

TIME. Oh laughie, laughie, laughie, clapie, clapie, clapie but don't you see, once *I,* Time, was the *teller* of this tale. I was the *star* and played *all* the parts: the seasons, the shades, the *windy day.* I spoke the lines of a face, the drips that made the canyons, the philosophical arguments 'tween Hegel and Kant.

LILY. She said Kant.

TIME. But as The Great Longing Deity gains power I, and my thoughts, are reduced. Shrunk to serials. Vaudevilles disguised as…culture. MUSICAL THEATER! Now I, *we*, are forced to play *stock* characters. Time is fixed to the atomic clock. I am captured in the hourglass. Trapped in the cuckoo clock and digital phone. Treated as something to be checked and put aside. A time piece. A side kick. But there is a last vestige. Part of me remains. Free. Essential. Inside of here. *(Listening to the heart of an Audience Member:)* Bubum. Bubum. Bubum. That is me. Hidden from view. Leave this place, now, before I am drained from you completely. I BEG YOU!

No one? Not a single soul?

> *(A* TICK *and three* DAISIES *enter and go to their band positions.)*

TIME. *(Horrified at the sight of the* DAISIES:*)* Ahhhhhhh!…

> *(The* DAISIES *and the* TICK *are ready.)*

TIME. The band has entered. The *play* begins. *(To the audience:)* You are doomed.

> *(The* DAISY / TICK *band plays the overture.* TIME *sinks into the background in despair. Five* FLOWER GIRLS *awaken with screams and determination.)*

FLOWER GIRLS DEITY. Yaaaaaaaaaaaa! We Flower Girls, minions of The Great Longing Deity,

PRIME DEITY. Mary

SUSAN. Mary

SUBPRIME DEITY. Mary

THE MARYS DEITY. And The Marys

LILY. They're all named Mary.

FLOWER GIRLS DEITY. We Flower Girls must awaken The Great Longing to begin the tale. Oh, fill our dependency to *(An echo:)* dreams, dreams, dreams, dreams.

LILY. Dreams, dreams, dreams.

SUSAN. Someone's talking from the audience.

PRIME DEITY. Ignore it and sing!

> *(The* FLOWER GIRLS *sing a Pindaric Ode ritual to awaken* THE GREAT LONGING. *They do so while jonesing and in complete choreographic unison. They are aware that they are in a performance. Most of their movements/ expressions are a pantomime of gestures indicating each and every word they say. Examples are: on "violin" they act like they're playing the violin; on "dulcet" they indicate being soothing; on "ruse" they indicate dirty scheming, etc. The effect should be a bit manic, clean [unison transitions from one word to another], clear*

[they should communicate the song above all antics], marvelous in how intricate it all is, and look like a group of amateur junkies choreographed a song together. During the choruses, they caress the Curtain and/or themselves. Their caressing should become erotic and erotically neurotic. Filthy in fact.)

FLOWER GIRLS DEITY.
AHH AH AH AH AH
AH AH AH AH AH

(SUBPRIME coughs a wretched smokers hack full of phlegm and age.)

FLOWER GIRLS DEITY.
AH AH AH AH AH
AH AH AH AH AH
THE GREAT LONGING, OUR DIETY
'TIS BUILT WITH ODES AND BONHOMIE.
STITCHED WITH A VIOLIN PATCHED BY OUR DREAMS
THEN DIPPED AND CLEANED IN SENTIMENTAL
STREAMS.

PRIME and SUBPRIME DEITY.
TO NOURISH THEE WE MUSE
AND SING OUR SOFT BERCEUSE.

THE MARYS DEITY.
AND IN OUR HAZY HUMID HUES
WILL BREACH A KIND AND DULCET RUSE

FLOWER GIRLS DEITY.
A DIETY THAT GIVES THE GALLANTRY
REMEMBERING REMEMBERED MEMORY.

LILY. MEMORY.

FLOWER GIRLS DEITY. THE GREAT LONGING,

LILY. THE GREAT LONGING.

FLOWER GIRLS DEITY. OUR DIETY

LILY. OUR DEITY.

FLOWER GIRLS DEITY. ENVELOPE SIGHS, CARESS ENNUI

LILY. ENNUI.

FLOWER GIRLS DEITY. AWAKE SWEET GOD OF ACHE AND
BLISSFUL LORE.

LILY. BLISSFUL LORE.

FLOWER GIRLS DEITY. COME WRAP US IN NOSTAGLIA'S
PARAMOUR.

LILY. PARAMOUR.

FLOWER GIRLS DEITY. THE GREAT LONGING.

LILY. THE GREAT LONGING.

FLOWER GIRLS DEITY. OUR DIETY.

LILY. OUR DEITY.

FLOWER GIRLS DEITY. OUR DIETY.

LILY. *(Maybe trying to get the audience to sing along at this point:)*
OUR DEITY.

FLOWER GIRLS DEITY. OUR DIETY.

LILY. OUR DEITY.

FLOWER GIRLS DEITY / LILY. OUR DIETY!

PRIME DEITY. *(Not knowing what audience member she's talking to but knowing the direction it is coming from:)* WILL YOU STOP THAT!

LILY. Sorry.

SUSAN.
AHH AHH AHH AHH AHH AHH AHH AHH
AHH AHH AHH AHH
AHH AHH AHH AHH

FLOWER GIRLS DEITY.
WE PLEDGE TO THEE THIS LOT:
IN REVERIE WE'RE CAUGHT.

SUSAN.
JUST LIKE THE BIRDS AND BUTTERFLIES
THAT LONG FOR SONG, IN CLOUDLESS SKY.

THE MARYS DEITY.
BUT TRAPPED WITH FINGERS DRENCHED WITH DRIP
THEY FLUTTER, FLOP, THEY FLIP AND RIP.

FLOWER GIRLS DEITY.
SO TOO HAVE WE BECOME THE STORY OLD
PRAY HOLD US EVERMORE IN STORY TOLD

(A canon:)

OH PLEASE, OH PLEASE, OH DIETY, OH DIETY, OH PLEASE,
OH PLEASE, OH DIETY, OH DIETY, OH PLEASE, OH
PLEASE, OH DIETY, OH DIETY, OH PLEASE.

(A man painted to look the same color as the curtain pokes his head out of the top of the curtain—through the slit. He is THE GREAT LONGING. *His body, the curtain, moves as he speaks.)*

THE GREAT LONGING. I AM THE GREAT LONGING! God of nostalgia. Manifested as a stage curtain.

FLOWER GIRLS. *(The final chord of the song:)* AHHHHHHHH!

PRIME DEITY. Manifested as a stage curtain as theater is the world of dreams.

SUBPRIME DEITY. And dreams are what The Great Longing suckles.

SUSAN. Without them our dear deity would shrink away.

THE MARYS DEITY. And we would grow old instead of how we are.

FLOWER GIRLS DEITY. Forever young.

PRIME DEITY. *(Admiring her youth which is not there:)* I love theater.

TIME. Well some would say theater is not the realm of dreams but the blending of dreams with what is here and now.

THE GREAT LONGING. Mother, nobody wants to hear your HIFALUTIN' BLABBER.

TIME. Everybody wants possibility, thought and complexity.

THE GREAT LONGING. And boobies.

> *(THE GREAT LONGING points to TIME's dress which is shrinking to create a reveal of her breasts.)*

THE GREAT LONGING / FLOWER GIRLS. *(This laughter goes on for a very, very, very long time. It is crazed and if you think it's crazy enough, make it crazier.)* WA HA HA HA HA HA HA HA HA!

LILY. *(To an audience member:)* Oh! Oh! That clock gave birth to that curtain.

> *(Everyone gets nervous, not knowing what to do with the talking audience member.)*

LILY. That clock gave birth to that curtain and now the curtain wants to see its mother's boobies.

THE GREAT LONGING. *(Sotto Voce:)* What's happening?

SUSAN. *(Seeing the LILY for the first time:)* There's a personified *flower* in the audience!

> *(All the FLOWER GIRLS look into the audience.)*

FLOWER GIRLS DEITY. *(As if they are demon Lennie Smalls:)* Flower!

THE GREAT LONGING. DON'T LOOK AT THE AUDIENCE.

FLOWER GIRLS DEITY. Flower Girls go to flower!

THE GREAT LONGING. TO LOOK AT THE AUDIENCE IS FORBIDDEN.

LILY. Oh Mary. Mary Oh. Oh. You have a pimple.

PRIME DEITY. *(Covering her pimple:)* I do not.

LILY. You do too.

FLOWER GIRLS DEITY. *(Seeing that it's true:)* Ahhhh!

THE MARYS DEITY. That flower can see the here and now!

LILY. *(To the* MARYS*:)* And you have wrinkles.

FLOWER GIRLS DEITY. Ahhhhh. The here and now exposes all our imperfections.

SUBPRIME DEITY. Quick, Great Longing take us into dreams.

FLOWER GIRLS DEITY. *(They pronounce banished "ba-ni-shed".)* Where blemishes are banished with Romeo.

TIME. Worklights!

> *(The worklights turn on.)*

ALL. *(In horror:)* Worklights.

> *(They all cover their faces.)*

THE GREAT LONGING. *(Hiding:)* Mary, kill the worklights.

> *(The* FLOWER GIRLS *stumble about the stage, with their faces covered, looking for the off switch.)*

TIME. *(To audience:)* Quickly focus. That flower, though slightly obnoxious, has brought the truth of here and now to this fiction. Suddenly I see our way to freedom. I'll use my chicanery and bring an end to nostalgia by infesting this story with a Lily.

LILY. Really!

TIME. *(Taking center stage to perform a soliloquy, as she is wont to do, and also speaking in verse, the language of the flower:)*
For Lily with your fragrant snares
You force the dreamer to the now.
"Come stop and smell the present tense"
You call and so all fall in line.
Your open outstretched petals hail
And give a pause within the step.
Your style proper, strong, and sweet
Will prop this moment in the air;
Your stigma, blatantly pronounced,
Does proclaim carpe diem's route.
Born in the dirt, you're grounded, so
You know the here and now does count.
Yes Lily, you, will be instilled
in Longing's long and sucking tale
And free us from the reign of reverie.

LILY. It's true! You don't have to audition to be in the theater.

SUBPRIME. Got the worklights.

(SUBPRIME MARY pulls the worklight switch off the wall and we return to beautiful theatrical lighting.)

THE GREAT LONGING. That's the last aside you'll ever get mother. Now, welcome: The ingénue of the ages.

TIME. DO WE REALLY have to hear another story of some love-lorn waif?

THE GREAT LONGING. THIS IS MY WORLD MOTHER!

TIME. I am your parent not your mother or father. Time has no gender.

FLOWER GIRLS DEITY. *(A short/quick gross out:)* Eww.

THE GREAT LONGING. ENOUGH! I give you an epic romance. Twixt Bride and Groom.

FLOWER GIRLS. Groom! Groom! Groom groom groom.

TIME. There is more to life than epic romance. What about a nice succinct multi-cultural folktale about liberation?

THE GREAT LONGING. *(Mocking:)* Multi-Culti?

TIME. Starring say, Time and—

LILY. And a Lily.

TIME. Yes. Mary, fetch the flower.

SUSAN. Flower!

THE GREAT LONGING. Mary don't you break that fourth wall.

> *(SUSAN tries to stop herself from breaking the fourth wall but her momentum crashes her through it.)*

ALL. *(Shocked that she broke the fourth wall:)* Huh!

LILY. Oooo, she broke the wall.

SUSAN. Flower!

THE GREAT LONGING. Mary, don't you touch that flower.

> *(It's too late [she touches the flower when GREAT LONGING says, "flower"]. Touching the LILY gives her an electric shock. When she pulls away from the LILY she is suddenly different.)*

SUSAN. But we can wrap ourselves in profundity through the scrutiny of the inanimate object come to life.

ALL. *(Shocked at her sudden intelligence:)* Huh!

TIME. *(Perhaps a little turned on:)* Oh. My.

SUSAN. Please welcome to the stage: The Lily.

THE GREAT LONGING. Don't you dare.

TIME. I'll get the spotlight.

LILY. I've never been in a spotlight before.

TIME. Never?

LILY. I'm a left-over and discarded organic flower raised in a bodega under halogen lights.

THE GREAT LONGING. Left-over! Discarded! ORGANIC! You bring this un-purchased organic lily to my theater and you know I grow my own flowers on my farm in Ecuador.

TIME. *You* don't grow it, you force your sister, The Dirt, to grow everything for you.

FLOWER GIRLS. *(With disgust:)* Dirt!

LILY. Dirt?

TIME. God of Here and Now.

THE GREAT LONGING. I've asked you not to talk about the D.I.R.T.

TIME. You've made my baby a slave.

THE GREAT LONGING. She likes living on the factory farm.

TIME. You force her to manufacture ache and tripe: all your items of homogeneous dreck.

THE GREAT LONGING. You like nothing I make.

TIME. What is there to like? You have created a monotheistic fear-based culture so tight and limited, so intent on safety and order, on the perpetuation of tradition, that you have banished intimacy by creating a distance between the user and the maker so vast, all things have become technology.

THE GREAT LONGING. Nobody understands you when you talk like that Mother.

SUSAN. Are you referencing Heidegger?

ALL. *(A collective gasp:)* Huh!

TIME. *(Even more turned on:)* Methinks some semblance of a former life still exists in that Flower Girl.

LILY. Can I be in the play now?

TIME. Daisies. A little accompaniment please.

> (TIME *puts the spotlight on the* LILY. *The* BAND *plays an intro. Throughout the first verse the* FLOWER GIRLS *become entranced by the* LILY *as their addiction to story makes them fickle minions.)*

LILY.

> FROM SUN I'VE BEEN BEGAT
> REBORN WITHIN HER GLOW I FIND MY HABITAT—
>
> IS HERE ABOARD THE FLOORBOARD ROWS
> THE CRINKLED PAPER MOONS.
> ALL SORROW THAT HAS BEEN WILL GO
> FOR I WILL SING THE TUNE.
> OF LOVE THAT NOW WILL GROW.
> SO LOVE WILL EVER GROW.
>
> *(To audience:)*
>
> TO YOU I SEEK TO PLEASE
> TO CHEER AND CHANT, DECREE A HEART OF DEEP
> CERISE
>
> THE MARRIAGE GODDESS JUNO FED
> HER HERCULES TO BLOOM.
> FROM LIGHTNING GRIDS HER BREAST MILK DRIPPED
> AND GREW THIS FLOWER TO GROOM
> AND ONCE A LILY'S GROOMED
> IT'S FIT TO PLAY THE GROOM.

THE GREAT LONGING. A lily can't play the groom.

LILY. Why not?

TIME. Lily, don't fall into romantic cliché. Remember your purpose.

LILY. To woo the Bride?

TIME. To elevate the canned drivel of nostalgic narrative with here and now.

THE GREAT LONGING. Flowers aren't meant for the stage.

LILY. Flowers are brought to the theater all the time.

THE GREAT LONGING. As gifts. As trinkets. Not as the central character.

LILY.

> AND SOME WILL PUT ME IN THE DARK.
> THEY'LL SAY MY LOVE IS CAIN'S CURSED MARK
> AND COULD NOT BE TRUE—
>
> LOVE FIT FOR THE CENTER STAGE.
> THEY'LL STUNT THIS GOAL FROM FLOWERAGE
> AND TRY TO SUBDUE—
>
> LOVE THAT MAKES THE WORLD APPLAUD
> THAT FLOWERS MORE THAN AARON'S ROD
> AND THAT WILL DEBUT—

THE GREAT LONGING. Mother, what's that Lily doing?

TIME. It's stealing the show!

THE GREAT LONGING. Flower Girls, don't listen to that Lily. We don't know where it came from. Were there any regulations in its growth? Why look, that Lily has but five petals. Everyone knows lilies should have six petals.

LILY. *(About to cry from being ridiculed:)* It's true. I was born with but five petals. *(Breaking free from sorrow to triumph:)* Just like a star! *(With grand vocal athletics:)*

UPON THIS WOODEN O
I'VE BROKEN FREE FROM PEWS: THE TRAP OF STA-TUS QUO

MY SCENT WILL BRING YOU JOY AND CHEER
MY LOVE IS BORN TO BREED
FROM RHIZOME TO THIS LILY HERE
IS ALL YOU'LL EVER NEED.
SO LOVE MAKES ITS PREMIERE
AND YOU WILL ENDEAR.

> *(TIME applauds with the audience and shouts Brava and things like, "Five is the new six" for a very long time.)*

THE GREAT LONGING. Flower Girls. Plug mother into the wall.

FLOWER GIRLS DEITY. *(Attacking TIME:)* Yaaaaaaaaa!

> *(The FLOWER GIRLS plug TIME into the wall.)*

THE GREAT LONGING. That Lily is no star. Why, I do believe it's diseased.

FLOWER GIRLS DEITY. *(The FLOWER GIRLS all run into the audience:)* AHHHHHHH!

THE GREAT LONGING. FLOWER GIRLS, COME OUT OF THE AUDIENCE!

LILY. I'm not diseased.

THE GREAT LONGING. Nobody wants to hear from a weak little flower.

LILY. Obviously they do.

THE GREAT LONGING. Everybody wants the Bride story. Isn't that right?

FLOWER GIRLS DEITY. *(Quietly with anticipation:)* Oh yes.

> *(The following is a sexual game THE GREAT LONGING plays with the FLOWER GIRLS. All of them partake and come back onto the stage. He is winning them back.)*

THE GREAT LONGING. Everybody wants a story about a perfect day?

FLOWER GIRLS DEITY. Oh yes.

THE GREAT LONGING. A special day that never ends.

FLOWER GIRLS DEITY. Yes Curtain.

THE GREAT LONGING. Do you want to tell the story?

FLOWER GIRLS DEITY. *(A sudden sexual tinge:)* Yes Curtain.

THE GREAT LONGING. Do you really want to?

FLOWER GIRLS DEITY. Yes Curtain.

THE GREAT LONGING. How much do you want to?

FLOWER GIRLS DEITY. Give us the story to tell. Oh give it to us.

THE GREAT LONGING. Tell the curtain what you want.

FLOWER GIRLS DEITY. Don't tease us Curtain don't oh. Oh. Oh.

THE GREAT LONGING. Get down on those knees and beg to tell the story.

FLOWER GIRLS DEITY. Oh work it. Work it.

THE GREAT LONGING. Genuflect to tell the story.

FLOWER GIRLS DEITY. Work it.

THE GREAT LONGING. You want to tell the Bride story?

FLOWER GIRLS DEITY. Oh yes, let us tell the Bride story.

THE GREAT LONGING. You want that big epic Bride story?

FLOWER GIRLS DEITY. Yeah. Epic. Oh oh.

THE GREAT LONGING. The bride's gonna be at the *center* of the story.

FLOWER GIRLS DEITY. Oh. Yes the center. Get her in the center.

THE GREAT LONGING. Oh, I'll get that bride in the center.

FLOWER GIRLS DEITY. Oh Curtain. Oh.

THE GREAT LONGING. Yeah, say my name.

FLOWER GIRLS DEITY. Oh Curtain. Oh. The story.

THE GREAT LONGING. You wanna tell it!

FLOWER GIRLS DEITY. Oh. Oh. Oh.

THE GREAT LONGING. I'm gonna let you tell it.

FLOWER GIRLS DEITY. Oh! God! Yes!

THE GREAT LONGING. You're gonna tell *it*, yes you are, do it, tell it, tell iiiiiiiiiiiit.

FLOWER GIRLS DEITY. Oh oh oh oh oh oh oh oh oh oh oh oh oh—
ONCE UPON A TIME!

(The FLOWER GIRLS *have epileptic fits of ecstasy on the floor. Once they are done they are in blissful reverie.)*

THE GREAT LONGING. Take that, Mother.

FLOWER GIRLS DEITY. *(In blissful post-ecstasy:)* Once upon a time there was a curtain.

THE GREAT LONGING. Who opened to reveal a sorrowful Bride Hopeful.

*(*THE GREAT LONGING *opens to reveal a little girl Bunraku puppet who is naked. Eventually the* MARYS DEITY *and* SUBPRIME *will puppeteer her [*SUBPRIME *will be the voice].)*

LILY. *(Scared:)* Ahhh!

FLOWER GIRLS DEITY. What?

LILY. She's naked.

PRIME DEITY. Nudity sells tickets.

LILY. But she can't be naked; she's the Bride.

SUBPRIME DEITY. But she can't afford clothes 'cause she works in a sweatshop.

THE MARYS DEITY. Making toxic badminton birdies.

PRIME DEITY. Until true love arrives and saves her from life's drudgery.

LILY. Now is my chance. I'll woo the Bride's sorrow to rosy picture hue and so become the lead in the play.

TIME. *(Sotto Voce:)* Lily, forget the Bride.

LILY. Never!

TIME. I brought you into this tale to be an end to institutionalized nostalgic narrative.

LILY. But everybody loves the romantic lead.

TIME. Wouldn't you rather be a flower who people stopped to smell?

LILY. I can't let other people smell me. My scent is saved for the Bride.

TIME. Only pain can come from such plebeianism.

LILY.
IF PAIN IS GAINED FROM LOVING
AS GENIAL A SOUL AS SHE
THEN PLEASE INFLICT ME HERE AND NOW
WITH CRUSHING LIMBS THAT SQUEEZE ME SO
INTO THAT QUAINT AND NAKED GAIT.

LILY. *(An idea:)* Ooo, I know, she wears a pillowcase.

TIME. What?

LILY. She's so poor she can only afford a pillowcase that she tries to make look like a wedding dress.

PRIME DEITY. That's not part of the story.

SUBPRIME DEITY. But it's good.

THE MARYS DEITY. Yeah.

> *(The* FLOWER GIRLS *put a pillowcase wedding dress on the* BRIDE PUPPET *during the following.)*

LILY. And she had a Lily.

FLOWER GIRLS DEITY. *(All but* SUSAN:*)* What?

LILY. *(Making it up as it goes along:)* A rhizome, which the Bride Hopeful planted and grew in the confines of the sweatshop. A flower companion she loved dearly.

TIME. *(Sotto Voce:)* Lily, you are helping them stoop to the lowest common denominator of archetypical sexism. What's next, the evil step-mother?

LILY. Oh. I know, she had an evil step-mother.

PRIME DEITY. *(Pointing to* TIME:*)* An evil step-mother who was a cranky academic.

SUBPRIME DEITY. Yeah she was a femi-nazi academic.

SUSAN. I'm not sure I feel comfortable with that.

TIME. Agreed, can we please transcend just a little.

THE MARYS DEITY #1. A lesbian femi-nazi academic

THE MARYS DEITY #2. Who read Hegel.

TIME. Enough with the sexist homophobic anti-intellectualism.

SUSAN. I love Hegel.

FLOWER GIRLS DEITY. *(All but* SUSAN:*)* A lesbian femi-nazi academic who read Hegel and wore ugly clothes. *(Attacking* TIME *and forcing her into the Evil Stepmother outfit:)* YAAAAAAAA!

TIME. What are you—stop that. Don't you know who I— I mean really, no, not the tweed, etc.

LILY. Gag that Stepmother. Let the Bride sing.

> *(*PRIME DEITY *gags* TIME *and the* BRIDE PUPPET *sings and is puppeteered.)*

BRIDE PUPPET.
I DREAM OF RIBBONS
SO EXQUISITE, CHEEKS AGLOW

OH-OH-OH-OH-OH
I DREAM AN ARABESQUE
A BALL-ROOM PICTURESQUE

OH-OH-OH-OH—

OH A HEART DOES QUAKE
THINKING OF THE BRIDAL AISLE I'LL TAKE
MINIATURES ATOP
A CAKE. CONNOISSEURS STOP
IN MY WAKE. THE STAKES
SIGNED AND SEALED WITH BUT A KISS, AN ACHE.

OH OH OH OH

LILY / BRIDE PUPPET.
WHEN YOU LIVE A TROUBLED LIFE,
DESTINED TO THE PAIN AND STRIFE,
AS WE BOTH DO,
TO DREAM THE DAY AWAY'S A PLEASURE,
IT'S THE MEANS WITH WHICH WE'LL MEASURE
HOW TO CRAWL THROUGH.

BRIDE PUPPET. I DREAM OF I DO'S

LILY. HONEYMOONS

LILY / BRIDE PUPPET.
IN GRAND CHATEAUS.
OH-OH-OH-OH-OH

BRIDE PUPPET. I DREAM I'LL FIND THE ONE

LILY. WITH FELIX MENDELSSOHN.

LILY / BRIDE PUPPET. OH-OH-OH-OH

BRIDE PUPPET / LILY.
OH A DRESS THAT FLOATS,
UP ABOVE THE CROWD WHERE CLOUDS PROMOTE—
BRIDAL MAID BIRDS, WHO SING
AND DOTE, MAJESTIC WORDS THEY,
DO DENOTE THE QUOTE,
WE AND YOU HAVE LEARNED BY RIPPLING ROTE.

BRIDE PUPPET.
HERE COMES THE BRIDE ALL DRESSED IN WHITE
HERE COMES THE BRIDE ALL DRESSED IN WHITE

BRIDE PUPPET / FLOWER GIRLS.
HERE COMES THE BRIDE ALL DRESSED IN WHITE
HERE COMES THE BRIDE ALL DRESSED IN WHITE

BRIDE PUPPET / LILY / FLOWER GIRLS.
WHEN YOU LIVE A TROUBLED LIFE,
DESTINED TO THE PAIN AND STRIFE,
AS WE ALL DO,
TO DREAM THE DAY AWAY'S A PLEASURE,
IT'S THE MEANS TO WIN THE TREASURE,
THAT YOU ARE DUE.
OH DREAMS.

LILY. Bride Hopeful.

BRIDE PUPPET. Yes Lily.

LILY. Each night I dream I awake and find you and each morning I awake and my dream has come true.

BRIDE PUPPET. Oh.

> *(The* BRIDE *kisses the* LILY. THE GREAT LONGING *closes. All the* FLOWER GIRLS *except* SUBPRIME *are downstage of the curtain. The* LILY *and* SUBPRIME *[and* BRIDE PUPPET*] are upstage and so not seen.)*

THE GREAT LONGING. THIS IS UNACCEPTABLE.

FLOWER GIRLS DEITY. Yes Curtain.

THE GREAT LONGING. Flower Girls I entrusted you with the Bride's story.

FLOWER GIRLS DEITY. Yes Curtain.

THE GREAT LONGING. You can't tell the Bride's story if you can't get it right.

FLOWER GIRLS DEITY. Yes Curtain.

THE GREAT LONGING. A Bride can't marry a flower and if you don't tell the real story you'll never get to the wedding.

FLOWER GIRLS DEITY. *(Sticking their heads out of various places in the Curtain:)* Wedding wedding wedding.

SUSAN. But the Bride really loves the Lily.

THE GREAT LONGING. *(Swatting* SUSAN *away:)* The Bride is obviously a child and children do not marry, do they?

FLOWER GIRLS DEITY. No Curtain.

THE GREAT LONGING. Children must grow up and let go of their love for interloping organic flowers.

FLOWER GIRLS DEITY. Yes Curtain.

THE GREAT LONGING. And so I give you the *aging* of the Bride.

(THE GREAT LONGING Curtain opens to reveal the BRIDE PUPPET and the LILY still kissing. Suddenly she starts having spastic fits. The BRIDE PUPPET flails about the stage in great pain. Eventually she is pulled violently down into the dress as if she were being eaten by a shark. A little blood spews.)

BRIDE PUPPET. Ahhhhhhhh!

(The dress shakes and shrieks. An older version of the BRIDE [what we'll call BRIDE DEITY], forces herself to grow out of the dress. It appears as if she has been under the dress the whole time. She looks haggard and hoary. SUBPRIME tries to maneuver her but the BRIDE DEITY slaps her. She runs, crying, to the other FLOWER GIRLS.)

LILY. Bride?

BRIDE DEITY. I think I'm the Bride as adult.

LILY. You're very beautiful.

BRIDE DEITY. Am I?

LILY. Of course.

BRIDE DEITY. I've never been featured before. Usually I just play factory wench number 11.

LILY. I'm in the story now too.

BRIDE DEITY. They told me I was too old to be the bride.

LILY. I'm the groom.

BRIDE DEITY. What?

LILY. You just kissed me.

BRIDE. Did I?

LILY. We're lovers.

BRIDE DEITY. Lil, we need to talk.

LILY. What about?

BRIDE DEITY. Well I like you and all—

LILY. Like?

BRIDE DEITY. It's just, well… I've changed and I'm not what I used to be and, well—

LILY. YOU LOVE ME.

BRIDE DEITY. Um.

LILY. YOU LOVE ME NOT?

BRIDE DEITY. Well—

LILY. YOU LOVE ME.

BRIDE DEITY. About that—

LILY. YOU LOVE ME NOT
THINK HOW YOU ONCE LOVED ME?

BRIDE DEITY. I don't know Lil.

LILY. WHY WOULD YOU NOT LOVE ME?

BRIDE DEITY. Maybe we need a little space.

LILY. *SPACE?*

PRIME DEITY. Yeah distance.

SUBPRIME DEITY. So the new grown-up Bride went out for a stroll in the garden.

THE MARYS DEITY. Where she saw a hot guy.

> *(The* MARYS DEITY *puppeteer a cardboard cutout of a hot guy.)*

SUSAN and LILY. No!

FLOWER GIRLS DEITY. *(All but* SUSAN:*)* Yeah.

PRIME DEITY. And she forgot all about that Lily.

> *(The* BRIDE DEITY *flirts with and sings to the Cardboard Man. The* LILY *sings to the* BRIDE.*)*

BRIDE DEITY. DO YOU CARE FOR ME

LILY. OR DOES HE NOT

BRIDE DEITY. ARE YOU THERE FOR ME

LILY. IT'S ME YOU'VE GOT

LILY and BRIDE.
THINK, HOW YOU COULD LOVE ME
WHY WOULD YOU NOT
LOVE ME

PRIME DEITY. And as the Lily looked out its window it saw the Bride, hanging out by some daisies, affix herself to the cruelest of deeds.

> *(Three human-size* DAISIES *enter.* BRIDE DEITY *pulls a petal off* DAISY #1 *with each line of her song. The* LILY *watches in horror.)*

BRIDE DEITY. HE LOVES ME

DAISY #1. *(In pain:)* Ahhhhhhh!

BRIDE DEITY. HE LOVES ME NOT

DAISY #1. No, no, no, no: Ahhhhhhhh.

BRIDE DEITY. HE LOVES ME

DAISY #1. Pleeeeeeeease.

BRIDE DEITY. HE LOVES ME NOT

DAISIES. *(Meaning stop:)* Stah ah ah ah ahp!

BRIDE DEITY. WHY WILL HE LOVE ME

DAISY #1. Mooooooooother!

BRIDE DEITY. WHY WILL HE NOT LOVE ME

PRIME DEITY. But little did the Lily know, the worst was yet to come.

FLOWER GIRLS DEITY. *(All but* SUSAN:*)* Enter the Flower Girls.

DAISY #2. Not the Flower Girls.

> *(The* FLOWER GIRLS *run on howling.)*

FLOWER GIRLS DEITY. AWOOOOHAHAHAHYAYAYAYAGRGLE-HUHU!

BRIDE DEITY.
> HE IS A FIGURE
> WRAPPED UP IN PANCAKES
> ROCKING CHAIRS, COFFEE BEANS,
> AND SUNDAY STROLLS.
> WRAPPED UP LIKE CHRISTMAS.
> WRAPPED UP LIKE TENDER STORIES OF OLD.

> *(*BRIDE DEITY *and* FLOWER GIRLS *begin to pick apart the other* DAISIES *during the following verse. The* DAISIES *scream. The* LILY *sobs.)*

BRIDE DEITY and FLOWER GIRLS.
> DOES HE CARE FOR ME?
> OR DOES HE NOT?
> IS HE FAIR TO ME?
> WHAT HAVE I GOT?
> WHY DOES HE LOVE ME?
> WHY DOES HE NOT
> LOVE ME?

PRIME DEITY. Now the Lily saw that The Bride had no real love for flowers.

FLOWER GIRLS DEITY. *(Demonic laughter:)* Wa ha ha ha ha ha ha ha!

LILY. But the Bride will soon learn what true love is when she meets the alternative. Enter a realistic Groom.

> *(The* LILY *points to a guy in the audience and gestures for him to come on stage.)*

LILY. Yes, you in the plaid.

(The guy comes up. It should seem at first as if he really is an audience member.)

LILY. And he sings.

(The man doesn't know what to do.)

LILY. Sing!

(He spontaneously sings and is now our GROOM DEITY.)

GROOM DEITY.
    I THINK OF PORNOGRAPHIC IMAGES WHEN I MAKE
        LOVE TO YOU.
    PAST LOVERS.
    SOMETIMES OTHERS,
    STILL WHO I HAVE NOT YET MET.
    MADE UP NAKED QUILTS OF VARIOUS BODY PARTS.
    THE PERFECT BREAST,
    A POCKET OF A SPINE,
    SOFTER HAIR,
    A WHISPER, SUPERIMPOSED OVER AND SOMETIMES
        MIXED WITH YOU.
    "PLEASE STAY HARD"
    THAT'S WHAT I'M THINKING. I THINK.
    PLEASE LET ME LOVE YOU
    OH LET IT WORK
    WHY CAN'T I LOVE YOU
    WHY DOES IT HURT
    TO LOVE YOU.

*(*PRIME DEITY *slaps the* GROOM.*)*

PRIME DEITY. What are you doing?

GROOM DEITY. I'm being honest.

SUBPRIME DEITY. You weren't hired to be honest.

THE MARYS DEITY #1. You're supposed to *act* like a man.

THE MARYS DEITY #2. Not actually be one.

GROOM DEITY. Then what do I say?

FLOWER GIRLS DEITY. Just shut up and look suitable.

LILY. You have a choice Bride Hopeful. That Groom or me.

SUSAN. And the Lily, waiting in anticipation for the Bride's answer,

PRIME DEITY. *(Trying to force the rejection of the* LILY *on the* BRIDE:*)* The Bride *knowing* what she must do,

GROOM DEITY. The Groom eyeing the bosom of the lady in the front row,

SUBPRIME DEITY. The nibbling flower girls,

THE MARYS DEITY. And the dying desecrated daisies—

ALL. All sing:

BRIDE, GROOM, FLOWER GIRLS, LILY, and DAISIES.
WILL YOU COME FOR ME
OH WILL YOU NOT
WILL YOU TAKE ME FROM
OR WILL YOU STOP
WHAT HAVE I LEFT TO GIVE
WHAT HAVE I NOT

(*Everyone, except the* LILY, *backs up behind the proscenium.*)

LILY. WHAT HAVE I NOT—

(THE GREAT LONGING *closes. The* LILY *is in front of the curtain alone.*)

THE GREAT LONGING. Lily. This story is my story. Is that understood?

LILY. She killed those flowers and she's thinking of marrying that awful groom.

THE GREAT LONGING. Do not try to take this story from me or I will have my Flower Girls tear you to pieces.

LILY. You want her to wed some guy she doesn't really care about, who doesn't really care about her so you can eat their aspirations of a better life.

THE GREAT LONGING. Yes.

LILY. I won't let you do it. I'll take over the story.

THE GREAT LONGING. I warned you Lily.

LILY. Well I'm warning you. If you do this to her I will make you obsolete.

THE GREAT LONGING. (*Taking control of the story:*) And so, as the Bride Hopeful held the fallen petals in her hand, she suddenly saw the flowers for what they truly were: beacons of her failure.

LILY. What?

THE GREAT LONGING. That damn five-petaled organic Lily.

LILY. No.

THE GREAT LONGING. That flower said it loved her but what had its love gotten her. Nothing. In fact the Lily's love was intervening in the only chance of happiness left to her.

LILY. She can be happy with me.

THE GREAT LONGING. No. She would end this childish charade and destroy the Lily.

(THE GREAT LONGING opens and the BRIDE DEITY is revealed holding scissors. A slasher movie sound cue.)

LILY. Amelia?

BRIDE DEITY. I'm sorry Lily.

(She cuts a petal off the LILY. It is truly horrible. The LILY is in great pain.)

FLOWER GIRLS DEITY. Again! Cut it again!

(The STEPMOTHER crawls on making silent movie eye gestures.)

STEPMOTHER. Hmmmmm.

PRIME DEITY. What's Evil Stepmother doing?

SUSAN. She's acting with her eyes. She says: "Stop this. It's not the Lily's fault. You must let go of this notion of a wedding. You don't have to marry. You could live like me."

BRIDE DEITY. I will not become an old maid lesbian femi-nazi academic evil step-mother. I will marry. I may not get all the success in life I deserve but I will have an idea of it.

(BRIDE DEITY goes to a spotlight.)

BRIDE DEITY.
WHEN I WAS YOUNGER
ALL MY TEARS I'D MAKE UP

(A fake cry.) Boo hoo hoo hoo.

JUST A SHOW I'D TAKE UP
WITH A WHIM.

THEN ALL MY SORROW
WAS A GAME TO GARNER
MOM'S DEEP SOOTHES TO DARN HER
DAUGHTER IN SOME WEDDING TRIM.

I'D LAY ABOUT IN COOL SILK DREAMING
TULLE ABOUND WITH FUTURE SCHEMING
OF THE WIFE I'D BE.

I'D WALK THE AISLE WITH GREAT SENSATION.
BAIT THE BOYS WITH VEILED SALVATION
OF A LIFE DECREED.

BUT NOW THAT I AM OLDER,
AND MY SORROW'S NOT AFFECTED,
ALL THE BOYS HAVE PLAYED THEIR PARTS
AND LEFT ME HERE REJECTED.

SO I'M TEETERING ON THE EDGE OF
TOO LITTLE TOO LATE,

TOO LITTLE TOO LATE,
TOO LITTLE TOO LATE.

I'LL LIVE IN MY DREAMS OF GRANDEUR
BUT SETTLE, CONFLATE.
AND STOP!
TEETERING ON TOO LITTLE TOO LATE

I HELD OUT FOR LOVE THAT WAS REQUITED
TWO KIDS AND DOG, BUT NOW DECIDED
THE DATE CAN'T WAIT.

'CAUSE I'M TEETERING ON THE EDGE OF
TOO LITTLE TOO LATE,
TOO LITTLE TOO LATE,
TOO LITTLE TOO LATE.

EXPEDIENT LOVE HAS FOUND ME
RELINQUISHED, SEDATE,
TEETERING ON TOO LITTLE, TOO LATE.

TRUE, THE MAN I GOT, HE'S NOT SO HANDSOME.
AND NO ONE ELSE HAS COME AND PAID THE RANSOM
OF TIME'S DEBATE.
MY FATE SOUL MATE
IS LATE.

LILY.
BUT OH IF LOVE DID SHOW,
WHAT GRAND VIRTUOSITY.
YES OH, IF LIVE COULD GROW...

BRIDE DEITY.
NO. PLANNED...RECIPROCITY.
FOR I'M TEETERING ON THE EDGE OF
TOO LITTLE TOO LATE,
TOO LITTLE TOO LATE,
TOO LITTLE TOO LATE.

I'LL LIVE IN MY DREAMS OF GRANDEUR
BUT SETTLE

FLOWER GIRLS DEITY. YOU'LL SETTLE

BRIDE DEITY. I'LL SETTLE

FLOWER GIRLS DEITY. SHE'LL SETTLE.

BRIDE DEITY. I'LL SETTLE.

FLOWER GIRLS DEITY. GO SETTLE.

BRIDE DEITY. I'LL SETTLE.

FLOWER GIRLS DEITY. JUST SETTLE.

BRIDE DEITY. I'LL SETTLE.

FLOWER GIRLS DEITY. COME SETTLE.

BRIDE DEITY. I'LL SETTLE

FLOWER GIRLS DEITY.
SETTLE, SETTLE, SETTLE, SETTLE, SETTLE, SETTLE, SETTLE, SETTLE.

> *(Musically this "Settle" section can go on for an extremely long time. Eventually the* BRIDE *should have a break down. The music stops. She pulls herself together and sings the final line.)*

BRIDE DEITY.
I'LL SETTLE
FOR LITTLE AND LATE.

LILY. But that suitor is not suitable. You don't want to marry someone who thinks of other women while he makes love to you?

BRIDE DEITY. You think I don't think about my chiseled firefighter calendar when I masturbate? Or movie stars or the cute guy who sat next to me on the bus, who pressed his leg against mine just a little deeper than a lack of intention would imply? I am not in this for the reality.

LILY. There are ideals. You're supposed to live up to them. *(To the* FLOWER GIRLS:*)* Tell her.

PRIME DEITY. We don't care.

SUBPRIME DEITY. As long as we get the wedding.

THE MARYS DEITY. And catch the bouquet.

FLOWER GIRLS DEITY. So we may long for future wedding days.

BRIDE DEITY. Enough! I have been waiting my whole life for my perfect groom. To the point where I have become haggard and hoary. *(To audience:)* Not whorey *(She gestures as if jerking someone off into her face, or an array of lewd mimes)* but hoary *(She gestures with an ugly/old gesture)*. I will marry. I will be a regular bride who marries a regular groom and be secretly filled with longing but I will not be a single lonely societal failure.

LILY. Then marry me.

BRIDE DEITY. What?

LILY. I love you and have always loved you.

PRIME DEITY. *(Pushing the* GROOM *into action:)* Do something, Groom.

GROOM DEITY. I thought I was supposed to be quiet.

FLOWER GIRLS DEITY. STEP UP TO THE PLATE!

GROOM DEITY. *(Taking center:)* Sports metaphor make man take action. *(He pumps himself up into the role of Man.)* Marriage isn't between a woman and a plant.

LILY. What about the frog prince?

GROOM DEITY. That was a frog.

LILY. *(Condescending to him:)* I understand that but—

SUBPRIME. And he was a Prince in disguise.

BRIDE DEITY. If you can tell me you're a prince Lily, then perhaps I would see fit to marry you.

GROOM DEITY. You're not even a man.

STEPMOTHER. Hmmm-hmmmmm.

(STEPMOTHER *acts with her eyes.*)

SUSAN. Evil Stepmother says: "What about the Cheyenne girl who married the king of the buffalo. Or the one who married a rattlesnake or—"

LILY. Yeah what about those?

GROOM DEITY. Multi-culti folklore marriages aren't real marriages.

LILY. Say that to the buffalo.

GROOM DEITY. I am a man and so a winner and so suitable for The Bride. *End of story!*

LILY. I'm more a man than you'll ever be—

GROOM DEITY. A man has legs, Lily. A man ventures out into the world. You are a one-of-a-kind flower loser in a pot.

BRIDE DEITY. Lily, I've nothing to look forward to but the past. There are no princes anymore. There are no knights. There is just… *(Looking at the* GROOM:) This. And dreams to keep the this more like that.

LILY. No. If this is the story that happens I won't let it be your story. From now on it's my story. All mine. *End of story.* Exclamation point. Fade to black. Curtain falls.

BRIDE DEITY. Lil—

LILY. Applause. Curtain rises. Lights return. Applause. Applause. Bow. Bow. Bow. Curtain falls. Applause Applause Applause. Curtain Rises. Standing O. Flowers thrown. For me. A simple Lily. Flowers? You shouldn't have. Humility. Thank you. Thank you. Hold flowers to your heart. Point to a person you pretend to know. Point to a person you pretend to know. Thank You. Thank You. Applause. Cheers. Brava. Hand to heart. Hand to heart. Applause. Cheers. Brava. Curtain falls!

BRIDE DEITY. Lily—

LILY. Oh no you don't. Encore. Encore. Give us more. Curtain Rises. Bow. Bow. Bow. Thunderous Applause. Feet Stamp. We demand more. Hold up a hand. Insist on their calm. "No, give us more", hold up a finger. "If you insist, I'll do one more." Gratitude. Applause. Calm. Quiet. Quiet. Silence. A pin could drop but who would dare to drop it. Encore. Period. End of story. Curtain falls.

BRIDE DEITY. Okay Lily—

LILY. Riotous Roar. Applause. Applause. Applause. Curtain rises. Nod head. Hands full of flowers. Nod head. Wipe a tear. Show them the tear on your finger. Turn, exit. Curtain falls.

THE MARYS DEITY. Is it done?

LILY. Backstage crew cheering. Supporting characters cheering. Old Man Joe, who's been pulling the curtain for 80 years, since he was a little boy growing up in the depression working this theater so he could bring home a little money for his mother and sisters to eat. Just a little. Enough to buy a piece of bread and on Christmas a potato. Ever since father died from the tuberculosis. Old Man Joe who has seen over thirty thousand performances in this theater, hardened and callused-hand Old Man Joe is weeping. "Oh Lily, it was the greatest performance this theater has ever seen," "Oh Joe, you don't know what that means to me." Applause. Applause. Applause. Walk backwards. Thanking everyone. Find the railing. Descend the stairs. Open the dressing room door. Thank you. Thank you. Thank you. Applause. Applause. Applause. Gently close door. Muffled sounds of excitement behind the door. Sanctuary. A moment to one's self. Exhale. Put down the flowers. Rest your limbs. Sit in front of the makeup mirror. Look at yourself. Melancholy. A deep sorrow. Alone. Did it happen and if so what does it all mean? And who cares if you're always alone. A knock at the door. Your agent. "Oh darling you were magnificent." Feign humility. Don't be greedy. Ask her about herself. A knock at the door. The producers. "You were magnificent. Lily, I'd like you to meet insert famous person." "You were magnificent." "Thank you. Thank you. I loved your last picture." "Oh it was nothing to what you do. A real star." "Thank you. Thank you." "Darling, your fans. They await you. Do not keep them waiting in the cold." "Yes you're right." Fur coat. Only a slip on underneath. Pen in hand. To the stage door. Flash. Flash. Screams. Someone faints. Sign. Sign. Sign. Underline the signature. Period. Exclamation point. "We love you. We love you. We love you." *(To the* GROOM DEITY:*)* You're not the only winner. I am a winner too. I am—

> *(The* LILY *painfully uproots itself. It takes a long time. Green sap sprays. It wears high-heel roots and stumbles about the stage. The* LILY *almost passes out. The* BRIDE *comes to its rescue holding it up.)*

BRIDE DEITY. Lil?

LILY. Yes?

BRIDE DEITY. I'll you make a deal. You are a flower. But unlike any flower before you, you have pulled yourself free of your roots.

LILY. Yes.

BRIDE DEITY. It could be that you are a man under a curse.

LILY. Really?

(PRIME *snorts [like a laugh].*)

BRIDE DEITY. If you can break this curse, and return to me a man in *(Looking at her watch:)* ...four hours time, I will agree to wed you. But if you fail then, you agree, this Groom will be *my* groom.

LILY. Agreed.

BRIDE DEITY. But only four hours. I will not wait another second. I will be wed.

PRIME DEITY. Can the wedding take place in the garden?

THE MARYS DEITY. *(Demon Lennie Smalls again:)* Flowers.

BRIDE DEITY. Of course.

SUBPRIME DEITY. *(Evil sexual desire:)* Let's go mail order the wedding supplies from Ecuador.

THE MARYS DEITY. *(Evil sexual desire:)* Outsourcing.

(MARYS DEITY *and* SUBPRIME *exit.*)

SUSAN. Lily?

PRIME DEITY. *(Grabbing SUSAN in a punishing reprimand and dragging her off.)* Come on Mary.

SUSAN. Ah.

BRIDE DEITY. *(To the LILY:)* Goodbye brave Lily. Goodbye brave childhood.

GROOM DEITY. You don't really think that flower has a chance to become a man do you?

BRIDE DEITY. *(Looking at The LILY with melancholy:)* No.

(*The curtain closes.*)

LILY. I will become a man.

THE GREAT LONGING. No Lily, you will be become one of my keepsakes. Not dead and not living. Pressed inside a book for all of time.

LILY. You'll see.

THE GREAT LONGING. Flower Girls! Press that flower in The Book.

FLOWER GIRLS DEITY. *(Entering:)* YAAAAAAAAA!

(SUBPRIME brings out a giant Bible. The MARYS try to force the LILY into the Bible. EVIL STEPMOTHER tries to speak with her eyes.)

SUSAN. *(Interpreting EVIL STEPMOTHER's eye-speak:)* WAAAAIT! Evil Stepmother says, Mary, you don't have to do this. You're an individual. You have opinions and feelings that are separate from the group. You enjoy reading Hegel.

THE GREAT LONGING. Mother stop trying to steal my minion.

SUSAN. She says, "Break from stock character conformity and embrace your individuality already!"

THE GREAT LONGING. Mary!

SUSAN. My name is not Mary. My name is Susan Stewart. I live in Queens and I want to go home.

STEPMOTHER. Hmm-hmmm-hmm-hmmm?

(SUSAN de-gags the EVIL STEPMOTHER.)

STEPMOTHER. Susan Stewart? Critical theorist Susan Stewart? Author of *On Longing*?

SUSAN. Yes, I don't know, I think so, I can't remember, it was so long ago I started watching this…play.

STEPMOTHER. I thought there was something special about you.

SUSAN. There is! I won't participate in nostalgic narrative any longer.

THE GREAT LONGING. But everybody loves nostalgia.

SUSAN. "NOSTALGIA IS A SADNESS WITHOUT AN OBJECT!"

(Everything stops. Lights focus on SUSAN. She is allowed her moment in the spotlight and speaks to everyone.)

SUSAN. "A sadness which creates a longing that is inauthentic because it does not take part in lived experience…the past it seeks has never existed except as narrative."

(Lights return to normal.)

STEPMOTHER. Oh Susan.

SUSAN. I free you of your Evil Stepmother tweed.

(SUSAN strips TIME's Evil Stepmother outfit off. TIME looks around and then runs into the audience and off.)

TIME. I AM FREEEEEEEE!

THE GREAT LONGING. MOOOOOTHEER!

PRIME DEITY. *(Looking into the audience:)* The Evil Stepmother is disappearing into the void.

THE GREAT LONGING. DON'T LOOK INTO THE AUDIENCE.

SUBPRIME DEITY. How can we find her if we can't look into the audience?

THE MARYS DEITY. Curses.

PRIME DEITY. Who's gonna play the Hegel reading femi-nazi lesbian evil stepmother in bad clothes now.

(They all look at SUSAN.)

SUSAN. Oh no.

FLOWER GIRLS DEITY. Yaaaaaaaa.

(They grab SUSAN and put her in the Stepmother outfit. The LILY pushes the Bible open and stumbles out.)

SUSAN. (As STEPMOTHER.) Lily. The Curtain may be adept at creating a reveal and a frame and a barrier but a window provides an exit.

LILY. What?

(The FLOWER GIRLS drag the new STEPMOTHER off-stage.)

SUSAN. An exiiiiiiiiiit.

(It is just the LILY and THE GREAT LONGING on stage now. LILY sees the windowsill. THE GREAT LONGING tries to reach the LILY but it can't.)

THE GREAT LONGING. Lily, don't you get up on that windowsill.

LILY. I will leave and I will take this story with me.

THE GREAT LONGING. Lily, you don't have to go in the book if you don't want to. We can repot you. You don't have to end your life in obscurity. As a failure. Lily. Listen to me. You'll never become a man and you will have sacrificed yourself for nothing. What about your legacy: to be a keepsake? Everyone wants their life to mean something. Don't you want to foster the preciousness of memory? LILY, YOU GET BACK BEHIND THIS PROSCENIUM THIS INSTANT!

LILY. I will become a man. I will wed the Bride. This is my story now. Goodbye… Curtain.

(The LILY jumps through the window. Blackout.)

End of Act I

THE GHOST WARRIOR
Act Two: An Act in Iambic, Song, and Haiku

"When an individual is protesting society's refusal to acknowledge his
dignity as a human being, his very act of protest confers dignity on him."
—Bayard Rustin

*(When the audience returns from intermission they discover that what once was
a proscenium set-up is now in the round.* MASTER SUNFLOWER *is
trying to plant* DAISY #3 *from "The Deity" back into the earth. When the
characters in "Ghost Warrior" speak to the audience it is directly, not looking
over heads.)*

MASTER SUNFLOWER. Dear Daisy, victim of a frenzied love,
be strong and bear your pain while garden tries
to plant and patch you back in patch of earth

(The DAISY *falls to the ground.)*

MASTER SUNFLOWER. It is no good. The Daisies won't take root.

(A TICK *enters.)*

MASTER SUNFLOWER. The Garden spy arrives and brings us news
of humans who attack we flowers with
their every move and longing whim. Speak, Tick.

TICK. It's what we feared. The humans plan a wedding
to be held on garden ground.

DAISY #3. Oh horror.

MASTER SUNFLOWER. Where Flower Girls, with absentmindedness
will wrench us from our mother Dirt then leave
us to be trampled to a death.

(They sob.)

MASTER SUNFLOWER. If only Dirt would send her star.

TICK. A star?

MASTER SUNFLOWER. She promised in a prophecy a star.
"A Lily flower, born petals five, will fall
from mortal's soil and free Dirt from her cell.
Then use her to destroy the Curtain's reign
and bring an end to flower suffering."

TICK. And you believe that?

MASTER SUNFLOWER. It is the only hope.
Alas it seems our champion has lost
its way and we are destined to become

but rubble underfoot a wedding's rage.
So Tick do take unrooted Daisies far
from this barbaric land and let them die
in peace.

TICK. I swear to stop the Daisy's pain.

> *(The* TICK *drags* DAISY #3 *off-stage.)*

MASTER SUNFLOWER. Oh Mother Dirt if you've but any will
do send your champion so we may live.

> *(Lights focus on the* LILY, *who is falling/floating from the windowsill. It sings the entire time is falls.)*

LILY.
> THE FLOATING DOWN
> A FLOWER'S DEED
> IS TO SEED
> TO SEED
>
> AS TEARS DESCEND, DECREE
> THE CHEEK
> HOME
> BUT WITH THE WEIGHT OF ALL THAT'S WRONG
> WILL CLING THEN STREAK
> AND FALL TO
> LOAM.
> SUBMERSE INTO THE EARTH
> TO NURTURE CRUEL GREAT LONGING'S
> TOME.
>
> A FLOWER FALLS
> TO FIELD AND FLOW
> TO GROW
> TO GROW
>
> UPHOLD, PROTECT, PROMOTE
> AND SOW
> A MOLD
> AND SO IT'S STAYED THROUGHOUT ALL TIME
> WE DRIFT DEVOUT
> AND SLOWLY
> FOLD
> INTO THE HEAVY DEW
> TO DO, TO BE WHAT WE ARE
> TOLD
>
> AND I WAS DESTINED TO THE SAME:
> TO LOLL AND LANGUISH AS MY LOVE IS TAMED,
> TO WILT AWAY AS CAMEO,

TO BE REBORN AND TO TIPTOE
INTO AN UNREQUITED LIFE.
WELL I WILL BREAK THIS CYCLE RIFE
WITH WHAT I CAN AND CANNOT BE
I'LL FLOWER INTO THE NOBILITY
OF A MAN.
CENTER STAGE!

MY FLOATING DOWN'S
A FLOWER FREE
TO BE
TO BE.
TO WIN, TO WED THE DAMSEL SO.
OH-OH
YES A MAN'S LIFE I WILL ATTAIN,
I'LL BE RENOWNED.
AND HOW I WILL BE CROWNED.
SO THEN WHAT I WILL SEED
IS WEDDING'S BLISS, A BRIDAL KISS,
AND LOVE FROM ALL
THE GROUNDLINGS.

OH OH OH
OH OH OH
SO FLOWER FALL

(The LILY *lands in the garden and passes out.)*

LILY. Ow.

*(*MASTER SUNFLOWER *appears.)*

MASTER SUNFLOWER. Could it be? The Chosen Flower has come?
Alas, four petals I do count not five.
She is but one more casualty of humans:
pulled from her roots, then used, and dashed to ground.
Oh how we flower kind do suffer so.
I'll grow my roots and move to other side
and try to ease the hurt she now must weather.

*(*MASTER SUNFLOWER *crosses the stage very slowly.)*

I did not say the movement would be quick.

(She keeps going very slowly.)

MASTER SUNFLOWER. A flower's roots do not grow fast you see.

(She keeps going very slowly.)

This play has been inspired by the Noh.

(She keeps going very slowly.)

The Noh who like Butoh, well, move so slow.

(She keeps going very slowly.)

Jesus Christ.
Now work I to bring love to heal her pain.
For pleasure can be found in suffering
and Lily drops into a flower's bed.
(Licking the LILY's *butt:)* Rarrrrrrr.

> *(*MASTER SUNFLOWER *voraciously licks the* LILY's *butt for an extremely long time.)*

LILY. *(Waking up and enjoying the attention:)* Oooo, ahhh, ohhhh— *(Coming to its senses:)* What are you doing?

MASTER SUNFLOWER. Verse.

LILY. What?

MASTER SUNFLOWER. A flower is not a base and common breed
that speaks in crass and trite demotic talk.
Its language is a pampered poetry
that strives to match its rich and vibrant hues
its sensuous ambrosial perfumes.

LILY. Oh.

MASTER SUNFLOWER. A flower's speech is flowery and so
we will converse in strict iambic verse.

LILY. Fun.

MASTER SUNFLOWER. Yes.

LILY. Oh no I can't.

MASTER SUNFLOWER. You can't or won't?

LILY. I can't engage in the activities of flowers because I have to become a man.

MASTER SUNFLOWER. Excuse me?

LILY. A curse has been placed on me that has turned me into a Lily but really I am a man so I should probably talk kinda boring. Fuck.

MASTER SUNFLOWER. Dear Lily please, I Master Sunflower be.
I am director of the garden flowers
and if I say you speak in verse, then verse
is what will tumble from your trilling tongue.

LILY. Agreed. For now, while flower form I take,
but once the curse does lift than no, I'll speak
explicitly in grunts and gab about
like men who are composed of expletives.

MASTER SUNFLOWER. Why would a flower so fierce and fresh reject
The call to beautify?

LILY. It is for love.
I take this quest to wed the bride in spotlight.

MASTER SUNFLOWER. To wed! For shame! Why long to wed The
    Bride?
A wicked creature who does tear at flower limbs
to satisfy her love-me-love-me-not
pathetic desperation. To kill The Bride
would be a better goal and free yourself
from blind complicity in Longing's rein.

LILY. I'll not stand back and let you speak this way
of my betrothed who is a gem, an innocent.
It's not her fault. She has been forced to cruelty
by wretched Curtain and its minion bitches.
No, Bride, she is a wonder of the world!
Her beauty does surpass the hanging flowers
in Babylon; her eyes contain a blue
that breaks the Barrier Reef; the earthquake
who toppled Colossus of Rhodes would cease
its rage upon one glance at my sweet bride;
her breasts outshine Egyptian pyramids;
her soul so pure the statue Zeus bows down
to kiss her feet. You dare insult her so.
(Showing off what it has just done:) Verse.

MASTER SUNFLOWER. Well Lily I applaud your strong devotion
but still the wedding is a monstrous beast
who uses and commodifies our kind
until we are but sad cliches who none
do stop to hail or praise.

LILY. Hyperbolize
away but I do wish to be a groom,
like in the story books, who has but one
bright soul who signs a pact to love me true.

MASTER SUNFLOWER. True love does come from loving all the world
not hoping for the love of one to grant
their love on you. Come Lily, don't you be
a selfish soul who holds its love so tight
but cherish what you are: a flower who gives
its sacred love to every passerby.

      *(*MASTER SUNFLOWER *licks an audience member.)*

LILY. Are you suggesting I become a whore?

MASTER SUNFLOWER. What better way to live than spread delight?
How come you to this puritan and trite
perspective of the world?

LILY. I'm sorry I
am not as worldly wise as you would like.
I am a simple man raised in a pot,
inside a room, not in a flower bed
where lusty limbs may love who they would like.

MASTER SUNFLOWER. Then know you nothing of the flower bot'ny?

LILY. I'm not a flower but a man who has been cursed.

MASTER SUNFLOWER. A flower's pageantry I feel we need
to teach the Lily of its worth and lore.
Come, enter Baby's Breath, and school this Lily.
The Baby's Breath crosses into the playing space.

LILY. You want a Baby's Breath to school me? Please.
I know my worth as man and won't be taught
from such a minuscule herbaceous breed
whose role is to accessorize a flower.

BABY'S BREATH. You lily-livered sell-out fucker—

*(*BABY'S BREATH *attacks the* LILY *physically strangling it.)*

MASTER SUNFLOWER. Baby's Breath stop. Let go and count to ten.

*(*BABY'S BREATH *lets go of the* LILY.*)*

BABY'S BREATH. One, two, three…

*(*BABY'S BREATH *continues counting, trying to control itself, under the following speech.)*

MASTER SUNFLOWER. Now Lily, listen closely to these words
before your ignorance does greater harm.
The Baby's Breath was born to stop and smell
not be a plant that fills all empty space.
It's vicious humans, who do serve Great Longing,
they are the ones who saddled her as filler:
To frame all other flowers in bouquet.

BABY'S BREATH. The role of sidekick has been forced on me.
But being thus, I have accompanied
the bride, the gift, the garden flowers and know
the lore and prophecies that all do tell.
And so I am the best to school the lily.

MASTER SUNFLOWER. *(To* LILY:*)* Apologize.

LILY. I'm sorry Baby's Breath.

BABY'S BREATH. Sure, fine.

MASTER SUNFLOWER. Now introduce the flowers who haiku.

LILY. Haiku?

BABY'S BREATH. Haiku is what we flowers do
to raise our pride and celebrate our kind.

(Breaking verse:) The Flowers participating in today's Haiku-Off are:

> *(FLOWERS enter, doing a flower fashion show. Each flower gets its moment
> to shine before the next flower is called.)*

BABY'S BREATH. The Tulip:

> *(The TULIP enters.)*

BABY'S BREATH. The Poppy:

> *(The POPPY enters.)*

BABY'S BREATH. The Rose:

> *(The ROSE enters.)*

BABY'S BREATH. The Lilac:

> *(The LILAC enters.)*

BABY'S BREATH. The Pansy:

> *(The PANSY enters.)*

BABY'S BREATH. And The Pink Lady Slipper!

> *(PINK LADY SLIPPER enters. Once PINK LADY SLIPPER has
> had her due—)*

BABY'S BREATH. We present to you: The Garden Flowers.

> *(The FLOWERS all parade around as if in the final moments of a fashion
> show.)*

MASTER SUNFLOWER. But final flower who joins the cause to raise
the pride of Lily and rejoice our kind?
Dear audience, we give this role to you.

> *(BABY'S BREATH passes a cue sheet around the audience which is cut to
> look like a leaf.)*

BABY'S BREATH. Please take this leaf and pass it 'round. That's right.
A leaf, you see, with lines of text that float
upon its face. This is a cue-sheet that
contains the lines Forget-Me-Not will speak

MASTER SUNFLOWER. This character is yours to play as group.

BABY'S BREATH. *(To audience:)* And so we ask when you do hear the cue
please speak your lines in unison with verve.

MASTER SUNFLOWER. Should we rehearse?

BABY'S BREATH. I think we should.

MASTER SUNFLOWER. Okay.
Let's have the cue and we will give you pace.

BABY'S BREATH. Forget-me-not this is your practice cue.

> *(They conduct.)*

FORGET-ME-NOT. *(Reading from their cue sheet leafs:)* A cue we take and
now give back to you.

MASTER SUNFLOWER. Once more for luck to help the slow catch up.

BABY'S BREATH. Forget-me-not this is your practice cue.

> *(They conduct.)*

FORGET-ME-NOT. A cue we take and now give back to you.

MASTER SUNFLOWER. *(If it is messy it's okay to make fun of the audience with
this line and if it was great, then celebrate them with the line:)* Without flaw.

BABY'S BREATH. Now! Tulip! Take the dew! And speak haiku!

FLOWERS. Haiku! Haiku! The Tulip speaks Haiku!

> *(A spotlight shines on TULIP.)*

TULIP. Your sturdy stamen:
innocent yes, tested no,
soon perhaps with me.

> *(The FLOWERS mumble with gossip as if to say: ooo that TULIP is trying
> to get up in the LILY's business.)*

LILY. No sorry Tulip Flower I stand firm
just like my stamen that does stand for Bride.

> *(The FLOWERS are offended.)*

BABY'S BREATH. Lilac verse the Lily to your wonder.

LILAC. Lily heed Lilac
Our stigma *and* stamen stick
To take all comers.

LILY. That's nasty.

> *(The FLOWERS are flabbergasted.)*

BABY'S BREATH. Pansee is french for "thought" so give us yours.

PANSY. Look! Pansy gives face!
Her color upstages Bride
Making Lily doubt.

> *(The FLOWERS are turned on.)*

LILY. Doubt not, oh dowdy Pansy, Bride still reigns.

(The FLOWERS *are disgusted.)*

BABY'S BREATH. But can you handle, the Pink Lady Slipper.

FLOWERS. *(A sing-songey chant that suggests they think* PINK LADY SLIP-
PER *is as sassy as her name implies:)*
Pink Lady Slipper
Pink Lady Slipper

PINK LADY SLIPPER. Pull picks Pink Lady
To use as muse. A slipper,
Too hot for Bride's foot.

(The FLOWERS *are inspired.)*

LILY. That's true Pink Lady, no Bride would ever wear
A flower resembling, how should I say?
A gonad, testes, ball sac, family jewel?

(The FLOWERS *are furious.)*

LILY. No, actual jewels are for her princess feet
If she wore you, each time her *(Indicating itself:)* prince caressed
Her foot she'd have to turn her head and cough.

(The FLOWERS *are stunned.)*

BABY'S BREATH. Rose's turn.

RED ROSE. Lily come hither.
Our mingled fragrance then tempts
the dreamer to live.

(The FLOWERS *are excited by this.)*

LILY. My fragrance is for Bride to keep and dab
as kisses on her wrists and sumptuous neck

(The FLOWERS *are disturbed by this.)*

BABY'S BREATH. Poppy.

POPPY. A flower's scent dies
when trapped and kept as keepsake.
Best let it roam free.

(The POPPY *blows glitter pollen from its hand. This is a challenge, as if
slapping the* LILY *in the face with a glove. The* FLOWERS *cheer this.)*

MASTER SUNFLOWER. A flower's challenge.
Let Lily rise to haiku.
Give her morning due.

(Sun shines on the LILY.)*

LILY. *(Counting its fingers to make sure the five-seven-five syllables are right:)* The
Poppy will kill.
Existing in pipes and lungs:
turning life to dreams.

> *(The* LILY's *outstretched palm is facing the* POPPY *as if to say, "Talk to the
> hand." The* FLOWERS *are incensed by its offensive Haiku.)*

POPPY. The Poppy, if grown
as flower and not as poison,
is an innocent.

LILY. Poppy stop your game.
Take responsibility
for duplicity.

ROSE. Open dear Lily
and see possibility.
Embrace love not spite.

LILY. The Rose she'll cut you,
prick your style 'til its dry,
And then she'll smile.

> *(More shout outs: the haiku competition has gotten as vociferous as a vogue-off.)*

TULIP. Come to Tulip friend.
I can give you pleasure just
greater than the rest

LILY. Look flower I already told you no
I am a man and so can't love a flower.

PANSY. The falling flower,
who tries to transform to man,
brings foolery home.

FLOWERS. Ohhhhhhhhh.

LILY. *(Insulted:)* Hey.

> *(The* LILY *takes center stage.)*

Pansy's opinion
matters not to one as I
for man transcends plant.

FLOWERS. Oh!

RED ROSE. Shame on Lily's words!
Self hatred is a drought
that feeds itself dead

PINK LADY SLIPPER. *(Snapping during her line:)* Work! Work!

LILY. Some flowers will snap
but here they stay still and dumb
accepting their role.

POPPY. Mother Dirt gives roots
to ground her children in pride
not to loath what is.

LILY. Mother Dirt did curse
a man into a lily.
I'll water her down.

LILAC. This Lily is sick
to threaten precious Dirt.
Flowers live by her.

LILY. This Lily denies
the boundaries of flowers:
for it is a star!

BABY'S BREATH. This Lily is no star with petals four!

LILY. I had five petals but one of them got cut off.

GARDEN. Uh! THE CHOSEN FLOWER.

(A low rumble starts to enter the FLOWERS' bodies and voices. It grows until the FLOWERS are speaking in tongues and praising the DIRT. The praising of the dirt and tongue speak turns into an orgiastic desire for the LILY. They chase the LILY around the space. The LILY is about to escape when—)

MASTER SUNFLOWER. *(With great urgency to stop the LILY from leaving:)* Now! Baby's Breath do tell the tale of Dirt.

(The FLOWERS all position themselves for story time with breathy excitement.)

FLOWERS. Oh! Oh! The tale of Dirt. Oh! Oh! The Tale!

(BABY'S BREATH waits for all eyes to be on her before beginning. The story she tells is one she has been waiting her whole life to tell. It is the most important moment of her life and she tells it as if a priest were teaching Jesus of the importance of his second coming.)

BABY'S BREATH. When Time began there was but only Time.
Who would perform her words and wants alone
to vast and empty space. So lonely Time
did think, "A child I'll birth to love me so."
And thru her longing for a child she made
a curtain.

FLOWERS. Booooooo.

BABY'S BREATH. Yes. Time's first child was not
the loving audience that she had hoped.

For when a being comes from ache, *its* ache
can never satiate. So ache is what
Great Longing did. It hoped for better times
instead of praising Time for what it was.
So Time, decided to begin again.
Her second child, the baby of this clan,
was named The Dirt.

FLOWERS. Hooray!

BABY'S BREATH. And loved Time so.
For Dirt is here and now within each breath
and watches Time with wonder in her gaze.
And Dirt became the favorite child of Time.
She learned from Time how to create. She made
the flower, folklore, song, and bumblebee
and nurtured us with here and now. With licks
and love!

LILY. With licks and love?

MASTER SUNFLOWER. *(Licking an audience member:)* Yes licks and love.

FLOWERS. Intimacy, the best of Dirt's creations.

(They all lick audience members.)

BABY'S BREATH. But jealousy befell our mythic tale.
Neglected Longing hated baby Dirt,
so trapped her on its farm in Ecuador.

PANSY. Where miles of manufactured flowers take
And take.

TULIP. They suck and feast upon The Dirt,
'til she is used into a uselessness.

MASTER SUNFLOWER. So man may purchase love in flower form.

LILAC. But truly, little does he care for love,
for fellow men, and what kind Dirt does give.

RED ROSE. For if he did would not he cherish all
the imperfections in our petal calls?

POPPY. The wilted sorrow, the speckled shade, and bite
sized hole that gives a dimple to the rose?

TULIP. Would not he praise us planted in the ground
instead of pulling at our rooted life
and suffocating us in cellophane?

RED ROSE. Then adding to our insult, injury,
he wraps us even more with tacky, cheap
computer-graphic-flower paper prints.

PINK LADY SLIPPER. "Just in case you can't see the flowers wrapped inside, I'm gonna give you a diagram of what the gift was intended to be."

BABY'S BREATH. We're packaged like a story in a frame.
We're packaged like the past, which Curtain took
and put within a box. Then sealed that box
with ribbons and with rules so tightly wound
that none may open it and see the past
for what it truly is:

LILY. The here and now.

MASTER SUNFLOWER. Yes!

BABY'S BREATH. But Dirt has made a prophecy and flung
it from a windowsill to garden's ground.
"A Lily flower, born petals five, will fall
from mortal's soil and free The God of Here
and Now from factory farm. Then use her to
destroy the reign of longing and so end
this flower suffering."

(*All eyes on* LILY.)

GARDEN. The Chosen Flower.

LILY. Oh no, you can't be serious.

BABY'S BREATH. Your quest is thus: To free the present Dirt
and bring nostalgia to narration's end.

LILY. No really—

MASTER SUNFLOWER. Yes. You are the chosen flower.

LILY. (*To* BABY'S BREATH:) You made that story up because I insulted you.

BABY'S BREATH. In truth I wish I had but fate is fate

LILY. You want me to sacrifice myself to save the Dirt so you don't have to do it yourself.

PINK LADY SLIPPER. You're the one who's so proud of your manhood.

LILY. What's that supposed to mean?

PINK LADY SLIPPER. Act like a man.

TULIP. Step up to plate and lead flowers in revenge.

RED ROSE. A rose revolt

PANSY. Carnation coup,

DAISIES. (*From wherever the band is:*) a gang
of daisy chains!

POPPY. A poppy putsch!

LILAC. A Bluet
Brigade

PINK LADY SLIPPER. where mutinous mums make way.

FLOWERS. YES!
THE FLOWERS ARE FINISHED WITH STANDING BY
AS NATURAL BEAUTY IS COMMODIFIED.

    (They roar.)

MASTER SUNFLOWER. Calm my flowers!
Calm yourselves. Rightly riled you be but calm
give Lily point to say it's due anew.

LILY. Just to be clear. You want me to travel to Ecuador, free the Dirt, who
is the god of here and now, then lead a revolt against the Great Longing
deity, consumption, and corporate greed?

MASTER SUNFLOWER. Well, yes, this is our wish spoke *plainly* thus.

LILY. I could not be the hero you do seek:
a soul whose love is limited as such
and cares not that the world will fall from grace,
as long as grace is found in Bridal smile.
I've passively watched our kind tortured. No,
crusaders should be worldly wise and fit,
not draining dry from unrequited love.
And yes my roots do dangle free from earth's
sweet hold, where you are safe in her caress,
but *I'm* the one who pulled myself from soil.

GARDEN. What?

LILY. I made myself the hero in this tale
For love and not for revolution's game.
And I've not long to turn myself to man
and break the curse that keeps me from my Bride.
And if I fail then love I lose and love
Is all I want from life. And though I think
Your quest is just: to tear Great Longing down,
'tis not this lovelorn Lily that you need
to triumph in this mighty task. Best ask
The ant, the leaf, intrepid centipede.
Have Baby's Breath uproot itself and lead.

FLOWERS. The Lily does deny the hero's task.
OH SHAME ON WEAK AND PASSIVE FLEUR-DE-LIS

MASTER SUNFLOWER. Quiet now! Oh goading garden do tame.
We ask forgiveness for our rancor game.

LILY. That's okay.

MASTER SUNFLOWER. Truth be told their anger's just!
Though try you to persuade us from our truth,
that Dirt has brought her steward from above,
your arguments do prove the point we make.

RED ROSE. You say you're weak in nerve and body too.
That lack of love has sapped away the sap
that gives you verve, but no.

TULIP. To pluck yourself
from Pot's hard case takes plenty power and pluck.

BABY'S BREATH. As for your Bride and quest to change to man
could not this manhood be a metaphor?

LILY. What?

TULIP. Of course! The curse to break is one of fear.

MASTER SUNFLOWER. For men, at least the kinds in storybooks
who wish the damsel's heart and hand to take,
do set themselves to tasks of daring deeds.

PANSY. They champion the weak, well, such as we.

POPPY. And when they do succeed none can deny
their manhood for their manliness is fact.

LILY. I said I'd make that curtain obsolete
And so I will

GARDEN. Hooray—

LILY. But should I fail?

MASTER SUNFLOWER. All I can say is die all must. But still,
to die in cause is *living,* not to die.
To die in fear is *waiting* for the call.
To love and lose is loving after all.

BABY'S BREATH. Now you, Forget-me-not. With me. Let's go.

FORGET-ME-NOTS. And flowers do not wait, they are the call
to live and love to take each breath with grace.

LILY. I do agree and so I'll *bloom* to man.

FLOWERS. Hooray the Lily takes its cornered call.

LILY. But how will I, a flower, with three hours time,
Now make my way to Ecuador and back?

(TIME *enters in a* WIND *costume.*)

WIND. Wind.

GARDEN. What?

WIND. The Lily can fly to Ecuador on the wind.

LILY. Time?

WIND. 'Tis I.

LILY. What are you doing here and why are you dressed like that?

WIND. It's Time darling. I'm always here.

MASTER SUNFLOWER. Then be here in verse.

WIND. What?

MASTER SUNFLOWER. Director of this world am I and so
insist you speak in verse or venture forth.

WIND. Look we don't have *time* for this. If the wedding takes place between
the Bride and Groom, the Curtain will take back the story for *all* of Time.
Me.

MASTER SUNFLOWER. *Rhyming* couplets then.

WIND. Oh now,

MASTER SUNFLOWER. Stop being such a prude and just resign.

WIND. A prude you say.

MASTER SUNFLOWER. Just rhyme

WIND. Okay then fine.

MASTER SUNFLOWER. Now that the form is settled please do tell
About the Curtain and where it does dwell.

WIND. No fear, Oh Flowers do not be afraid.
The power of that drapery does fade.

> *(To* LILY:*)*

For in your leap from pot and windowsill
you stole Great Longing's tale, changed tale with will.
Such that a simple flower's mighty nerve
has bent proscenium into a curve.
Where now, my sweet, a flower will not be found
for Curtains cannot reach you in the round.

LILY. Truth?

WIND. Truth be told. But all the same.

LILY. The same?

WIND. You must fly off.

LILY. Partake in hero's game

TIME. To free the Dirt who's trapped in Torture's camp.

LILY. And win the title of a man.

WIND. Decamp
from Circle's safety zone of flower friends.

LILY. And though in certain terms I risk my death
I will break free mean Casting's shibboleth.

WIND. Except you need the wind to fly you south
so Wind I'll play and wind comes from my mouth.
And know, with me it will not be a bore
for I will lecture as we fly to Ecuador.

LILY. Oh no.

WIND. Oh yes. The only way to carry you
to factory farm and all the captured, who
can aid you in your revolution's aim,
is if I'm freed from Garden's rhyming game
And speak in *lecture* form. For wind is made
when speech is great and cuteness makes Wind fade.

(Pause as all look to MASTER SUNFLOWER.*)*

MASTER SUNFLOWER. Fine.

WIND. *(Running to the* LILY *with excitement:)* I'll quote from my favorite collection of essays: Susan Stewart's *On Longing.*

LILY. *(Not great:)* Great.

(As she speaks WIND *begins to blow stronger. The* LILY *is violently flown about. The* FLOWERS, *who are rooted are less affected by her blowing.)*

WIND. "Speech leaves no mark in space;"

LILY. *(Being slightly blown and feeling the danger:)* Oh.

WIND. "Like geniture, it exists in its immediate context and can reappear only in another's voice."

LILY. *(Worried:)* Oh Okay.

WIND. "Another's body, even if that other is the same speaker transformed by history. But writing contaminates; writing leaves its trace, a trace beyond the life of the body."

(A petal is blown off the LILY.*)*

LILY. *(Showing its petal:)* Ahhhhhh!

WIND. Oh sorry.

LILY. "Oh sorry," that's all you say.

MASTER SUNFLOWER. I knew that breaking form would ruin the day.
LILAC. Look what she's done with all her stormy spiel.

RED ROSE. Tempestuous torrent taunts, her squalling squeals.

POPPY. Her winded rants, conceited shower of puff.

BABY'S BREATH. Her whirling wafting wails.

WIND. Okay enough!
Ha, wafting, puff, your humor is immense.
What's next a joke of blowing flatulence?

PINK LADY SLIPPER. Somebody farted.

WIND. Now that my friends is where I draw the line.
And so the Wind is gone. I do resign.

MASTER SUNFLOWER. Oh Wind we all apologize for sure.

TULIP. Yes sorry Wind, for tooting like a sewer.

WIND. Then I continue with Susan Stewart?

LILY. But what if I should lose another petal?

WIND. To rhyme or fly your choice

LILY. Okay I settle.
For love is worth the sacrifice of beauty.
So lecture on and fly me to my duty.

WIND. *(Excited:)* It'll be just like a book on tape.

MASTER SUNFLOWER. Well then the garden wishes you adieu.

FLOWERS. Farewell fierce flower, who helps us in our coup.

LILY. I will not fail you in this task. I swear.
You will be liberated and *I* wed.

> *(WIND blows as WIND speaks.)*

WIND. To understand nostalgia's use as a tool for oppression we must first examine the gigantic and the miniature.

LILY. Oh dear.

WIND. "The eschatological nature of the minia

LILY. *(Blown in a hurricane:)* Ohhhhhhhhhh

WIND. *(Blowing the hurricane:)* tuuuuuuuuure—"

> *(The LILY is blown off stage. The WIND follows.)*

MASTER SUNFLOWER. And now flower bed sing of what we will wreck.
Inspire the Lily on her troubled trek.
Give word to her and melody to Wind
we gentle and unique to vengeful kind.
Yes rise from dirt, in figurative ways
but literally too in fits of craze.

TULIP. What?

MASTER SUNFLOWER. The Lily, she has shown the way for all.
And though it pains me to reject The Dirt,
it is through leaving home that one does grow.

> *(MASTER SUNFLOWER painfully uproots herself. TULIP pukes.)*

MASTER SUNFLOWER. Uproot yourselves and take your battle cry.
> *(The FLOWERS are terrified by they idea. MASTER SUNFLOWER sings a song of revolution to inspire them.)*

MASTER SUNFLOWER.
> AT NIGHT THE SUNFLOWER DREAMS OF SUNSHINE AND
> SOIL.
> WE GROW AMIDST UNFETTERED ACRES,
> WHILE CHARMING HONEY MAKERS
> THAT TICKLE AND CARESS.

POPPY.
> AT NIGHT THE POPPY'S DREAMS ARE FREE OF ALL TOIL.
> WE SOW OUR SEEDS IN EASY BREEZES,
> ATTRACT THE BEES WITH TEASES
> NO SICKLE TO DISTRESS.

MASTER SUNFLOWER.
> BUT IN OUR SUNSHINE GOLD
> WE'RE BOUGHT AND THEN WE'RE SOLD.
> SNIPPED WITH CLIPPING CUT AFFLICTIONS.

POPPY.
> AND SOON MY BREEZY PLAY
> TURNS TO A TWEAKING PREY.
> RIPPING DREAMS FOR THEIR ADDICTIONS.

POPPY and MASTER SUNFLOWER.
> OUR PAIN IS SO BRIGHT
> WE'RE KILLED FOR TRITE DELIGHT.
> SLAUGHTERED FOR BIOLOGIES

POPPY. *(Pulling herself out of the earth:)* AND KISS ME, LOVE ME PLEASE-
ES.

BABY'S BREATH.
> FOR WHEN THEY DIE
> THOUSANDS OF BLOSSOMS WILL DIE TOO.
> PLACED IN THEIR GRAVES
> WHERE AND HAIR AND FINGERNAILS
> STILL GROW
> BUT FLOWERS
> NEVER DO.

RED ROSE.
>AT NIGHT THE RED ROSE FEARS THE HARSH BRUISING
>>TOUCH
>BUT DREAMS OLFACTORY ORGASMS
>WITH DANGLE DROOPS OR SPASMS
>TO LURE THE DEW FROM DAWN.

TULIP.
>AT NIGHT THE TULIP DREAMS OF GOD-FEARING DUTCH
>WHOSE FETISH CRAZE DOES PRAISE OUR SPECIES;
>WHO BREED US, FEED US FECES
>ENSURING LOVE WILL SPAWN.

RED ROSE. *(Tearing her roots from the earth:)*
>BUT SOON MY DANGLE KICKS
>TURN TO THEIR MANGLED PICKS
>PULLING, JABBING, NEVER GENTLE.

TULIP. *(Tearing her roots from the earth:)*
>AND SOON MY BREEDING DREAMS,
>BECOME THEIR GREED EXTREMES.
>OVER-PLANTING'S MADE ME MENTAL.

PANSY/LILAC. *(Tearing themselves up from the earth:)*
>THEIR LOVE IS SO BRIGHT
>WE'RE KILLED FOR LITE DELIGHT,
>SLAUGHTERED FOR APOLOGIES,

PINK LADY SLIPPER. *(Pulling itself up from the earth:)* AND KISS ME
>LOVE ME PLEASES.

BABY'S BREATH.
>FOR WHEN THEY LOVE
>THOUSANDS OF BLOSSOMS PAY THE DUE:
>SEALED IN A BOOK
>WHERE WISHES AND ENNUI
>STILL LIVE
>BUT FLOWERS
>NEVER DO.

>>*(TICK and DAISY #3 enter with snare drum and bugle [perhaps other band member DAISIES on portable instruments come with them].)*

TICK and DAISIES.
>AND WHEN INJUSTICE DOES TAKE PLACE
>FROM ALL THE STRONG WHO TYRANNIZE
>IT IS THE RIGHT OF THOSE DISGRACED
>TO THEN FIGHT BACK AND EUTHANIZE
>THOSE WHO ABUSE.
>HOW THEY WILL LOSE.

FOR MEEK WILL SEEK TO STOP THEIR HATEFUL ENTER-
PRISE.

FLOWERS and TICK.
SO NOW THE FLOWERS DO DENY YOU YOUR JOYS.
AT NIGHT WE CLOSE AND PLOT DESTRUCTION.
A WEDDING RUINATION.
TO PICKLE AND SUPPRESS.
AND WE WILL USE YOUR HEADS AND LIMBS AS OUR
TOYS.
TO GARNISH ALL OUR CELEBRATIONS.
OUR NUPTIAL CONGREGATIONS
WILL TRICKLE
WITH YOUR BLOODY MESS.
JUSTICE IS OUR RIGHT.
WE'LL MURDER AND WE'LL FRIGHT
SLAUGHTER ALL YOUR EULOGIES

BABY'S BREATH.
AND AS WE DIE
MILLIONS OF HUMANS MAY WE SLAY.
HUNG UPSIDE DOWN,
SO BLOODY DRIPS
FALL ON THE EARTH WHERE WE'LL
REGROW,
BUT HUMANS
WILL DECAY.

MASTER SUNFLOWER. And the Lily will use its fragrance to cover the stench of…

FLOWERS. ROTTING FLESH!

(Lights out.)

End of Act II

THE LOVE ACT
Act Three: A Dream Ballet

"Pity we haven't got a bit of rope."

—Samuel Beckett

(A bare stage other than a couch outline on the floor.)

(This act is a dance act performed as a series of pratfalls, lazzi routines, and dance. The dialogue is spoken within, between, and around the movement.)

(On one side of the stage is a sign that says, "Ecuador Factory Farm" and on the other side, a sign that says, "Garden." The LILY *is blown on.* WIND *enters behind.)*

WIND. *(Reading from and holding a copy of Susan Stewart's* On Longing:*)* "THE ESCHATOLOGICAL VISION OF ALLEGORY MAKES THE READER THE PRODUCER OF THE TEXT IN THE SENSE THAT CLOSURE CAN BE ACHIEVED ONLY THROUGH CONVERSION. OUR READER," *(Not from the book:)* or audience member or uprooted flower, *(Back to the book:)* "BECOMES A CHARACTER, A FIGURE WHO LOOKS FOR SIGNS AND CLUES. A READER OF CORRESPONDENCES BETWEEN THE SIGNS OF THE WORLD, THE IMMEDIATE ENVIRONMENT OF EVERYDAY LIFE, AND THE SIGNS OF THE STORY."

(The LILY *hits a wall and a third petal falls off. If the audience shows signs of being saddened by the* LILY's *loss of another petal,* WIND *says:)*

WIND. It's fine.

(If not she'll skip the line "It's fine" and just continue with:)

WIND. So you Lily, you will study these signs as we continue our travel from the Garden to the Ecuador Factory Farm.

*(*WIND *begins to put the* LILY *in a being-blown-by-the-wind pose.)*

WIND. You will study them until closure, and so conversion to the here and now, is attained. For only then will you be strong enough to free the God of Here and Now. To your right is the story.

*(*BRIDE *and* GROOM DEITY *enter and go to the right of the* LILY *[or change* WIND's *line to fit where they enter to]. They lay down to sleep. There is no bed. Just a floor [perhaps a bed outline is in place].)*

WIND. *(Gesturing to the audience and the playing space:)* All about you is the world, and within you is the immediate environment of everyday life. Begin.

(The LILY *begins a slow Butoh walk/blow across the stage.* GROOM DEITY *falls asleep during the following.)*

BRIDE DEITY. *(A capella—very slow and sad:)*
I'M TEETERING ON THE EDGE OF
TOO LITTLE TOO LATE
TOO LITTLE TOO LATE
TOO LITTLE TOO LATE

I'LL LIVE IN MY DREAMS OF GRANDEUR
BUT SETTLE…CONFLATE
AND STOP
TEETERING ON TOO LITTLE TOO…

> *(BRIDE DEITY falls asleep. They snore. The lights dim and fantasy lights come in. BRIDE LOVE and GROOM LOVE enter dancing. We are in a dream ballet. BRIDE and GROOM DEITY are asleep in the same spots we saw them fall asleep in. They continue to sleep through the rest of The Love Act [until woken up].)*

BRIDE LOVE. *(Noticing the audience. Upset:)* Oh. Hello.

GROOM LOVE. *(To audience. Upset:)* The guests have arrived. Already.

> *(The FLOWER GIRLS LOVE enter riding SUSAN in grand monster chaos. They are unruly brats on the special day. The GROOM tries to calm them down and they pay no attention.)*

FLOWER GIRLS LOVE. Ya! Ya! Ride Evil Stepmother Ride, etc…

GROOM LOVE. Hey Girls, Flower Girls, young ladies, don't, hey don't, behave yourself, now stop that, what are you, act your age, this is the big day, hey, you have obviously had too much sugar, Flower Girls you listen, hey don't treat the Evil Stepmother that way, what are you, Mary you tell Mary to get Mary and Mary to, hey *(Etc.).*

BRIDE LOVE. Story time.

> *(The FLOWER GIRLS instantly stop their torture and ruckus to listen to the BRIDE.)*

BRIDE LOVE. Eden is a garden with only kind insects. Lady bugs and butterflies. A world lacking the mosquito. And leaves the size of hammocks. This used to be so gorgeous. It makes my mouth water. All that former lushness. Even the word lush makes my mouth water. And freshness. The smell of the good kind of life. Where the death is mixed in with the life and smells *only* sweet instead of like a "just dessert." Eden is where I'll go for my honeymoon. And I'll be happy.

FLOWER GIRLS LOVE. NO MORE TALK.

> *(The FLOWER GIRLS do a taking-over-the-space dominance dance. A bit like a tornado. SUSAN is forced to dance and participate with them throughout the rest of The Love Act. The BRIDE and GROOM get swept up in the chaos.)*

THE MARYS LOVE. *(Dropping out of the dominance dance:)* I'm hungry.

PRIME LOVE. I'm hungry.

SUBPRIME LOVE. *I'm* hungry.

BRIDE LOVE. Give the Flower Girls some nuts.

FLOWER GIRLS. *(Attacking him:)* YAAAAAAAA!

GROOM LOVE. I DON'T HAVE ANY NUTS.

BRIDE LOVE. *(Blaming* GROOM LOVE*:)* We're still waiting on the nuts?

GROOM LOVE. *(Blaming* SUSAN*:)* You let Time be free and now the outsourced party supplies don't know when to get here.

BRIDE LOVE. The decorations, the cake, cocktail napkins and couch.

GROOM LOVE. And there's nowhere for mama to sit.

BRIDE LOVE. *(Reprimanding the audience:)* And the guests have all arrived early.

FLOWER GIRLS. *(Panicked:)* And the bouquet. We're missing the wedding bouquet.

> *(The* FLOWER GIRLS *do a tantrum dance of impatience.)*

BRIDE LOVE. Do something Groom!

GROOM LOVE. *(Looking in his tux and trying to sooth the* FLOWER GIRLS*:)* I might have some fuzzy pretzels.

> *(The* FLOWER GIRLS *grab the handful of fuzzy pretzels from the* GROOM. *They do a devouring food dance during the following.* SUSAN *tries to get some but is beaten back. The* BRIDE *takes a pretzel.)*

BRIDE LOVE. Lint laden pretzels?

> *(The* BRIDE *has an extreme overdramatic moment where she thinks she's going to puke, then that she was poisoned and last that she's choking and dying. The* FLOWER GIRLS *stop their dance and watch.)*

BRIDE LOVE. How long have those been in there?

GROOM LOVE. Since I last wore this tux.

BRIDE LOVE. You're not wearing a new tux for our wedding?

> *(The* BRIDE *has an extreme overdramatic moment of rage. A tantrum. She squinches up her face, punches the air, screams to the heavens, falls to the ground kicking and screaming. The* FLOWER GIRLS *try to imitate her.)*

GROOM LOVE. *(In defense:)* *Your* dress looks like a pillowcase.

BRIDE LOVE. I HAVE SENTIMENTAL ATTACHMENTS TO THIS DRESS.

> *(The* BRIDE *has an extreme overdramatic moment where she is hurt by his insensitivity. She is first insulted, then must get away from the* GROOM, *then*

is bereft sobbing. The FLOWER GIRLS *imitate her. When it's over the* BRIDE *returns to normal and the following is all done in the style of method acting—not pretend sincere but actually honest.)*

BRIDE LOVE. Are we stuck?

GROOM LOVE. Stuck?

BRIDE LOVE. With our decision?

GROOM LOVE. Well I think at this point, yes.

BRIDE LOVE. It's just, I wanted to marry you. I did but that was over an hour ago and we are such different people now and with all this waiting, I have time to think about the Lily.

(The GROOM LOVE *breaks down crying.)*

BRIDE LOVE. No. Bad Bride. Bad. Watch. Watch.

(They break method. An overdramatic moment where the BRIDE *beats herself up: she punches an invisible opponent and then runs into the spot where she punched and gets hit by an invisible fist, she self-flagellates, and she rolls a toilet on stage and puts her head in the toilet.)*

LILY. Don't stick your head in the toilet.

WIND. Lily! Focus!

(The LILY *focuses.)*

BRIDE LOVE. *(Going to the* GROOM:*)* Don't be mad at me. Hold me. Hold me.

(The BRIDE *clings to the* GROOM. *He tries to rid himself of her but she is stuck on him. They walk the space with her stuck on him. They run. They hop. They run in circles. They shake. The* FLOWER GIRLS *join the cling. He gives up and decides to hold her back.)*

PRIME LOVE. What do we do now?

GROOM LOVE. We wait.

(They do the dance of impatience.)

BRIDE LOVE. *(As if being attacked in her brain.)* It's not working. Oh God they're coming. I feel them. The options. THE OPTIOOOOOOOOOONS.

(The BRIDE *breaks free and does an option dance. Does she want to go left, right, up, down, back, forth, etc.?)*

BRIDE LOVE. I can be anything I want to be. I'm a successful business woman. I'm a hard-core dyke. I am a fierce tranny. I can try all the things I've never tried.

(She grabs the various FLOWER GIRLS *and tries sexual activities with them. Eventually she goes down on a Flower Girl. She comes up horrified.)*

BRIDE LOVE. I JUST ATE PUSSY!

(She runs to the GROOM who comforts her.)

BRIDE LOVE. *(Sobbing:)* There are too many different kinds of tomato soup.

GROOM LOVE. There are no options. *(He slaps her to wake her out of her craze.)* It's just you and me. *(Slap.)* Look at me. *(Slap.)* Just you and me. Forever.

BRIDE LOVE. *(Horrified:)* Ahhhhhhhh!

SUBPRIME LOVE. What do we do?

BRIDE LOVE. Burn the apartment down.

FLOWER GIRLS LOVE. Burn mother fucker burn!

(The FLOWER GIRLS do a light-the-house-on fire fraternity dance during the following dialogue.)

BRIDE LOVE. *(Pulling a lighter out of her body somewhere.)* I've got the lighter fluid.

GROOM LOVE. What if you get caught?

BRIDE LOVE. You do it.

GROOM LOVE. Ladies first.

BRIDE LOVE. Why ladies first?

GROOM LOVE. Etiquette.

BRIDE LOVE. Blame.

GROOM LOVE. Chivalry.

BRIDE LOVE. Cowardice.

GROOM LOVE. *(It is absolutely true:)* Not true.

BRIDE LOVE. You go first.

GROOM LOVE. Why me?

BRIDE LOVE. It's your apartment.

GROOM LOVE. It's our apartment.

BRIDE LOVE. Tomorrow it's our apartment. Today it's yours.

GROOM LOVE. So.

BRIDE LOVE. So if I burn it down it's vandalism. If you burn it down it's frivolous expenditure.

GROOM LOVE. What's the difference?

BRIDE LOVE. The latter is chivalry. The former is blame. *(Raging at him:)* You're the mother fucking Groom, you're supposed to know what chivalry is. No sorry, hold me, hold me.

(Everyone runs to the GROOM *to be held. He runs away. They chase him during the following.)*

GROOM LOVE. Let's wait and see how it looks.

BRIDE LOVE. The decorations?

FLOWER GIRLS LOVE. The bouquet!

GROOM LOVE. It was so perfect in the catalogue and the factory farm White Rose will make the best centerpiece for the bouquet.

BRIDE LOVE. *(Going towards the* LILY:*)* But maybe an organic flower would be better.

LILY. *(Breaking:)* Yeah.

TIME. Lily, focus!

(The LILY *focuses. The* BRIDE *does a look at me dance, trying to get the* LILY's *attention.)*

BRIDE LOVE. *(Regarding the* LILY *focusing not on her:)* Look at me. Look at me. Yoohoo. Yoohoo. Why won't the Lily look at me?

GROOM LOVE. Dunk her!

(The FLOWER GIRLS *grab the* BRIDE *and dunk her head in the toilet.)*

PRIME LOVE. Who do you want to marry?

BRIDE LOVE. Um.

(They dunk her.)

SUBPRIME LOVE. Who do you want to marry?

BRIDE LOVE. I—

(They dunk her.)

THE MARYS LOVE. Who do you want to marry now?

(The dunk her.)

GROOM LOVE. Wait! *(He runs to the window.)* I thought it was the truck with the couch and the cocktail napkins and plates and the forks and food and the rest of the wedding band.

BRIDE LOVE. *(Pulling her head out of the toilet:)* Was it?

FLOWER GIRLS. *(In great overdramatic despair:)* NOOOOOOOO!

(The FLOWER GIRLS *roll around on the floor in a despairing impatience dance.)*

GROOM LOVE. *(During their dance.)* Girls. Girls. Young Ladies. Hey. Now come on. Stop that. If you, if you roll on the floor your dresses will get dirty. Hey. Hey. NOBODY EVER LISTENS TO ME.

(The GROOM *rolls around on the floor in a pay-attention-to-me dance. He stands. He's had enough. He's gonna act the man now. He dances a Man-thru-the-ages dance. It incorporates all the things that archetypical men get nostalgic for: sports, old westerns, horseback riding, winning, being in a band, drinking, smoking pot, doing cocaine with the guys, watching a pole dancer. He uses* PRIME *for this. He puts her in the cake and makes her pop out.)*

(The BRIDE *turns and sees* PRIME *giving him a lap dance... She acts as if she just caught her husband cheating on her and has an extreme overdramatic reaction. She points at* PRIME, *she points at the* GROOM, *she calls up a friend [one of the* FLOWER GIRLS]*and vents on the phone.)*

(She and the FLOWER GIRLS *do a dance of hating men.)*

(The GROOM *apologizes with his lapel flower. The* FLOWER GIRLS *protect her. He gets down on his knees and begs. She is tempted but The* FLOWER GIRLS *pull her away and scold her. He goes to church, confesses, gets a boring job, mows the lawn, takes out the trash, then gets down on his knees and begs her. She wants to forgive him. The* FLOWER GIRLS *point to the couch outline. The* BRIDE *agrees he can come back but has to sleep on the couch outline. The* FLOWER GIRLS *and* BRIDE *storm off.)*

(He lies down in the couch outline and sleeps. He does a toss and turn dance. A dream within a dream ballet begins:)

(The BRIDE *joins him on the couch. They embrace in forgiveness and reconciliation. He wants to go down on her. He puts his head under her pillowcase wedding dress. He is pleasing her. Suddenly he is choking. He pops his head out.)*

(He does a choking dance.)

(He puts his hand in his mouth and pulls out a LILY. *The* BRIDE *points and laughs. The* FLOWER GIRLS, *this time lead by* SUSAN, *run on and laugh at him. They throw and beat him with lilies, which come out of the* BRIDE's *vagina [hid in her pillowcase wedding dress]. The* GROOM *wakes screaming.)*

GROOM LOVE. AHHHHHHHHH!

(The BRIDE *runs to comfort him. In the style of method.)*

BRIDE LOVE. Shhhhh. It was just a nightmare within a dream ballet.

GROOM LOVE. I'm sorry.

BRIDE LOVE. What for?

GROOM LOVE. History.

BRIDE LOVE. It's all over now.

GROOM LOVE. Let's do something. Go out. Live a little.

BRIDE LOVE. Let's dance!

(A disco beat. The BRIDE *and* GROOM *dance as if at a nightclub.)*

GROOM LOVE. *(To* FLOWER GIRLS:*)* Don't just let it be us making fools of ourselves.

BRIDE LOVE. Yeah, join in.

FLOWER GIRLS LOVE. *(To* SUSAN:*)* Dance creature dance.

(The FLOWER GIRLS *force* SUSAN *to dance various disco routines.)*

BRIDE LOVE. Look, Evil Stepmother is dancing disco.

GROOM LOVE. Now that is charming.

BRIDE LOVE. Who knew she could be so delightful?

GROOM LOVE. This is what living is!

BRIDE LOVE. You know what would make this moment even more memorable?

GROOM LOVE. If an entire room full of guests all began to follow the Evil Stepmother in her dance?

BRIDE LOVE. I would never forget a moment like that.

(The FLOWER GIRLS *aggressively get audience members to join a group dance. The dance can be random dancing or an actual group dance made by the choreographer that is akin to, but not actually [no pop culture references in my play please], group dances like the electric slide or the hustle. When they dance they chant the following [at the very least three times].)*

FLOWER GIRLS LOVE. *(This is done in a rhythm devised by the* FLOWER GIRLS:*)* Ya. Ya. Do it. Dance the Evil Stepmother dance. Do it. Have fun. Do you want/your memory/to be that of saying no to life. You better have fun. Smile when you dance.

(Suddenly the drumming stops and everyone is in mid-dance. SUSAN *falls to the floor [passed out].)*

FLOWER GIRLS. That was stupendous. Great job wedding party. Give yourself some applause. You deserve it. That's it. Don't overdo it. Settle down.

(The FLOWER GIRLS *spray the audience [like they're bad cats] with spray bottles and get them back in their seats.)*

LILY. I CAN'T TAKE IT ANY LONGER. I WANNA DANCE.

BRIDE LOVE. Lily?

(All eyes on LILY *and its story.)*

WIND. Do not allow your travel to become a nostalgic narrative.

LILY. But I can do the Evil Stepmother's wedding dance too. Watch.

(The LILY *dances.)*

WIND. *(A comment on how stupid the* LILY's *dance is:)* Exactly. Move smaller! Slower. Like this.

(She demonstrates her Butoh moves. The LILY *moves with her.)*

LILY. But they're taking the story from me 'cause this…is boring.

WIND. We will start from the beginning.

(Starting at the top of On Longing—*not really but acting as if it is the top:)*

WIND. "THE ESCHATOLOGICAL VISION OF ALLEGORY MAKES THE READER THE PRODUCER OF THE TEXT IN THE SENSE THAT CLOSURE CAN BE ACHIEVED ONLY THROUGH CONVERSION."

*(*WIND *blows* LILY *all the way back to where it started its first Butoh walk.)*

LILY. Nooooooooo!

WIND. "OUR READER," *(Not from the book:)* or audience member or uprooted flower, *(Back to the book:)* "BECOMES A CHARACTER,"

LILY. STOP!

WIND. "A FIGURE WHO LOOKS FOR SIGNS AND CLUES."

LILY. PLEASE.

WIND. "A READER OF CORRESPONDENCES BETWEEN THE SIGNS OF THE WORLD, THE IMMEDIATE ENVIRONMENT OF EVERYDAY LIFE, AND THE SIGNS OF THE"

LILY. I CAN'T TAKE IT ANYMORE.

WIND. YOU WILL TAKE IT LILY. WE WILL QUOTE FROM SUSAN STEWART AND WE WILL TRAVEL FROM THE GARDEN TO ECUADOR UNTIL YOU LEARN TO LET GO OF INSTITUTIONALIZED NOSTALGIC NARRATIVE.

LILY. I don't know what that means.

WIND. Like marriage.

LILY. Being married is being loved.

(The WEDDING PARTY *applaud this.)*

WIND. Married love, hopeful love, is ephemeral. It stays behind in its picture book as Time moves on. No one can outlast Time. No one endures. The here and now is forever here but the heartbeat always stops.

LILY. *(A discovery:) It* doesn't stop. You stop it. You're a killer of love. Maybe if you'd get some every so often you wouldn't have created such an asshole Curtain.

WIND. How dare you. You have no idea what it's like to be a single parent raising two opposing avatars.

LILY. I know what it's like to grow up without love. To have a caregiver who doesn't care. Who views you as less than. Someone… something to be abandoned.

WIND. I NEVER ABANDONED ANYONE!

> *(The* WIND *blows off the* LILY's *fourth petal [leaving it with only one].)*

LILY. You gave up on your child curtain. *(A discovery:)* And on Susan Stewart.

WIND. What?

LILY. *(A discovery:)* Secretly you love her.

WIND. I don't know what you're talking about.

LILY. You quote her every chance you get but then abandon her to play your role of the Evil Stepmother. You've turned her into a side-kick.

WIND. No.

LILY. You don't like dreaming of love because you don't know how to love.

WIND. Lily we must get to Ecuador, please you're distracting us from the flight.

LILY. I will use the Evil Stepmother's wedding dance to travel the rest of the way.

WIND. Lily, you must listen.

LILY. A person who has no love might as well not exist.

WIND. If you do this you'll become a toy of The Great Longing.

LILY. This is my story. And you are no longer in it.

> *(*TIME *is danced off.)*

LILY. To Ecuador.

> *(The* LILY *dances off to Ecuador. The* WEDDING PARTY *all begin to follow the* LILY. *A man-size curtain enters, pushing them back.)*

THE GREAT LONGING. DON'T YOU DARE FOLLOW THAT LILY'S STORY.

THE MARYS LOVE. It's The Great Longing.

SUBPRIME LOVE. Did someone put you in the dryer?

THE GREAT LONGING. *(Sobbing, to the* BRIDE:*)* The tale is being taken from me. And so I'm shrinking.

ALL. Poor Great Longing.

THE GREAT LONGING. I have been forced to adapt to our modern times. And am reduced to a more cost effective representation.

ALL. NOOOOOOOOO!

THE GREAT LONGING. And now the Lily is making its way to Ecuador.

BRIDE LOVE. You mean it might succeed in becoming a man?

THE GREAT LONGING. *(Punishing her:)* You just *had* to make a deal with it.

BRIDE LOVE. Does that mean the Lily and I might wed?

THE GREAT LONGING. *(An epileptic fit:)* Ahhhhhhh.

GROOM LOVE. What's happening?

THE GREAT LONGING. I'm shriiiiinking again.

SUSAN. Wait. *(She runs to the piano and sits.) Now* shrink.

> *(She plays/sings a New Orleans Jazz style version of "The Great Longing" song, sung in Act I.* THE GREAT LONGING, *as it shrinks more and more, does a strip-tease to the song. It is a glorious number [don't feel the need to rush it but make it choreographically specific]. The whole time, while* THE GREAT LONGING's *body is enjoying performing the strip, its face is horrified. During the striptease the man-size curtain outfit gets taken off to reveal a torso-sized curtain outfit. The torso-sized curtain outfit gets stripped/ shrinks and is now a curtain skirt. The curtain skirt gets taken off and* THE GREAT LONGING *is about to be naked on stage but* PRIME LOVE *runs on with a box of cocktail napkins and puts one strategically on* THE GREAT LONGING, *covering its privates.)*

THE GREAT LONGING. A cocktail napkin?

PRIME LOVE. The wedding supplies have arrived!

WEDDING PARTY. *(All but* BRIDE LOVE:*)* Hoooray love can come to pass!

PRIME LOVE. Everything's here but the bouquet.

SUBPRIME LOVE. The tracking number has indicated that the centerpiece of the bouquet, the White Rose, will not be here for at least another hour.

BRIDE LOVE. We can't have a wedding without the bouquet.

> *(*THE GREAT LONGING *makes a bouquet out of napkins.)*

THE GREAT LONGING. I have to do everything myself. Nostalgic narrative. Burlesque. Flower arrangements. Here. A bouquet!

BRIDE LOVE. I can't have a cocktail napkin bouquet. This is my special day.

> *(*BRIDE LOVE *throws the cocktail napkin bouquet at* THE GREAT LONGING's *face. He does a slapping dance where he slaps* BRIDE LOVE *over and over all around the space.)*

THE GREAT LONGING. Reality is unimportant. You must imagine your special day.

> *(He continues to brutally beat her.* BRIDE DEITY, *unconscious, behaves as if getting beaten.* THE GREAT LONGING *slaps* BRIDE LOVE *right*

next to BRIDE DEITY. *Eventually he is beating them both. This is a truly disturbing and scary moment with no schtick.)*

THE GREAT LONGING. You think dreams are fun. Dreams are for survival. Now dream. Do it. Do it. DO IIIIIIIIIIT!

(He spits on them. They lay beaten. He walks center. BRIDE DEITY wakes up. She weeps. GROOM DEITY wakes as well. Everyone waits to see what she will do. While quietly crying, she writes a dream down on a cocktail napkin. She hands it to BRIDE LOVE who hands it to GROOM LOVE who hands it to GROOM DEITY.)

GROOM DEITY. *(Reading:)* Love.

(The FLOWER GIRLS take the napkin and attach it to THE GREAT LONGING.)

THE GREAT LONGING. More.

(BRIDE LOVE writes down another one. She hands it to BRIDE DEITY who hands it to GROOM DEITY who hands it to GROOM LOVE.)

GROOM LOVE. *(Reading:)* Romance.

(The FLOWER GIRLS take the napkin and attach it.)

THE GREAT LONGING. Yes. More.

(The BRIDES writes down two more and hand them to the GROOMS.)

GROOMS. *(Reading:)* A wedding.

THE GREAT LONGING. Yes. Give it to me. Build me back. Bring back the curtain.

(The WEDDING PARTY attach cocktail napkins to THE GREAT LONGING. They say very general words like: a house, a family, safety, a car, success, happiness, comfort, care, etc. as they attach the napkins. The FLOWER GIRLS continue attaching [reducing their words to a inaudible whisper]. The BRIDES and GROOMS step aside and face out. The rest of the act is performed in the style of method. It should be horribly sad and quiet.)

BRIDES. What if we're not right for each other?

GROOMS. People are never right for each other.

BRIDES. Right.

GROOMS. *(Not wanting them to cancel:)* We could cancel if you want.

BRIDES. We've come this far.

(Blackout.)

End of Act III

THE LIVING PERSON ACTS
Act Four: A Silent Film

"Gather ye rosebuds while ye may
Old Time is still a-flying:
And this same flower that smiles to-day
To-morrow will be dying.

The glorious lamp of heaven, the sun,
The higher he's a-getting,
The sooner will his race be run,
And nearer he's to setting.

That age is best which is the first,
When youth and blood are warmer;
But being spent, the worse, and worst
Times still succeed the former.

Then be not coy, but use your time,
And while ye may, go marry:
For having lost but once your prime,
You may for ever tarry…"

—Robert Herrick

(The audience sits in the middle of the stage. Projection screens surround them on all four sides.)

(A silent movie begins. Incidental music plays [taken from the various songs throughout the play]. The dialogue is text upon the screen, as in old silent films. In the original production this was done as a stop-motion silent movie with originally designed dolls. It could be done as a live-action film as well. It is eerily saturated with color and not a black and white film.)

(A title appears:)

"The Living Person Acts: Part Four. Welcome to the Factory Farm."

(The LILY appears. The camera pulls back and we see the LILY walking through rows of flowers on a farm. It meets a normal looking WHITE ROSE.)

(Title I appears:)

Lily: Hello Rose.

(Title II appears:)

White Rose: Hello Lily. I've come to the technology farm to become a perfect specimen so I may be the centerpiece of the wedding.

(A montage of what the WHITE ROSE dreams appears: being cherished, smelled, loved, carried in a beautiful bouquet down an aisle.)

(Title III appears:)

Lily: I've come to become a man and marry The Bride.

(Title IV appears:)

White Rose: Good luck Lily.

Lily: Good luck Rose.

(The LILY and WHITE ROSE part ways. The LILY approaches a help desk.)

(Title V appears:)

Diana: Welcome to the Factory Farm.

Lily: I'm here to free The Dirt from distance and so become a man and wed The Bride.

Diana: Right this way.

(The LILY goes on a tour of the Flower Farm.)

(Title VI appears:)

Diana: In order to win the prize you must become the perfect specimen.

(The LILY looks at itself in a mirror. It does not look good. The LILY enters The Factory Farm Fitness Center. The LILY takes an Aerobics class. It enjoys this.)

(Title VII appears:)

Diana: Lily, that form of exercise will not give you the strength you need. This is your personal trainer Pope John Paul.

(The LILY is introduced to JOHN PAUL.)

(JOHN PAUL takes the LILY through a plethora of exercise routines: weight lifting, playing basketball with a lot of guys, on the football field getting pummeled. LILY is not successful at any of these things.)

(The LILY wants to give up but looks up at the TV screen while its on the treadmill and sees a montage of The BRIDE.)

(The BRIDE is running smiling through a field, with the LILY, they caress each other, walk on the beach, etc. She bends in to kiss the LILY and the close-up on her lips turns into the end of the montage.)

(We're back in the gym. The LILY doubles its effort.)

(The LILY is in boot-camp. Climbing ropes, crawling through mud with a machine gun, going through target practice, doing pushups. DIANA points out that the LILY's efforts are still not working.)

(Title VIII appears:)

Diana: To truly win you must go to greater lengths. This is your stylist Ron.

(LILY is introduced to RON. The LILY's face is cleaned of makeup, it is waxed, it enters a spray-on tanning booth and is sprayed, it's forced to drink protein powder, its given a toupee and a tuxedo.)

(DIANA and RON confer that, no, it's still not working.)

(Giant scissors are brought out. The LILY doesn't want to go through with it.)

(Title XIV appears:)

Lily: Wait! I don't have to become an actual man to win the Bride, just a metaphorical one.

(RON, DIANA, and JOHN PAUL all laugh demonically.)

(Title X appears:)

Diana: Oh Lily, nobody believes in metaphor anymore.

*(The LILY sees the TV Bride montage again.
It agrees to be made a man.)*

(The LILY lays down on a surgical bed. It turns to the flower next to it and sees the WHITE ROSE.)

(Title XI appears:)

Lily: White Rose, what are you doing here?

White Rose: I'm about to undergo perfection surgery so I can become the centerpiece of the wedding.

(The WHITE ROSE undergoes surgery. Instead of looking like she's had plastic surgery, she looks more like a republican politician's wife [if such a wife were a white rose].)

(Title XII appears:)

Lily: You turned the White Rose into a republican!

(RON, DIANA, and JOHN PAUL laugh demonically.)

(The WHITE ROSE waves goodbye and is shipped to the wedding.)

(Title XIII appears:)

Diana: And now prepare for your treatment!

(RON, DIANA, and JOHN PAUL give the LILY electric shock treatment. Its final petal falls off.)

(A crackling, a changing of channels, chaos, blurred images and suddenly things come back into focus and we see the Dirt talking directly to the camera. This is a different kind of film. No longer silent. It is a collage of history: weddings, flowers, parades, political actions, etc, and the various things the two characters talk about. It is shot from the LILY's perspective [so we don't see LILY during the film] and throughout the film we continually see the face of DIRT superimposed over everything.)

DIRT. Lily! Lily wake your ass up.

LILY. Where am I?

DIRT. You are trapped in technology on the factory farm. You have but a short time to free me and save the Garden.

LILY. Dirt?

DIRT. Nice to meet you.

LILY. You're…

DIRT. Fabulous?

LILY. Yes.

DIRT. Thank you.

LILY. What happened?

DIRT. You let The Great Longing's triumvirate give you electric shock treatment so you could become…a man.

LILY. I don't feel like a man.

DIRT. I don't imagine you would.

LILY. I failed.

DIRT. And now you're just a petalless lily in a tuxedo.

LILY. *(Taking its toupee off.)* With male pattern baldness.

DIRT. Yes.

LILY. And the Bride could never love that.

DIRT. Do you love the Bride, Lily?

LILY. Of course I do. Did. Will. Sometimes. Often. Have told myself to. Want to. I do. But, I think, deep down inside, the real reason I asked her to marry me was because everybody loves the romantic lead.

DIRT. And you want people to love you?

LILY. To treat me as more than less than.

DIRT. And marriage is a way to accomplish that?

LILY. After everything I've been through…pulling myself from my pot, losing my petals, staying celibate and still being as alone as when I started… being married doesn't seem like such a special thing anymore. Now it's like a video cassette player.

DIRT. Okay?

LILY. Something so old and plastic and everyday that it's become removed and distant. I don't know how it works. And when it breaks I have no idea how to fix it or if it should even be fixed. And the institution of marriage is so large.

DIRT. Like looking up close at the skin of an elephant and trying to figure out what it is?

LILY. Yes. So large with its billion dollar industry and century-old traditions… I couldn't possible understand it. And it is so small,

DIRT. As an atom,

LILY. So small in its thinking, so limited, exclusionary, and sexist…so small I'm finding it hard to keep caring about it.

DIRT. And?

LILY. And the miniature and the gigantic together create a felt lack. A felt lack that is essentially…nostalgia.

DIRT. Someone's been hanging out with my parent Time.

LILY. But if marriage won't make me the center of the story what will?

DIRT. Traditionally it is a sacrifice of the thing you want most.

LILY. But the thing I want most is to be center of the story.

DIRT. To be the center of the story or to be loved?

LILY. Is that so bad? Shouldn't everyone be loved? Doesn't everyone deserve their special day?

DIRT. Lily, what would it be like if you stopped equating love with equality?

LILY. What?

DIRT. What would it be like to stop equating love with loving?

(Slowly, during the following, the actual LILY *appears on stage. He wears a tuxedo and no makeup and looks like a man in a tux. Eventually, the film version fades away.)*

LILY. It would be an all day show.

DIRT. Okay?

LILY. *(On stage:)* I'd put on an all day show. With the help of friends. An all day show rehearsed in recreational centers, basements, and backyards. Performed for neighbors, strangers, friends who are family and family who are friends. People will sit in folding chairs, and there will be cardboard cut-out set pieces and mugging actors who sing songs on ukuleles, eat food, dance, drink too much, flirt with audience members, and genuinely think of the day as a special day. Not a perfect day but certainly a special one. One they won't forget. One that strives to inspire them to make a commitment to each other. A commitment to be there on the days when there is nothing and no one.

DIRT. You're saying, to love others, you want to create community theatre?

LILY. Yes.

>   *(Suddenly a rumble is heard and sparks start flying.)*

LILY. What's happening?

>   *(The technological world explodes. The Garden [our setting for Act V] is revealed. It is reminiscent of the Act II garden. Appearing in the center of it all is the actor playing DIRT.)*

LILY. Dirt?

DIRT. Yes.

LILY. You're…

DIRT. Fabulous. Yes!

LILY. But we were trapped in technology on the factory farm and now we're all the way back in the garden…how—

DIRT. Lily, simply by choosing to create community theater you have taken us from distance. And for the first time, since the industrial age, I, the God of Here and Now, am free.

>   *(In verse:)*

Now, hide ourselves amidst Forget-Me-Not
and let the Garden find their agency.
For here the revolutionaries enter!

>   *(The LILY and DIRT hide in the audience.)*

End of Act IV

THE MAD DEMON
Act V: Divine Madness

"Weddings are bad community theater"

—Anonymous

(All the GARDEN FLOWERS *enter [except* PINK LADY SLIPPER *and the* DAISIES*] or are revealed.)*

FLOWERS. *(Ululating:)* Lelelelelelelel.

MASTER SUNFLOWER. Do we have the Way?

RED ROSE. If Master Sunflower means do we wish to liberate the flowers from The Great Longing Deity's oppression, then yes, the Way is clear.

BABY'S BREATH. If Master Sunflower means do we wish to destroy the wedding, then yes, the Way is clear.

POPPY. If Master Sunflower means do we wish to wreak havoc amongst the Wedding Party—

TULIP. And by doing so bring an end to the tyranny of nostalgia—

POPPY and TULIP. Then yes the Way is clear.

MASTER SUNFLOWER. Do we have the weather?

BABY'S BREATH. The season is now.

PANSY. The sky is destined to a perfect summer blue.

LILAC. The weather forecast is memorably beatific.

POPPY. The weather has set expectations of the wedding to a standard of high.

FLOWERS. A perfect day for surprise, disruption, and disappointment.

MASTER SUNFLOWER. Do we have the discipline, command, and supplies needed.?

> *(Two deadheaded* DAISIES *enter. They look roughed up from their fight with the* FLOWER GIRLS *in "The Deity.")*

DAISY CHAIN. The daisy chain of command is present. What are our supplies?

BABY'S BREATH. Thorns?

RED ROSE. *(Displaying thorns:)* Check.

BABY'S BREATH. Opium?

> *(POPPY holds up a giant pipe.)*

POPPY. Check.

BABY'S BREATH. Excrement.

(*PINK LADY SLIPPER drags on a giant turd.*)

PINK LADY SLIPPER. Check.

BABY'S BREATH. Incurable Disease.

(*An INCURABLE DISEASE enters.*)

INCURABLE DISEASE. Present.

BABY'S BREATH. White Rose?

(*The TICK, dressed in a Delivery Man outfit, enters pulling on the republicanized WHITE ROSE.*)

TICK. I have purloined the delivery truck and captured the republicanized White Rose who was to be the centerpiece of the bouquet.

WHITE ROSE. Help me.

RED ROSE. We will use her to infiltrate the Wedding Party.

FLOWERS. Now is the time to strike.

MASTER SUNFLOWER. Wait. First do we have the leadership?

BABY'S BREATH. If Master Sunflower means has the chosen flower learned to be trustworthy, humane, courageous, intelligent and stern? Then we don't know.

TULIP. But if we wait for the Lily we could lose the weather, way, and terrain.

(*The GARDEN make worried sounds.*)

MASTER SUNFLOWER. We strike when time is right and pray to Dirt The Lily does arrive to help the cause.
So Daisies, Tick, go to your battle stations.

(*The DAISIES and TICK go to their band positions.*)

MASTER SUNFLOWER. And Flowers adorn yourself with fierce disguise.

(*The GARDEN all put WEDDING PARTY disguises on [bow ties, veils, Flower Girl baskets].*)

LILAC. (*Gesturing to the audience:*) But what about Forget-Me-Not?

PANSY. Forget-Me-Not can disguise itself as the wedding guests.

MASTER SUNFLOWER. Perfect. Forget-Me-Not on the count of three, turn your seats so they face all in this direction. One, two, three.

(*The audience members turn their seats. They are now all facing one direction together and they sit where the Act I stage originally was and now the Act V stage is where the audience sat in Act I. If they need help moving their seats the various FLOWERS can help them and MASTER SUNFLOWER should feel free to improvise with the awkwardness of this act.*)

MASTER SUNFLOWER. Gorgeous. You did that all so gracefully. Now, Baby's Breath give them lines to speak to help in their disguise.

(BABY'S BREATH *[and others]* hand out leaves to the audience.)

BABY'S BREATH. Keep these with you and when time is right I will conduct you. Don't read it now or you'll seem too rehearsed.

MASTER SUNFLOWER. And now, prepare to infiltrate the Wedding Party!

GARDEN. LELELELEL—

MASTER SUNFLOWER. SHHHHH!

GARDEN. *(Quietly:)* Lelelelelele.

(The GARDEN *sneak off. The* WEDDING PARTY *enters. The* BRIDES *[Deity and Love] and* GROOMS *[Deity and Love] enter. All eight* FLOWER GIRLS *follow them dragging* SUSAN STEWART. *They are all panicked.)*

BRIDE LOVE. Nothing is ready.

PRIMES. She's stalling because she knows this is a mistake.

BRIDE DEITY. *(Slapping* BRIDE LOVE:) Bad Bride.

BRIDE LOVE. *(Slapping her back:)* You've been undermining us the whole time.

BRIDE DEITY. *(Punching* BRIDE LOVE:) Why can't you just settle?

BRIDE LOVE. *(Pulling* BRIDE DEITY's *hair:)* Love the Groom you stupid bitch.

BRIDE DEITY. *(Dunking* BRIDE LOVE's *head in the toilet:)* Grow up.

BRIDE LOVE. *(Dunking* BRIDE DEITY's *head in the toilet:)* Be responsible. *(To* BRIDE DEITY:) Wait, who are you again?

BRIDE DEITY. I'm The Bride.

BRIDE LOVE. *I'm* The Bride.

SUSAN. You're all just stock characters.

FLOWER GIRLS. That's not true.

THE PRIMES. I'm Mary.

PRIMES. No, I'm Mary.

SUBPRIMES. I'm Mary.

SUBPRIMES. No, I'm Mary.

THE MARYS DEITY. We're Mary

THE MARYS LOVE. No, we're Mary.

FLOWER GIRLS. *(In perfect unison:)* Stop that. No, you stop that. Stop that. No, you stop that.

SUSAN. Not one of you has a solo part like me?

FLOWER GIRLS. WE WANT SOLO PARTS.

GROOMS. How could you say such a thing? Don't you know The Great Longing needs our group think and sentiment to keep it strong?

MARY DEITY #1 and MARY LOVE #1. *(Taking turns dunking each other in the toilet:)* You're right. Bad Mary. Take that Mary. Drink that pee water.

GROOMS. Hot.

BRIDES. Could you not be such a heterosexual cliche.

GROOMS. I'm a stock character.

> *(A door is rolled on. A doorbell.)*

ALL. *(Collective shock:)* Huh.

> *(Pause.)*

GROOM LOVE. You don't think?

BRIDES. The Lily?

FLOWER GIRLS. The White Rose?

SUSAN. Time?

> *(SUSAN is gagged. A doorbell.)*

BRIDES. Well, someone should answer it.

FLOWER GIRLS. We'll do it.

> *(The two sets of FLOWER GIRLS eye each other.)*

FLOWER GIRLS. We said we would answer it. Not you, us. Stop that. No, you stop that. Stop that! No, you stop that!

BRIDES. *(To the GROOMS:)* You do it.

GROOMS. Why me?

BRIDES. You're the man.

GROOMS. God damnit.

> *(Doorbell.)*

GROOMS. Oooo I know, we'll all do it.

WEDDING PARTY. Together.

> *(Everyone goes to the door together.)*

BRIDES. Open it.

WEDDING PARTY. One. Two. Three.

(*Everyone opens the door together. They all run together to the opposite end of the stage, as if it were going to be a bomb. In the doorway is a* DELIVERY MAN *[who is the* TICK *in disguise].*)

DELIVERY MAN. I present to you The White Rose.

(*The* WHITE ROSE *is given the spotlight. Fantasia music plays. The* BRIDES *are drawn to the* WHITE ROSE.*)

BRIDES. (*Mesmerized by its beauty:*) Appropriately pretty.

(THE GREAT LONGING *closes on the* WEDDING PARTY, *shutting them off from the audience.* **The curtain is made entirely of red cocktail napkins with dreams written on them. This is a scenic must.** *The Curtain, which should be larger than the Act I Curtain, should not be partially covered in red cocktail napkins but completely so. The magic of this moment is in seeing a massive stage curtain made entirely out of cocktail napkins. The audience, during the intermission, should be asked to write down their various dreams on red cocktail napkins. The illusion is that their dreams have been used to build the Act V Curtain. This takes a lot of work and manpower and I suggest starting this project on day one. I've seen it done full-out and it takes the audience's breath away and I've seen it done half-way and watched it do nothing for the audience, as it then becomes a gimmick rather than a wonder. I beg of you to choose wonder over gimmick.*)

(*The scene is backwards from when we started the play with the audience sitting on stage and the rest of the play taking place where the audience originally sat.*)

THE GREAT LONGING. (*A exclamation of triumph:*) WA HA HA HA HA HA! I'M BACK. RESTORED TO MY FULL GLORY. NOTHING CAN STOP THE REIGN OF LONGING. And you, you who have waited diligently for this moment, our climax, you will get to hear such favorite classics as: "With this ring I thee wed," the sumptuous pleasure of two "I do's," the delicious innocence of "you may kiss the Bride." Yes, tissues will be available, and best of all the white rose bouquet will be thrown and caught, providing you with a sequel that will embrace you here in never ending bliss. So please, please ladies, give introduction to: the Groom.

(*The* LADIES *all poke their heads out of the sides of the curtain and sing:*)

LADIES. (*All* BRIDES *and* FLOWER GIRLS:)
HE IS A FIGURE WRAPPED UP IN PANCAKES
ROCKING CHAIRS
COFFEE BEANS
AND SUNDAY STROLLS
WRAPPED UP LIKE CHRISTMAS
WRAPPED UP LIKE TENDER
STORIES OF OLD.

(The GROOMS *enter through the slit in the curtain and make their way stage left of the Curtain.* MASTER SUNFLOWER *and* POPPY *[who are disguised as* GROOMS*] whisper to each other.)*

GROOMS.
YOU LOVE ME.
YOU LOVE ME NOT.
YOU LOVE ME.
YOU LOVE ME NOT.
WHY DO YOU LOVE ME?

MASTER SUNFLOWER. Disguised as Groom we'll strike when time is right.

POPPY. And Flowers will be freed from dreamer's harm.

MASTER SUNFLOWER / POPPY / GROOMS. WHY DO YOU NOT LOVE!!

THE GREAT LONGING. And now, those harbingers of youth and charm, the Flower Girls.

(The FLOWER GIRLS *each enter from the slit. They dance and throw petals of flowers from baskets.* RED ROSE, TULIP, LILAC, PANSY *are dressed as* FLOWER GIRLS.*)*

FLOWER GIRLS. *(Acting the roles of sweet* FLOWER GIRLS *but ending up rather deranged in their desperate glee:)* Hee hee hee hee hee hee hee hee HEE!
WILL YOU CARE FOR ME?

(The FLOWER GIRLS *throw petals.)*

RED ROSE / TULIP / LILAC / PANSY. *(Aside:)* Petals they do throw.

FLOWER GIRLS.
OR WILL YOU NOT?
ARE YOU THERE FOR ME?

(The FLOWER GIRLS *throw petals.)*

RED ROSE / TULIP / LILAC / PANSY / PINK LADY SLIPPER.
(Aside:) The viciousness the horror

FLOWER GIRLS.
WHAT HAVE I GOT
WHAT HAVE I LEFT TO GIVE?

(The FLOWER GIRLS *throw petals.* TULIP *lunges forward. Rose holds her back.)*

TULIP. I'll kill you, you fuckers!

RED ROSE. *(Holding* TULIP *back and whispering to her:)*
Tulip save your hate

Soon bloody limbed Flower Girls
We will toss to ground.

TULIP. *(To other* FLOWER GIRLS:*)* Sorry. I was just thinking of something else. Continue.

FLOWER GIRLS and FLOWERS. WHAT HAVE I NOT.

THE GREAT LONGING. And to grace us all with beauty as perfect as a picture of a special day. Do you want her?

> (BABY'S BREATH *steps out holding the gagged* WHITE ROSE *hostage but looking like she's decorating the bouquet with herself.)*

BABY'S BREATH. Now guests! Pull out your cue sheets.

THE GREAT LONGING. I said do you want her?

> (BABY'S BREATH *conducts them.)*

GUESTS. Oh yeah.

THE GREAT LONGING. Do you want that Bride?

GUESTS. Yes Curtain.

THE GREAT LONGING. Do you really want her?

GUESTS. Don't tease us Curtain. Don't. Oh. Oh. Oh.

THE GREAT LONGING. Where do you want that Bride?

GUESTS. In the center! GET HER IN THE CENTER!

THE GREAT LONGING. Oh I'll get that Bride in the center.

GUESTS. OH CUUUUUUUURTAAAAAAAIN.

THE GREAT LONGING. I GIVE TO YOU…THE BRIDE.

> (*The* BRIDES *enter.* BABY'S BREATH *takes the* WHITE ROSE *to them and they hold the two* FLOWERS *as a bouquet. The* BRIDES *meet the* GROOMS *during the following. Everything slows down and the schtick falls away.)*

BRIDES.
> WILL YOU COME FOR ME
> OR WILL YOU NOT
> WILL YOU TAKE ME FROM
> OR HAVE YOU STOPPED
> WHY DO YOU LOVE ME
> WHY CAN YOU NOT LOVE ME

BABY'S BREATH. *(Aside:)*
Throughout all Time I have been known as filler.
A cherub who does frame the heroine.
But when you look up close to Baby's Breath,
am not I just as grand, as say, The Bride.

Man's distance from me is what keeps me small.
So distance must now end in flower revenge.

BRIDES.
>LOVE ME
>LOVE ME
>WHY WILL YOU NOT?
>LOVE ME
>LOVE ME
>WHY WILL YOU NOT?
>LOVE ME
>LOVE ME
>WHY WILL YOU NOT?
>LOVE ME
>LOVE ME
>WHY WILL YOU NOT?
>LOVE ME
>LOVE ME
>WHY WILL YOU NOT?

>*(The* WEDDING PARTY *sing to the audience, in a cannon, during the following.)*

THE GREAT LONGING. Dearly beloved. We are gathered here today, in the shadow of me, and in the face of this audience to join together this man and this woman. If any person can show just cause why they may not be joined together. Let them speak now or forever hold their peace.

WEDDING PARTY. *(In a canon that stops on the word "peace":)*
>LOVE ME. LOVE ME. WHY WILL YOU NOT. LOVE ME. LOVE
>   ME. WHY WILL YOU NOT LOVE ME?
>LOVE ME. LOVE ME. WHY WILL YOU NOT LOVE ME? LOVE
>   ME. LOVE ME. WHY WILL YOU NOT LOVE ME?
>LOVE ME. LOVE ME. WHY WILL YOU NOT—

SUSAN. *(Gagged:)* Hmmmmmmmm.

THE GREAT LONGING. Anyone? Anyone?

SUSAN. Hmmmmmmmm.

THE GREAT LONGING. Your last chance.

SUSAN. Hmmmmmmmm.

THE GREAT LONGING. Well then—

MASTER SUNFLOWER. FLOWERS! REVEAL YOURSELVES!

>*(The* FLOWERS *throw off their disguises.)*

WEDDING PARTY. Hey! You're not part of the Wedding Party. Why, you're revolutionary flowers in disguise!

GARDEN. LELELELELELE!

(MASTER SUNFLOWER and BABY'S BREATH pull the Curtain open so that TULIP, RED ROSE, POPPY, PINK LADY SLIPPER, and INCURABLE DISEASE can push the WEDDING PARTY upstage of the Curtain. MASTER SUNFLOWER and BABY'S BREATH then close it. The SUBPRIMES have escaped being stuck behind the Curtain.)

SUBPRIMES. WHAT'S HAPPENING?

THE GREAT LONGING. THEY'RE USING ME TO SHUT YOU OUT.

(The SUBPRIMES attack the two FLOWERS.)

SUBPRIMES. YAAAAAAAA!

(Tableau vivants [with dialogue] begin. Every time MASTER SUNFLOW-ER and BABY'S BREATH get the curtain closed The SUBPRIMES do different things to them [stomping feet, head butts in their guts, pulling their pet-als, etc] to take control of the Curtain, open it up, and reveal what's happening behind. The first scene reveals RED ROSE stabbing the BRIDE LOVE with her thorns while WHITE ROSE stands by in horror.)

RED ROSE. Yaaaaaaa!

WHITE ROSE. What are you doing?

RED ROSE. Painting the White Rose red.

(BRIDE LOVE's blood sprays on WHITE ROSE.)

WHITE ROSE. Ahhhhhhh!

(The Curtain closes and opens to reveal PRIME DEITY and POPPY staring at the audience, as if watching TV, sharing a bag of chips, stoned out of their minds.)

PRIME / POPPY. Wow.

(POPPY gives a devious smile to the audience.)

(The Curtain closes and opens to reveal LILAC and PANSY punching the shit out of the MARYS DEITY.)

PANSY. *(Punching MARY DEITY #1 in the face:)* Does he love you now cunt?

LILAC. *(Punching MARY DEITY #2 in the stomach:)* How 'bout this time?

PANSY and LILAC. *(Slamming the MARYS DEITY's heads together:)* What about now?

(We open and close and PINK LADY SLIPPER is using her scrotum like flower self to tea bag GROOM DEITY [who is horrified].)

(The curtain closes and opens to show SUSAN rolling by with BRIDE DEITY's head in the toilet.)

SUSAN. *(Singing, the melody from the bridge of The Great Longing Song, through her gag.)* AHHH AHHH AHHH AHH AHH AHH AHH AHH AHH.

> *(The curtain closes and opens to* GROOM LOVE *getting a blowjob [with his back to the audience] by the* INCURABLE DISEASE.*)*

GROOM LOVE. Oh yeah. Oh that's nice.

> *(The* GROOM *orgasms, turns around, looks down, sees that his crotch is a giant pus infected sore [think red and putrid colored stringy things bulging out of his crotch].)*

GROOM LOVE. AHHHHHHHHH!

> *(He runs off and the* INCURABLE DISEASE *wipes its mouth and chases after him.)*

> *(We open and close and the* MARYS LOVE *are watching* TULIP, LILAC, *and* PANSY *dancing with a giant turd.)*

MARY LOVE #1. What is it?

MARY LOVE #2. Why I think it's a giant turd ballet.

> *(The other members of the* WEDDING PARTY *enter and watch like zombies to a show.)*

MASTER SUNFLOWER. FLOWERS! FERTILIZE THE WEDDING PARTY.

FLOWERS. LELELELELELELELE!

> *(The* FLOWERS *all throw pieces of poo at the* WEDDING PARTY. *The* INCURABLE DISEASE *throws the giant turd into the audience. It gets thrown around like a beach ball at a concert until the* INCURABLE DISEASE *gets it back. The* GROOM DEITY *drags on the beat up* PINK LADY SLIPPER.)*

GROOM DEITY. Wedding Party!

> *(Everyone looks stops and looks at* GROOM DEITY.)*

GROOM DEITY. Fight Back!

WEDDING PARTY. YAAAAAA!

> *(The* MASTER SUNFLOWER *and* BABY'S BREATH *try to close the curtain but The* SUBPRIMES *drag them away by the petals. The* WEDDING PARTY *fight their way through the poo slinging and begin tearing the petals off the* FLOWERS, *biting and stomping on them.)*

BRIDES. HERE COME THE BRIDES!

> *(The* BRIDES *enter with a giant [meaning at least 5' wide] container of cellophane [or something that would look like it] and wrap the* FLOWERS *up in it, creating a massive bouquet. At the last second a giant bow is attached to the bouquet.)*

WEDDING PARTY. We won! We won!

(TIME *[as* WIND*] enters.)*

TIME. Oh no you haven't.

PRIME DEITY. Who's that?

TIME. I am Time.

FLOWER GIRLS. So?

TIME. I am also a Hegel-reading lesbian earth mother who wears comfortable clothes.

FLOWER GIRLS. So?

TIME. I am also the Wind. Not *(Indicating a smelly fart:)* wind. But WIIIIIIIIIIND!

(*The* WEDDING PARTY *are blown asunder. The* FLOWERS' *cellophane is blown off, freeing them.* TIME *walks gently to* SUSAN.)

TIME. I quote from Susan Stewart's *On Longing*: "Nostalgia is a sadness without an object, a sadness which creates a longing that is inauthentic because it does not take part in lived experience...the past it seeks has never existed except as narrative." *(Breaking the quote:)* But I can heal that sadness by becoming the lived experience. Then I cannot lack for love. The heart can never be taken from me.

(TIME *takes* SUSAN's *gag off.)*

SUSAN. I thought you were cut from the story.

TIME. I had to relinquish my disdain for narrative in order to make my way back.

SUSAN. I didn't think I'd see you again.

TIME. I'm sorry I allowed them to force you into my role of Evil Stepmother.

(TIME *tears the Evil Stepmother outfit off of* SUSAN.)

SUSAN. You freed me.

TIME. No, you freed me.

SUSAN. No you freed me.

TIME. No you freed—

(SUSAN *kisses* TIME.)

FLOWER GIRLS. Eww.

MASTER SUNFLOWER. Now, Garden, strike. While prejudice distracts.

GARDEN. LELELELELELELELELE!

WEDDING PARTY. AHHHHHHHHHHHHHHH!

(The LILY *pops up in the audience.)*

LILY. WAIT!

GROOMS. That audience member is talking to us.

LILY. I'm not an audience member.

> *(The* LILY *runs up to* BRIDE DEITY *and kisses her in the grandest romantic way.)*

ALL. *(Collective gasp:)* Huh!

BRIDE DEITY. Lily?

GROOMS. Look, it's a man.

FLOWER GIRLS. It can't be.

FLOWERS. It certainly looks like a man.

LILY. I am and I'm not. But all the same I freed the Dirt!

ALL. *(A collective gasp:)* Huh!

DIRT. *(Standing up in the audience:)* Flowers! Gild that Lily.

FLOWERS. Lelelelelel!

> *(During the ululating The* FLOWERS *grab the* LILY's *tux and tear it off revealing a gold sequined tux underneath.)*

BRIDE LOVE. Lily?

LILY. Bride?

BRIDE DEITY. Lily, I have a confession to make. I'm not an individual. This is my other self.

LILY. Fantastic.

> *(The* LILY *kisses* BRIDE LOVE. *It then swings the two* BRIDES *in and they kiss each other.)*

GROOM LOVE. Hey!

LILY. Oh shut up.

> *(The* LILY *kisses the* GROOM LOVE.*)*

GROOM DEITY. *(Horrified:)* Ahhhh!

BRIDES. What?

GROOM DEITY. *(Horrified:)* I liked that.

LILY. *(To the* BRIDES:*)* Brides?

BRIDES. Yes?

LILY. I have a question for you.

BRIDES. *(Putting their hands out as if they're going to get a ring:)* Yes.

LILY. Wait.

(The LILY *goes to* TIME.*)*

LILY. I'm sorry about what I said before, about you being a killer of love.

TIME. You were right.

LILY. No. You are love. *(The* LILY *dips* TIME.*)* And I have a question for you too.

(The LILY *kisses* TIME.*)*

TIME. But I'm with Susan now.

LILY. That's great because I have a question for Susan as well.

SUSAN. Oh yes!

(The LILY *kisses* SUSAN.*)*

INCURABLE DISEASE. What about me?

LILY. Yes. You too Incurable Disease. Because, if you live long enough you play all the parts.

TIME. And forgiveness is a way to love.

(The LILY *tongues The* INCURABLE DISEASE.*)*

LILY. Yes. It all comes down to this, and I don't want you to answer now, because there's nothing worse than watching people say yes, under public pressure, when what they really mean is no, but I have a question for you all.

*(*LILY *goes to an audience member.)*

Even you.

(The LILY *kisses the audience member.)*

And you.

(The LILY *kisses another audience member.)*

And the ushers.

(The LILY *kisses an usher.)*

(Pointing backstage:)

And the techies.

ALL. Oh the techies, get the techies!

(Everyone runs upstage of the curtain to get the techies. They drag two of them out.)

LILY. I have a question for the techies who have been working so hard all evening long. And my question to you all is—

(The Curtain closes behind the LILY *[so it is alone onstage with just* THE GREAT LONGING*].)*

THE GREAT LONGING. DON'T YOU DARE!

LILY. What?

THE GREAT LONGING. You come in here and turn my story into a wanton hippie love-fest.

LILY. You're included in this proposal too, Great Longing.

THE GREAT LONGING. Disgusting.

LILY. I love nostalgia and now realize the past and present can be joined as equals.

THE GREAT LONGING. You don't get to pop out of nowhere and make the rules.

LILY. Flowers have been around just as long as Curtains and now we're making our own rules.

(THE GREAT LONGING *attacks the* LILY.)

THE GREAT LONGING. AHHHHHHH.

(*A plethora of* GREAT LONGING *hands pop out of the curtain and attack the* LILY. *At one point they are pulling the* LILY's *arms as if it were on a cross.*)

LILY. Jesus.

THE GREAT LONGING. You'll never be the center of the story! Never! NEVER!

(THE GREAT LONGING *beats the* LILY *into a bloody pulp.*)

LILY. That's true. It's your story now Dirt.

(*Dirt's theme music plays. She enters from the audience and does a soiling dance on* THE GREAT LONGING. THE GREAT LONGING *improvises: "What, what are you doing, stop that, no, oh no, don't rub that there, no, no, please, not my tassel, oh…etc.*)

THE GREAT LONGING. What did you just do?

LILY. She soiled you with here and now.

THE GREAT LONGING. No. It can't be. Not the here and now. It didn't happen. *(To the audience:)* Don't look at the Dirt. Look at me. Imagine perfect velvet contours. I'll take you back to dreams.

LILY. It won't work Great Longing. Their butts are sore and they wanna go home.

THE GREAT LONGING. *(Shaking:)* No! No! Nooooooooooooo!

(THE GREAT LONGING *falls to the ground revealing the naked actor behind it and the whole cast having an orgy. Positions and partners can be figured out for each production separately. What is important is that* SUBPRIME

LOVE *is being pleasured by the* POPPY, SUSAN *and* TIME *are getting it on*, BRIDE DEITY *and* GROOM DEITY *are making out, and that a multitude of sexual preferences are represented including multiple partners, and a masturbator and someone simply amidst it all reading a book or crocheting. The* INCURABLE DISEASE *sees the naked* GREAT LONGING *and gets excited. It chases* THE GREAT LONGING *offstage.)*

THE GREAT LONGING. *(Running offstage and hiding its privates:)* AHHH-HHHHH!

LILY. Dirt, you did it. You defeated The Great Longing.

DIRT. We did it. The reign of nostalgia has come to an end.

ALL. *(Having a collective orgasm:)* Hu-hu-hu-hu-ray.

MASTER SUNFLOWER. *(Post-coital:)* Now the Flowers are free to love who they wish to love.

BRIDES. As are the Brides.

GROOMS. And the Grooms.

POPPY. And we can all marry and pleasure each other.

SUBPRIME LOVE. *(Being pleasured by* POPPY:*)* Aye Papi.

PRIME DEITY. Wait a minute. Isn't group love similar to group think?

PRIME LOVE. Yeah I thought you said cliché was bad.

THE MARYS. And isn't a group wedding one of the biggest clichés of all?

LILY. *(With great pleasure:)* Well, yeah.

MASTER SUNFLOWER. But isn't it what you do with the cliché that elevates it?

BRIDES and GROOMS. You mean cliché doesn't have to be a reductive commodity?

TIME. *(Embracing the* DIRT:*)* And good and evil can be evil and good.

ALL. Yes! Relativism has won the day.

> *(Enter* THE POPE *with a machine gun.)*

THE POPE. NEVER!

> *(*THE POPE *fires its bullets into everyone. Fabric blood [red for the people and green for the* FLOWERS *and red and green for the* LILY*] sprays everywhere. It looks like Christmas.)*

RED ROSE. The Pope shot us all.

ALL. You asshole Pope.

THE POPE. *(Eating a Twinkie:)* It wasn't my fault.

> *(*THE POPE *exits.)*

THE MARYS DEITY #1. Didn't the Pope die or resign or something?

TIME. He's a stock character; one pope passes and another pope pops up in his place.

TULIP. But what are we to do? We're all bleeding to death.

> *(Everyone suddenly feels the pain of getting shot.)*

SUSAN. Lily, wasn't there something you were going to ask before you defeated The Great Longing.

LILY. Right.

TIME. Whatever it is, you'd best do it quickly as we are coming to our end.

MASTER SUNFLOWER. Wait, if we're all about to die, then let's add in some manipulative underscoring.

PANSY. Ooo, I love manipulative underscoring.

SUBPRIME DEITY. And a choir. Let's have a choir.

FLOWER GIRLS DEITY. Good idea.

FLOWER GIRLS DEITY and HALF THE FLOWERS.
AHHH AHH AHH AHH AHH
AHHH AHH AHH AHH AHH.

> *(They continue singing their "Ahhhs" under the following dialogue.)*

SUBPRIME LOVE. And dancing.

PRIME LOVE. *(Making her blood cloth float around:)* While throwing things that float.

> *(The FLOWER GIRLS LOVE and the other half of the FLOWERS dance and throw their blood fabric streams during the rest of the play. Others can join in.)*

BRIDE LOVE. And make the overly sentimental theatrical gestures start small and crescendo to the end of the play.

GROOM LOVE. That's the best.

> *(Everyone sings and dances small [they will grow to a crescendo by the end of the play].)*

BRIDE DEITY. Lily, do you have enough life in you to sing?

> *(All stop.)*

LILY. I'll try.
THE FLOATING DOWN
A FLOWER FREE
TO BE
TO BE

> *(The LILY falters and BRIDE DEITY helps.)*

BRIDE DEITY.
 AS TEARS DESCEND,
 DECREE
 THE CHEEK
 HOME
 BUT WITH THE WEIGHT OF ALL THEY LEARN
 MUST CLING

LILY. THEN FALL

BRIDE DEITY / LILY.
 AND SEEK TO
 ROAM
 DISPERSE UPON THE EARTH
 ADJOURN FROM YEARNING
 TOMES

BRIDE DEITY. I love that verse.

GROOM DEITY. What else do you love?

BRIDE DEITY. Your hairy chest.

GROOM DEITY. Really?

BRIDE DEITY. Yeah.

GROOM DEITY. Well I love your nose.

BRIDE DEITY. You do?

GROOM DEITY. Of course.

GROOM LOVE. *(To* BRIDE LOVE:*)* Do you love anything about me?

BRIDE LOVE. I love the morose optimism of Beckett.

GROOM LOVE. Me too.

WHITE ROSE. I love my boyfriend's morning cock.

TICK. Me too.

SUBPRIMES. And bitchy humor.

PANSY and LILAC. Fuck you, you cunt.

SUBPRIMES. Oh yeah say it again.

PANSY and LILAC. Fuck you, you cunt.

LILY and BRIDES and GROOMS.
 A FLOWER FALLS
 MUCH FASTER THAN A WISH
 AND SO OUR LONGINGS LAY
 ARE LATE
 LOST
 AND WE ARE LEFT TO KNOW OUR FATE

TO LAND
TO LOSE
TO ACHE.
AND SO WE'LL DIE UPON THE GRATING FROST.

(THE GREAT LONGING *comes out, led by the* INCURABLE DISEASE *on a leash. The Haiku light shines.*)

THE GREAT LONGING. Come season of now
It's here The Great Longing falls
And grows to balance.

FLOWERS. Work the haiku!

(*The Haiku light ends.*)

TIME. Nice to have you back Great Longing.

(TIME *gently reveals her breasts to the audience as an act of joy and reconciliation with her child curtain. She makes what was meant to be a crass act into one of beauty. Then she puts a crass button on it by doing a little jiggle with them.*)

THE GREAT LONGING. (*Genuinely touched:*) Thanks ambiguously gendered parent.

(*Everyone continues with the dancing and singing.*)

LILY.
AND I WOULD RATHER END MY LIFE
WITH ALL THE SOUND, THE WIND AS FIFE ABOUND

SUSAN and TIME. WITH ALL THE SMELLS OF MORNING AIR

LILY / SUSAN / TIME.
TO SEE THE SUN ARISE AND BLARE
ITS COLOR ALL ABOUT THE WORLD

LILY / SUSAN / TIME / GREAT LONGING / INCURABLE.
IN THIS LAST MOMENT WE'VE UNFURLED
THE BEAUTY OF WHAT CAN BE HERE
IT TAKES AWAY ALL THAT I FEAR FROM DEATH

ALL.
OH THE BREADTH
FLOATING DOWN

THE MARYS. And I love that some of you have to pee and some of you are crying at the manipulative nature of a key change modulation.

GROOM LOVE. And because we're talking about what we love.

GROOM DEITY. And some of you want to stick your fingers down your throats

ALL. *AND I JUST LOVE IT!*
OH THE BREADTH FLOATING—

> *(They are about to hit the high point but* MASTER SUNFLOWER *brings them down.)*

MASTER SUNFLOWER. Wait bring it down. Let the Lily ask the question before we die.

> *(The light begins to fade.)*

LILY. Okay. This is what we're gonna do. I'll ask the question and then the lights will go dark. And in that moment of darkness, if you want to say yes, pout your lips like this. *(The* LILY *pouts.)* It is essentially a come hither pucker and it means, yes you'll make a commitment to *thinking* about marrying everyone and everything. And if your answer is no then leave your lips the way they are. And if your answer is no, you don't want to make a commitment to *thinking* about marrying everyone and everything, that's fine. Because everyone understands having mixed feelings about marriage and commitment and…thinking. And you may not want to marry a man and a flower and an Incurable Disease. And The Dirt knows there are moments in everyone's life when they're happy being single so it all makes sense. But of course I really want you to pucker. So with my dying breath I'll sing the final verse, pop the question, the lights will go dark and you will do what you will do.

> SO HERE I FRAY
> AND MELT AWAY
> AND FLOW
> AND FLOW
> INTO THE NEVERMORE I GO
> OH-OH
> AND THE KING'S LIFE I THOUGHT TO LIVE,
> TO LAST FOREVERMORE

ALL. TO BE RENOWNED

LILY.
> NO, I WON'T BE CROWNED
> INSTEAD I WILL RECEDE
> BUT NOT BEFORE WE DO ENJOY
> HOW WE'LL CONCEDE
> TO GROUNDLINGS.
> OUR MANIFOLD.
> OUR FLOWERGORY.

LILY / SUSAN / TIME / MASTER SUNFLOWER.
> OUR MANIFOLD

TIME / SUSAN / MASTER / LILY / BRIDES / GROOMS.
> OUR FLOWERGORY

TIME / SUSAN / BRIDES and GROOMS / FLOWERS / LILY.
OUR MANIFOLD

ALL. OUR FLOWERGORY.

ALL. Will you, marry me?

(The lights reach black.)

End of Play

Appendix

WHITE ROSE BANTER

The following White Rose dialogue is all loosely part of the script. The information must be said but the performer playing The White Rose should feel free to improvise (barring any pop-culture references). The White Rose is a host who hangs out with the audience during all the intermissions and pre-show, chatting them up. She should be someone we all want to get instructions from (so if improvising, try to stay away from nasty humor that is exclusionary). Also if improvising try to stay away from ruining the surprises that have been built into the play. An example is: if they ask why there isn't any food or drink allowed in The Love Act, make something up that isn't the real reason: "Because we hang you upside down in this Act and we don't want the floor to get messy."

Pre-Show.

(Right before the audience is let into the theater The WHITE ROSE *enters the lobby with a megaphone or her gong and a loud voice.)*

WHITE ROSE. Hello Everybody! Gather round please. Come on. Chatty Kathys in the back with the wine come on. Gather round. We are about to begin and I have some important information. If you do not listen to this you will not be able to relieve your bladder for five whole hours. Get your booties over here. Ladies and Gentlemen. And gender ambiguous people! My name is The White Rose and I will be your guide throughout this evening.

(She holds up a sign that says "Applaud." The Audience applauds or if they don't she encourages them to.)

WHITE ROSE. Thank you, that's so sweet. Some Important information! We have divided what you're about to see into five distinct sections. They are called The Deity (Part One), The Ghost Warrior (Part Two), The Love Act (Part Three), The Living Person Acts (Part Four) and The Mad Demon (Part Five). Five parts with intermissions, of fifteen minutes a piece, breaking them up.

Very important information! During these intermissions we ask you to leave the theater and hang out in the building where you are now or within earshot of the building. We ask that you take all your belongings or check them downstairs in the coatcheck. In those breaks you may stretch your legs, grab some snacks or a drink from the cafe, hang out with the cast in the open dressing room downstairs, enjoy the intermission performances that will be happening throughout the building, and above all talk with your fellow audience members. In fact why don't we practice that right now. Will everyone turn to the person on your left and say "Hi, how are you?"

(They do this.)

WHITE ROSE. Now turn to the person on your right and say, *(In a mock scolding voice:)* "I'm having a conversation."

(They do this.)

WHITE ROSE. Good practice.

Very Important Information! Your third intermission, between The Love Act (Part Three) and The Living Person Acts (Part Four) has been set aside for cellphone/texting use. During this time we encourage you to communicate with the outside world. What I like to call the cellular community.

Very important information! During the rest of the play **and the other intermissions** we ask you to not turn your communicating devices on. This means during the first two intermissions no calling your friends, searching the internet, tweeting or texting—what I call chimping: *(She acts like a monkey who is texting:)* Ooo ooo ooo.

If you absolutely must talk to the cellular community before the third intermission make sure you do it before you enter the theater for the first time. For we are conducting an experiment: what would it be like if, during two out of three of the intermissions, you stayed engaged with the audience members, creators, and physical intimacy of the play? So help us with our experiment please.

One last thing: feel free to bring food and drink into the theater. There is no dinner break in this play, only the fifteen minute intermissions, and we want to make sure you keep your energy up. And try not to drink too much too soon. Pace yourself as you have a long way to go.

And speaking of go. Here we go folks. Ushers and ticket takers: open the gates and let these people in.

(She holds up the "Applaud" sign.)

WHITE ROSE. Thank you, that's so nice.

Deity/Ghost Warrior Intermission

(At the end of The Deity, the house lights come up and The WHITE ROSE *enters.)*

WHITE ROSE. Okay everyone that concludes The Deity (Part One) and it is now time for our first intermission. We ask you to make your way into the rest of the building, make sure you take your things with you and we will see you in fifteen minutes. Oh and don't forget, no talking on the cellphone or chimping this time.

Top of Ghost Warrior

WHITE ROSE. Okay everybody, The Ghost Warrior is about to begin. You may enter the theater, etc…

Ghost Warrior/The Love Act Intermission

WHITE ROSE. Intermission #2 has begun. We have to do another change over in here so please clear out of the theater and don't forget to take your things. And I know you're all jonesing to check those emails and update that Twitter but be strong. All you have to do is get through this intermission and the next part of the play and you'll have fifteen whole minutes dedicated to the cellular community. Be strong. Also no food or drinks are allowed in the theater during The Love Act so make sure if you eat or drink something you can do it in fifteen minutes. And see you in fifteen.

Top of The Love Act

WHITE ROSE. "The Love Act" is about to begin. The theater is open. Etc.

The Love Act/The Living Person Acts Intermission

WHITE ROSE. You made it to the cellular community intermission. Congratulate yourselves. This is the intermission where we encourage you to only use your cellphones to communicate. Try your best to ignore the people around you and text away. Of course we have to do it outside of the theater because we have another change over so make sure you bring your things with you.

Very important information.

This is your final intermission. That's right this is the last break. There is no intermission between "The Living Person Acts" and our climax "The Mad Demon" so make sure you take that bathroom break while talking on the phone. See you in fifteen.

Top of The Living Person Acts

WHITE ROSE. We're back folks. Turn off those cellphones and get in that theater and find yourself a seat. Feel free to bring food in this time. Here we go people. Our hero is about to enter its inner cave.

DRESSING ROOMS

The open dressing room is the place where all the actors have their makeup stations and costumes. It is open to the audience once at the first intermission and for the rest of the performance. Performers should not be in character in the open dressing room but should feel free to be themselves, talk to their fellow cast members, audience members they know, or audience members they don't know. It's essentially a party.

The closed dressing room is for hiding any costumes/performers that haven't been revealed yet (example: the Act II performers and costumes need to be kept secret in the first intermission but should join the open dressing room in the second and third intermissions) and where performers can get changed if they want privacy while doing so. The Lily is the only cast member who needs an actual break during the intermissions (as all other cast members have breaks during the various acts they're not in).

KYOGENS

Some of the Kyogen ideas should be created from scratch (devised by the company) and some of them are part of the script and need to be in the intermissions in order to give the audience the full experience of the play.

Script Kyogens

Playwright's Monologue: the most important Kyogen. It should play during all three of the intermissions and audience members should be encouraged to watch it. It's essentially a video program note from the playwright. In it the entire cast (or others) perform a different paragraph or sentence from The Playwright's Monologue.

The Discussion Disco is also a part of the play. It's essentially a dance party in the open dressing room. During it you can talk about the themes of the play while dancing or simply dance.

Context Corner: this is a small library created somewhere in the building. As programs must only be handed out at the end of the performance, audience members can go, during the intermissions, to the Context Corner and read or learn about the history of myths, marriage, Susan Stewart, The Hero's Journey, Theater of the Ridiculous, Noh, Kyogens, The Act-Up ashes action, Flower Farms, the various collaborators' earlier works, etc.

PLAYWRIGHT. Eight years old and I attend my first wedding. Princess Diana rides in a bullet proof glass pumpkin across the TV screens of the world. My family wears our pajamas to the wedding and everyone agrees it is a perfect day.

At nine I attend my second wedding. I am the ring bearer, so wear a tux for the first time. I am proud. Though soon I become a wallflower, while the family complains about the effeminacy of the groom.

Ten years old and the only gays I *know* I know are a couple down the street, who, in fear that they might molest me, I am told to stay clear of.

At twelve, I become aware of AIDS, on the same day puberty enters my life. AIDS awareness happens in the form of The Pope preaching abstinence to fight AIDS. Puberty comes in a wetdream that consists of two boys humping each other while the Greek goddess Thetis, aside a Pegasus, reads their wedding vows. After this dream I am afraid to masturbate because I think, since I am gay, I will give myself AIDS. But ultimately I decide my overwhelming desire to have sex means I must bring an end to AIDS.

I attend my first AIDS Walk in San Francisco by telling my mom I am spending the night at my friend Marcy's. Instead Marcy and I drive three hours to the city, sleep in her used Chevy Sprint and walk. So many gays. A community. I see men pushing men in wheelchairs who wear matching rings, but are not lawfully wedded family members, and a Sister of Perpetual Indulgence passes on an incurable disease called glitter. Thank you sister. I wish the marching gays would kiss me and think, if I pout my lips they'll be drawn to me by the power of the protruding lip. I walk the whole march like this:

(The Playwright pouts.)

Marcy says, "Why are you pouting your lips like that?" I reply, while pouting, "I don't know what you're talking about."

After this day I learn about a group of AIDS activists, who took urns to D.C. and dumped the ashes of their longtime companions on the White House lawn. It is a reaction to George Bush continuing Ronald Reagan's horrendous disregard of the epidemic.

At seventeen I move to San Francisco and attend my first orgy in the middle of Castro Street on Halloween night. I am dressed like a zombie cater waiter and wear a tux around my ankles. The crowd chants: Gay Sex! Dyke Sex! Let's have some Fag Sex! I find a boy in a wedding dress and for the sheer pleasure of satisfying the imagery, we jerk each other off amidst cumber-bun and tulle, as drummers drum, onlookers take pictures, and everyone smiles. Three people costumed as Princess Diana, Ronald Reagan, and Pope John Paul II are seen having a three-way. It seems to me the most perfect of days.

In my twenties I start attending orgies in New York city but soon get bored. The sex parties are always dark. Why can't they look like weddings: flowers and grandmas dancing and tuxedos and cake and cock all mixed together? Eventually I do attend weddings that are, if not orgies, at least a combination of cake and cock.

As a cater waiter I pay the bills by serving mini-cheese souffles and pretending like I don't see the thirteen-year-old girls giving blowjobs to the boys underneath the tables while the parents drink, grandma dances disco, and the staff roll their eyes at the monotony of people who think they are undergoing a special day but are, from an overworked cater waiter's perspective, just reenacting the millions of special days that have come before. My work-mate Jose and I do it in the silver closet.

In 2004 I attend my first gay wedding at the same time George W. Bush is elected President, primarily because people don't want gays to marry. The wedding is typical: grandma dances disco; the guests both participate and are asked to be silent observers. It is an all day affair (or at least a five hour one) and some people can't wait for it to be over and some people love every moment and some are trapped somewhere between.

This is also the year Ronald Reagan dies and, inspired by Princess Diana's funeral a few years before, thousands of people descend on Washington to throw flowers on the white house lawn. A little while after that Pope John Paul II dies and the flowers are thrown again. The icon three-way ends in a pile of cellophane and sentiment and I begin writing *The Lily's Revenge*.

Other Kyogen Ideas

Box Office Boogie: a gogo flower or flower girl dances in the Box Office.

Outdoor Originals: Cast members perform their own performance art pieces outside the theater (all having to do with one of the themes of the play).

Cafe Camp: Flower Girls all call each other and everyone else Mary back and forth for fifteen minuets.

Marriage Bashing: three items that represent Prop 8, Gay Marriage, and the Institution of Marriage. Audience members can choose which one they'd like to bash. Maybe little piñatas.

Wedding Party Photo Shoot Booth: get your picture taken with the wedding party. Cut-out heads on the Bride and Groom so anyone can play either character.

Critics Soap Box: Stand on the soap box and tell the people what you hate and love about the play so far.

Carpe Diem Demonstration: How to stay in the moment. Various clowning (physical) ways to practice staying in the moment.

The Cake Smash: Smash cake in your loved one's face (comes with paper towels).

Peepshow Marriage Booth: Put a quarter in a slot and raise a screen that will reveal a Groom willing to propose to you. Could have various romantic settings as backgrounds (a moonlight night in Paris, in a gondola).

Songs We Flushed: Songs that have been cut from the show are performed in both the male and female bathrooms. They are switched in the next intermission.

SONGS WE FLUSHED FROM THE SHOW

No sheet music exists for the "Songs We Flushed From the Show." If you would like to perform them, feel free to listen to the tracks on the audio recording (available on iTunes under *The Lily's Revenge*) and learn the compositions from ear. In the case of the "Donut Song", there is no music available and new compositions to the lyric are encouraged.

THE NIGHT

THE NIGHT WILL GO TO BED
SHE WORKED THE GRAVEYARD SHIFT
AND NOW IGNORES THE NOISE THE DAY DOES TREAD
SHE FILLS HER EARS WITH COTTON
A BLINDFOLD 'ROUND HER EYES
TO DARKEN DAY, THE ROTTEN ROGUE
TO BLOCK THE RUDENESS OF THE STATUS QUO
OH OH OH OH OH, THE STATUS QUO.

THE NIGHT WILL TRY TO SLEEP
SHE'LL TOSS AND TURN AND ACHE
THE TRUCKS WILL CHURN AND BLARE THEIR MONSTER
    BEEP
THE SLAMMING DOORS, THOSE LEECHES
THAT SUCK THE CALM FROM NIGHT
THE DAY OH HOW SHE SCREECHES SO
HER DOMINANCE ON ALL THE WORLD SHE'LL CROW
OH OH OH OH

SO WHEN IT'S TIME FOR NIGHT TO WAKE
DO NOT YOU FEIGN SURPRISE
IF FEAR SHE FREES FROM FINGERED FOLDS
TO KNOT YOU UP IN CRIES
TO TEACH YOU SO OF WHAT IT IS
TO ACHE FOR SLUMBER'S REACH
TO BROWN THE YOUTH UNDER YOUR EYES
IT IS NOW YOU THE NIGHT WILL LEECH.

THE ARROGANCE OF YOU WHO THINK
YOUR WAY IS ALL THERE IS
WILL FIND THE NIGHT SEEPED IN YOUR DREAMS
UNTIL YOU WAKE WITH SCREAMS
ALL THROUGH THE NIGHT YOU'LL TOSS AND TURN
THE NIGHT'S SAD PLIGHT YOU'LL LEARN
FOR WHEN THE DAY NEXT COMES HER WAY
YOU'LL SLUMBER THROUGH HER NOISE AND LIGHT
AND WISH YOU COULD BUT FALL ASLEEP
IN ALL HER NORMALCY AND TRITE

SO TOMORROW DAY YOU'LL CREEP
INTO THE PRECIOUS LIGHT
AND BLACKEN OUT DAY'S BLATANCY SO NIGHT MAY
    SLEEP
YOU'LL OIL ALL THE CREAKING
YOU'LL TIP-TOE THROUGH THE STREETS
YOU'LL QUIET ALL YOUR SHRIEKING DEEDS
AND TO THE DAY YOU'LL WHISPER FEARFULLY AND
    LOW
SHHH
THE NIGHT HAS GONE TO BED.

THE DONUT SONG

GROOM LOVE.

BEAUTY COMES AS BEAUTY GOES
AND ALL THE LITTLE UNCONQUERABLE
OBSTACLES COLLECT,
UNWANTINGLY EXPOSED
ONCE BEAUTY GOES

AT THE DUNKIN DONUTS
A BEAUTIFUL GIRL SAT ACROSS FROM ME
ON THE NOD

IF SHE HAD BEEN UGLY
I WOULD HAVE BEEN REPULSED
BY THE DROOL THAT TRICKLED DOWN HER FACE
BUT BECAUSE SHE WAS A BEAUTY
I SAT AND WATCHED THE DROOL
GLISTEN IN THE FLORESCENT LIGHT
LINGERING IN
SUSPENDED FLIGHT
SLOWLY MADE ITS WAY TO HER SLIGHTLY EXPOSED NA-
    VEL

HER NAVEL SVELTE AND SMOOTH AS SUNSHINE
DEFINED BY YOUTH AND HEROIN FOR DINNER
COLLECTED HER DROOL
LIKE A PLASTIC WADING POOL.

SHE WAS IN HER OWN REALITY
SHE CROSSED THE MEMBRANE SEA
HEADED TO THE PLACE OF 99% NEVER USED
AND SHE WAS FREE

AND I FELT AN URGE TO TAKE THE GIRL HOME WITH
    ME

CLEAN HER HOMELESS SUN TANNED BODY
HAVE HER TELL ME ALL HER TROUBLES
LET HER SLEEP IN MY TWIN SIZED BED
WITH ME IN MINOR
RELATIVE
SAFETY

IF SHE HAD BEEN UGLY
I WOULD HAVE LAUGHED OR LOOKED AWAY
'CAUSE TRAGEDY IS MUCH TOO TRAGIC
WHEN ACCOMPANIED BY FAILED BEGINNINGS

AT THE DUNKIN DONUTS
I HAD A FRENCH CRULLER
AND A TWIST
AND BEAR CLAW
TWO SUGARED
A CREAM FILLING
HALF-A-DOZEN DONUTS
FILLED MY BODY
SENDING ME INTO A SUGAR COMA

AS IS SAT
JITTERING
DROOLING UNEXPECTEDLY
DOWN ONTO MY SLIGHTLY EXPOSED WHITE AS COT-
    TAGE CHEESE CONVEX NAVEL

THE GIRL AWOKE
SHE STARED AT ME
SUGAR CLUNG TO
THE CORNERS OF MY MOUTH
AND SLOWLY FELL DOWN
TO THE WHITE GLARING FLOOR
AS I SMILED
AS I TRIED TO SMILE
AT THE GIRL

THE GIRL SHE QUICKLY LOOKED AWAY
AS IF CAUGHT STARING AT A TRAGEDY
A FAILED BEGINNING
THEN SHE STUMBLED TO THE STREET
AND DISAPPEARED INTO THE PRETTY

BRIDE LOVE.
SOMETIMES WHEN YOU TALK OF YOUR EX LOVER
IT MAKES ME FEEL AS IF YOU WOULD
RATHER BE WITH HER
AND I KNOW YOU DON'T
WANT TO BE

BUT IT'S STILL HARD FOR ME
ALL THE SAME

AND I DON'T THINK THAT IT IS
JEALOUSY
AS MUCH AS IT'S THAT
I FEEL LIKE WE AREN'T BUILDING
OUR OWN STORIES
'CAUSE OUR STORIES CONSIST OF THE TIMES WE USED
    TO HANG AND TELL STORIES OF YOUR EX LOVER

AND WELL THAT'S NO FUN.
WHAT AM I GOING TO TELL OUR GRANDCHILDREN?
"ONCE GRANDPA AND I WENT ON A PICNIC
AND HE TALKED THE ENTRE TIME OF HIS
FIRST LOVE"
SOMETIMES I REQUIRE
YOUR NEED TO BE WITH ME
AS CO-DEPENDENT AS THAT MAY BE

GROOM LOVE.
MY EX-LOVE SHINED AS
BRIGHT AS MOONLIGHT
THE BEST LIGHT
WE DANCED 'TIL FOUR AM
THEN SUNBATHED BY THE SEINE
WE LAY IN BED AND DREAMED OUR DAYS
WE ROWED OUR OARS SO FAR AWAY
FROM HERE.

BRIDE LOVE and GROOM LOVE.
BEAUTY COMES AS BEAUTY GOES
AND ALL THE LITTLE UNCONQUERABLE
OBSTACLES COLLECT
UNWANTINGLY EXPOSED
ONCE BEAUTY GOES

HOW IT USED TO BE

BRIDE HOPEFUL.
OH ME HOW IT USED TO BE
OH MY HOW IT MAKES YOU SIGH
OH WHY DID THE WORLD AGREE
THE KEY IS TO MODIFY

THEY CHANGED ALL THE WORDS AND WAYS
NO THEE, NO MORE THOU

NOW IT'S "YOU," "HEY," OH WOW
HOW I DISAVOW THESE DAYS

LILY.

YOU WEREN'T HOW IT USED TO BE
I LEARNT THIS FROM YOU NOT THEE
I'VE COME TO BELIEVE
THE PAST WE SHOULD LEAVE
SO NOW YOU AND ME CAN SEE

THE PRESENT OF BEING HERE
THIS PLEASANTRY'S A FRONTIER
SURPRISING AND NEW
THE NOW'S QUITE A COO
I DO DISAVOW YOUR FEARS

BRIDE HOPEFUL.

OH ME HOW IT USED TO BE

LILY.

OH MY WHAT A SUPPLE SKY

BRIDE HOPEFUL.

WE'LL SIGH AND JUST DISAGREE
TO BE IS FOR THEE, NOT I

LILY.

BUT CHANGING A WORD OR WAY
OF HOW AND OF WHO
TRUE LOVE CAN IMBUE
BRINGS YOU AND MY VOW THIS DAY

THE WAY OF THE WORLD

BRIDE PUPPET.

THERE'S THE ONE OF THE PRINCE WHO DID KISS THE
     BEAUTY
WHO HAD PRICKED AND THEN SLEPT
WHAT A LOVELY DUTY
BUT TO SLEEP AND AWAKE TO FIND LIFE IS GRANTED
AND THE DANGERS HAVE BEEN SORTED
AND YOUR FUTURE HAS BEEN PLANTED

LILY.

LIKE ME.
THERE'S THE ONE WITH THE GIRL WHO DID EAT THE
     APPLE
SHE DID BITE AND THEN SLEPT
TO GET TO THE CHAPEL

YES SHE DREAMED AND AWOKE TO FIND LOVE HAD
    FOUND HER
AND THE WICKED WITCH HAD FALLEN
AND HER MIRROR IT HAD CROWNED HER
LIKE ME.

BRIDE PUPPET.
THERE'S THE ONE OF THE GIRL AND THE INCANTATION
THAT DID SWITCH A DEAR PRINCE
TO A LOWLY STATION
YES A FROG WAS THE PRINCE AND A WITCH HAD CURSED
    HIM
AND TO SHARE HIS BED FOR THREE NIGHTS
WAS THE WAY OUR GIRL REVERSED HIM

LILY.
OOOOO-WEEEE.

LILY/BRIDE.
STILL THE WAY OF THE WORLD IS TO DREAM AND
    CHERISH
ALL THAT'S PAST AND TO LEARN
WHO DOES THRIVE AND PERISH
WE CAN SLEEP AND AWAKE AND FIND WISHES
    GRANTED
SO DREAM AWAY TO SAVE THE DAY
AND HAVE A LIFE ENCHANTED
WITH ENNUI

ALICE IN SLASHERLAND

Qui
Nguyen

About the Collaboration
Geeking Out Onstage

When the idea of Vampire Cowboys first began taking shape in the spring of 2000, with the first collaboration between playwright/fight director Qui Nguyen and director Robert Ross Parker, New York Comic Con wasn't even in existence; conventions of that sort were still mainly relegated to dingy hotel conference halls with zero Hollywood presence, and superhero movies had yet to meet their James Gunns, Josh Whedons, and Christopher Nolans. In 2000, geek was still very far from chic, so to create a theatre company whose main focus was to mix theatrical spectacle with stories of zombies, superheroes, and ninjas seemed like an idea meant for a different multiverse. But like any young Peter Parker trying to figure out if his webshooters would keep him from going splat on the concrete, at some point a superhero just has to take a leap. So in the spring of 2003, Vampire Cowboys launched into New York City, and in the process of getting their first production grant, producer Abby Marcus would create the term that would define them, become their mission, and name a new theatrical genre that would one day become a sort of beacon for all bullied outsiders who longed to see shows written for them. That term on that first grant proposal would be "Geek Theatre."

The "Geek Theatre" of Vampire Cowboys is a mixture of pop culture fun and strong imaginative theatricality. All their productions use puppetry, music, original songs, multimedia, and loads of first class fight choreography to tell their stories. But underneath, the part that isn't always the focus of their marketing blurbs is the thing that has won them so many dedicated fans. Amidst all the spectacle and fights, the company always highlights diversity, strong female characters, and stories that are built on character, heart, and those often ignored by mainstream pop culture as the centerpieces of all their shows. They make superheroes for those who don't often get to see people that look like themselves on stage and screen saving the world.

In their decade-long history, riding the same wave that has earned Hollywood billions, Vampire Cowboys has had an incredible run of sold-out productions and critically-acclaimed shows, and has since witnessed a new generation of young theatre professionals follow in their footsteps at creating "Geek Theatre." They've became the first and only theatre organization to ever be officially sponsored by New York Comic Con and in 2010 earned a prestigious *Village Voice* Obie for their consistency at making outstanding work. They are, as the *Village Voice* called them, New York's "best army of geeks."

§

Alice in Slasherland *is loads of bloody fun (quite literally). It has lovable teen characters, hysterical demonic monsters, badass fights, gallons of blood effects, and a fun adventure mixed with a lot of heart. Artistically speaking, it also pushed our company in new directions. Unlike our previous shows where we utilized puppetry to create spaceship battles, dragon fights, and special effects,* Alice in Slasherland *was the first time we used a puppet as main character who would require the same physical flexibility and emotional expressiveness of a human actor to deliver everything from dialogue to fight choreography. The VC team has always encouraged me to "write the impossible." So with that philosophy in mind,* Alice in Slasherland *doubled down on that objective and the outcome became the perfect Halloween show for our company that's known for weaving awesome pop-culture stories and innovative onstage theatricality.*

—Qui Nguyen, Playwright

Mission Statement: Vampire Cowboys

Vampire Cowboys is an Obie Award-winning "Geek Theatre" company that creates and produces new works of theatre based in action/adventure and dark comedy with a comic book aesthetic. The company actively pursues the mating of different genres with varied theatrical styles to create an eclectic structure to tell its stories. The company aims to bridge the gap between mass media entertainment and the performing arts, exposing the community to challenging, thought-provoking live entertainment rooted in today's pop culture vernacular.

About the Author

Originally from Arkansas, Qui Nguyen is a playwright, TV writer, and Co-Founder of the Obie Award-winning Vampire Cowboys. His plays include *Vietgone* (commissioned by South Coast Rep); *War is F**king Awesome* (Sundance Theatre Lab); *Samantha Rai and the Shogun of Fear* (Children's Theatre Company); *She Kills Monsters* (The Flea, Buzz22 Chicago/Steppenwolf, Company One); *Soul Samurai* (Ma-Yi Theater/Vampire Cowboys); *Krunk Fu Battle Battle* (East West Players); *Aliens vs. Cheerleaders* (Keen Teens); *Trial By Water* (Ma-Yi Theater); *Bike Wreck* (EST); and the VC productions of *Six Rounds of Vengeance, The Inexplicable Redemption of Agent G, Alice in Slasherland, Fight Girl Battle World, Men of Steel, Living Dead in Denmark, A Beginner's Guide to Deicide,* and *Vampire Cowboy Trilogy.* He is a proud member of New Dramatists, The Playwrights' Center, Ensemble Studio Theatre, and the Ma-Yi Writers Lab. For TV, he writes on the Emmy Award-winning children's cartoon *Peg+Cat,* airing on PBS.

Cast of Characters

LEWIS, a young nerdy fan-boy who accidentally opens a rift into Hell. Think Michael Cera, but even more virginal.

MARGARET, a young nerdy cheerleader. She's both sweet and tough when needed. She's also Lewis's best friend and the girl he's been in love with since "forevs."

ALICE, a young teenage girl recently risen from the dead. Though dark-eyed and attractive, she has forgotten how to be human since her death and spends the course of the story "re-learning" how to be normal. Whenever she's "hungry," she acts & moves like the girl from "The Ring." When satiated though, she talks and moves like a regular (but badass) girl.

EDGAR, a demonic teddy bear that fancies Alice in a romantic way. Though he's from Hell, his speech and demeanor are very much influenced by contemporary hip-hop and he sounds remarkably like Tracy Morgan. This actor also plays the following roles:

DUNCAN, high school quarterback.

GARRETH, a demon with a French accent.

TINA, head cheerleader. Queen Bee of the Mean Girls. Will ultimately end up being the big bad of the story. This actor also plays the following roles:

HURT, a fat demon that hungers for human flesh.

MATILDA, a winged demon.

DEPUTY BARROW, a victim.

JACOB, the slasher of slasherland, he's this story's Michael Myers. This actor also plays the following roles:

T-BONE, a mugger.

BURNOUT, a fat demon that hungers for human flesh.

TOMMY, high school bully.

SHERIFF DUNWOODY, a victim possessed by Garreth.

Acknowledgments

Alice in Slasherland received its World Premiere on March 18th, 2010, produced by Vampire Cowboys (Abby Marcus, Producer) at HERE Arts Center. It was directed by Robert Ross Parker with the following cast and crew:

ALICE	Amy Kim Waschke
LEWIS	Carlo Alban
MARGARET	Bonnie Sherman
EDGAR, DUNCAN, GARRETH	Sheldon Best
TINA, HURT, MATILDA, DEPUTY BARROW	Andrea Marie Smith
JACOB, T-BONE, BURNOUT, TOMMY, SHERIFF	Tom Myers
Scenic / Lighting Designer	Nick Francone
Costume Designer	Jessica Shay
Sound Designer	Shane Rettig
Video Designer	Matthew Tennie
Puppet Design / Construction	David Valentine
Production Stage Managers	Danielle Buccino
Assistant Stage Manager	Marina Steinberg
Props / Gore	Lex Friedman
Publicity / Press Rep	Jim Baldassare
Photographers	Jim Baldassare, Theresa Squire

Bonnie Sherman, Sheldon Best, Carlo Alban, and Amy Kim Waschke in the world premiere of *Alice in Slasherland,* produced by Vampire Cowboys in March 2010. Photo: Theresa Squire.

ALICE IN SLASHERLAND
by Qui Nguyen

Prologue

(In the darkness...)

LEWIS. *(Voiceover:)* I looked, and behold, there was the fourth emissary; and his name was Death; and Hades followed with him. He was given the authority to kill with sword and wrath and the Earth shuddered for the end was near.
– Revelations 20:13

(Projection: Twenty years ago...
In pitch black, we hear the sound of fast breathing and rain.)

ALICE. Oh god oh god oh god oh god oh god oh god oh god oh god.

(ALICE, a young girl, runs onto the dark stage carrying a lit flashlight. She tries to quiet herself as she frantically finds a corner to hide.)

Shhhhhhhhh...shhhhhhhh...shhhhhhhh...

(We see that she's wet from rain and drenched in blood. Clearly some very bad shit has just gone down.
In the darkness, we hear another set of footsteps approaching. As they do, ALICE holds her breath as she turns off her flashlight.
In the darkness, we hear the footsteps getting closer.
And closer...
And closer...
Lightning flash; and we see the large ominous blood-covered figure of JACOB standing onstage with a large machete in hand and a Halloween mask covering his face.)

JACOB. *(With a deep gravelly voice:)* Late...

(We hear him moving about in the darkness. Occasionally we see more flashes of lightning which show JACOB at different points on the stage on each flash.)

Late...

(Finally, after a tense while, we hear him exit the stage completely.
ALICE sits in the darkness alone for a bit, too scared to move. But as she realizes that JACOB has indeed left, she turns on her flashlight and cautiously looks around. Seeing that she's alone, she begins to stand up. As she does though, we see that JACOB is standing directly behind her.)

(She tries to run away, but it's too late. He grabs her.)

ALICE. AAAAAAH!!!

>*(Blackout!*
>*Projection: ALICE IN SLASHERLAND.)*

ACT I

Scene One

>*(Projection: CHAPTER ONE: NOT ALL ANGELS FALL FROM HEAVEN*
>*Projection: Present night…*
>*Video: LEWIS'S VIDEO BLOG.)*

LEWIS. Yo, whazzup, whazzup, whazzup! It's yo' boy, Lewis, coming straight at ya from the internets! And do I got some news for you tonight! Tonight, my cool cats and hot hotties, yo' boy is making an appearance at Tina Carpenter's Halloween party out in Country Club Terrace! Cause, you know, no party can truly "groovis" without ya boy Lewis. And for all y'all wondering about if my soon-to-be main squeeze is gonna be in attendance? Well, fear not, yours truly is accompanying the Magnificent Margaret May herself.

>*(LEWIS shows a picture of Margaret May to the camera. She's indeed super-cute. A mixture of nerdy cuteness and cheerleader sexy.)*

BLAM! Look at that hotness. So hot. So sexy. So nice!
And check it: tonight—tonight's the night it all gets real for Margaret and me cause tonight is the night I finally lay down what's the what's up on all the feelings that I'm feelin' for my girl.
It's gonna be like—

>*(His voice drops an octave:)*

"Yo, Margaret, what's up?"
"Hi, Lewis, you looking all sexy up in here looking like Wolverine and shit."
"Baby, you know you the only girl in this place that can make my claws go SNIKT!"
And she'll be all like "Aw, now you making me blush."
And then I'll lay it down all Barry White smooth with "Yo, Margaret, can we pause and get real for a hot second? Do you mind if we get real?"
And then…that's when I drop…the L-bomb.
Wish me luck. This has been a long time comin'. Peace!

>*(Cut to…*
>*Lights up on the party where we find a very drunk TINA, head cheerleader and host of this shindig, dressed in a truly outrageous naughty devil costume. She's stumbling around, drinking straight from the bottle, and holding a fancy-looking hand mirror.)*

(She spots DUNCAN, *high school football star, who's chilling.)*

TINA. Hey there sexy, do you wanna see something scary?

*(*TINA *shoves her hand-mirror at* DUNCAN's *face.)*

Little Lucifer's Angel.

DUNCAN. Yo, say what?

TINA. "Little Lucifer's Angel." Say it three times in a mirror on Halloween night and the devil will appear.

DUNCAN. Man, that's some straight up slumber party bullshit.

TINA. Fine. Then if you don't want to do something scary, then do you want to do something drunk?

DUNCAN. Like what?

*(*TINA *gives* DUNCAN *a flirtatious smile.)*

TINA. Me.

*(*TINA *grabs* DUNCAN *and pulls him into a dark corner giggling and smiling. Focus shifts to* MARGARET, *a cheerleader [but in this moment dressed in a Halloween costume], awkwardly wall-flowering.* LEWIS, *dressed in a Wolverine costume strolls up with two cups in his hand.)*

LEWIS. Wow, some party, huh?

MARGARET. I guess.

LEWIS. Tina really has a lot of friends.

MARGARET. All the slutty ones do.

LEWIS. Haha, that's funny. You're funny.
Um, here's your drink.

MARGARET. What is this?

LEWIS. Something, something, with vodka.

MARGARET. Mmm. Tastes like loose morals.

LEWIS. That's strange. Mine just tastes like a gateway-drug towards a lifetime of broken dreams.
Not really. It actually just tastes like pineapple.

MARGARET. Thanks for coming with me tonight, Lewis. I hate these things. It's always like night of the living sorostitutes up in these parties.

LEWIS. I don't know. I think it could be fun.

*(*MARGARET *shoots* LEWIS *a look.)*

I'm serious. This could be a nice night. Life changing even.

MARGARET. Life changing?

LEWIS. You never know. Maybe something could happen that could change everything.

MARGARET. Like what?

LEWIS. Like...uh...

    (LEWIS suddenly clams up.)

MARGARET. *(Looking at* LEWIS's *costume:)* So what is this costume supposed to be?

LEWIS. I'm a superhero. Snickety Snikt. I got claws.

    (LEWIS gives MARGARET *a big smile.)*

MARGARET. You look cute. Superhero apparently looks really good on you. It really brings out your eyes.

LEWIS. Thanks!

    (Manning up:)

So...um...

    (Speaking lightning fast:)

Can we "get real" for a second?

MARGARET. What?

LEWIS. *(Still talking way too fast:)* Can we "get real"? You know "get real." Can we get real for hot second, Miss Margaret May?

MARGARET. Uh. Sure?

LEWIS. Well—um—we've been friends for a long time, right?

MARGARET. Yeah.

LEWIS. And in that time we've been tight, right? Shared some good memories?

MARGARET. Yeah.

LEWIS. *(Calming down:)* And, well, the thing is—
AND sometimes with friends like us, things happen that would make one pause to say—

    (DUNCAN reappears.)

MARGARET. Holy shit!

LEWIS. Yes, that's actually what I was going to—

MARGARET. Is that Duncan Price!?!

LEWIS. D-Duncan Price?

MARGARET. Oh my God, Lewis, I heard Duncan broke up with Penelope Taylor. Can you believe that? Penelope fucking Taylor!

LEWIS. I can't say I've been keeping up.

MARGARET. Lewis, I've had a crush on Duncan Price like forevs. FOREVS!

LEWIS. You have?

MARGARET. Have you ever seen his abs? They're fucking man-tastic! If I could, I would put every inch of his fine ass body into my mouth.

LEWIS. Wow, that's…slightly pornographic.

MARGARET. Oh God, I should make my move tonight, shouldn't I? Spit some game.

LEWIS. Well, I don't know about—

MARGARET. You know what? You're right. I'm going to talk to him. You said it, this could be life changing. I should do it. Oh my God, Lewis, I'm going to do it. I'm so glad you're here.

LEWIS. Yeah, me too—

MARGARET. Thanks, Lewis! Wish me luck!

(MARGARET *exits.)*

LEWIS. *(As* MARGARET *exits:)* Okay. Um, bye. I love you.

(TINA *enters.)*

TINA. NERDBOY!

LEWIS. Oh God…

TINA. NERDBOY! What the fuck are you doing here at my party?

LEWIS. Oh, hi Tina! Nice…costume. It's very…wow, I don't think I'm old enough to look at you.

TINA. Don't "Hi Tina" me! What are you fucking doing in my fucking house? Are you here to rob me?

LEWIS. No.

TINA. I think you're fucking robbing me, robber!

LEWIS. I'm not robbing you.

TINA. I'm gonna call the police. POLICE!

LEWIS. Tina!

TINA. I'm just fucking with you, Lewis. Get a clue.

(TINA *eyes down* LEWIS.)

You know what, Lewis Diaz? You don't look so bad tonight.

LEWIS. I don't?

TINA. No. Not at all. Almost yum even.

LEWIS. Thank you?

TINA. *(Looking at* LEWIS's *Wolverine costume:)* Have you been working out?

LEWIS. No, these are fake—

TINA. Do you wanna do something scary?

LEWIS. Like what?

　　　　*(*TINA *sticks the mirror into* LEWIS's *face like she did earlier with Duncan.)*

TINA. Little Lucifer's Angel.

LEWIS. Seriously? Isn't that what little kids do at parties?

TINA. Well, if you don't wanna do something scary, then do you want to do something drunk?

　　　　(As LEWIS *looks around, he sees* MARGARET *flirting with* DUN-CAN.)*

MARGARET. You are so hot!

DUNCAN. And you are so…right about that assessment.

LEWIS. Actually, you know what?
Hand it here. Let's have some fun. Just you and me.
Little Lucifer's Angel, Little Lucifer's Angel…
Little…
Lucifer's…
Angel.

TINA. …

LEWIS. Aaaaaaaaah!

TINA. *(Legitimately upset:)* Oh my God! What?

LEWIS. Nothing. I'm just being…funny. You know. Haha?

TINA. So since scary didn't work out, do you wanna maybe do something… drunk?

LEWIS. Sure. Like what?

TINA. *(Smiling coyly:)* Me.

LEWIS. …

TINA. So?

LEWIS. Yeah, you know what? I'm all good.

TINA. What?

LEWIS. I'm good.

TINA. FUCK YOU, NERD BOY!

LEWIS. I don't mean anything by it, it's just I have feelings for—

TINA. Fuck you! You know how many guys wanna get up on this? On this? It's like a fucking water-park slip-and-slide down there.

LEWIS. Tina, calm down.

TINA. FUCK YOU, LEWIS DIAZ! Lick my asshole, asshole!

> (*TINA storms off.*
> *LEWIS turns, silently watching* MARGARET *and* DUNCAN *flirt and begin kissing. He exits.*
> *As lights fade on* MARGARET *and* DUNCAN, *we see [with some scary sound support] a dark disheveled* ALICE *quickly cross the back of the stage behind them [Think creepy girl from "The Ring" movies].*
> *Cut to…*
> *We see* LEWIS *walking home through a very suburban neighborhood trying to use his car-keys to "beep" his car.*
> *As he does, we see the rotting decaying image of* ALICE *appearing in the background.*
> *As* LEWIS *turns to see what's behind him, a hand reaches out from the darkness and grabs him.*)

LEWIS. Aaaaaaah!

> (*It's not Alice, but a mugger.*)

T-BONE. Shut the fuck up, kid!

LEWIS. What? Who?

T-BONE. I said shut the fuck up.

LEWIS. Wait. Who are you? What do you want?

T-BONE. Well, I'm a guy with a gun holding you by the throat in the middle of the night. So does it really fucking matter?

LEWIS. Good point.

T-BONE. Give me your fuckin' wallet!

LEWIS. What?

T-BONE. Your fucking wallet, bitch! Now!

LEWIS. Here! Take it!

T-BONE. See how that easy that was. You get to live and it only cost you…

> (*Reaching into Lewis's wallet:*)

An expired condom?

LEWIS. Hehe, I was, uh, hanging out with cheerleaders tonight?

T-BONE. Oh yeah? Well, it certainly doesn't look like you got lucky, now did it?

> (*T-BONE points his gun at* LEWIS.)

LEWIS. No, don't! I'll give you whatever you want!

T-BONE. Sorry, kid. That's not how this goes down. I don't dig on eye-witnesses. It's a professional standard, really.

> (T-BONE *pulls the hammer back on his gun. As he does, we see* ALICE *in the far background walking across the stage.*
> *Then suddenly and supernaturally fast, she's on top of* T-BONE.)

T-BONE. What the hell?

> (ALICE *pulls him into the darkness.*)

T-BONE. Oh God! Get off me, GET OFF ME!!!

> (*There's a struggle, we hear gunfire, and then a huge spray of blood.*
> LEWIS, *who's been watching in total disbelief, starts to leave. But before he can escape,* ALICE *is in his face.*)

LEWIS. (*Terrified:*) I'm—uh—just going to go…home…now. Okay?

> (*She slowly walks up to him.*
> *He freezes in fear.*)

Oh god.

> (*She stands face to face with* LEWIS.
> *She suddenly grabs him and kisses him on the mouth. She then suddenly passes out in his arms.*)

Um. Hello? Hello? Are you okay?

> (*Cut to…*
> *Margaret's bedroom.*
> *Lights up on Margaret's bed. At the angle we're at, we only see her head-board. She is completely hidden behind it.*)

MARGARET. This is crazy. I can't believe this is happening.

EDGAR. Believe it, baby.

> (MARGARET *suddenly sits up. We can see her, but not the other person lying in bed with her.*)

MARGARET. Shut up. I don't do this. This isn't what I do. Why did I pick you up? I just saw you in Tina's bedroom and picked you up and brought you home? I don't do that. I don't steal things. What kind of dumb slut am I?

EDGAR. What's with the hate, baby?

MARGARET. Don't call me baby! This is a nightmare.

EDGAR. You keep pouring the hate-arade like you do, I'm gonna take it personal.

MARGARET. Oh God, why did I have to drink so much!?!

EDGAR. Don't blame the alcohol, sweet stuff.

MARGARET. I'm going fucking crazy. I am.

EDGAR. You're not going crazy.

MARGARET. I'm not? Then how do I explain you, huh? What the fuck are you doing in my bed?

EDGAR. Look, hot stuff, it's all good. Things don't always go as planned— I was looking for my girl tonight, but instead I found you. We'll make it work.

MARGARET. Wait. You were looking for your girlfriend?

EDGAR. Yeah, but that can wait til morning. Now come to bed and let's cuddle.

MARGARET. No.

EDGAR. You don't believe I can be cuddly?

MARGARET. No, I can totally believe you can be cuddly. That's not what's hard to believe. It's just…the talking is weird. And the walking.

EDGAR. And why's that? Talk to your honeybear.

MARGARET. Do not refer to yourself as honeybear!

EDGAR. Come on, hot stuff. Let me give you some love.

MARGARET. Will you stop? I said no!

EDGAR. How bout a hug then? Everybody can use a hug.
A little huggy wuggy for Margie Wargie? I'll let you stick your nose into my tum tum. Rub it around a little.

MARGARET. Um…

EDGAR. I wub you.

MARGARET. Stop it.

EDGAR. I weely weely wub you.

MARGARET. Fine. Just come here.

> (MARGARET *picks up* EDGAR *so we can see him.*
> *As it turns out, he's just a wee little talking teddy bear.*
> *He hugs* MARGARET.)

MARGARET. Yeah, I guess you are cuddly.

EDGAR. *(Lecherously:)* Mmm, so are you.

MARGARET. Ew, gross. Get off me.

EDGAR. *(Singing:)* When I get that feeling
I get that sexual feeling.
Sexual!

> (*Cut to…*
> LEWIS *is bringing* ALICE *into his bedroom.*)

LEWIS. Shhhhhh. You have to be really quiet, okay? If my mom finds out you're in my room, she'll kill me.

ALICE. Hehehehe.

LEWIS. No, that's not funny. Seriously. She really will kill me.

(ALICE *begins rummaging around Lewis's bedroom. She's very feral-like. She finds a stack of dirty magazines.*)

LEWIS. Oh, hey! Don't look at those. Those aren't mine. I'm keeping those for a friend. I just look at them because I think they're funny…

ALICE. Hmmm…

LEWIS. You have no idea what I'm saying, do you?

(ALICE *doesn't respond.*)

If you understand what I'm saying, blink twice.
Laugh.
Scream.
Rub your boobs.
Nothing at all, huh?
Like I can say anything to you right now and you wouldn't have a clue. Like… actually those are my magazines and I masturbate all the time!

(*Suddenly scared that she might understand him:*)

But not really. I'm not like a pervert or anything, it's just that I'm a teenage boy and I have way too much free time on my hands.
Like when I say too much free time, I mean I sorta have no life whatsoever besides school and my video blog that no one actually ever sees except for like these two older German guys in Germany who totally have a crush on me in a totally NAMBLA pedo kind of way.
Like thank you for saving my life this evening, but it's sorta not that big of a deal since, ya know, I'm not really that big of a deal.
Like I'm a total fucking loser.
Like all I wanted to do tonight was tell Margaret, this girl I've been in love with since like forever, how much I dig her and yet I still fucked that all up. Because I fucking suck. Like totally.

(ALICE *nuzzles her head onto* LEWIS's *chest.* LEWIS *smiles.*)

Wow. You know you're really easy to talk to.

(*Light shifts to Tina's house.* TINA *is stumbling around her home. She's holding her hand-mirror.*)

TINA. (*Talking to herself and impressed by her own "come-on line":*) You wanna do something drunk? Like me?

(*The monstrous* JACOB *appears. He's gigantic and still wearing the same Halloween mask we saw when he was chasing* ALICE *down.*)

TINA. *(Spotting* JACOB*:)* Hey. Party's over, perv. Get out of my house. Did you hear me? I said party's fucking over. Go home.
By the way, this is a pretty fucking stupid costume. What are you supposed to be anyways? A Halloween janitor? Yeah, that's real sexy.

> *(Lights shift back to Lewis's room.)*

LEWIS. So do you speak maybe French or Spanish or something?
Bonjour?
Hola?
Ni-Hao Ma?
Moshi Moshi?
Anything?

> *(*ALICE *pulls back her matted hair and smiles at* LEWIS*.)*

You know if it weren't for the fact that you're totally mad creepy, you're actually very pretty.

> *(Lights shift back to Tina's house.*
> *In the background behind* JACOB*, we see the shadows of demonic creatures moving around.)*

TINA. Hey, who the fuck are they? Party's over, assholes! Go home!

> *(We hear the demonic creatures make noises. It's all very demonic-y.*
> *Lights up on both Tina's and Lewis's homes. We see them both now simultaneously.)*

LEWIS. So, um, can I get you anything?
You can borrow anything you want. T-shirts. Shorts. Anything. Tomorrow, we can get you some real clothes.

TINA. Uh…what are you guys doing in my house?
Are you here to rob me?

> *(*LEWIS *reaches on the ground and picks up a stuffed rabbit.)*

LEWIS. Do you like stuffed animals? This is Mister Nick.

> *(He tosses it to* ALICE*. As it lands in her hands…)*

TINA. *(Trying to change the vibe:)* Do you want to do something drunk?

> *(*JACOB *suddenly sticks his machete through* TINA*'s chest as the stuffed animal hits* ALICE*'s hands.)*

TINA. Aaaaaah!

ALICE. *(As if feeling Tina's pain from afar:)* Aaaaaah!

> *(*TINA *dies.* ALICE *goes crazy.* LEWIS *holds onto* ALICE *to calm her down as* JACOB *lords over the fallen* TINA*. Demonic hands reach out and pull* TINA*'s body into the darkness.*
> *Lights go down on Tina's house and shifts completely to Lewis's home.)*

LEWIS. Shhhh! Holy shit. It's just a stuffed animal. You're really not into stuffed animals, are you? Look, you're safe here. Shhhhh. You're safe.

(ALICE *cowers into the corner.*)

Uh, okay, if you want to chill out there, that's okay. Um, look, I'm just going to go to the bathroom to wash up. Feel free to take anything you want and put on some clean clothes, alright? Just try to relax, okay? We'll figure out everything in the morning.

(LEWIS *begins to leave...*
ALICE *runs up and blocks him from walking out.*)

Uh...you're sorta in my—

(ALICE *takes him by the hand and leads him back to the corner where she was cowering. She makes him sit with her. She cuddles up to him.*)

Okay, or we can do this.

ALICE. *(Slowly and almost painfully, she speaks the first words she's spoken in twenty years:)* Alice.

LEWIS. What? Your name's Alice?
That's funny...cause my name's Lewis and yours is Alice.
You know...like the story?
Alice in Wonderland?
Which this situation actually doesn't resemble at all.
Like in any way.
Not even in theme.
Huh.
Well, I guess that was a pretty useless observation.

(ALICE *smiles at* LEWIS.)

You're going to be okay, Alice, I promise. It's all going to be okay.

(ALICE *and* LEWIS *cuddle.*)

Scene Two

(*Projection: CHAPTER TWO: IT'S SO NOT OKAY*
Projection: Five days later...
MARGARET *runs onto stage screaming. Her cheerleading uniform is covered in blood. She's in a high school classroom.*)

MARGARET. OH GOD! Oh god oh god oh god oh god!

(LEWIS *&* DUNCAN *jump out of the shadows and grab* MARGARET *and cover her mouth. They cower under a desk.*)

LEWIS. Shhhhhhhhh!

MARGARET. Lewis! Duncan! Th-th-there's demons everywhere.

LEWIS. Shhhhh. We gotta keep quiet, okay? We don't want to draw attention.

MARGARET. They killed our Algebra teacher.

LEWIS. I know. They also ate Principal Tolson as well.

MARGARET. Oh God.

LEWIS. Look at me. We're going to be okay. We just have to maintain a low profile for right now. You're with me?

MARGARET. Yeah, I'm with you.

LEWIS. Good.

DUNCAN. Guys, we can't just hide here. We gotta do something.

LEWIS. I told you, Duncan, for right now, we hide.

DUNCAN. What kinda pussy ass shit is that? I say we grab some mother-fuckin' guns and shoot them whackass motherfuckers.

LEWIS. Duncan, actually, now that I think about it—oh my God—that sounds like...A HORRIBLE FUCKING IDEA! Did you not just hear her? They killed our Algebra teacher and our principal. And where are we supposed to find some—quote—motherfuckin' guns—

MARGARET. End quote!

DUNCAN. All's I'm saying is...she's sporty, you're smart, with our powers combined, we can go all Captain Badass on those bitches.

LEWIS. This isn't a fucking football game, Duncan. You can't just audible your way around a demon.

DUNCAN. There's no such thing as demons. Even if they were, it ain't like we're powerless. Yo, these muscles ain't just for looks. Ain't that right, Melissa?

MARGARET. My name's Margaret!

DUNCAN. Whatevs. So what do you say, geek?

LEWIS. I say—

>   *(Crash!)*

Hide!

>   *(HURT & BURNOUT, two demons, slowly creep into the space as the teens hide.)*

HURT. Fee-Fi-Fo-Fum!
I'm in the mood to eat a few teenage bums.

BURNOUT. Doesn't look like anyone's here.

HURT. Don't be a dum dum, dum dum! You just have to sniff for 'em.

BURNOUT. Sniff, sniff, sniff.

(HURT *swipes the desk away that* LEWIS, MARGARET, *and* DUNCAN *are hiding under.*)

HURT. Boo.

LEWIS, MARGARET, & DUNCAN. Aaaaaaah!

HURT. Oh, lookie there, brethren! Snacks!

BURNOUT. I do enjoy me some snacks.

HURT. Yum, yum.

LEWIS. Stay back!

BURNOUT. We're going to enjoy eating your skin...

DUNCAN. Did that motherfucker just say he was gonna eat our skin?

HURT. We will bathe in your blood and feast upon your virgin flesh.

MARGARET. Actually, none of us are virgins, asshole!

LEWIS. *(This is news to* LEWIS*:)* Since when!?!

DUNCAN. Fuck you, motherfuckers. Do you know who you're talking to? I'm an All-State Blue Chip Quarterback. I bench two-fifty and run the 40 at under five.

LEWIS. Duncan, stop!

HURT. Impressive.

BURNOUT. This human offers to be eaten first.

HURT. Very noble.

BURNOUT. We will delight in sucking the marrow from your bones.

DUNCAN. The only thing you two are gonna be sucking on is gonna be my dick!

(*The demons rip off* DUNCAN's *dick and throw him offstage.*)

DUNCAN. Aaaaaah!

LEWIS. Oh God.

HURT. That food was far too loud.

BURNOUT. It was.

HURT. Maybe the other two cows will be less noisy.

MARGARET. Um, Lewis. What do we do?

LEWIS. Hey demons, you don't want to eat us. We're really...fattening?

MARGARET. What?

LEWIS. Yeah, you don't want to get fat, right? That would be really unhealthy.

HURT. Is this creature calling us fat?

BURNOUT. I don't like being called fat.

LEWIS. Fuck it.
Aaaaaah!

> *(LEWIS suddenly tries to attack the demons by surprise. They knock him away easily. They grab MARGARET.)*

MARGARET. Help!

HURT. This one looks absolutely delicious.

BURNOUT. Want to split her?

HURT. Yes. Let's.

MARGARET. Lewis. Help!

LEWIS. *(Getting back on his feet:)* No don't! Take me instead.

BURNOUT. Instead? There's no instead, little human. There's only firsts and seconds.

HURT. She's firsts.

BURNOUT. You're seconds.

MARGARET. No, stop!

BURNOUT. I like it when they fight. It makes them all salty.

> *(Suddenly, ALICE appears. She's now decked out looking all super awesome.)*

ALICE. Surprise, bitches. Remember me?

> *(HURT and BURNOUT toss MARGARET aside.)*

HURT. The Harbinger!

BURNOUT. Harbinger.

ALICE. I'm not a harbinger!

> *(ALICE attacks them. With feral grace, ALICE beats the shit out of her foes. She stabs one and bites the neck out of the other. They both die.)*

ALICE. *(With blood all over her lips:)* Mmmm. Violence tastes yummy.

LEWIS. Margaret, are you alright?

MARGARET. What the hell is happening?

LEWIS. Well. Um. Hell is.

MARGARET. What?

LEWIS. Hell is happening. Like literally.

MARGARET. Uh. Okay. What?

ALICE. Your world's being consumed by Hades through a dimensional rift that was created five nights ago on the Devil's holiday.

MARGARET. What did that bitch just say?

LEWIS. There's a hole. Bad shit is coming out of it.

MARGARET. This is a joke, right?

LEWIS. No. No joke. Hell's a-coming. We have to stop it.

MARGARET. And how are we going to do that?

ALICE. There's a conduit.

MARGARET. A what?

ALICE. A conduit. An object or thing that acts as a key keeping the rift open. We destroy the conduit, we close the rift.

LEWIS. We have to get to Tina Carpenter's. Like now.

MARGARET. Tina's?

JACOB. *(Voiceover:)* Late…

> *(Lights come up on* JACOB *walking down the hallway.* ALICE *senses this.)*

ALICE. Shhhh!

JACOB. Late…

ALICE. Shit!

LEWIS. Who the fuck is that?

ALICE. Jacob.

MARGARET. Another demon?

ALICE. No. Worse. He's the third emissary.

LEWIS. A what?

ALICE. One of Lucifer's archangels.

LEWIS. Wait, you said he's the third one? There's two others? We should get the fuck out of here.

MARGARET. Where's Edgar?

LEWIS. What?

MARGARET. Edgar. The bear.

> *(Lights go down on the team, now we're purely focused on* JACOB *in the hallway.*
> EDGAR *enters.)*

JACOB. Late…

EDGAR. Hey there, Jacob.

JACOB. Late…

EDGAR. You and I got some shit to deal with. You keep messing with my girl Alice, that means you mess with me, motherfucker. And, me, I'm gonna enjoy sending your overgrown ass back to the badlands, baby! Nobody fucks with my girl, ya dig?

(JACOB grabs EDGAR and picks him up by the throat.)

EDGAR. I ain't scared of you.

JACOB. Alice...

EDGAR. Yeah. You ain't gonna see her. Cause she's long gone—

ALICE. *(Coming to her friend's aid:)* I'm right here—

EDGAR. Or she's right here.

ALICE. Edgar, what are you doing?

EDGAR. Alice, go away. I promised you I'd get you some revenge. This motherfucker's mine. Come on, asshole, let me see what you—

(JACOB tosses EDGAR out of the way.)

LEWIS. What do we do?

ALICE. We fight.

MARGARET. With what?

(LEWIS notices something behind a bench.)

LEWIS. Hey, look, a random pile of weapons!

(Each of them grabs a different object to protect themselves.)

ALICE. Butcher knife.

LEWIS. Baseball bat.

MARGARET. *(Picking up a tennis racket:)* I'm so going to die.

(JACOB begins marching towards ALICE. ALICE and the team immediately begin attacking JACOB. They stab him, hit him, kick him, but he's unstoppable.)

ALICE. Okay. Maybe this isn't such a good idea right now.

LEWIS. Might I suggest running?

MARGARET. To my car!

ALICE. GO!

*(The team runs away.
A spotlight on JACOB as he slowly marches downstage after them.)*

Scene Three

(Projection: CHAPTER THREE: LOVE IN THE TIME OF CANNIBALISM
Projection: Four days earlier...
Video: LEWIS'S VIDEO BLOG.)

LEWIS. Whazzup, whazzup, whazzup, my cool cats and hot hotties. It's yo' boy, LEWIS, coming straight at ya from the internets like a knucklehead. Well, as it turns out, for all y'all keeping score at home, the Magnificent Margaret May and I did not end up hooking up at Tina Carpenter's Halloween party after all. But yo' boy did end up meeting himself a lady. And this girl is a-sizzlin'. Like Shakira and shit. And she's—right now—in his...bedroom. WHAT! That's right. She's kicking a bit of that dark gothchick vibe, but that's all right. Lewis likey. Lewis definitely likey.
Hold up, here she is. Come on out, Alice. Psst.
It's alright. I'm just doing my video blog. Don't be shy. No one really ever watches these. Say hello to Hans and Sigmund.

> *(In the background, we see ALICE come onto screen. Her eyes are completely black. As she appears, the screen begins becoming very jumpy and staticy, like the bad footage from "The Ring." Suddenly it all goes black. And then out of nowhere, we see ALICE very close up to the screen [With a very loud sound support to help make the audience jump]. She gives a very evil smile. Blackout. Cut to...*
>
> *The high school. MARGARET is at her locker talking to EDGAR who's hanging out literally inside her locker.)*

EDGAR. She's not going to be here. This is stupid.

MARGARET. Shut up, Bear.

EDGAR. It is.

MARGARET. And what? You think you're going to find your girlfriend hanging out in my bedroom? No way. At least this way you won't freak out my mom while she's renovating the house.

EDGAR. Your mom's hot.

MARGARET. Shut up.

EDGAR. She is. I think she wants me.

MARGARET. You're a stuffed animal.

EDGAR. Yo, that's racist.

MARGARET. That's not racist.

EDGAR. You're suggesting that your mom wouldn't date me because of something as small as my genetic makeup.

MARGARET. Your genetic makeup is all fuzz and cotton stuffing.

EDGAR. Racist.

MARGARET. That's not racist!

EDGAR. Uh-huh.

MARGARET. Fuck you, just get in my backpack.

EDGAR. Oh hell's no.

MARGARET. Get in my backpack, Bear.

EDGAR. No.

MARGARET. You can't just hang out inside my locker.

EDGAR. I'm not planning on hanging out in your locker. But I'm certainly not gonna ride in your backpack like some ventriloquist dummy. I ain't nobody's dummy, ya dig?

MARGARET. Then how am I supposed to bring you around. I can't just let you walk down the hallway by yourself, now can I?

EDGAR. Carry me.

MARGARET. Oh, I'm not going to carry you.

EDGAR. Why?

MARGARET. I'm a grown woman. Grown women don't carry teddy bears.

EDGAR. You're 15.

MARGARET. I'm 17.

EDGAR. Wow, I'm sorry, what a remarkably huge difference. I wasn't aware I was talking to an elder statesman—

MARGARET. Fuck you. Get in my backpack. Now.

EDGAR. Or what?

> (MARGARET *slams the locker door on him. She stands there patiently waiting.* EDGAR *knocks on the door.*)

EDGAR. Um. Okay. I'll get in your stupid backpack.

> (MARGARET *opens the door.*)

MARGARET. Okay. Go.

EDGAR. A "please" would be nice.

MARGARET. Get in my motherfucking backpack now, motherfucker! Please.

EDGAR. Yeah. You'll be calling me motherfucker alright after I fuck *your* mother.

MARGARET. Shut up.

(LEWIS and ALICE enter. ALICE is dressed all gothic-y super-hot. Clearly a teenage boy has picked out her clothes.)

LEWIS. Hey Margaret.

MARGARET. Hey Lewis!

LEWIS. Looks like you survived your evening with Duncan intact.

MARGARET. *(Distracted by the new girl on LEWIS's arm:)* Yeah. That experience actually ended up being pretty anti-climatic. Why'd you head out so early from the party? You didn't even say good-bye.

LEWIS. I got busy.

MARGARET. Um, who's this?

LEWIS. This is Alice. She's an…exchange student.

EDGAR. Mmmm! Mmmm-hrm-mmm!

MARGARET. Shut up!

(MARGARET abruptly slams her backpack into some lockers.)

EDGAR. Owwww!

LEWIS. What was that?

MARGARET. Nothing—um, something—my mom got me one of those digital pet thingies. It keeps going off.

LEWIS. Oh yeah? Can I see it? I love Japanese things.

MARGARET. NO! I mean it's lame.
SOOO, Alice, where are you from?

ALICE. *(Talking slow and creepy:)* Hungry.

MARGARET. That's funny you don't look Hungarian. Hehe. Get it? No? Okay.
Um, Lewis? Can I ask you something privately?

LEWIS. Sure. What?

MARGARET. *(Pulling LEWIS away from ALICE:)* What is up with her?

LEWIS. What do you mean?

MARGARET. *(Imitating Alice's creepy voice:)* "Hungry."

LEWIS. Well, clearly, English isn't her first language.
And she has a…cold.

MARGARET. And why is she dressed like that?

LEWIS. Like what?

MARGARET. Like that. Like, I mean, seriously, where'd she get her clothes? The slutty section from Halloween Adventure?

LEWIS. I think she looks nice.

MARGARET. She looks like a teenage boy's wet dream.

LEWIS. *(Suddenly embarrassed:)* Yeah. Weird. It must be cultural.

MARGARET. I don't like the way she's looking at me.

LEWIS. What do you mean, she's not looking at you in any weird—

(TOMMY, *the school's bully, enters.*)

TOMMY. Whaddup, fags.

LEWIS. Shit.

TOMMY. Saw you two at Tina's party. How'd it go? You two end up fucking?

LEWIS. Shut up, Tommy.

TOMMY. Hey, "Huey Lewis," what's with the Asian goth chick? Where'd you find her? Mail order?

MARGARET. Fuck off.

TOMMY. I'm sorry, Buffy the Carpet Layer, is this actually *your* girlfriend? Shoulda figured. I always knew you loved the pussy.

LEWIS. Hey! Back off.

TOMMY. Or what? You'll tell on me? Eat my dick, gaytard. "Herro, new girl! Do you understandee Engrish? Do you need some big beef for your pink taco?"

MARGARET. Leave her alone.

TOMMY. Yo, dyke, just cause you're cheerleading now don't make you any less of a dork. You best respect.

(LEWIS *throws a punch at* TOMMY. *It lands, but doesn't affect him at all.* TOMMY *grabs* LEWIS *by the back of the neck.*)

TOMMY. Lewis, not even in your fuckin' dreams can you imagine a life in which your weak ass is badder than my badass.

(MARGARET *steps towards him.*)

TOMMY. And since you've probably eaten more pussy than me, I think that makes you damn man enough for me to smack. So I'd second guess that step, bitch.

(TOMMY *pushes* LEWIS *into* MARGARET. LEWIS's *hands land on* MARGARET's *breasts. They both freak out.*)

LEWIS. Let's get out of here!

(LEWIS *and* MARGARET *run away, leaving* ALICE *all alone.*)

TOMMY. See ya, fags.

And yo, Lucy Liu, let me know if you want any of this big egg-roll to be dipped into your sweet-and-sour sauce, kay?

> (*As* TOMMY *leaves laughing,* ALICE *stares at him. She begins to drool. She wipes her mouth and gives an evil grin. With jagged and stilted movement, she begins following him like a possessed demon.*
> *Cut to...*
> TOMMY *in the workout room, lifting weights.*)

TOMMY. *(Singing:)* Whoa, I'm half way there!
Whoa, living on a prayer.
Take my hand, we'll make it I swear.

> (ALICE *suddenly appears behind him.*)

TOMMY. Whoa-OHHH!
Holy shit, you scared the hell out of me.

> (ALICE *smiles at* TOMMY.)

TOMMY. What are you looking at, huh?

ALICE. Yummy.

TOMMY. Oh, you like this, huh?
So I guess you're done hanging out with geeky and dyke-y?

> (ALICE *nods and smiles.*)

TOMMY. So what are you doing back here, huh? This is the boy's locker-room.

> (ALICE *shrugs her shoulders and gives* TOMMY *a flirtatious look.*)

TOMMY. Oh. Um...

> (ALICE *giggles. It's sweet.* TOMMY *smiles at her.*)

TOMMY. Hey, look. You know I was just kidding with all that big egg roll stuff.
My name's Tommy by the way.

ALICE. Alice.

TOMMY. Alice. Nice to meet you, Alice.
So where are you from?

> (ALICE *is suddenly possessed and points to the ground. Though* TOMMY *doesn't hear this, the sounds of demons quietly laugh in the background.*)

TOMMY. Um, you're Australian?

> (ALICE *leans in.* TOMMY *goes to kiss her. She bites him.*)

TOMMY. Ow!
The hell?

> (ALICE *smiles and giggles.*)

TOMMY. So you're a bit freaky, huh? I can handle that. Come here.

(He picks her up and begins kissing her neck. ALICE *bites him again. It draws blood.)*

TOMMY. OW! Okay, maybe not. Jesus Christ, that fuckin' hurt. Okay, maybe I'm not so into this.

*(*TOMMY *tosses* ALICE *off. She spits blood into his face.)*

TOMMY. What the fuck!?!

(Her face suddenly goes from flirty to very very serious. Her body stiffens and she begins speaking in Latin.)

ALICE. *Via, concursu, tempus, spatium—*
Audi me ut imperio!

TOMMY. What the fuck are you saying?

ALICE. *(Her voice turns demonic:) Perio!*

TOMMY. Oh shit—

ALICE. *Pereo! Pereo! Pereo!*

*(*ALICE's *eyes turn black and she leaps onto* TOMMY.*)*

TOMMY. Aaaaaaaah!

(Cut to…
LEWIS *and* MARGARET *looking for* ALICE.*)*

LEWIS. Alice! Alice!

MARGARET. Did you hear that?

LEWIS. Hear what?

MARGARET. It sounds like someone getting killed.

LEWIS. That's stupid.

*(*TINA, *completely zombied out and wearing the exact same costume from the first night [but now covered in dried blood] slowly creeps down the hall.)*

LEWIS. Hey Tina!

MARGARET. Hey!

LEWIS. Great party the other…night.

MARGARET. Yeah. Good times.

LEWIS. Tina?

MARGARET. Hey Tina, are you okay?

*(*TINA *smiles. A cup's worth of blood spills out from her mouth.)*

MARGARET. Oh my God!

(MARGARET and LEWIS stare at TINA in horror. MARGARET finally breaks the tension with…)

MARGARET. You are still totally wasted! What the fuck is that? Jäger?

(TINA stumbles off.)

MARGARET. Bitch.

(LEWIS goes back to calling for ALICE.)

LEWIS. Alice!

MARGARET. Lewis, seriously, this is ridiculous. She's fine.

LEWIS. Alice!

MARGARET. Lewis!

LEWIS. Look, you don't have to help me. Why don't you go hang out with the football players or something?

MARGARET. What is that supposed to mean?

LEWIS. Alice!

MARGARET. Hey, I'm talking to you!
What's up? You suddenly got all strange-ranger on me.

EDGAR. Mmmm-mmm!

MARGARET. Shut the fuck up!

LEWIS. I'm the one being strange?

MARGARET. One sec.

(Opens up and talks into her backpack:)

Will you stop!?

(MARGARET tosses her backpack into her locker. We hear EDGAR banging around in it.)

EDGAR. Let. Me. Out of this motherfucker!!!

(He suddenly kicks the door open.)

LEWIS. What the—

EDGAR. If you shove me back in there again, woman, I swear to Christ I will do creepy things to you in your sleep.
I'm not fucking around. You left your gym socks in there. Jesus Christ, you might look like heaven, but your feet stink like all hell.

LEWIS. Uh, Margaret? Talking bear, talking bear.

MARGARET. Hehe. You might be wondering what this thing is, right?

EDGAR. This thing has a muhfuckin' name. And that muhfuckin' name is Edgar.

LEWIS. Your name's Edgar.

EDGAR. That's right, bitch. Where's my girl at?

LEWIS. Who's your girl?

EDGAR. You know—lady hotness vibing with the dark hair, eyes, and soul.

MARGARET. You mean Alice?

EDGAR. Yeah, that girl's my girl. Where is she, dickhead?

LEWIS. I, uh, lost her.

EDGAR. You what?

LEWIS. Wait, how do you know her?

EDGAR. Look, buster, you need to find her before some truly bad shit hits, you get it? And when I say bad, I don't mean just bad. I'm talking straight up end of the world bad.

LEWIS. Wait. How the fuck do you know so much?

EDGAR. Come here.

(LEWIS approaches.)

EDGAR. I'm a talking fucking teddy bear. Have you ever met a talking fucking teddy bear?

LEWIS. No.

EDGAR. Well if you did, you'd know that—

(Suddenly grabs LEWIS by the ear. It hurts him a lot.)

WE'RE WISE AS A MOTHERFUCKER! And when a talking fucking teddy bear says some evil apocalyptic shit may go down, then some evil apocalyptic shit…WILL. GO. DOWN. Dumbass.

(EDGAR throws LEWIS to the ground.)

LEWIS. I don't think I like that bear.

EDGAR. Now where's my girl at?

(Shell-shocked, ALICE stumbles onto stage. She looks a bit less "demonic" now.)

ALICE. Lewis?

LEWIS. Alice? What's wrong?

ALICE. Hold me. Please.

LEWIS. Alice, you're talking.

MARGARET. She can talk now?

LEWIS. Are you okay? You're shaking.

ALICE. Just hold me, Lewis. I just need you to hold me.

(ALICE walks over to LEWIS and embraces him. As it turns out, after ALICE feeds, she returns to being a normal teenage girl.)

MARGARET. Um, I'll see you in class. Later.

(MARGARET isn't able to watch and just walks away.)

LEWIS. Alice, what is it?

ALICE. I did something bad.

LEWIS. Whatever it is—

ALICE. I don't want to be bad.

LEWIS. You're not bad.

ALICE. I can't go back, Lewis. I can't. I can't I can't I can't.

LEWIS. Shhhhh. Everything's going to be alright, Alice. I promise. Look. I even found your freaky talking teddy bear.

EDGAR. What's up, hot stuff?

ALICE. Oh God, they're coming after me, aren't they?

EDGAR. Don't worry, baby. We'll stop them. Who's your honeybear?

LEWIS. Stop who?

(Cut to…
Projection: Five days later…
Projection sequence: We see shots of Lewis's hometown. Buildings are on fire, homes are wrecked, stock news footage of riots and police gear.)

RADIO. *(Voiceover:)* As violence continues to escalate in El Dorado Hills, Sheriff Emil Dunwoody has issued a full evacuation of the Country Club Terrace neighborhood to begin immediately.

(Spotlight comes up on SHERIFF DUNWOODY addressing the press. The images continue in the background.)

SHERIFF DUNWOODY. The highest concentration of criminal activity does seem to be focused in this area of town. I know that there's been some outrageous claims circulating that the perpetrators are of some kind of supernatural origin, but on the record, these are just criminals—yes, violent and dangerous criminals that clearly show no indication that they have any respect for human life—but they are criminals nonetheless and I can assure you we will have this situation under control in the quickest amount of time possible. We do ask for all our citizens to stay indoors during the evening hours and do not—under any circumstance—attempt to drive north of the city towards the Country Club Terrace area. That neighborhood is very very unstable right now. Avoid at all costs. Thank you. And may God be with us all.

(Cut to…

LEWIS, ALICE, EDGAR, and MARGARET in a car. They are going down a long dark road towards Country Club Terrace. The roads are littered with wreckage. LEWIS is at the wheel as MARGARET stares down ALICE who's in the back seat.

Note to the designers: The car will be "traveling" towards the back of the stage, so the audience will be looking at the back end of the vehicle and the "backs" of the actors.)

LEWIS. Is he still behind us?

EDGAR. No, it looks like we lost him.

LEWIS. For someone who only stalks about, he really moves freakishly fast.

EDGAR. Thus him being a hell demon.

(ALICE notices MARGARET glaring at her.)

ALICE. Why are you looking at me like that?

MARGARET. I don't trust you.

ALICE. You don't have to come with us.

MARGARET. This is my car, bitch.

ALICE. And this is my hatchet.

MARGARET. And this…is my bird!

ALICE. That's a finger.

MARGARET. What? Do people not flip each other off in Hell?

EDGAR. Ladies! There's no need for all that. Do you two need a hug? Cause I will hug the shit out of you. Just stick me in between y'all and hug away.

ALICE. Shut up, Edgar.

MARGARET. Why don't you shut up!

LEWIS. Actually, can you all shut up? You're making it really hard to concentrate. There's like dozens of cars wrecked out here. It'd be nice to—

(Suddenly and out of nowhere, MATILDA, the second emissary, a flying winged demon, jumps onto the hood of the car.)

ALL. Aaaaaaaaaaaah!

LEWIS. DEMON!!!

(LEWIS swerves the car back and forth trying to sling the demon off. It doesn't work.)

EDGAR. Brake hard right!

(Suddenly LEWIS swerves the car hard slinging MATILDA off.)

MARGARET. Wait. Stop. Is she dead?

(*MATILDA stands back up and unfurls her wings.*)

LEWIS. Everybody, hold on! I'm throwing it in reverse!

(*LEWIS throws the car in reverse and drives backwards away from the demon.
MATILDA extends her wings and flies at the team.
As LEWIS speeds down the highway in reverse, MATILDA closes ground.*)

MARGARET. Hit the brakes, Lewis!

(*LEWIS slams on the brakes, this time MATILDA slams face first into the car.*)

LEWIS. Haha! We got her!

(*MATILDA raises her head. She's fine.*)

LEWIS. We don't got her—We don't got her!
Everybody out!

(*Everybody jumps out of the vehicle as MATILDA climbs back on it and rips it apart.*
MATILDA *grabs* EDGAR.)

EDGAR. Hey! Somebody save my furry ass!

MARGARET. What the hell is that thing?

ALICE. It's Matilda. The second Emissary.

LEWIS. How do we kill it?

ALICE. With violence. Lots and lots of violence.

(*The team pulls out their weapons and attacks.
As a fighting unit, the team is pretty useless. MATILDA has them all on the ropes pretty quickly. Right when it looks like MARGARET will be killed, ALICE's eyes turn black.
ALICE leaps onto MATILDA and bites a chunk out of her.
MATILDA throws her off. ALICE lands on her feet, blood covering her lips. She smiles.*)

ALICE. (*Demonically:*) *Via, concursu, tempus, spatium, audi me ut imperio! Perio! Perio! Perio!*

(*MATILDA suddenly stiffens. Blood begins to run out from all her orifices. MATILDA's head then explodes. ALICE collapses.*)

MARGARET. WHAT! THE! FUCK!?!

LEWIS. What the fuck just happened?

EDGAR. Oh shit.

MARGARET. That bitch just destroyed my car!

EDGAR. Oh fuck. This isn't good, guys. Alice, you gotta keep that in check, baby. Seriously.

LEWIS. Keep what in check?

MARGARET. That bitch destroyed my car.

EDGAR. There's a demon inside her. It's getting stronger the more hell is unleashed.

LEWIS. There's a demon in her?

EDGAR. How far are we?

MARGARET. Considering I don't have a car anymore. Far!

LEWIS. Actually, it's not that bad if we take a shortcut through the woods.

MARGARET. You mean the demon-infested ones?

LEWIS. Yep. Those would be the ones.

EDGAR. I don't think we got a choice here.

MARGARET. And what are we supposed to do? Carry Alice? Look at her. She's wrecked. LIKE MY CAR.

LEWIS. Alice?

ALICE. No. I'm good. We should go. Let's go.

LEWIS. You sure?

ALICE. Yes. What's the worst that can happen, right?

MARGARET. We could all die.
But, ya know, don't listen to me.

> *(The team exits. Blackout.)*

End of Act I

ACT II

Scene One

(Projection: CHAPTER FOUR: BADNESS FALLS
Projection: Five nights ago...
Movement sequence: two teenagers fooling around in a parked car to Bonnie Tyler's "Total Eclipse of the Heart" playing in the background. JACOB kills them.
Cut to...
Two kids smoking pot. JACOB kills them.
Cut to...
A kid vandalizing a wall, JACOB kills him.
Cut to...
Three girls pillow-fighting in their underwear. JACOB kills them.
Cut to...
Two boys pillow-fighting in their underwear. JACOB kills them.
Cut to...
In an unrelenting series of death, we see JACOB slaughtering teenagers left and right. As it all culminates, we see JACOB standing in the middle of the stage with dead bodies all around him, playing air-guitar with his bloody machete. Flames explode all around him as he throws the "devil horns" hand signal into the air like a heavy metal rocker.
And right when we think he's become just a silly rock 'n roll headbanger, he suddenly turns very cold and kills an "audience plant." He walks away slowly.
Cut to...
Projection: Present night...
The team is resting in the woods.)

LEWIS. Hey.

ALICE. Hey.

LEWIS. How are you feeling?

ALICE. Like Hell.

LEWIS. That's funny. You're funny.

(The two smile at each other. MARGARET sees this and some jealousy rises up in her.)

MARGARET. OKAY! So, let me get this right, you're a demon, correct?

ALICE. What?

MARGARET. You're a demon. You kill people. You're like evil and shit. One with the devil?

LEWIS. Margaret.

MARGARET. No, Lewis. She might be all schoolgirl cute right now, but how much longer before she goes all homicidal blacked-eyed girl on us? On a scale of one to ten, how demon-y are you right now? Do you want to eat our skin yet or are you satiated for the time-being because you chomped out demonic Tinkerbell's throat back there?

LEWIS. Alice isn't going to hurt us.

MARGARET. How do you know that? I don't know that.
The bitch can kill speaking Hebrew!

LEWIS. Latin.

MARGARET. Whatever. Can you kill things by speaking Latin? I can't. I can't even kill things using a big fucking knife, yet she tosses around some Catholic school education and, blam, motherfuckers are blowing up. That's. Evil!

LEWIS. Margaret, stop it. She's not a demon.

MARGARET. Not yet anyways. But Edgar said it, the more time passes, the more devil-horny she's gonna get.

EDGAR. Margaret, that's completely unfair—

ALICE. But she's right though, Lewis.

LEWIS. Alice.

ALICE. She's right. There is a demon inside me.

LEWIS. But you were once just a normal girl, right?

ALICE. Once. A long time ago.

EDGAR. You ain't got to apologize to nobody, Alice. Just cause we are what we are don't mean we gotta be stuck being evil. Every man has a right to save their own soul. This is our time for redemption.

LEWIS. Were you ever human?

EDGAR. Hell no. Demon. One hundred percent and proud. What-WHAT?

ALICE. We should move.

LEWIS. I'm all rested up.

EDGAR. Me too.
Yo, sweet Margaret, how you holding up?

> (*At some point in the conversation,* MARGARET *fades out and turns away from the group. She's now facing upstage and we can't see her face.*
> *The team parts and a spotlight falls on the back of* MARGARET's *head. It's clear that something's up.*)

LEWIS. Um, Margaret? Are you okay?

EDGAR. Yo, pretty thing, you alright?

(The team slowly approaches. Suddenly, with light, sound, & video support, MARGARET *turns around, her face has turned demonic.)*

MARGARET. *(In a demonic voice:)* You will all fucking die! Your flesh will be consumed by the emissaries of Hell and your corpses will be used as instruments for my sexual pleasure! *Via temporis, iam clamo ad te, via spatii te iubeo aperire. Aperi!*

*(*MARGARET *suddenly turns to* LEWIS *and then explosively vomits blood all over him for an extended period of time.*
MARGARET *stands back up. She's suddenly back to normal, but woozy.)*

MARGARET. *(Normal:)* Uh, I don't feel so good.

*(*MARGARET *passes out.)*

LEWIS. What the fuck was that!?!

EDGAR. That would be the bad guy.

LEWIS. Oh. Holy shit. I need to go do a number one now.

(Cut to…
SHERIFF DUNWOODY *is investigating Country Club Terrace. He has his pistol out and sprints to a door. He knocks on the door.)*

SHERIFF DUNWOODY. El Dorado Hills Police Department! Anyone home?

(No one answers.)

(Into radio:) Deputy, you still with me?

DEPUTY. *(Voiceover:)* Still here, Sheriff. Horseshoe Lane is clear. No residents.

SHERIFF DUNWOODY. Shady Lane's also clear. I just have one last house left to sweep, but it looks like Country Club Terrace is officially fully evacuated.

DEPUTY. *(Voiceover:)* Wait just a minute, sir. There seems to be some activity at 2108 Gaines.

SHERIFF DUNWOODY. The Carpenter's estate?

DEPUTY. *(Voiceover:)* Hey! You over there! All residents are supposed to be— Aaaaaaaaaaaaaaaaaaaaaaaaaaaaaaaaaaaaaaaaaaaaaaaaaaaaaah!

SHERIFF DUNWOODY. Deputy?
Deputy?

GARRETH. *(Voiceover. Demonic:)* Iratus malum nex supervenio!

SHERIFF DUNWOODY. Hang tight, Deputy! I'm coming!

*(*SHERIFF DUNWOODY *races down the street. We watch him pass burning homes and collapsed houses. He finally arrives to the front steps of the Carpenter's house.)*

Deputy Barrow? Deputy Barrow?

(The DEPUTY's *severed head rolls onto stage.)*

Oh God!

GARRETH. *(Voiceover:) Iratus malum nex supervenio!*

(We see the enormous shadow of GARRETH, *the first emissary, overtake the stage.)*

SHERIFF DUNWOODY. Aaaaaah!

(Cut to…
LEWIS *runs out trying to zip his fly.)*

LEWIS. Aaaaaah!

*(*EDGAR *enters behind him.)*

LEWIS. What the fuck are you doing?
You scared the shit out of me!

EDGAR. Alice wanted me to follow you.
To keep you safe.

LEWIS. You're here to keep me safe?

EDGAR. That's what I said.

LEWIS. Seriously?

EDGAR. Yeah.

LEWIS. You. Here. For my safety.

EDGAR. That's correct.

LEWIS. No offense, but you're a teddy bear. The last two fights we've been in, you got bear-snatched.

EDGAR. I know that.

LEWIS. So what could you possibly do to protect me?

EDGAR. Good point. I should go. Good luck maneuvering your way through these demon-infested woods by yourself. Bye now.

LEWIS. Whoa, wait just a minute there, bear. Where you going?

EDGAR. Well, you obviously don't want my help so why should I bother helping you? If you get in a jam, I'm sure you are more than capable of figuring out how to defend yourself from whatever kind of demon, slasher, or emissary of the devil you might run across. And if not, you'll be dead, so who cares?

LEWIS. Okay, wait. You can stay.

EDGAR. Okay. Pee.

(LEWIS walks to a corner and tries to pee.)

EDGAR. Look, Lewis, I'm glad we have this time together. I wanted to talk to you about something.

LEWIS. What's that? Curious if I had any honey?

EDGAR. Ah, cute, Winnie the Pooh jokes. Clever.
Stay away from Alice.

LEWIS. What?

EDGAR. You heard me. Stay away from her. She's mine. The other one with the boobs is all yours, but Alice, she's my lady, ya dig?

LEWIS. Look, bear, if Alice digs on me, she digs on me. Deal with it.

EDGAR. Wow, little nerdboy gets a little kissy kissy action and now he thinks he's Indiana fucking Jones.

LEWIS. Fuck off.

EDGAR. Look, don't make me do this.

LEWIS. Do what?

EDGAR. …

LEWIS. …

EDGAR. Please.

LEWIS. Did you just say "please"?

EDGAR. Yes. Please.
I love her.

LEWIS. You what?

EDGAR. Just back off, alright? Or I'll kick your ass.

LEWIS. What?

EDGAR. You heard me.

LEWIS. Yeah? How? You're a fucking teddy bear. Getting hit by you would be less painful than getting hit by a fucking Nerf-gun.

EDGAR. Don't fucking push me, Lewis.

LEWIS. And you know what? What if I did back-off on Alice? How is that going to help you at all? You're a teddy bear! What the fuck are you going to do with her? Hump her ankles? You can't do shit. You don't even have a dick. You're a—

(EDGAR jumps up and kicks LEWIS's ass. It's funny.)

LEWIS. Ow! Okay! You hit really hard for something so friggin' fuzzy.

EDGAR. You're a pussy.

LEWIS. Well, you're…short.

EDGAR. Good one.

LEWIS. Shut up.

> *(We see* JACOB's *shadow slowly approach.)*

EDGAR. Um, Lewis?

LEWIS. Shut up. This really fucking smarts. You got me right in my eye.

EDGAR. Lewis!

LEWIS. What?

EDGAR. Shhhhhhh! Over there!

> *(*LEWIS *sees* JACOB.*)*

LEWIS. We should go get the girls.

EDGAR. Fuck that. I say we take out that motherfucker ourselves.

LEWIS. No way.

EDGAR. Don't be a pussy, Lewis. Let's get our man on!

LEWIS. No. The girls are our priority. If you really care about Alice, you know she wouldn't want you to fight Jacob alone.

EDGAR. Man, whatever.

LEWIS. We should go.

EDGAR. …

LEWIS. Um, if I pick you up, I think we could there a lot faster.

EDGAR. Uhhhh! Just do it.

LEWIS. Sorry.

> *(*LEWIS *lifts* EDGAR *and runs off.*
> *Cut to…)*

ALICE. Why don't you like me?

MARGARET. What?

ALICE. Why don't you like me?

MARGARET. Cause you're a fucking bitch.

ALICE. How am I a bitch?

MARGARET. It's not really a certain action or quality, it's really the whole persona. You emanate bitch.

ALICE. I think it's jealousy.

MARGARET. No, I think it's your fucking face, that's what I think it is.

ALICE. Right.

MARGARET. Fuck off.

ALICE. You know, whatever it is that Lewis sees in you, I really just don't get it.

MARGARET. What Lewis sees in me?

ALICE. I mean he's a good guy. Smart, funny, willing to drive into Hell—literally—to save the world. And you…you're just holding him back. There's really not much more to you than just hair and boobs, now is there? Besides being really really pretty, you're basically a fucking retard.

MARGARET. Fuck you!
My brother's retarded.

ALICE. What?

MARGARET. My brother. He's retarded. Mentally speaking. In the literal sense. He's retarded. That's the proper use of the word "retard."
And what do you mean "what Lewis sees in me"?

(Abruptly, LEWIS and EDGAR rush in.)

LEWIS. Guys! We got company. Hide!

EDGAR. It's Jacob.

ALICE. What?

LEWIS. Margaret, come with me!

(LEWIS blows out the fire. The stage goes dark. The team splits up into two different spots on stage. LEWIS and MARGARET hide together while EDGAR and ALICE hide at a different spot.
JACOB enters. For a tense while, he tracks back and forth slowly. It's very reminiscent of the prologue. After seeing no one there, he begins to leave. However, as he does, Margaret's cell phone goes off.)

MARGARET. Shit.

(JACOB suddenly rushes towards MARGARET. LEWIS jumps in the way, JACOB knocks him out. ALICE rushes to defend, but JACOB grabs MARGARET and tosses her in the way. MARGARET collides into ALICE. As they try to get up, JACOB knocks them out as well. EDGAR steps up.)

EDGAR. Yo, ugly! Why don't you fight someone your own size?

(JACOB looks down and drop kicks EDGAR far offstage.)

EDGAR. Aaaaaaaaah!

(Suddenly, we hear demonic sounds.)

TINA. *(Voiceover:)* Bring me the one!

> *(*JACOB *examines who's lying on the ground. He makes a decision and reaches down to grab* LEWIS.*)*

Scene Two

> *(Projection: CHAPTER FIVE: HELL'S A BITCH*
> *Lights come up on* JACOB *with an unconscious* LEWIS *over his shoulder.*
> LEWIS *slowly wakes up.)*

LEWIS. Where the fuck—
Hey, how come you're not killing me? Not that I'm complaining—thank you for not killing me, but—
Hello?

JACOB. Late…

> *(*JACOB *places* LEWIS *in front of a door.)*

LEWIS. Wait. Where am I?

> *(*LEWIS *looks around and sees where he's at. He's at Tina's house, but it now looks way demonic-y.)*

LEWIS. Holy shit. This is Tina's house. You brought me to Tina's house? Why would you do that? Why'd you bring me here? WHY AM I HERE!?!

> *(*JACOB *walks away.*
> LEWIS *sticks his head into the house.)*

LEWIS. Tina?

TINA. *(Voiceover. Demonic-y:)* TINA DOESN'T LIVE HERE ANYMORE!

> *(Demonic hands reach out and pull* LEWIS *into the darkness.)*

LEWIS. Aaaaaah!

> *(Cut to…*
> MARGARET *and* ALICE *are walking through a Suburban neighborhood.)*

ALICE. *(Calling:)* Edgar! Edgar!
Where the fuck is that bear?

MARGARET. Look, Alice, I need to say something.

ALICE. We don't have time—

MARGARET. No. Please.

ALICE. What is it?

MARGARET. I'm…sorry.

ALICE. What?

MARGARET. I'm sorry about, you know, giving you such a hard time. I'm sorry I've been such an ass and that you're a raging bitch and that the fact that your face makes me want to puke makes me want to puke and that you dress like a total slutbag. But the bottom line is I just want to save Lewis now and make sure he's safe. You're the only one who's strong enough to save him, so…I'm sorry. You're a good person.

ALICE. I am?

> *(A very creepy smile emerges on* ALICE's *face.)*

MARGARET. Are you smiling? Um. That's a really creepy smile.

> *(Lights come up on a sign that says "Welcome to Country Club Terrace." Below, we see* SHERIFF DUNWOODY *standing in dark. He's facing away so we can't see his face.)*

MARGARET. Holy shit. Is that a cop over there?

ALICE. What?

MARGARET. Alice, he can totally help us out.

ALICE. Margaret—

MARGARET. Officer! Officer, oh my God, I'm so happy to see you. We need help. One of our friends is—

> *(*SHERIFF DUNWOODY *turns. He is possessed. With, ya know, evil. Note:* GARRETH *[Or whoever is possessed by Garreth] should speak with a French accent.)*

SHERIFF DUNWOODY. *(Demonic:) Iratus malum nex supervenio! Perio!*

ALICE. Stop!

SHERIFF DUNWOODY. *Perio! Perio! Peri—*

> *(Suddenly realizing who he's speaking to:)*

Wait. Is that you, my little Dewdrop?

ALICE. Dewdrop?
Garreth, is that you?

SHERIFF DUNWOODY. *(With French accent:)* Alice. My Dewdrop! They said you had gotten out. Told me to look for you. And, look, here we are. Reunited once again. As it should be.

ALICE. Garreth, get out of that body.

SHERIFF DUNWOODY. Hehehe. What? Do you not like my new skin, Alice? I like it. Very robust. But perhaps, maybe—

MARGARET. *(As* GARRETH:*)* You prefer this one?

ALICE. Stop it.

SHERIFF DUNWOODY. Oh, you've grown dull, Alice. That's not good, not good at all.

MARGARET. What the fuck? Don't do that!

SHERIFF DUNWOODY. We used to have fun, you and I. But now look at you. You're all into being human again.

MARGARET. Do you know him?

ALICE. It's Garreth. He's an emissary.

SHERIFF DUNWOODY. Is that all I am to you?

ALICE. And my ex-boyfriend.

MARGARET. What?

SHERIFF DUNWOODY. Quick question, love.

MARGARET. Are you going to eat this? Because this human looks to be one tasty little treat.

SHERIFF DUNWOODY. Where the fart-knuckles am I? Who are you people?

ALICE. Get out of her now.

MARGARET. Now that's a provocative sentence indeed.

SHERIFF DUNWOODY. Would you prefer I get inside of you?

MARGARET. Don't you miss what we had?

SHERIFF DUNWOODY. How we used to tear each other apart?

MARGARET. The things I could do to you now that we're corporeal again.

SHERIFF DUNWOODY. The pleasures of the flesh, Alice.

MARGARET. The mere idea is making my mouth water.

SHERIFF DUNWOODY. Question.

MARGARET. Is it making you all wet as well?

ALICE. Garreth…

MARGARET. Shhh.

> (MARGARET *kisses* ALICE. ALICE *gives in and kisses back. However, after a bit—*)

ALICE. No. Stop.

MARGARET. Wow, I suddenly feel very gay.

ALICE. Garreth, get out of that body now.

SHERIFF DUNWOODY. Or what?

ALICE. Or I'll rip you out.

MARGARET. You're a really good kisser. I really liked that. Wait. Am I gay?

SHERIFF DUNWOODY. You can't harm me, Harbinger. My true form is hidden deep within this vessel. For you to get to me, you'd have to kill this body. And seeing that you're trying your best to be good again, you wouldn't kill me, would you? You're a good girl now.

(*ALICE* slugs SHERIFF DUNWOODY *in the stomach. He vomits out a very small, very teeny demon.*)

GARRETH. *(Shaking off vomit:)* Dammit! You are such an asshole.

SHERIFF DUNWOODY. What? Where?

GARRETH. Come back here, vessel! I need your body to protect me!

SHERIFF DUNWOODY. No! Stay away from—

(GARRETH *jumps onto the* SHERIFF *and tries to climb back into his mouth. The* SHERIFF *throws him off. Seeing no other way in,* GARRETH *tries to burrow into the* SHERIFF's *stomach. Blood flies everywhere. The* SHERIFF *dies.*)

GARRETH. Dammit, that did not work. You! Tasty treat. Your body will have to suffice.

(GARRETH *jumps onto* MARGARET *and tries to climb down her throat.*)

MARGARET. Alice! Help!

(*ALICE* walks over and grabs GARRETH!)

GARRETH. Alice. Let me go. Please. For old times sake.

ALICE. Garreth, it was so good seeing you. Seriously, it really was. But unfortunately, this relationship is officially over.

(*ALICE* squashes him.
Cut to…
LEWIS *is tied up.* TINA, *looking all sexy and hot, is staring out a window with her back to the audience.*)

LEWIS. Um, hey, are you going to kill me? Cause if you're not going to kill me, I could really use the bathroom right about now. Um, Tina? Right, "Tina doesn't live here anymore." Who are you again?

(TINA *turns to look at* LEWIS. *She gives him a smile and a wink. She then snaps her fingers. Music begins playing [A basic Jazz riff].*)

TINA. *(Singing:)*
    I'M THE BADNESS,
    THE QUEEN OF SADNESS,
    I'M THE EVIL THAT BRINGS THE WHACKNESS,
    I'M THE PRINCE OF LIES, I'M THE KING OF PAIN
    I'M FROM THE DEPTHS OF HELL TO BEGIN MY REIGN

OF DEATH AND DESTRUCTION
ON THIS CREATION
THAT'S BOUND FOR HORRIFIC ANNIHILATION
BELIEVE ME I'LL DESTROY EVERYTHING I SPY
CAUSE ALL I WANT IS ALL OF YOU
TO DIE DIE DIE

SO IF YOU NEED A NAME FOR YOUR NEW CONQUEROR
LUCIFER IS MY PREFERRED MONIKER
BEELZEBUB WILL WORK AS WELL
I ALSO DIG ON THE PRINCE OF HELL

I'M THE BADNESS,
THE QUEEN OF SADNESS,
I'M THE EVIL THAT BRINGS THE WHACKNESS,
I'M THE PRINCE OF LIES, I'M THE KING OF PAIN
HERE TO KILL THE WORLD SO GET OUT OF MY WAY

AND I'M BRINGING ON THE NIGHT
I'M THE ANTI TO THE CHRIST
THE DARKNESS TO THE LIGHT
AND IN THIS NEW BODY, I'M JUST TOO TIGHT
AND I'M GONNA FUCKING FUCK ALL OF YOU MOTHER-
FUCKERS ALL THE FUCK UP!

(Spoken:) So to answer your question, my name's Lucifer, but you can call me Lucy for short!!

LEWIS. I won't let you hurt Alice!

TINA. Lewis, who said I was out to hurt her?
Did you really think she was the good guy in this story?

LEWIS. What?

TINA. She's not just turning into a demon, darling. She's my fourth and final horseman. "I looked and behold, there was the fourth emissary, and his name was death. He was given the authority to kill with sword and wrath and the Earth shuddered for the end was near." Revelations: I'm gonna kick your ass.

> *(Cut to...*
> MARGARET *and* ALICE *approach Tina's house.* ALICE *doesn't look good. Her eyes are dark. She's looking a bit more undead now.)*

MARGARET. Here we are. Tina's is the last house on the left.

> *(ALICE swoons.)*

MARGARET. Alice, are you okay?

ALICE. Oh God.

MARGARET. Alice?

ALICE. Hungry.

MARGARET. I think I might have a granola bar on me.

ALICE. No. No, please.

MARGARET. What? You don't like granola?

ALICE. *(Demonically enhanced:)* BACK OFF!

MARGARET. Whoa! What's with the sudden Linda Blair?

ALICE. *Via, concursu, tempus*—NO!

MARGARET. Alice?

ALICE. Margaret.
RUN.

MARGARET. Alice?

> *(ALICE looks up at MARGARET. Black stuff oozes from her mouth. She gives MARGARET an evil smile.)*

MARGARET. Oh shit …

> *(ALICE leaps at MARGARET. MARGARET tries to fight her off. ALICE bites into MARGARET, blood sprays everywhere. As ALICE is drenched in Margaret's blood, she snaps out of her trance.)*

ALICE. Oh God. Oh God no. NO!

> *(ALICE runs away. As she does, we see MARGARET lying on the ground slowly bleeding.)*

MARGARET. Fucking fuck.

> *(MARGARET is still alive and begins trying to get back up. As she does, we see JACOB enter and stand over her. He pulls out his machete and points it at her.)*

MARGARET. No. Don't.

> *(JACOB raises his machete.)*

JACOB. Late …

> *(Suddenly EDGAR appears.)*

EDGAR. Yo, motherfucker! Get the fuck away from my lady!

MARGARET. Edgar?

EDGAR. Yo, what happened to you?

MARGARET. Alice.

EDGAR. Shit. She's losing it.
Alright, Jacob, it's time we finally finish this.

MARGARET. You can't fight him. You're too…small.

EDGAR. My lady, who said this was my fighting form? I'm a demon after all. And demons are awesome.

(A spotlight falls on EDGAR.*)*

Converting to battle mode! *Verto magnus monasteriense!*

*(*EDGAR *stretches out his arms. And then in an amazing super theatrical display,* EDGAR *transforms from tiny little cute teddy into a human-sized badass teddy bear / demon hybrid.)*

MARGARET. Wow…

*(*MARGARET *passes out.)*

EDGAR. Margaret? Margaret!

JACOB. Late…

EDGAR. Alright, Jack. This one's for my ladies. Time to boogie.

(In a very messy and bloody fight, EDGAR *and* JACOB *go at it.* EDGAR *is heavily wounded. But in the end,* EDGAR *is able to disarm* JACOB *and stab him through with his own machete.)*

EDGAR. Boo-yah…

*(*EDGAR *collapses. Onstage, we look at the fallen bodies of* JACOB, EDGAR, *and* MARGARET.*)*

Scene Three

(Projection: CHAPTER 666: APOCALYPSE NOW-ISH
Projection: Present night…
Lights come up on Tina's house. It is completely Hellish now.)

TINA. Are you sad?

LEWIS. Shut up.

TINA. I think you're sad.

LEWIS. I think you're ugly.

TINA. Oh, I don't think so. I see the way you're looking at this body. You likey.

LEWIS. No, I don't.

TINA. Who are you trying to fool, Lewis? I'm the devil. Every dirty thought you have ever had that's crossed that naughty little mind of yours is inspired by yours truly.

LEWIS. Don't touch me.

TINA. Mmmm. Virgin flesh. So yum.

LEWIS. I'm not a virgin.

TINA. Oh, don't be shy. I knows when I've found myself a Mary when I see one. And I found myself a Mary. I'll be honest, if it weren't for the fact that killing you would so ruin my evil plans, I would eat you up whole. Literally.

(A very bloody, very messed up looking ALICE enters…)

LEWIS. Alice?

TINA. Harbinger! How are you, love? You look absolutely…well, you look like shit.

LEWIS. Alice, can you hear me?

TINA. Of course she can hear you. She's evil, not deaf. Mmmm, and can you feel that? Now that's some darkness and malice! The kind only a teenage girl can produce.

LEWIS. Alice, where's Margaret and Edgar?

TINA. Lewis, tact! Please. You shouldn't ask that. A woman never likes to kill and tell. Or was that kiss? Well, in this instance, it's definitely kill.
But if you really want to, Harbinger darling. You can tell him. Tell him what you did with Alice's friends.

ALICE. *Via, concursu, tempus—*

(TINA places a finger on ALICE's mouth to shut her up.)

TINA. Oh, no. You don't want to do that, love. Killing Alice's boyfriend here would definitely be bad for all in the room.

LEWIS. Alice, no…

TINA. Isn't my fourth emissary just so cute, Lewis? The Harbinger of Death itself incubating deep inside her like a fine wine. Or demonic chicken. Whatever. And now, she's finally ready to kill God's lamest creation—humanity. Isn't that right, love?

(ALICE looks over to TINA. She smiles. And then slugs TINA in the face.)

ALICE. Wrong, bitch.

LEWIS. Alice!

(ALICE goes and unties LEWIS.)

ALICE. Sorry for taking so long.

LEWIS. We have to find the conduit.

(TINA pulls herself off the ground.)

TINA. Wow, see, now that was really fucking rude. If you're not going to be my Harbinger of Death, Alice, then don't just stand there pretending. That made me look stupid. And no one makes the big bad look stupid.

ALICE. Yeah, you're too busy handling that on your own.

TINA. Oh clever. So very very clever. How clever are you going to be when I rip your fucking lips off?

> *(TINA attacks ALICE. ALICE tries to fight the best that she can, but TINA's too powerful. She knocks ALICE on her ass.)*

TINA. Oops, bitch fell down.

ALICE. *Via, concursu, tempus—*

TINA. Con queso, chimichanga, taco bell!

> *(TINA slugs ALICE in the mouth.)*

TINA. Who do you think gave you those powers in the first place? Latin can't hurt me!

> *(MARGARET enters.)*

MARGARET. Then how about pointy things?

> *(—and tosses a knife into TINA's face. TINA falls. EDGAR enters as well and runs to ALICE's side.)*

ALICE. Edgar, is that you?

EDGAR. In the flesh, baby.

ALICE. Holy shit, Edgar, you look…well, you look good.

MARGARET. Lewis, are you alright?

LEWIS. I'm better now.

TINA. *(Standing back up and pulling the knife out of her face:)* Alright, all you fuckers wanna battle? Then let's fuckin' battle.

ALICE. Oh, it's on. It's on like classic Pong.

> *(Badass music pipes in.*
> *And now, in the greatest fight sequence ever to be seen on a theatrical stage, ALICE, LEWIS, MARGARET, and EDGAR go at it against TINA the Devil. The team drops in Kung Fu, Capoeira, Muay Thai, Krav Maga, and any other awesome fight form they can muster to battle TINA. And it really looks like they're gonna win. But…and here's the big but—)*

TINA. I'm the devil, motherfuckers. You can't beat me with kung fu.

> *(TINA takes each of them out.)*

TINA. Now, Alice, if you're not gonna willingly be my emissary of death, destruction, and evil bad things. Maybe I have to do this the old fashion way. With, you know, some killing you and then possessing your corpse like I did this one. And look at how great that turned out. Don't I look smashing as a fucking ginger?

> *(TINA pulls out a hand-mirror and admires herself.)*

LEWIS. Margaret, the conduit! The conduit.

(MARGARET goes for it, but TINA hits her in the face.)

EDGAR. I got it!

(EDGAR goes for it, TINA does the same to him, but with magic. As she laughs at the fallen EDGAR and MARGARET, LEWIS sneaks up and quickly snags the mirror out of her hand.)

LEWIS. Hey! Devil! Go to hell!

(LEWIS breaks the hand-mirror.
TINA starts screaming "in pain"
…which slowly evolves into a laugh.)

TINA. You idiot. You really thought you'd beat me by throwing the ring into the volcano? You guys are fucking lame!

(To ALICE:)

Now you, let's get back to the business of killing you. And let's do this old school style, shall we?

(Using Alice's own weapons against her, TINA goes to land a killing blow on ALICE.)

LEWIS. No, stop!

(LEWIS runs up and grabs onto TINA.)

TINA. Let go of me!

LEWIS. Leave her alone!

TINA. Get off me!

(TINA cuts LEWIS.
Then, suddenly, she screams in pain at the same time as LEWIS. They're connected.
Realizing that TINA hurts when he does, LEWIS grabs a weapon and cuts his arm twice. Each time, TINA screams in agony.)

MARGARET. Lewis, what are you doing?

LEWIS. I looked, and behold, there was the fourth emissary; and his name was Death; and Hades followed with him. He was given the authority to kill with sword and wrath and the Earth shuddered for the end was near.

TINA. Don't.

(LEWIS impales himself with the blade.)

MARGARET. NO!

(As LEWIS bleeds out, the devil feels his pain.)

TINA. *(Demonically:)* Aaaaaagh!

(As LEWIS lies bleeding as the stage begins imploding, TINA collapses on the ground. As she does, using projections and sound FX, we see the demonic shaped

shadow of Lucifer float out of TINA's *body. It writhes in pain before it gets sucked back into Hell.*
The theatre suddenly goes black.
A spotlight slowly comes up on our heroes. MARGARET *still holding* LEWIS *in her arms.)*

MARGARET. Lewis.

LEWIS. We did it.

MARGARET. No, no, stay with me.

LEWIS. I love you, Margaret May. I always have. I always will. Keep Alice safe.

MARGARET. Lewis, I—

(LEWIS *goes limp in* MARGARET's *arms.)*

MARGARET. Lewis?

ALICE. He did it.

EDGAR. Lewis was the conduit?

ALICE. He closed the rift. He saved us all.

EDGAR. Margaret? Margaret, are you okay?

MARGARET. I never got to tell him.

ALICE. Oh, Margaret.

(ALICE *puts her arm around* MARGARET. *The three heroes walk off stage together with their heads hung down.*
Cut to…
Video: MARGARET'S VIDEO BLOG
It's Margaret's video blog. She's holding a shot glass of bourbon.)

MARGARET. What's up, sexy bitches! It's your girl, the Magnificent Margaret May, coming straight at ya from the internets. And tonight's a pretty somber night for your girl here. One year ago, she lost her boy Lewis to some truly whackass whackness. And the worst part was I never got to tell him some very important things. So take a lesson from your girl Margaret May, if you dig someone, make sure they know it. Don't ever live in regret. Cause ya never know when the mothafuckin' devil might show up and take everything away. This is to you, Lewis, wherever you are. I love you.

(MARGARET *takes the shot.*
Suddenly, a very scary LEWIS *appears in the background.)*

Lewis?

(*Blackout!* MARGARET *screams!)*

End of Play

PHOEBE IN WINTER

Jen Silverman

About the Collaboration
Embracing the Bold and the Strange

Clubbed Thumb (and its seminal summer theater festival Summerworks) has been a valued artistic compass in the downtown theater for nearly two decades. Founded in 1996 as the brainchild of two young actresses, Maria Striar and Meg MacCary, who were dismayed by waiting around for other people to give them opportunities, and by what a lot of those opportunities consisted of, Clubbed Thumb's now long-standing mission of producing "funny, strange, provocative" work has helped evolve them into one of New York's most important (and adventurous!) artistic trailblazers.

What's their secret? It would have to be fearlessly fierce Maria Striar, founding artistic director. By keeping their fingers—or thumbs, really—on the pulse of who and what is hot before anyone else sees it coming, and taking risks on new and untested plays and playwrights by mounting some of the most killer productions around, Striar and her staff have gifted the downtown theater community with the most inventive, zany, and boldly outrageous work out there. Because of their proven track record of identifying, supporting and producing writers who go on to become artistic trendsetters in the field, you can't see a show in New York or turn on your TV without encountering artists who have passed through Clubbed Thumb's doors. Award-winning writers like Lisa D'Amour, Rinne Groff, Sheila Callaghan, Anne Washburn, Sarah Ruhl, and Jordan Harrison have found a home there. Actors like Merritt Wever, Heidi Schreck, James Urbaniak, Michael Showalter, Maria Dizzia, Elizabeth Meriwether, Michael Zegen and hundreds more have gotten a launch doing Clubbed Thumb's signature left-of-center, female-heavy, cutting-edge work that makes you laugh and think in equal measure. It's also undeniable that some of the best directors in the country flock to Clubbed Thumb. Anne Kauffman, Ken Rus Schmoll, Annie Dorsen, and even Tony Award winner Pam MacKinnon (also Clubbed Thumb's chairman of the board), have all staged plays there. Purposefully flexible, scrappy, and badass, Clubbed Thumb's work has brought forth and incubated incredible talent that has resonated on stage and screen far beyond New York, cementing them as a singularly unique and critical downtown tastemaker.

§

I deeply respect Clubbed Thumb's fearlessness, ingenuity and integrity, and being the beneficiary of these was magnificent. Phoebe is a strange play, a slightly askew play, a play in which accumulated destruction and chaos are as much a character as the people in it. Pre-Maria, the response to it had often been, "What else do you have?" Clubbed Thumb gave me a wholehearted invitation into a little family in which the stranger something is, the harder it's embraced—and this is the kind of gift that a playwright never forgets.

—Jen Silverman, Playwright

Mission Statement: Clubbed Thumb

Clubbed Thumb commissions, develops and produces funny, strange and provocative new plays by living American writers. Their plays vary in style and content, but are always intermission-less, 90 minutes or under, and unproduced in New York City. They feature substantial and challenging roles for both men and women, are questioning, formally inventive, theatrical, and, somewhere in the text, they contain a sense of humor. While the comany's emphasis is emerging artists, they provide a home for artists at all stages of their careers to make unique work and take risks in a safe and well-supported environment.

About the Author

Jen Silverman is a New York-based playwright raised in Asia, Europe, and Scandinavia and the United States. Her work has been produced Off-Broadway by The Playwrights Realm (*Crane Story*), Off-Off Broadway by Clubbed Thumb (*Phoebe in Winter*), regionally at InterAct (*The Dangerous House of Pretty Mbane*), and commissioned and produced by Playwrights Horizons Theater School/NYU (*That Poor Girl and How He Killed Her*). *The Roommate* was selected for the 2015 Humana Festival at Actors Theatre of Louisville.

She is an affiliated artist with New Georges, Ars Nova, The Playwrights Realm, The Lark, and Youngblood/EST, was a workspace resident with the Lower Manhattan Cultural Council (LMCC), and received a Playwriting Grant from the New York Foundation for the Arts. She is a two-time MacDowell Fellow and has developed work with Playwrights Horizons, Bay Area Playwrights Festival, NY Stage and Film/Powerhouse, Williamstown, PlayPenn, the O'Neill National Playwrights Conference, Seven Devils, New York Theatre Workshop, and The New Harmony Project. Her play *The Hunters* was selected for the 2014 Cherry Lane Theatre Mentor Project (mentor Lynn Nottage). Her play *Still* won the 2013 Yale Drama Series Award, and was published by Yale University Press. She is the recipient of the Kennedy Center's Paula Vogel Playwriting Award and a Leah Ryan/ Lilly Award. Education: Brown, Iowa Playwrights Workshop, Juilliard. More information: www.jensilverman.com.

Cast of Characters

PHOEBE, early 20s, female

BOGGETT, early 30s, female

DA CREEDY, 60s, male

JEREMIAH, late 20s, male

ANTHER, mid-20s, male

LIAM, early 20s, male

Place

A house in a northern country.

Time

Now or soon.

Playwright's Note

Destruction accumulates. Dishes that are broken in Scene 3 stay on the floor throughout. When Liam gets into the bath, the bathwater stays bloody for the rest of the play. The characters should seem entirely unaware of this.

Also: the metaphors of the play are strongest when the cast is most diverse. If cast this way, there should be no scenario in which the family is all Caucasian, and Phoebe or Boggett are the only actors of color. The family itself should contain multiple ethnicities.

There is no intermission.

Acknowledgments

Phoebe in Winter premiered at Clubbed Thumb's Summerworks at The Wild Project on June 7th, 2013. It was directed by Mike Donahue, with the following cast and crew:

PHOEBE. . . . . Chinasa Ogbuagu
BOGGETT. . . . . Jeanine Serralles
DA CREEDY. . . . . .Gerry Bamman
JEREMIAH . . . . .Christopher Ryan Grant
ANTHER . . . . .Chris Myers
LIAM. . . . . Bobby Moreno

Production Manager. . . . . Cody Westgaard
Stage Manager. . . . . Devorah Jaffe
Set Design . . . . Jason Simms
Costume Design . . . . Kaye Voyce
Lighting Design . . . . .Burke Brown
Sound Design . . . . Stowe Nelson
Fight Choreography . . . . J. Allen Suddeth
Dramaturgy. . . . . .Christine Scarfuto

All production groups performing this play are required to include the following credits on the title page of every program:

> *Phoebe in Winter* was initially produced at The Wild Project in June 2013 by Clubbed Thumb, an Obie Award-winning company that commissions, develops, and produces funny, strange, and provocative new plays by living American writers.

Jeanine Serralles in *Phoebe in Winter,* Clubbed Thumb Summerworks
Festival, New York, New York (2013). Photo: Heather Phelps-Lipton.

Phoebe in Winter
by Jen Silverman

1.

(Darkness.

Far far away, a huge explosion rocks the world. Lights up.

DA CREEDY *sits in his rocking chair, eating an apple.* BOGGETT *the maid crouches by the fire. Outside, it snows.* DA CREEDY *takes a huge juicy bite of his apple and then stops, mid-chew. He examines the apple for a long close beat. Speaks with his mouth full.)*

DA CREEDY. It isn't the season for such things.

BOGGETT. Ah?

DA CREEDY. Unseasonal.

BOGGETT. Ah.

DA CREEDY. Ungodly.

BOGGETT. Ah!

DA CREEDY. Apples in winter. Oranges in winter. Pears in winter. You don't listen to me when I speak. You daydream.

BOGGETT. I do not. They're imported.

DA CREEDY. Ah.

BOGGETT. From warmer places.

DA CREEDY. Ah!

BOGGETT. From places where it's not winter.

DA CREEDY. Exactly!

BOGGETT. Exactly?

DA CREEDY. The world has become a smaller place. That makes it more dangerous.

> *(The sound of footsteps outside.* DA CREEDY *sits upright.* BOGGETT *bolts to her feet in anticipation.)*

BOGGETT. Liam!

DA CREEDY. *(A hand outstretched:)* Wait!
We must let things occur at their own natural time.

DA CREEDY. Such is the problem with a smaller world. One feels that things must occur at one's own natural time. This is dangerous.
Sit, Boggett!

> (BOGGETT *sits. The sound of someone knocking snow off their boots outside.*)

BOGGETT. Do you think it's Liam?

DA CREEDY. Perhaps.

BOGGETT. Perhaps all the boys together?

DA CREEDY. It may be.

BOGGETT. But especially Liam?

DA CREEDY. The boys left together. It does not necessarily follow that they must return together.

BOGGETT. It's Liam. And he's brought us presents.

> (*The door opens.* BOGGETT *is on her feet again, eager.* ANTHER *enters.* BOGGETT *cannot conceal her disappointment.*)

BOGGETT. Anther.

ANTHER. Da Creedy! It's so good to see you!

> (DA CREEDY *takes another bite of his apple.*)

DA CREEDY. *(Through his mouthful:)* It's cold.

ANTHER. It's me!

DA CREEDY. Shut the door properly, it's cold.

BOGGETT. Where are the others?

> (ANTHER *shuts the door properly.*)

ANTHER. I survived! Are you happy to see me?

DA CREEDY. Ah.
Yes. Let's see you.
Turn for me. Turn.

> (ANTHER *turns in a circle.*)

Mmm. Yes. You've done well for yourself. No holes.

ANTHER. No holes.

DA CREEDY. No bits missing. That I can see. Are there?

ANTHER. No bits missing.

DA CREEDY. Well that's good then.

BOGGETT. Where's Little Liam?

DA CREEDY. You won, did you?

ANTHER. I don't know.

DA CREEDY. You don't know?

ANTHER. It was a war, Da Creedy, nobody knows if you've won in a war.

DA CREEDY. Ah?

ANTHER. It's the people from the outside who can tell if you've won. They can see it, you see. Properly. You can't see it properly from the inside of it.

DA CREEDY. Ah.

ANTHER. It's like a boa constrictor, actually. If you'd been eaten by a boa constrictor. And I were to ask you what the boa constrictor looked like.

DA CREEDY. Dark.

ANTHER. Ah?

DA CREEDY. Dark, I'd say.

ANTHER. Ah! Yes. That's good. Dark. Yes. I'd say it was dark.

BOGGETT. *(Beside herself:)* Your brothers, Anther! Your brothers!

DA CREEDY. Sit down, I say! My sons are like imported fruit. They will arrive at our door when the season is right.
(To ANTHER*:)* Sit. Boggett, attend to Anther.

> *(He walks out of the room.*
> BOGGETT *watches* ANTHER *with hungry eyes.)*

BOGGETT. They say the women there are pretty. Real pretty.

ANTHER. Leave me alone.

BOGGETT. You think they were pretty?

ANTHER. I didn't see many women so often.

BOGGETT. I hear they don't even paint their faces. Don't even pluck their eyebrows. Born perfect.

ANTHER. I don't know.

BOGGETT. You don't know?

ANTHER. I don't remember.

BOGGETT. You don't remember.

ANTHER. I saw things burning mostly. Some of them might have been women.

BOGGETT. You leave a woman back there behind you?

ANTHER. No!

BOGGETT. No?

ANTHER. No!

BOGGETT. Did Liam?

> *(DA CREEDY returns with a bottle of whiskey.*
> *The sounds of footsteps outside.* BOGGETT *and* ANTHER *are on their*
> *feet.* DA CREEDY *calmly pours two more shots.)*

ANTHER. Da…there's someone at the door.

DA CREEDY. Could be.

> *(Someone knocks snow off their boots right outside. The door opens.* JEREMIAH
> *enters, explosive. He takes up all the space.)*

ANTHER. Jeremiah!

JEREMIAH. Da Creedy!

DA CREEDY. *(Lifts the shot:)* Well, there's one for all of us.

JEREMIAH. *(Fast and hard:)* Father, it's so good to be back. As I came in through the countryside I looked at all of it—the winter trees, the shapes of things in winter, the darkness of winter—and I thought it was beautiful. There are strange red birds in the jungle. They have feathers like blades. Their voices sound like human voices, and in the early dark of morning, you think you've been surrounded by the enemy as you slept.

DA CREEDY. *(To* ANTHER:) He's full of conversation.

JEREMIAH. Do you remember the birds, brother?

ANTHER. No.

JEREMIAH. No?

ANTHER. I don't remember anything.

DA CREEDY. Bottoms up.

> *(ALL drink.)*

Let's have another.

JEREMIAH. I shot at them, Father, I would shoot at them when I could. The whole way back here I thought: I will wake up in the morning in my old bed and there will be no red birds.

> *(DA CREEDY pours more shots.)*

JEREMIAH. To health and hearth and the hunt.

ANTHER. Indeed.

DA CREEDY. Ah.

> *(They toast and drink.)*

Tomorrow.

ANTHER & JEREMIAH. Ah?

DA CREEDY. A feast.

BOGGETT. A feast?

DA CREEDY. For my sons. Who are home.

JEREMIAH. We ate strange fruits in the jungle, Father. Things swollen like organs and glossy like disease, we ate fruit that was darker than our own blood. You remember the fruit, brother, surely?

ANTHER. *(Close to an outburst:)* I do not. I do not remember. It is too far away.

JEREMIAH. I've dreamed of a good winter meal, beast and peas. I've dreamed of your cooking, Boggett.

> *(He pinches BOGGETT. She backs away.*
> *Footsteps at the door.)*

BOGGETT. Liam!

ANTHER. Liam?

DA CREEDY. Ahh.

> *(The door is kicked open with a CRASH.*
> PHOEBE *stands in the doorway, flushed and glowing with cold, a machine gun pointed at them.)*

PHOEBE. Good afternoon, friends. Don't get up.

2.

> *(Darkness. On the other side of the world, the sound of rapid machine gun fire. A landmine detonates. Then silence.*
>
> *Lights on the living room.*
>
> PHOEBE *sits by the fire with her gun in her lap. The men sit arranged around her. They all keep a wary eye on her as* BOGGETT—*very gingerly—pours her tea.* JEREMIAH *is deeply shaken but fighting to stay in control.*
>
> *A long awkward beat as she sips.)*

JEREMIAH. *(Abruptly, explosively:)* Now see here. I object. I object to this, you see. You can't just march in here and drink our tea. We don't know who is drinking our tea and that is an insult. Do you understand? If we knew you, we might have invited you. But *I* don't know you.

ANTHER. *I* don't know you.

BOGGETT. *I* don't know her. Either.

> *(*DA CREEDY *clears his throat. They are silent.)*

DA CREEDY. Is it good?

PHOEBE. The tea?

DA CREEDY. Yes, the tea.

PHOEBE. It's all right. Thank you.

DA CREEDY. Would you like an apple?

PHOEBE. An apple?

DA CREEDY. To accompany your tea.

PHOEBE. I don't know what that is, an apple.

DA CREEDY. *(To* BOGGETT:*)* Fetch her an apple.

BOGGETT. An apple!

DA CREEDY. To accompany her tea.

>   (BOGGETT *offers an apple, tentatively.)*

PHOEBE. It looks strange. Is there poison in it?

DA CREEDY. Boggett, is there poison in the apple?

BOGGETT. No!

DA CREEDY. No, there is not poison in the apple.

>   (PHOEBE *takes it. She takes out a hunting knife. She plunges it into the apple, sudden and violent. They recoil. She licks the juice.)*

DA CREEDY. What do you think?

PHOEBE. It tastes cold.

>   *(Beat.)*

DA CREEDY. Why, if I may ask, have you been good enough to come by our humble home?

PHOEBE. Ah! Yes. You might want to know that.

ANTHER. We do.

BOGGETT. You see, we do.

DA CREEDY. It would help.

JEREMIAH. She should go.

>   (PHOEBE *clears her throat. They all lean in.)*

PHOEBE. My name is Phoebe.

ANTHER. Phoebe?

BOGGETT. Phoebe.

PHOEBE. Maybe you know it.

JEREMIAH. That's a strange name.

PHOEBE. Or maybe you know my face.

ANTHER. No.

PHOEBE. *(To* JEREMIAH, *a challenge:)* Or perhaps you do.

    *(*JEREMIAH *looks away sharply.)*

JEREMIAH. Of course we don't know your face, don't be ridiculous.

DA CREEDY. What sort of a name is Phoebe?

PHOEBE. You see, this is the situation at hand. I have come from a distance. See you that I alone have come; that my hand shall take hold of judgment; that the foot of my enemies shall slide; that the night is come, that the time makes haste to come.

    (Beat.)

DA CREEDY. Ha?

ANTHER. Judgment?

JEREMIAH. She's mad.

PHOEBE. Judgment. Do not think that I came to spread peace upon the earth. I came not to spread peace, but the sword.

DA CREEDY. Ah?

ANTHER. The *sword?*

JEREMIAH. Ask her to leave, Father.

PHOEBE. That is to say: you killed my brothers. I had three.
So now you will be my brothers.
And I will live here and you will care for me.
And a man's enemies shall be they of his own household.

    (Beat.)

ANTHER. Who killed?

PHOEBE. You did.

ANTHER. I did?

PHOEBE. Or he did.

JEREMIAH. *I* did?

PHOEBE. *(To* DA CREEDY:*)* Or you did.

DA CREEDY. *I.* Did not.

PHOEBE. These are your sons, are they not?

DA CREEDY. They are.

PHOEBE. *(To* ANTHER:*)* This is your brother, is he not?

ANTHER. Well, he——

PHOEBE. *(To* JEREMIAH*:)* And this is yours.

JEREMIAH. Well yes, but—

PHOEBE. And it was a man who killed my brothers. And you are all three men. And you, sir, are a man who fathered men. Am I correct in this so far?

DA CREEDY. Ah. Hum.

JEREMIAH. I argue. I argue. I must disagree. There are many men who have killed many men. We all look the same in war. So do you.

PHOEBE. Yes. And that is why one must stand for all.

(A strange knowing beat between PHOEBE *and* JEREMIAH*.)*

JEREMIAH. I think you should leave.

PHOEBE. I only just arrived.

JEREMIAH. I think you should get out.

BOGGETT. I think she should leave too.

ANTHER. One must stand for one. And another for another. And if another killed your brothers, that's not our fault. Although we're sorry. I'm sure if I thought about it, I would be sorry.

JEREMIAH. What he's saying is, it's not our problem.

PHOEBE. Oh but you misunderstand. Of course it is.
An eye for an eye, a tooth for a tooth, and a brother for a brother.

DA CREEDY. There's one missing.

PHOEBE. Pardon me?

DA CREEDY. Liam. He hasn't come home. In this household, there are only two brothers. And you demand three. So this is clearly not the household to satisfy you. There are others. Why don't you pay them a visit.

PHOEBE. No. I've come this far and this is where I've stopped. If you're missing a third son, then you must be the third son to me.

DA CREEDY. I'm old. I limp when I walk. If I walk. My eyes are clouded. If I were to read, the words would swim on the page. So I do not read.

PHOEBE. But you must. You must read.

DA CREEDY. I must?

PHOEBE. So that you can read to me. A bedtime story. I demand to be read to.

DA CREEDY. I am too old to be your third brother.

PHOEBE. That may be so. But still, you must. What *should be* has been replaced—forever, now—by what *is.*

(A long beat.)

DA CREEDY. Ah.

PHOEBE. Yes.

DA CREEDY. I haven't been young in such a long time.

PHOEBE. You'll enjoy it.

DA CREEDY. Hmm.

PHOEBE. Your knees will bend better. Your back will last longer.

DA CREEDY. And my hearing?

PHOEBE. It will become crystal clear.

DA CREEDY. I shall want to engage in rough sports. As I did in my youth. Wrestling, perhaps. Boxing. The javelin.

PHOEBE. Horseback riding.

DA CREEDY. Something more violent. The hunt, perhaps. A hunt.

PHOEBE. Being my third brother will be the best thing you've ever been.

DA CREEDY. *(Dreaming of it:)* Ah…hm…

PHOEBE. What time is dinner?

(BOGGETT *strides over to* PHOEBE.)

BOGGETT. You need to leave. I don't like you here. I don't want it. There's something about you like a bad bone, like a bad old penny, like the number thirteen and no salt over the shoulder. Get. Go on, get out.

(PHOEBE *lifts the gun so the muzzle rests against* BOGGETT's *chest.)*

PHOEBE. *(Very gently:)* I don't recall addressing you. And here you've spoken out of turn.

(The men stand as one.)

JEREMIAH. Wait.

ANTHER. No need for that here.

JEREMIAH. I'll kick you out myself.

ANTHER. We're a civilized household.

DA CREEDY. You may stay for dinner.

ANTHER. Father!

JEREMIAH. Father!

BOGGETT. Da Creedy!

DA CREEDY. Boggett, I believe, was about to cook us a feast.

JEREMIAH. Father *really!*

DA CREEDY. A roast of some sort. A cooked beast. Have we any beast?

BOGGETT. *(Shaken:)* I—there may be—some sort of—

DA CREEDY. Then prepare it.

> *(A beat.*
> BOGGETT *turns and walks toward the kitchen.* PHOEBE *lets her go, not breaking eye contact until* BOGGETT *herself turns away. When she has reached the door:)*

PHOEBE. I did not have a maid.

DA CREEDY. No?

PHOEBE. Nor a sister. Nor a mother. In my previous family. Therefore, here in this family which I have adopted, no maid will be needed.

> *(*BOGGETT *stops in the doorway.)*

JEREMIAH. We have found her necessary.

PHOEBE. We must get rid of her.

ANTHER. We can't get rid of her. She—prepares things. She fixes them.

PHOEBE. This is no longer a world in which things get fixed. This is a world of inadequate replacements. You are my inadequate replacements and I'm satisfied. She is unsatisfactory to me. She replaces nothing.

DA CREEDY. Perhaps, if only for the length of a meal, she might replace a—a beloved pet. Whom you lost. Tragically.

> *(*BOGGETT *is tense.* PHOEBE *considers this.)*

Anther, perhaps you might give our guest a tour of the house.

ANTHER. A tour?

JEREMIAH. A tour??

DA CREEDY. A tour. So that she has something to occupy her. While dinner is prepared.

JEREMIAH. I'll do it.

> *(*JEREMIAH *brushes past* ANTHER. *Faces* PHOEBE. *A tense beat in which everyone waits. Then* PHOEBE *walks toward* BOGGETT, *brushing past her, too close.)*

PHOEBE. *(To* BOGGETT*:)* You can be the dog.

3.

> *(*BOGGETT *in the kitchen. Upset.)*

BOGGETT. If Liam were here, he'd never tolerate this. He'd never tolerate anyone to be rude to his favorite Boggett. He'd never tolerate. A *stranger.* Just waltzing in. A *dog*. Can you even. The *dog*. I've never. My whole life in this family and I've been insulted a thousand times and I've *still* never. I just. URRGHHH.

> (BOGGETT *unleashes aggression for the first time since childhood. Or maybe ever.*
> *She stops, transfixed. Amazed.*
> *That felt good.*)

BOGGETT. *(Experimentally:)* AGGGRRHHHGHHHHH.

> *(It still feels good.)*

BOGGETT. UUUUUUGGGGAAAAAAAAAAAAAARGHHH!

> *(It's the best she's ever felt.)*

That's what Liam would say. That's what he'd say.

> *(She picks up a plate and smashes it.)*

And that's what Liam would *do*.

> *(Another plate.)*

That's what he'd DO.

> *(Another plate, more plates.)*

And THAT.
And THAT.
And THAT.

> *(Beat. BOGGETT stands in the shards of a number of dinner plates, exhausted and elated. She gets an idea.)*

BOGGETT. Oh!

4.

> *(JEREMIAH stands with PHOEBE in the doorway of a bedroom. He is giving her the tour, brusque and cold.)*

JEREMIAH. And this is a bedroom. And that was a hall. And before that was a staircase.

PHOEBE. Whose bedroom is this?

JEREMIAH. *(Impatient:)* What?

PHOEBE. Who sleeps here?

JEREMIAH. Nobody sleeps here.

PHOEBE. Then I will.

JEREMIAH. You can't sleep here.

PHOEBE. Why not.

JEREMIAH. You can't, is why not.

PHOEBE. You don't seem to understand, Jeremiah. I'm your sister now. I will need a place to sleep.

JEREMIAH. You are not my sister.

PHOEBE. And you are my brother.

JEREMIAH. I am *not* your brother.

PHOEBE. And your brothers are my brothers. And your food will be my food and your maid will be my dog and your father will be my brother. And so this bedroom will be my bedroom. Simpler like that. One shouldn't share a bed with one's brother. *(Beat—needling:)* Should one?

JEREMIAH. Father's a fool to give you dinner.

PHOEBE. I'll put a nightstand…here. Perhaps one of you will carve it for me. And a new little bed, one that is more my size. Right here. We'll pluck all the geese naked to fill the mattress, like my old brothers did. And I'll hang all my pictures on the walls. When I have pictures again.

JEREMIAH. You don't belong with us.

          (PHOEBE turns back toward him. Very sober.)

PHOEBE. No that's you. Who doesn't belong. Not among your own kind. Not anymore.

JEREMIAH. *(Shaken:)* I don't know what you mean.

PHOEBE. Don't you?

          (Beat.)

JEREMIAH. Did Liam tell you to come here?

PHOEBE. I know things the people who love you don't know. And *you* know things the people who love you don't know. And that gives us a commonality. That's almost the same thing as family.

JEREMIAH. Did he give you our address?

PHOEBE. Was he planning to take me back here, you mean? Make me his honorable bride?

JEREMIAH. Answer the question!

          (Beat.)

PHOEBE. Right here.
Right…about…here. Is where I'd put a nightlight.

JEREMIAH. …A nightlight.

PHOEBE. I like to see in the dark. I like to know what's coming.

(Beat. JEREMIAH *is close to losing his control.)*

JEREMIAH. Phoebe.

PHOEBE. Yes?

JEREMIAH. What happened there—it was an accident. It happened so fast. You have to know that. You can't look at me like that. You have to know.

PHOEBE. I don't. I don't know.

JEREMIAH. It was so hot we could hear the jungle fruits rotting as they grew. The sound of putrefaction, Phoebe, have you heard it?

PHOEBE. The last time he came to my bed. He said, "Some day when this is all over, we'll go home together." As if I didn't already have a home. As if you all weren't destroying it.

JEREMIAH. Listen to me!

PHOEBE. But now—here I am at last. In some approximation. Home. Isn't that sweet? I think it's sweet.

JEREMIAH. If you haven't ever heard it, the sound of rotting, I don't think you can understand.

PHOEBE. I've heard it. So what?

JEREMIAH. I never meant for things to go so far.

PHOEBE. Didn't you?

JEREMIAH. He was weak. You saw that. I tried to make him a man.

PHOEBE. You tried to make him unkind, like all the rest of you.

JEREMIAH. The way Liam talked about you—as if no one else were going to your bed at night. But Liam couldn't see it, could he. He thought he was special. He thought he loved you.

PHOEBE. He loved you too, big brother. And you put a bullet between his eyes. What is that, do you think? Is that love? Or is that just family?

*(*JEREMIAH *loses his control. He puts his hand around her throat. Calm, victorious, she doesn't move.)*

PHOEBE. Oh look. There he is.
There is Jeremiah.

*(*JEREMIAH *drops her. A beat.* PHOEBE *smiles.)*

JEREMIAH. I don't want that. That's not what I want.

PHOEBE. Of course it is. Of course it is what you want. Don't lie to little sister. She knows her brothers through and through. *(Very gentle:)* I'm not here to destroy you. In fact, I would like to think we have an understanding.

JEREMIAH. An understanding.

PHOEBE. I would like to think that neither of us will misremember the truth.

JEREMIAH. Which truth?

PHOEBE. That you've never seen me before. And I've never seen you. And you killed no one. And no one came to me in the night.
And you are my brother.

JEREMIAH. We can feed you.

PHOEBE. You are my flesh and blood.

JEREMIAH. Things like that can't be so easily built.

PHOEBE. Things that are easily destroyed should be easily built. No? Big brother?

JEREMIAH. *(A concession:)* Little sister.

(ANTHER *comes in, out of breath.)*

ANTHER. I've been calling.

(JEREMIAH *and* PHOEBE *move away from each other.)*

PHOEBE. We didn't hear you.

ANTHER. *(Glancing between them:)* Are you all right?

PHOEBE. Of course.

JEREMIAH. I'll just go freshen up before dinner.

(JEREMIAH *turns and stalks out. Beat.)*

ANTHER. I hope Jeremiah wasn't rude to you.

PHOEBE. Of course not.

ANTHER. I'm sorry. I want to apologize for him. On his behalf.

PHOEBE. That's gentlemanly of you. But I don't need it.

ANTHER. He killed ants as a child. Nothing bigger. It made Liam cry. Liam is the youngest.

PHOEBE. I know who Liam is.

ANTHER. You do?

PHOEBE. Jeremiah was just informing me.

ANTHER. He didn't mean it. To insult you or to offend you. Or if he did, he didn't mean to mean it. It's just—one becomes different. After things. Certain large-scale things.

PHOEBE. I don't think Jeremiah has ever done something he did not mean. And neither have I. It is one reason we see eye to eye.

(Beat, ANTHER *glances at her, uncertain.)*

ANTHER. *(Re. Phoebe's gun:)* Do you want to put that down?

PHOEBE. Oh. I forget about that. It's just a weight. Like carrying an arm. Or a baby. Don't pay any mind to it.

ANTHER. It's hard for either of us to ignore a gun. You understand.

> *(Beat.* PHOEBE *smiles at him. It's a very sweet smile. He looks away immediately. She takes off the gun. She puts it down with a flourish, on the bed.)*

PHOEBE. Does that feel friendlier?

ANTHER. Somewhat.

PHOEBE. Good. I want us to feel friendly.

> *(Beat.)*

Did you kill ants?

ANTHER. What? No.

PHOEBE. No?

ANTHER. Not really.

PHOEBE. No, or not really?

ANTHER. One does things. One is in the moment and one acts. Later, one does not quite remember. It did not define one's character, you see, the action. It defined the moment.

PHOEBE. I see.
And what defines the character, Anther?

> *(Beat.)*

ANTHER. We should go freshen up for dinner.

PHOEBE. I'm going to live in this room.

ANTHER. You can't live in this room.

PHOEBE. I have already started. I have already begun living in this room.

> *(Beat,* ANTHER *is stymied.)*

PHOEBE. Have you ever had a mother?

ANTHER. *(Uneasy:)* Well of course I've had a mother.

PHOEBE. What was she like?

ANTHER. Like?

PHOEBE. How did you recognize her in the mornings? How did you know her to be your own?

ANTHER. She smelled familiar.

PHOEBE. Come here.

(She holds out an arm.)

Come *here.*

(ANTHER approaches cautiously.)

Smell me.

(Beat. ANTHER smells her.)

PHOEBE. What do I smell like?

ANTHER. Smoke. Dirt. Gunpowder.

PHOEBE. And isn't that familiar?

(ANTHER looks away.)

PHOEBE. I think you put your face against a woman's neck once, and she smelled like this. You put your face against her neck and later you gave her money. It wasn't your mother though.

ANTHER. *(Recoils:)* Don't talk like that.

PHOEBE. *(Puts her hand on his arm.)* We all need something in this world. And those who don't take what's given and mold it into what they need are the ones who go without.

(ANTHER looks at the hand on his arm.)

ANTHER. *(Softer:)* Stop.

PHOEBE. You seem kind.

ANTHER. I do?

PHOEBE. You do.

ANTHER. I think you're wrong.

PHOEBE. I think you're scared.

ANTHER. I'm always afraid these days.

PHOEBE. I used to be afraid of everything. And now there's nothing in the world to scare me.

ANTHER. That must be nice.

PHOEBE. You miss your mother, don't you?

(Beat.)

ANTHER. This was her bedroom.

PHOEBE. If you have a bad dream in the night, come stand in the door. You'll hear my breathing and you'll smell my smell and you won't feel afraid.

5.

(Darkness. The sound of a tank rumbling past, far on the other side of the earth.

Lights up. Dinner is served. Everyone around the table. PHOEBE *sits beside* ANTHER. *She is comfortable as the littlest sister.)*

PHOEBE. Please pass the peas.

JEREMIAH. *(Passes to* DA CREEDY:*)* The peas.

DA CREEDY. *(Passes to* ANTHER:*)* The peas!

ANTHER. Have the peas, Phoebe.

*(*ANTHER *would pass to* PHOEBE *but* BOGGETT *swoops in and takes the peas. Staring straight at* PHOEBE: *a calculation.)*

PHOEBE. The dog has got the peas.

ANTHER. May we please have the peas?

PHOEBE. The dog has got the peas, Anther.

ANTHER. Boggett, would you please pass me the peas?

PHOEBE. Is it common for a pet to disrupt dinner?

JEREMIAH. Boggett, give Anther the peas.

ANTHER. Phoebe, would you like some beast?
Da Creedy, pass Phoebe the beast.

DA CREEDY. *(Correcting him:)* "Liam."

PHOEBE. I would like the peas.

ANTHER. Have some beast.

PHOEBE. Peas.

JEREMIAH. Beast!

PHOEBE. Peas!!

DA CREEDY. There's no need to shout at the table, brothers. My hearing has improved immensely.

PHOEBE. How wonderful for you.

DA CREEDY. It is! It is wonderful. And my sight! And my knees! And my knuckles, are they not the knuckles of a young man?

PHOEBE. I'm immensely gratified on your behalf. *I,* however, would like THE PEAS.

ANTHER. *(Diplomatic:)* Would you like *first* some beast and *then* some peas?

PHOEBE. *(Tightly:)* I suppose.

JEREMIAH. *(Passes:)* The beast.

DA CREEDY. *(Passes:)* The beast!

ANTHER. *(Passes:)* Have the beast, Phoebe.

> (—But BOGGETT *intercepts the beast. She balances it on the peas and maintains her baleful stare.)*

PHOEBE. *(Flatly:)* Your dog has intercepted my beast.

ANTHER. Really now Boggett!

JEREMIAH. Stop being childish, can't you see we're at dinner!

DA CREEDY. Nevermind the beast, a young man should consume nothing but brandy. That's what I think.

> (BOGGETT *picks up the bottle of brandy, and drops it on the floor. It smashes.* PHOEBE *leans back—now she's intrigued.)*

JEREMIAH. Now see here!

ANTHER. Boggett what are you doing! This is a civilized occasion!

JEREMIAH. She needs a beating. One used to beat the help.

DA CREEDY. *(Curiously:)* When did one beat the help?

JEREMIAH. In the olden days, one beat the help. It spurred the onset of progress.

ANTHER. She's very confused. It's a very confusing time.

PHOEBE. She is not confused. She has something to say.

> *(All of them look at* PHOEBE.*)*

(To BOGGETT:*)* Go ahead.

> *(All of them look at* BOGGETT.*)*

BOGGETT. Liam has not returned. In his absence, given the dictates of our guest, a third brother is required. I and only I must take on the role of Liam. Not the maid. Not the dog. No other option is acceptable to me.

> *(The men are shocked.* PHOEBE *smiles.)*

DA CREEDY. You?

BOGGETT. Me.

JEREMIAH. *You* want to be Liam.

BOGGETT. Every family of three brothers must have a youngest brother.

DA CREEDY. That's my job. Being Liam. She said that would be my job.

BOGGETT. You can be Boggett, if you need a job.

DA CREEDY. *(Appealing to* PHOEBE:*)* You said I could be Liam.

PHOEBE. *You* said you were too old.

DA CREEDY. And then *you* said that I was *not* too old. You said that I can walk upright, like the young. Breathe deeply, like the young. Engage in foolish fantasies, like the young.

PHOEBE. I said that the world is a state of aftermath and in a state of aftermath, many things are permissible. I did not say that you—specifically— were the best choice.

JEREMIAH. This is obscene.

(Beat. PHOEBE looks at JEREMIAH.)

PHOEBE. Do you wish to elaborate?

JEREMIAH. Liam is absent. It is vulgar for either Boggett or Da Creedy to be Liam.

PHOEBE. On the contrary. If he were here, it would be harder to be Liam. Given his absence, anything becomes possible.

(Beat—JEREMIAH retreats.)

PHOEBE. Let us return our attention to the matter at hand: who will stand in for the youngest son?

DA CREEDY. I will.

BOGGETT. *I* will. Or your food goes uncooked, your beds go unmade, flies will invade, cockroaches will follow, I will break your dishes and perhaps late at night, when you're curled in your soiled sheets dreaming wastelands and nightmares, I will slip into your filthy rooms and deliver a swift hatchet to your heads. One by one. Head after head.

PHOEBE. The family dog makes a convincing argument. Years of observing the speech of humans has made her eloquent.

DA CREEDY. Whose side are you on!

PHOEBE. My own. *(Beat—to BOGGETT.)* Come here.

(BOGGETT approaches her.)

Make a muscle.

(BOGGETT does.)

Make another.

(BOGGETT does.)

Stand like a man.

(BOGGETT does.)

Look at me like a man.

(BOGGETT looks PHOEBE up and down, a long measuring glance. Both cold and sexual.)

PHOEBE. *(Impressed despite herself:)* Very good. *(To* DA CREEDY:*)* Now you stand over there.

(DA CREEDY approaches her.)

Make a muscle.

(DA CREEDY does.)

Make another.

(DA CREEDY does.)

Stand like a man.

(DA CREEDY does.)

Look at me like a man.

(A long beat. Finally:)

PHOEBE. *(To* BOGGETT:*)* Congratulations. You have been selected to be Liam.

BOGGETT. Thank you.

DA CREEDY. This is unbelievable.

BOGGETT. *(To* PHOEBE, *with some respect:)* You're a little viper.

PHOEBE. I started as a viper then turned into a girl. You started as a dog and turned into a man. I don't see much of a difference between us except that I, from the beginning, was meaner, faster, stronger.

BOGGETT. That remains to be seen.

PHOEBE. Doesn't it?

(They study each other.)

DA CREEDY. This is all very disturbing. *(To* BOGGETT:*)* Fetch me the brandy. I need brandy.

BOGGETT. Fetch it yourself.

DA CREEDY. *(Outraged but reasonable:)* I am an old man. I do not fetch my own liquor.

ANTHER. Would someone please pass the peas?

(BOGGETT and DA CREEDY stare at each other—a heaving contest of iron wills.)

DA CREEDY & BOGGETT. *(Together, referring to the other:)* Boggett will do it.

6.

(PHOEBE in the bedroom alone. She explores the space with quiet ecstasy. She can't quite bring herself to sit on the bed yet. She gives it the reverence it deserves. BOGGETT appears in the doorway, dressed in Liam's old clothes. Beat. She enters.)

BOGGETT. You got the old lady's room.

PHOEBE. My room now.

(BOGGETT walks around the room. PHOEBE lets her. BOGGETT stops by the bed.)

BOGGETT. She and Da Creedy stopped sharing a bed after the youngest son. The king retreated to his living room, the queen to her tower.

PHOEBE. And the land grew cold.

BOGGETT. The land has always been cold.

PHOEBE. And where did you come from?
Did you crawl your way out of an apple like a baby worm?

BOGGETT. Boggett drifted downstream in a basket and they took her in. Or perhaps a cow gave birth to a baby Boggett. Or else the king fucked a girl in the next town over and took home a new little Boggett. Maybe it was that. That's none of my concern now. The youngest son crawled his way out of the jungle.

PHOEBE. And tell me about that.

BOGGETT. It was bloody and vicious and tangled. I loved every second of it.

PHOEBE. Did you?

BOGGETT. I did.

PHOEBE. And the killing?

BOGGETT. I threw away my weapons so I could use my bare hands.

PHOEBE. And the threat of being killed?

BOGGETT. I used to walk naked through fields sown with landmines. Just in the off-chance that I'd be blown sky-high.

PHOEBE. How did it feel?

BOGGETT. It was like an early morning run and a fresh cup of coffee.

PHOEBE. That's great.

BOGGETT. I think so. I think it's great.

PHOEBE. But perhaps factually incorrect.

BOGGETT. Fuck that. I don't care about that.

(Beat.)

Little Liam was a pretty little boy. He fell down and skinned his knees. Or his brothers pushed him. Either way he cried. Boggett always hit the older boys when they made him cry. Then later he got bigger. Later Little Liam went off to war. I'm almost sure he cried there.

PHOEBE. He did. Once or twice. *(Catches herself:)* Most likely.

BOGGETT. *(Sharp-eyed:)* Did he?

PHOEBE. I would imagine.

>	*(Beat.)*

BOGGETT. I'm what Liam never could have been. The strongest. The fastest. The best of the three. That's me now. The youngest prince.

PHOEBE. The favorite brother.

BOGGETT. *Your* favorite brother.

PHOEBE. *(Smiles.)* That remains to be seen.

>	*(Beat. BOGGETT sidles closer and closer to PHOEBE. PHOEBE lets her, easily. BOGGETT walks a circle around PHOEBE, studying her.)*

BOGGETT. You're very pretty.

PHOEBE. Thank you.

BOGGETT. It's good to have a pretty sister. I wouldn't want an ugly one.

PHOEBE. Nobody wants an ugly sister.

BOGGETT. That's very true. Brothers, on the other hand, must be brutish.

PHOEBE. If they are not brutish, then they are not brothers.

BOGGETT. How true. And fathers, what do you think of fathers?

PHOEBE. What functional good do they do, may I ask?

BOGGETT. Indeed, what?

PHOEBE. Did Da Creedy grow things? Did he repair them?

BOGGETT. Indeed not.

PHOEBE. Did he give birth to things? Did he clean them?

BOGGETT. He did neither.

PHOEBE. Or maybe he defended things? Maybe he clubbed things to death and dragged them indoors.

BOGGETT. I can't say that he did. He had ideas about things.

PHOEBE. But the world is no longer a place for those with ideas.

BOGGETT. It's a place for us. You and me. To take what we're owed.

PHOEBE. I have.

BOGGETT. Pardon me?

PHOEBE. I have taken what I was owed.
This world? Right here? I like it this way.
But perhaps brother is dissatisfied.

  (Beat. Challenging. Then BOGGETT *smiles.)*

BOGGETT. If little sister is happy, then I'm happy.

PHOEBE. How delightful to find that we are in accord. It is rare for a family to be in accord.

BOGGETT. Rare and yet, when it occurs—

BOGGETT & PHOEBE. *(Together:)* Delightful.

  (A beat. Razor-edged. They measure each other up. BOGGETT *stretches out on Phoebe's bed, testing the bounds of their alliance.)*

BOGGETT. The old queen's bed is very comfortable.

PHOEBE. I hadn't tested it yet.

BOGGETT. Not a lump. Not a pea.
Fit for the littlest sister.

PHOEBE. The frailest of the lot.

BOGGETT. Oh?

PHOEBE. *(Smiling:)* The weakest. The gentlest. Cheek of milk. Touch of feather.
That's me.
Now get the fuck out of my bed.

  *(*BOGGETT *stands, taking her own sweet time.)*

PHOEBE. I'm gratified to have you as my littlest brother. I believe a number of our principle goals and values are in firm accord. Don't you?

BOGGETT. It does seem like that. For the moment.

PHOEBE. For the moment.

  *(*PHOEBE *goes to the door, signaling that* BOGGETT *should leave.)*

Good night Liam.

BOGGETT. Good night little sister.

  (Beat. BOGGETT *maintains eye contact for one lingering challenging beat. Then leaves.)*

7.

(The living room, as in Scene 1.

PHOEBE *sits in Da Creedy's rocking chair, eating an apple.* JEREMIAH *reads the funnies.* ANTHER *reads over his shoulder as they drink from little glasses.* BOGGETT *sits in the most comfortable chair, with her boots on the furniture. She drinks straight from the bottle. Her steely gaze is often fixed on* JEREMIAH.

DA CREEDY *crouches by the fire, dressed as* BOGGETT *once dressed. Outside, the wind howls.*

PHOEBE *takes a juicy bite of her apple and then stops and examines the apple for a long close beat. Speaks with her mouth full.)*

PHOEBE. And you say these grow here?

ANTHER. Not in the winter. Nothing grows in the winter.

PHOEBE. And yet, it is here.

ANTHER. It came from somewhere else.

PHOEBE. Do these grow in my country?

JEREMIAH. No, nothing from here thrives there.

BOGGETT. I would. *(She finishes the bottle. To* DA CREEDY;*)* Fetch me another.

*(*DA CREEDY *leaves the room.)*

PHOEBE. Little brother.

BOGGETT. Yes, little sister?

PHOEBE. My little throat is parched.

*(*BOGGETT *takes* ANTHER's *brandy glass out of his hand. She gives it to* PHOEBE, *gallantly.)*

ANTHER. Give that back.

PHOEBE. Little brother, we must be polite to bigger brother.

BOGGETT. Little sister, drink your drink and be glad you have it.

PHOEBE. That's also a sound philosophical approach. But we must preserve the peace in our little family.

BOGGETT. *Peace?*

PHOEBE. Within our family, yes. The family is the microcosm of the world, after all.

(A beat. PHOEBE *returns* ANTHER's *drink.)*

ANTHER. Thank you.

PHOEBE. You're welcome. *(To* BOGGETT:*)* You see? The face of a brave new world.

*(*BOGGETT *sprawls back in the chair.)*

BOGGETT. I miss the war.

JEREMIAH. Nobody misses the war.

BOGGETT. I can do more push-ups than you. So shut up.

JEREMIAH. You cannot.

BOGGETT. I can.

JEREMIAH. You know you can't.

BOGGETT. I can and I will and also I can do more pull-ups.

JEREMIAH. *(Increasingly irritated:)* Were you using my bar? I told you not to touch my things.

BOGGETT. You're not using it. You're just sitting around getting fat.

JEREMIAH. My razor was missing this morning.

BOGGETT. Oh boo-hoo.

JEREMIAH. You've been in my room again haven't you. *(On his feet:)* I will thrash you if you go in my room again.

BOGGETT. *(On her feet:)* Just try it.

JEREMIAH. My muscle mass exceeds yours.

BOGGETT. My manhood eclipses yours.

JEREMIAH. You—that is not true! That is not true!

BOGGETT. Length *and* girth.

ANTHER. Brothers. Please.

PHOEBE. Listen to Anther.

ANTHER. Thank you, Phoebe.

PHOEBE. You're welcome, Anther.

*(*DA CREEDY *returns with a fresh bottle.)*

BOGGETT. You can just put it there, Boggett.

(He puts the bottle where she directs him.)

More to the right.

(He does.)

More to the left.

(He does.)

BOGGETT. Take it away. A cold drink on a cold day is uncouth. I prefer a hot toddy.

(*A beat.* DA CREEDY *removes the drink.*)

It is almost impossible to get good help these days.

ANTHER. (*Peace-keeping:*) It is difficult. But perhaps Boggett finds it difficult as well.

BOGGETT. Boggett's difficulties are not of concern to me. It is *my* difficulties that are of concern to me.

JEREMIAH. Little Liam is forgetting his place.

ANTHER. Little Liam is restless.

JEREMIAH. Then you'd better give him something to do before I give him a knock in the mouth.

BOGGETT. We'll see who gives who a knock in the mouth.

PHOEBE. Brothers, little sister is terribly upset when you fight. Stop it at once.

ANTHER. I'm sorry, Phoebe.

BOGGETT. He started it.

JEREMIAH. I will twist your face.

PHOEBE. We should go on a family outing.

JEREMIAH. It's winter.

BOGGETT. An outing where?

DA CREEDY. (*Returning with a hot toddy:*) I want to go.

(*They all look at him.*)

PHOEBE. (*Gently:*) But who will make dinner if you go, Boggett?

ANTHER. (*Kindly:*) And the fire must be hot for when we return.

JEREMIAH. We're running low on firewood.

PHOEBE. And the laundry, the laundry must be done.

BOGGETT. We should go hunting.

JEREMIAH. What would we hunt?

BOGGETT. Each other. We should hunt each other.

(*Beat between* BOGGETT *and* JEREMIAH.)

ANTHER. Like hide and seek?

BOGGETT. It would be like hide and seek but you kill what you find.

JEREMIAH. You can't play this game. Liam hides in stupid places and we find him and he cries.

PHOEBE. *(Intrigued, now:)* And the winner? What does the winner win?

JEREMIAH. Or he hides in stupid places, and we don't find him, and he cries.

BOGGETT. You. The winner wins little sister. All for himself.

PHOEBE. I must say I've always liked being the center of attention.

DA CREEDY. I want to play too.

JEREMIAH. You can't play. You're busy.

DA CREEDY. I want to play too!

BOGGETT. This is a game for men.

DA CREEDY. I WANT. TO PLAY. TOO.

ANTHER. Let Boggett play.

> *(Beat.)*

PHOEBE. Little brother, do you really think it's proper to let the maid play with you?

ANTHER. Little sister, a game is no fun if there are only a few players.

DA CREEDY. I'd be good. I'd be a good player. I'd hide so good. Nobody would ever find me again. Except when I came swinging down out of a tree. Or popping up from a hole. Or sliding from the shadows. Ready to crush. Ready to stab. Secret and silent and vicious. An unstoppable force of destruction. You'd be so glad you let me play.

PHOEBE. All right. But let us play inside. I am not yet adjusted to the cold.

ANTHER. None of us would want you to catch cold.

JEREMIAH. *(Sets his newspaper aside.)* I suppose there's going to be a lot of running and shouting and it will be impossible to read.

DA CREEDY. Yes, running and shouting! It has been such a long time since I ran and shouted!

BOGGETT. I will be It. You must all hide immediately. If I find you, I will kill you. Is that understood?

JEREMIAH. *(With a dark look:)* Perfectly.

ANTHER. But cover your eyes. No cheating.

> *(BOGGETT covers her eyes as everyone scatters to hide. She cheats on the counting.)*

BOGGETT. One two three fourteen sixteen twenty-one twenty-two thirty...

(Only JEREMIAH *doesn't scatter to hide. He stands behind her. A dark beat. Then he puts his hands around her throat.* BOGGETT's *eyes shoot open. She struggles. He chokes her. Then: a clattering. A banging of boots.* JEREMIAH *drops* BOGGETT. *She gasps for air.* PHOEBE, ANTHER, *and* DA CREEDY *stick their heads out of their hiding places, unaware of the violent act they just missed.)*

PHOEBE. Is there—?

ANTHER. Is someone—?

DA CREEDY. There's someone—

PHOEBE. The door, Boggett, see to the door.

*(*DA CREEDY *rises and goes toward the door. Before he reaches it, the door is kicked open with a CRASH.* LIAM *stands in the doorway, flushed and glowing with cold.*

There is a giant hole in his head, from which blood continually oozes. He cradles a gun across his chest. All of them freeze, eyes on him.)

LIAM. Good afternoon, brothers. Don't get up.

8.

*(*LIAM *in the bathtub, naked. His army uniform is discarded next to the tub.* BOGGETT *sits on the edge of the tub, still wearing Liam's clothes and a pair of combat boots. There is an easy familiarity between them. Although* LIAM *is soaking the dirt away, his gaping head wound still bleeds in a casual manner.)*

BOGGETT. Get your back?

LIAM. Oh yes please.

BOGGETT. Hard to reach.

LIAM. I think I have ringworm.

BOGGETT. Where?

LIAM. In the middle.

BOGGETT. I'll scrub.

*(*BOGGETT *scrubs* LIAM's *back. Long pause.)*

How is it?

LIAM. Feels good.

BOGGETT. No—being dead.

LIAM. It itches.

BOGGETT. Oh?

LIAM. All the time. Sort of just under the skin. So you scratch but it doesn't really ever stop itching.

BOGGETT. Could be ringworm.

LIAM. Maybe it's a combination.

> *(BOGGETT scrubs more.)*

LIAM. You look good.

BOGGETT. Thanks.

LIAM. That was my favorite jersey.

BOGGETT. I know.

LIAM. It looks good on you.

BOGGETT. I know.

LIAM. You look happy.

BOGGETT. I am.

LIAM. Did you miss me?

> *(BOGGETT stops scrubbing. She looks straight at LIAM. Dead honest:)*

BOGGETT. You're the only one I missed.

> *(LIAM smiles. It lights up his whole being.)*

LIAM. That makes me feel good. That makes me feel good to hear you say that, Boggett.

BOGGETT. "Liam."

LIAM. Sorry. "Liam."

BOGGETT. Your hair is filthy.

LIAM. Maybe you shouldn't touch it.

BOGGETT. I'll wear gloves.

LIAM. There's larvae, I think.

BOGGETT. And other things. Growing.

LIAM. I'll just let it soak for a while. Before you touch it.

BOGGETT. *(Re: head wound:)* Does it ever stop bleeding?

LIAM. Hasn't yet.

BOGGETT. That's a bother.

LIAM. You get used to it.

BOGGETT. Like the itching?

LIAM. I don't get used to that.

BOGGETT. I could give you a good scratch.

LIAM. Do you think it would help?

> (BOGGETT *scratches* LIAM's *back. He arches in pleasure.)*

LIAM. Mmm—ohhhh—yes, right there.

BOGGETT. Is it helping?

LIAM. Not really.

> (BOGGETT *stops scratching. She sits back and looks at* LIAM, *seriously.)*

BOGGETT. Jeremiah has become unmanageable.

LIAM. Ah.

BOGGETT. He threatened me, Liam. I will not have it.

LIAM. *(Alarmed:)* Ah.

BOGGETT. You're afraid of him. Still. Aren't you.

LIAM. Don't look at me like that.

BOGGETT. I want revenge, Liam. And you will want it too. You will learn to want it more than you want other things, like peace, or silence.

LIAM. I always thought you'd do a better job of it. Being the youngest son.

BOGGETT. You never stood up for yourself. That was your problem. I told you and I told you.

> *(Beat.)*

Does it make you sad?

LIAM. To see you doing a better job of it?

> (BOGGETT *nods.)*

LIAM. Not really. That sort of itches too, I guess. But in a way I can get used to. *(Hesitates:)* Bog—Liam?

BOGGETT. Yes?

> *(Beat.)*

What?

LIAM. Nothing.

BOGGETT. You're too dead to be timid, boy. Spit it out.

LIAM. Do you think she was happy to see me?

BOGGETT. Who? *(Beat—wary:)* Phoebe?

> (LIAM *nods.)*

BOGGETT. Oh lord.

LIAM. What?

BOGGETT. I knew from the second you walked in, there was something bad between you two.

LIAM. I think I'm in love with her.

BOGGETT. You absolutely are not.

LIAM. What if I am?

BOGGETT. Then we'll scrub that out of you along with the head lice and the ringworm.

LIAM. You don't like her.

BOGGETT. She's useful.

LIAM. If the whole world had been blanketed with napalm and there was one last single flower left and it was growing out of a festering mound of carcasses writhing with maggots, I would want to wade naked through the napalm and the festering and the maggots so that I could pick that flower and give it to her and say: "Look, I got you the one last single flower in the whole entire world."

(Beat—BOGGETT is nauseated—)

LIAM. That's how I feel.

BOGGETT. *(Gags.)* I just tasted a kidney.

LIAM. I think she's wonderful.

BOGGETT. Listen. It's great you want to wrestle bouquets from the jaws of maggots, but I don't think she's good for you. And also, I don't think she loves you.

LIAM. How would you know!

BOGGETT. She looks at you the way she looks at all of us. The way maggots look at a carcass.

LIAM. *(Deeply stung:)* I think you're wrong.

BOGGETT. All I've ever done is try to keep you from skinning your knees.

LIAM. *(Sharp:)* I have a big fucking gash in my head, I'm not worried about my knees!

(Beat. They stare at each other.)

BOGGETT. *(Softly, with some wonder:)* You *have* changed after all.

LIAM. *(Scared:)* I haven't.

BOGGETT. You have. Even you.

LIAM. *(Close to tears:)* I haven't, I haven't at all.

BOGGETT. Shhhh. Shhh OK? It's OK.

(She strokes his disgusting hair.)

Close your eyes. Lean your head back now. Shhh.

(LIAM closes his eyes. Relaxes into BOGGETT's touch. She sings.)

Rockabye Liam, in a tall tree
There's no one who loves you better than me
I'll guard you all night til the monsters are gone
And when the sun rises, I'll carry you home.

LIAM. *(Sleepy:)* Liam?

BOGGETT. Yes?

LIAM. I like it better like this.

BOGGETT. Like what?

LIAM. Like with two of me. Two Liams. I felt so lonely all the time for such a long time.

BOGGETT. You won't ever need to feel lonely anymore.

LIAM. Will you stay with me until I fall asleep?

BOGGETT. Yes. And then I'll wrap you up in a towel and carry you to your room and tuck you in.

LIAM. The way you always used to do.

BOGGETT. The way I always used to do.

LIAM. Thank you, Liam.

BOGGETT. You're welcome, Liam.

> *(They sit together, LIAM drifting, BOGGETT stroking his head. DA CREEDY lurks in the doorway, just in the shadows. Boggett's clothes do not fit him well. He is thin, malnourished, bitter. He watches them. BOGGETT realizes he's there. She lifts her head and looks straight at him. A beat between them. DA CREEDY leaves.)*

9.

> *(PHOEBE and the brothers in the living room. It is very civilized. JEREMIAH drinks fine wine. He reads a Very Large Book. ANTHER drinks fine sherry. He plays chess against himself. PHOEBE drinks a Shirley Temple. She stares moodily out of the windows.)*

JEREMIAH. This is a fine passage.

ANTHER. I've just made a fine move.

JEREMIAH. This author displays a fine command of logic and causality.

ANTHER. But then when I play the other side, I make fine moves as well.

(DA CREEDY creeps into the room. He refreshes everybody's drinks, then remains standing.)

JEREMIAH. *(Impatiently:)* Yes Boggett?

DA CREEDY. *(Tattle-tale:)* I'm sorry to interrupt, but I thought you should know the Liams are in your room again.

JEREMIAH. *(On his feet:)* They test my patience!

(He storms out of the room. DA CREEDY almost cracks a smile.)

ANTHER. Nobody likes a tattle-tale, Boggett.

DA CREEDY. I'm sorry.

PHOEBE. I don't think they were there at all.

DA CREEDY. I'm sure I don't know what you're talking about, miss.

(From the hallway, a thud and a yelp. Another thud, voices raised, a crash.)

ANTHER. *(Alarmed:)* Boggett, separate them. Boggett!

(DA CREEDY makes no move. Another crash, louder and closer, and more yelling. ANTHER gets up hastily and leaves the room. Beat.)

DA CREEDY. I meant to ask you, miss, how's the bed in the spare room?

PHOEBE. Quite comfortable, thank you.

DA CREEDY. You've seemed to be quite comfortable.

PHOEBE. I have been. That will be all.

(Beat.)

DA CREEDY. If I might trouble you with another question...

PHOEBE. What is it?

DA CREEDY. When do I get to stop being Boggett?

PHOEBE. Stop?

DA CREEDY. Yes.

PHOEBE. Stop being Boggett.

DA CREEDY. Yes.

PHOEBE. You can't stop being Boggett.

DA CREEDY. But—

PHOEBE. If you were to stop being Boggett, who would be Boggett?

DA CREEDY. You—you might. I thought.

PHOEBE. *(Laughs:)* I don't want to be Boggett.

DA CREEDY. Perhaps one doesn't need a Boggett.

PHOEBE. Of course we need a Boggett. It—prepares things. It fixes them. There can be no fine drinks and fine books and fine moves without a fine Boggett.

DA CREEDY. But there has to be a respite.

PHOEBE. But a respite for you would not be a respite for us. Surely you understand that.

DA CREEDY. There has to be room for change. For turnover.

PHOEBE. No no. Change is in the past. Turnover, unsteadiness, it is all in the past.

DA CREEDY. *(A quiet threat:)* If I am required to be Boggett for much longer, I can't hold myself responsible for what may occur.

> *(*PHOEBE *rises to her feet, wholly intimidating.)*

PHOEBE. Don't test me, Boggett. I'm no stranger to revolutions. Or the means by which one crushes them.

DA CREEDY. If I may be excused?

PHOEBE. You're dismissed.

> *(*DA CREEDY *leaves.* PHOEBE *sits back down.* JEREMIAH *re-enters the room. He nurses his lip.* ANTHER *follows.)*

JEREMIAH. The Liams are becoming unmanageable.

ANTHER. Liam The First said he wasn't in your room.

JEREMIAH. He's a liar. He always has been. Whose side are you on, anyway!

ANTHER. I'm not on anybody's *side,* Jeremiah, I think we can all get along peaceably. Being dead is a difficult adjustment. We should give him every benefit of the doubt.

JEREMIAH. We've all had a difficult time, Anther! One cannot create a new world by being given the benefit of the doubt! *(Beat.* JEREMIAH *sits— sulkily:)* And I don't like Boggett's attitude.

ANTHER. What's the problem?

JEREMIAH. Boggett is underperforming.

ANTHER. It's an adjustment, being Boggett when you haven't had to be.

JEREMIAH. There you go again with your adjustments. We are all making adjustments, Anther, but do you see myself or Phoebe or yourself, do you see us being discourteous in any way?

ANTHER. No.

JEREMIAH. No you do not. That is because we are forging a more civilized world. Is that not right?

PHOEBE. That is exactly right.

> *(LIAM and BOGGETT enter. BOGGETT is dressed in Liam's army uniform. LIAM is dressed as a civilian. A fresh bandage is wrapped around his head. As soon as he enters, LIAM's attention is fixed on PHOEBE, and JEREMIAH's is fixed on LIAM. PHOEBE tries hard not to look directly at LIAM, but she keeps sneaking glances.)*

JEREMIAH. Brother.

LIAM. Brother.

ANTHER. Good afternoon Liams.

JEREMIAH. You slept in.

ANTHER. You must have been tired.

LIAM. Liam drew me a hot bath last night, it put me right to sleep.

BOGGETT. *(At JEREMIAH:)* Until someone came storming in with his panties in a bunch.

JEREMIAH. *(At BOGGETT, to PHOEBE:)* Do you see? Discourteous.

ANTHER. *(Peace-keeping:)* You didn't have any nightmares, I hope?

LIAM. Not anymore, no. I just have the same dream over and over again.

ANTHER. What is it?

LIAM. One in which I itch.

BOGGETT. *(To LIAM, re: PHOEBE, sotto voce:)* You're gawking.

LIAM. *(To PHOEBE, soft:)* Hi.

> *(Beat. When PHOEBE responds, she's deeply uncomfortable. She can't quite look at him.)*

PHOEBE. Hello.

LIAM. I'm sorry about yesterday.

PHOEBE. Yesterday?

LIAM. I was filthy. I kept bleeding.

PHOEBE. It's perfectly all right.

LIAM. I would have liked to make a better appearance.

PHOEBE. It's fine.

> *(BOGGETT clears her throat loudly.)*

ANTHER. *(To LIAM & BOGGETT:)* Would you care for a drink?

LIAM. *(Still focused on PHOEBE:)* I can't drink. It just comes out of my pores.

ANTHER. Oh.

LIAM. *(To* PHOEBE*:)* You look…wonderful.

PHOEBE. *(Uncomfortable:)* Thanks.

LIAM. Better fed. Brighter. Like you belong here.

PHOEBE. I do. I do belong here.

LIAM. Yes of course, but I meant: as if you *always* belonged here. Since the past.

PHOEBE. The past is bad manners. One doesn't make reference to it.

LIAM. *(Flustered:)* Oh of course. I'm sorry.

>   *(Beat.)*

You've changed your hair. It looks good.

PHOEBE. Thank you.

LIAM. It also looked beautiful before. You used to brush it with your fingers.

PHOEBE. I don't remember that.

LIAM. *(Inviting her to laugh:)* I brought you a comb. You didn't know what it was.

PHOEBE. I don't remember those things.

LIAM. Phoebe—

PHOEBE. *(To the room:)* I would like a fine wine. Little sister is cold, and she would like somebody to please bring her a fine blanket and a fine wine and…

ANTHER. Where did Boggett go?

>   *(*BOGGETT *studies them, narrow-eyed.)*

BOGGETT. Get ahold of yourself, Liam.

>   *(*LIAM *takes off his jacket. He is going to put it over* PHOEBE*.)*

PHOEBE. No! No…thank you. I don't…that is not necessary.

LIAM. I don't want you to be cold.

PHOEBE. *(Low:)* You're standing too close.

>   *(A beat.* LIAM *backs up a step. He's sad.* BOGGETT *hits him with her shoulder.)*

BOGGETT. Put your jacket on, Liam.

JEREMIAH. I'm *trying* to read.

LIAM. Sorry.

BOGGETT. *(On top of him, sarcastic:)* Terribly sorry.

JEREMIAH. *(A warning:)* Phoebe!

ANTHER. *(Brightly:)* There's a dead bird in the backyard. Did anyone see it? Let's go see it.

JEREMIAH. What kind of bird?

ANTHER. A red one.

JEREMIAH. Here?

ANTHER. They've started flying into the windows now. They must be migrating.

JEREMIAH. There's nothing more delightful than a dead red bird in the snow.

> *(PHOEBE gets up. As she leaves the room:)*

LIAM. Where are you going?

PHOEBE. I've seen enough dead things.

10.

> *(JEREMIAH in the bath. Bubble bath. He drinks champagne. DA CREEDY comes in.)*

JEREMIAH. Boggett! This is not an appropriate time.

> *(DA CREEDY closes the door.)*

DA CREEDY. We have to talk.

JEREMIAH. I'm in my bath.

DA CREEDY. You are my eldest son. I have raised you. I have trained you. I have trusted in you.

JEREMIAH. How strangely you speak, Boggett. And how inappropriately.

DA CREEDY. There was a time when I was not Boggett! Can we not cast backwards to that time?

JEREMIAH. I'd rather not. It's uncomfortable for me.

DA CREEDY. But couldn't we—very briefly—recall the time when I raised you and held you and jostled you on my knee?

JEREMIAH. I am too old to be jostled on someone's knee, Boggett. But I am not too old to enjoy my bath.

DA CREEDY. But you have to remember! Once upon a time, I sat in my chair! My rocking chair! I ate an apple! A fresh apple! I had ideas! Such ideas they were!

JEREMIAH. Perhaps you did. Perhaps you did do those things. What is that to me, directly, in my current situation, my position if you will, here in my bath?

DA CREEDY. What I am saying is this: we have to get rid of Phoebe.

(Beat. JEREMIAH puts down the book.)

JEREMIAH. We can't get rid of Phoebe. Phoebe is our sister.

DA CREEDY. I was once a man with books. And now look at me. If I have fallen thus far, how far do you think you might fall?

JEREMIAH. Phoebe is necessary. The world has achieved shape and form because of Phoebe.

DA CREEDY. The world had a better shape and form before Phoebe arrived.

JEREMIAH. I must disagree.

(He picks up his champagne again. DA CREEDY knocks it out of his hand.)

JEREMIAH. What do you think you're doing!

DA CREEDY. Now listen to me and listen to me well. When Phoebe's world falls—and it will fall—which side do you want to be standing on?

JEREMIAH. You were home. You were here. You were safe, while we fought. And you wouldn't know this, but the smell soaked into the plants. If you picked a flower, it would smell like a slaughterhouse. If you chewed a blade of grass, it would taste like an infected wound. And that was the way the world looked for a long time.

(Beat.)

We can't come home to what we left. We have to come home to something new. And this is something new.

DA CREEDY. I just want things to go back to how they were.

JEREMIAH. That can't happen anymore.

DA CREEDY. Liam is home. Things will be different now that Liam is home.

JEREMIAH. Liam, Father? Liam was always weak, he was the only one of the three of us that died, and now he's home and there's two of him. Don't rest any of your hopes too strongly on his return.

DA CREEDY. You were always an opportunist. More than any of your brothers.

(Irritated, JEREMIAH gets out of the bath and pulls his bathrobe on.)

JEREMIAH. The champagne has spilled. You'd best mop it.

(He walks out. Beat. DA CREEDY alone. DA CREEDY sighs, a heavy sigh that comes from the bottom of his stomach. He sits slowly on the edge of the tub. His back hurts. He slips off his shoes. He dangles his feet into the tub water. He closes his eyes.)

DA CREEDY. Ah-h-h-h. I remember this.

(He is moved almost to tears by the feeling. BOGGETT appears in the doorway. She stands there watching him.)

BOGGETT. Feels good, doesn't it?

(DA CREEDY's eyes snap open.)

DA CREEDY. Go away.

BOGGETT. I might want to take a bath.

DA CREEDY. I'm cleaning. I'm cleaning the bath. Go away.

BOGGETT. Feels right, doesn't it. Feels civilized.

DA CREEDY. You're no son of mine.

BOGGETT. And I never wanted to be.

(Beat.)

Jeremiah, on the other hand…

DA CREEDY. I have disowned him.

BOGGETT. Flesh of your flesh, rib of your rib. That's Jeremiah. How does that feel, seeing him sit in the bath and refuse you?

DA CREEDY. I don't need a son who has no loyalty in his heart.

BOGGETT. I imagine it would feel terrible. I imagine it would be a fish-hook in the heart.

DA CREEDY. What are you doing here?

BOGGETT. I'm having a conversation with you.

DA CREEDY. They're sipping champagne and reading in the living room. Why don't you join them.

BOGGETT. I'm not interested in champagne and reading. I'm interested in war.

(Beat. DA CREEDY sizes up a potential ally.)

DA CREEDY. Is that right.

BOGGETT. That is.

DA CREEDY. You're on Phoebe's side. You can't trick me.

BOGGETT. Don't mistake me, old man. I'm on my own side.

DA CREEDY. And Liam?

BOGGETT. Liam and I are both Liam. We're on the same side. Whether or not he knows it.

DA CREEDY. What are you offering?

BOGGETT. No, what are *you* offering.

(Pause.)

DA CREEDY. I don't want her here.

BOGGETT. I could get behind that.

DA CREEDY. Or Jeremiah. If he's with her, he's against me.

BOGGETT. Jeremiah should be the first to go.

DA CREEDY. Ah.

BOGGETT. Ah.

DA CREEDY. What is Jeremiah to you?

BOGGETT. There is bad blood between us. That is all you need to know.

DA CREEDY. And Phoebe? Where is your bad blood with her?

BOGGETT. She is confusing to Liam at a time in his life when he cannot stand to be confused.

(Beat.)

DA CREEDY. You always did have an unhealthy interest in that boy.

BOGGETT. Unhealthy by whose standards?

DA CREEDY. By any. The way you look at him. As if you would devour him alive. *(Gestures to her clothes, her stance:)* I guess you did. In the end.

BOGGETT. Is there a point to this, old man? Or shall we discuss the terms?

DA CREEDY. Jeremiah toppled, Phoebe unseated. What other terms are there?

BOGGETT. Liam and I both stay Liams.

DA CREEDY. I have no objection to that.

BOGGETT. And we get the upper wing of the house.

DA CREEDY. The upper wing?

BOGGETT. You have the living room. We want the bedrooms. We can share the kitchen, at different times, and the bath. Also at different times.

DA CREEDY. And dinner preparations? And cleaning the bathroom? And making the beds?

(Beat. Both consider.)

BOGGETT. There's Anther.

DA CREEDY. There *is* Anther.

> *(They consider each other.)*

BOGGETT. Listen up old man. You don't like me much and I've never liked you. But in this current situation, we can both be useful to each other. There's no harm in that. Makes us something stronger than family. Allies. Maybe.

DA CREEDY. I've always thought you were spiteful. Cold. Ruthless. A face like a slab of frozen beef.
I find all of those attributes comforting in an ally.

> *(They shake hands.)*

DA CREEDY. What's our first move?

BOGGETT. We must create a distraction in the Kitchen long enough to establish our base of operations in the Living Room.

DA CREEDY. I can see you've given this some thought.

BOGGETT. Peace is a fragile thing, Da Creedy. It doesn't take much to shatter it. And once something is shattered, it can be rebuilt the right way.

11.

> *(PHOEBE, ANTHER, JEREMIAH, and LIAM at the dinner table. It is a very formal and elegant dinner.)*

PHOEBE. Brothers, please pass the beast.

> *(JEREMIAH picks up the platter and passes to LIAM.)*

JEREMIAH. Brother, please pass the beast to sister.

ANTHER. *(Passing to LIAM:)* Brother, pass the beast to sister, please.

> *(LIAM holds the platter out to PHOEBE. He watches her with large eyes. She can't look at him. She takes the platter abruptly.)*

LIAM. Have some beast, please, Phoebe.

PHOEBE. Where's the other Liam?

LIAM. Liam has a headache.

PHOEBE. And Boggett?

ANTHER. Boggett was feeling ill. Boggett took to bed after preparing dinner.

PHOEBE. Boggett has been sluggish of late. Sullen about the mouth.

ANTHER. Boggett's back has been hurting.

JEREMIAH. There's something funny about those two.

ANTHER. *(A mild protest:)* I'm sure they'll be fine by tomorrow.

JEREMIAH. I am beginning to hold them in distrust.

LIAM. *(To* PHOEBE:*)* Have you had the peas? They're quite good.

PHOEBE. *(Not looking at him:)* No thank you.

JEREMIAH. One should never trust anyone. That's my opinion.

LIAM. I can pass them if you'd like.

PHOEBE. I said no thank you.

JEREMIAH. *(To* LIAM:*)* Pay attention to your own dinner, not sister's.

LIAM. *(To* PHOEBE:*)* Do you not like peas? We can tell Boggett not to make them anymore.

JEREMIAH. Sit and eat your meal in silence or I will thrash you.

LIAM. *(To* PHOEBE:*)* I don't like them either, actually. I only ever ate them to be agreeable.

JEREMIAH. *(To* PHOEBE:*)* Little sister, do you not think it is impolite for one to be dead at the dinner table? We must begin holding ourselves to new standards, or else we shall never have any civilized dinners at all.

(LIAM *shoves his chair back violently and stands, in a towering rage.)*

LIAM. You can't talk to me like that anymore. Not anymore.

(A stunned silence.)

JEREMIAH. Pardon me?

LIAM. You heard me.

JEREMIAH. *(Suddenly on his feet as well:)* Maybe you'd like to repeat yourself.

ANTHER. Brothers! Brothers…

LIAM. I know what you did, Jeremiah. You and I, we know what you did.

ANTHER. What does he mean?

JEREMIAH. *(White-knuckled:)* And what about the things *you* did, little brother? Shall we discuss those?

LIAM. What were they? You tell me what I did to deserve such a betrayal.

ANTHER. What are they talking about?

JEREMIAH. You would have run away in the night, abandoned us for one of their women! Where was your loyalty? Where was your honor!

LIAM. You shot me in the head, brother, where was yours!

ANTHER. What are they saying? Make them stop saying such strange things.

JEREMIAH. *(Tightly:)* I don't remember that.

LIAM. Tell me, explain to me—

JEREMIAH. You're confused. You're very confused.

LIAM. I've never seen it all so clearly!

ANTHER. This is not civilized, this conversation, I can't stomach it—

JEREMIAH. Sit down, Liam, please—

LIAM. I said that to you too didn't I, I said *please*, I said *stop*—

JEREMIAH. Liam—!

(*PHOEBE whistles. They all stop.*)

PHOEBE. Is this any way to eat a civilized meal?

LIAM. (*To* PHOEBE, *wildly:*) You remember. He remembers. I remember. Perhaps there are things that Anther remembers. None of us here are talking about the things we remember.

PHOEBE. (*Straight to* LIAM:) That is because we no longer have a use for them.

LIAM. But I do. I do have a use for them.

PHOEBE. No. You may once, perhaps, have had a use for those memories. But they will not serve you here. They won't put dinner on the table. Boggett will. They won't heat you. The fire will. They won't soothe you. The bath will. Do you understand?

LIAM. I remember your lips against my lips. I remember your hair under my fingers. I remember I made you laugh. Once.

(*PHOEBE is shaken, but she holds onto the impenetrable logic of what she is saying.*)

PHOEBE. That was before I was your sister. Now I am your sister. I don't put my lips against your lips. You do not run your fingers through my hair. Neither of us needs to laugh. This isn't hard to understand.

LIAM. I loved you.

(*A beat that takes the oxygen out of the room.*)

I love you.

(*A beat.*)

Tell me you didn't love me!

PHOEBE. I didn't know you.

LIAM. I tried to take you away from all of it! Tell me you don't love me!

PHOEBE. You were a man! They were all men! I didn't know one of you from another!

LIAM. (*Raw:*) You did! You know you did!

PHOEBE. You, your men, you were a procession of blurs.

LIAM. But you came here for me! You came here to find me!

PHOEBE. You gave me your address and I used it. In what world could I *love* you, Liam?

> *(LIAM crosses the space between them in a heartbeat and has* PHOEBE *by the throat.)*

LIAM. That's not true, say it's not true.

PHOEBE. I wouldn't even have remembered your name if you hadn't written it down.

LIAM. *(Anguished:)* That isn't true! I was different from everybody else! Tell me I was different!

PHOEBE. You were weaker! I felt sorry for you!

JEREMIAH. Liam, I will kill you again if I have to!

> *(A breathless weightless beat. LIAM lets go of* PHOEBE. *Into the silence:)*

LIAM. *(Exhausted:)* At least you felt something.

ANTHER. Let's return to dinner. Let's eat dinner. Dinner is getting cold.

JEREMIAH. Something will have to be done about this. Dinner can't be disrupted.

LIAM. What if I were different. What if I didn't come from anywhere. What if it was just this world, this one in winter. And nothing ever came before winter.

PHOEBE. When summer comes you'll thaw, and we'll put you in the ground.

LIAM. Then love me until summer.

JEREMIAH. Sit down, Liam.

ANTHER. Please pass the beast.

LIAM.	JEREMIAH.	ANTHER.
Phoebe?	Liam?	Brothers?
Phoebe!	Liam!	Brothers?
Phoebe!	Liam!	Brothers?

> *(The kitchen explodes. Darkness.)*

12.

(Lights up. The living room. BOGGETT *and* DA CREEDY *build a barricade.* DA CREEDY *is beside himself with delight.* BOGGETT *is efficient. She carries a pickaxe.)*

DA CREEDY. Never saw it coming. The bastards. Never even guessed. Underestimated. That's their problem. Should never do that, underestimate. Thought: what can he do, the old man. Eating their beast. It was good beast. Passing the wine. Good wine. BOOM! Good boom. Never saw it.

(LIAM enters the barricaded living room. He's shaken, sooty, but undamaged.)

There's one of them now! Attack! Attack!

BOGGETT. It's Liam, sit down. *(To* LIAM:*)* We have a password now.

LIAM. Liam—the Kitchen exploded.

BOGGETT. There's a password before we let you through the barricade. It's "starfruit."

LIAM. Why is there a barricade in the Living Room!

DA CREEDY. Quick, come inside boy. Before they follow.

BOGGETT. "Starfruit." Say it fast.

LIAM. You've pickaxed the chairs.

BOGGETT. "Starfruit"!

LIAM. "Starfruit."

(BOGGETT lets him through the barricade.)

DA CREEDY. How's the enemy encampment, Little Liam?

LIAM. I don't want you to do anything to Phoebe.

DA CREEDY. I thought you said he was on our side.

BOGGETT. Go play sentry, old man. Let me handle this.

(DA CREEDY withdraws, disgruntled.)

LIAM. Liam!

BOGGETT. Yes, Liam?

LIAM. You shouldn't have done anything to Phoebe!

BOGGETT. Come here, Little Liam.

(BOGGETT leads him to a pile of homemade explosives.)

Do you see these? Do you know what these are?

LIAM. I don't want this.

BOGGETT. These are bombs. They are made to detonate. That is their nature. We are made to detonate them. That is our nature. Who are we to debate nature?

LIAM. I want to leave.

BOGGETT. You can't leave. There is no leaving.

LIAM. You can come. We'll both go. We can take Phoebe far away from this.

BOGGETT. Who do you think brought it here in the first place?

> *(Beat.)*

The seeds were planted in her. They grew up through her heart. Into her words. Into her eyes. Everything she saw and named and touched turned to this. And its inside you, too. Those seeds. Turning. Growing.

LIAM. Inside me?

BOGGETT. Inside you, Little Liam.
Don't you feel them there?

> *(Beat. LIAM does.)*

LIAM. How do I take them out?

BOGGETT. *(Genuinely surprised:)* Take them out? Look at you. You are in an age of power. A moment of power. You and I both. Why would we want anything less?

LIAM. I don't think I'm happy.

> *(BOGGETT laughs.)*

LIAM. Don't laugh at me!

BOGGETT. My sensitive little friend. When we win, we'll get the master bedroom. Da Creedy wants the living room. Jeremiah will be the Boggett and—

LIAM. I don't want the master bedroom!
I want Phoebe.

> *(Beat.)*

BOGGETT. And you can have her. If you stay.

LIAM. I can?

BOGGETT. All yours. Not your enemy. Not your sister.
A new Phoebe.
Phoebe will love you.
Morning and night, she will stay with you.
Would that satisfy you?

LIAM. What do I have to do?

BOGGETT. Keep her in the woodshed away from the house. Keep her tied up and she's yours.

 (Beat.)

LIAM. Tied up?

BOGGETT. Firmly tied up.

 (Beat.)

LIAM. What if it didn't have to be like this.

BOGGETT. But it always does, Liam. Somehow it always does. Which side are you on?

LIAM. But what if—

BOGGETT. Them or us?

LIAM. Boggett—

BOGGETT. That's not my name.
That's not my name, Liam.
Which side are you on.

DA CREEDY. *(Perched on top of the barricade:)* Intruder! There's an intruder!

 (ANTHER pokes his head around the door. He is dressed in as much armor as he could fashion from plates and pots and metal.)

ANTHER. I want Liam to come outside the barricade. Liam The First.

 (LIAM exits the barricade. Face to face with ANTHER. A beat between them: recognition.)

LIAM. Brother.

ANTHER. Brother. Can we end this?

LIAM. No, we can't end this.

ANTHER. If we just explained—if we just sat everyone down and explained to them—

LIAM. If you want it to end, you have to win. Or we do.

ANTHER. You and I have never been on different sides.

LIAM. Of course we have. The best preparation for war that we had was growing up together.

ANTHER. That's not how it was.

LIAM. No?

ANTHER. We were a happy family.
We played like brothers. We grew, as brothers.
When we became men, we went off to war, as brothers.

LIAM. And did we love each other, Anther, as brothers? Did we guard each other's backs?

ANTHER. Jeremiah was the one who bullied you.

LIAM. And you were frightened of him, so you let him.

ANTHER. I didn't *let*—

LIAM. You stood by.

ANTHER. He gave me orders.

LIAM. And you took them.
Your silence has always spoken louder than your words.

ANTHER. I'm not him. I'm not like him.

LIAM. No. You're worse.

> *(Beat.)*

This is how it will go. You will return to your camp. They will ask you: How is the enemy encampment? You will reply: It is weak. You will lower their guard.

ANTHER. Liam—slow down—

LIAM. And you will deliver a message to Phoebe. Tell her to meet me in the Bathroom.

ANTHER. In the—?

LIAM. And then you will perform your final act.

ANTHER. All I ever wanted was peace.

LIAM. But at *any* cost. At *any*. Peace at *any* cost is never peace—it's just cost.

ANTHER. I don't know if I can do this.

LIAM. Oh but you will. And do you know why?

ANTHER. Why?

LIAM. Because this time I'm the one giving you orders.
Take off your jacket. And come with me.

13.

> *(The kitchen. War zone. JEREMIAH has constructed his own barricade. He sharpens knives, creates catapults, all the toys of war. PHOEBE sits, without participating. She watches him. Both are singed, burned, disheveled.)*

JEREMIAH. We ate strange fruits in the jungle, Phoebe. I can't think of the names. And yet my mouth aches for sweetness.

> *(Beat.)*

JEREMIAH. What are you thinking?

PHOEBE. Guava, papaya, passion fruit, mango.

JEREMIAH. I'm sorry?

PHOEBE. Those were the fruits.

JEREMIAH. It's beautiful when you say it.

PHOEBE. You didn't know how to eat them. But you adapted. And now that you may have beast and peas whenever you wish, it's the jungle fruit that you want. When this is over, perhaps you will have the opportunity for a glass of champagne, a hot bath, a good dinner. But perhaps you will no longer desire those things. Do you understand what I'm saying?

JEREMIAH. I do not.

PHOEBE. This is not the world I wanted, brother. This isn't what I wanted.

JEREMIAH. We'll remake it. It will be better. You'll see.

PHOEBE. Jeremiah—

JEREMIAH. He's back!

> (ANTHER *re-enters the kitchen. Stopped by the barricade.*)

JEREMIAH. Password!

ANTHER. "Captain Jeremiah."

JEREMIAH. Let him back in Phoebe.

> (PHOEBE *lets* ANTHER *back in.*)

JEREMIAH. How was the enemy encampment?

ANTHER. Weak.

JEREMIAH. Is that so?

ANTHER. Deficient.

JEREMIAH. Are they armed?

ANTHER. Barely.

JEREMIAH. And their morale?

ANTHER. Lacking.

JEREMIAH. Very good. How did they welcome you?

ANTHER. I told them that I was a splinter-group.

JEREMIAH. Well done, soldier.

ANTHER. Thank you, Captain.

JEREMIAH. I've promoted myself to General. Given this time of conflict. Phoebe, how many hand-held explosives are we currently in possession of?

PHOEBE. I haven't counted.

JEREMIAH. Who has recovered the guns?

PHOEBE. I couldn't find them.

JEREMIAH. Do I have to do everything around here?

(JEREMIAH turns away, readying a stockpile of assorted weaponry.)

ANTHER. Liam asked me to give you this. *(Hands her a note.)* You need to go.

PHOEBE. What—?

ANTHER. Go!

JEREMIAH. *(Returning:)* Let them remain behind barricades in the Living Room. We must compromise the essential passageways. The corridors.

ANTHER. Very good sir.

JEREMIAH. We will begin with the air-conditioning. Perhaps one might spray rat poison through the vents. Anther, I will assign you field research in this area.

ANTHER. Yes sir.

(JEREMIAH studies ANTHER with cold calculation. It is utterly unnerving.)

JEREMIAH. Soldier.

ANTHER. Yes sir.

JEREMIAH. Take off your jacket, soldier.

ANTHER. Excuse me?

JEREMIAH. You heard me.

ANTHER. I don't understand.

JEREMIAH. You heard my order.

(A beat. ANTHER undoes his jacket. Holds it open. Nothing. JEREMIAH studies him, narrow-eyed.)

ANTHER. *(Scared:)* What's wrong.

JEREMIAH. Your shirt.

ANTHER. Jeremiah—!

JEREMIAH. Your shirt, soldier!

(After a long beat, ANTHER undoes his shirt. He has crude home-made explosive devices strapped to his body.)

JEREMIAH. *(Quiet:)* Any last words?

ANTHER. This wasn't my idea.

JEREMIAH. You took the wrong set of orders.

(He breaks ANTHER's *neck.* ANTHER *falls.* PHOEBE *stares.)*

JEREMIAH. They'll try any means. The enemy. Any means.

(Beat.)

JEREMIAH. Take the body outside.

PHOEBE. The ground won't thaw until spring.

JEREMIAH. I don't care what you do with it, Captain. Just get it out of my sight.

PHOEBE. Captain?

JEREMIAH. You've been promoted. Given this time of conflict.

14.

(The bathroom. Night. PHOEBE *sits on the edge of the bathtub. Waiting. She holds Liam's note.* BOGGETT *appears in the doorway.)*

BOGGETT. Not the Liam you were expecting?

PHOEBE. Where is the other Liam?

BOGGETT. Is the bath lovely and warm?

PHOEBE. I haven't been in it.

BOGGETT. Dip a toe, tell me.

PHOEBE. I don't want a bath.

BOGGETT. It's delightfully civilized, bathing. I should think you would have taken to it.

PHOEBE. I'm waiting for Liam.

BOGGETT. Oh, one Liam is as good as another, these days. I'll do nicely.

(Beat. She approaches PHOEBE. *Too close.)*

PHOEBE. *(Uneasy:)* You should go back downstairs to the war.

BOGGETT. I will.

PHOEBE. You should go now before you miss something.

BOGGETT. I'm taking a break. A respite. Every great leader needs a respite. Why don't you join me?

PHOEBE. In what?

BOGGETT. In my respite.

*(*BOGGETT *moves past* PHOEBE, *sensually, and slides fully-clothed into the bath. She stretches, eyes on* PHOEBE *the whole time.)*

BOGGETT. Why don't you read to me, little sister.

PHOEBE. Read to you.

BOGGETT. Your letter.

> *(Beat.)*

PHOEBE. It's personal.

BOGGETT. We're family.

PHOEBE. It wouldn't interest you.

BOGGETT. On the contrary, I will find it mesmerizing.
Unless there's something you wish to hide. In which case I wouldn't want to intrude.

> *(PHOEBE knows she is briefly outmaneuvered.)*

PHOEBE. *(Hostile:)* No, nothing at all. *(Clears her throat. Reads:)* "Dearest Phoebe."

BOGGETT. "Dearest." That's very nice. That, right there. "Dearest."

PHOEBE. *"Dearest* Phoebe. I know that there is history between us. Little of it is good."

BOGGETT. There's his self-effacing side coming out.

PHOEBE. "I hope that one day you can forgive me for my part in it. I do not, however, expect your forgiveness."

BOGGETT. "Forgiveness." What an antiquated word. I think it's gone out of usage these days. *(A beat, knowing there's more:)* A rather abrupt ending. Or does it continue?

PHOEBE. *(With finality, but lying:)* "Yours, Liam."

> *(PHOEBE folds the letter and puts it away.)*

BOGGETT. Rather abrupt.
I would have expected Liam to be rather less esoteric. To say, in essence:
Meet me.
Run away with me.
Let us escape.
—A romantic gesture, if useless.

> *(PHOEBE glances at BOGGETT, alarmed. They both know BOGGETT has the upper hand.)*

Are you sure you won't join me in the bath?

PHOEBE. What have you done with Liam?

BOGGETT. The Living Room has launched a counter-attack on the Kitchen, you know. Their forces met in the Hall.

PHOEBE. And Liam?

BOGGETT. The West Bedroom and East Bedroom will soon be involved. The Bathroom, little sister, will be involved. Don't think you can just slip out, no matter how Liam ended his note.

PHOEBE. Maybe Liam has changed, now that he's dead. Maybe he is capable of other things.

BOGGETT. Maybe he is, little sister. But you, on the other hand, claimed us. You sought us out. Where would you go that you wouldn't bring us with you?

PHOEBE. Maybe I have changed too. Maybe it is within me, to want something other than you.

BOGGETT. Is it?

PHOEBE. Maybe I want something else. Apart from this.

BOGGETT. Do you?

PHOEBE. I had three brothers.

BOGGETT. And then you had three more.

PHOEBE. Now I don't have any.

BOGGETT. Brothers are a slippery business these days.

PHOEBE. I thought about finding three new ones.

BOGGETT. Did you?

PHOEBE. But then I thought: if this is what accompanies three brothers, I would rather have one, perhaps. Or none at all. Live alone, even. In a small house somewhere.

BOGGETT. It's too late for that. You came here demanding three brothers, and that is what you got. You can't suddenly say you would have preferred just one.

(Beat.)

Kneel down by me, little sister. Look carefully at yourself.

(A beat. PHOEBE kneels on the other side of the bathtub. She looks at her reflection in the water, and BOGGETT looks as well.)

I admire you, you know.
Your shapely limbs. Your sleek form. Your ugly jaw. It is an ugly jaw. But it lends your face a certain strength.

PHOEBE. Does it.

BOGGETT. Your ugly chin. It is an ugly chin. But it bestows upon you a sense of direction.

PHOEBE. Direction?

BOGGETT. And your eyes. You have undeniably ugly eyes. But they do give you a distinctive air of self-sufficiency. Yes, it certainly is fortunate for you to have such ugly eyes.

PHOEBE. Are you done?

BOGGETT. I thought you were pretty but you're not very pretty after all. I see something in you, of course. Adaptability. Hunger. Those are traits that I value, personally. Not the traits of a deserter. But Liam. Liam is a deserter. What do you think he sees in you? Do you know?

PHOEBE. Things neither you nor I see. But he can see them because he values them. Maybe if I could see them, I would value them.

BOGGETT. Weakness. That's what he sees in you. Shared weakness. Nothing more than that.

PHOEBE. Let me tell you what I see in you.

BOGGETT. Yes?

PHOEBE. Ambition.

BOGGETT. Go on.

PHOEBE. That's it. Ambition.

> (BOGGETT *takes* PHOEBE's *head gently in her hands. She stares into* PHOEBE's *eyes.*)

BOGGETT. I have never met anyone else like you in the world, little sister. And I admire you greatly.

> (BOGGETT *plunges* PHOEBE's *head underwater.* PHOEBE *struggles frantically.*)

Shhhh. It will all be over soon.
It is no longer your turn to be The Phoebe.
It's my turn to be The Phoebe.
It is your turn to be The Liam. And The Liam is dead.

> (*Sings:*)

Rockabye Liam, in a tall tree
All good things must give way now to sleep
I'll guard you all night til the monsters are gone
And when the sun rises, I'll carry you home.

> (PHOEBE *stops struggling. She is dead.* BOGGETT *pulls her into the tub. She holds* PHOEBE *closely. She strokes her wet hair. Beat.* LIAM *enters, breathless. He stops when he sees them. Beat.*)

LIAM. What have you done.

BOGGETT. You would have left? Without even saying goodbye?

LIAM. How could you.

BOGGETT. And then what! And then you would have found yourself in trouble, and I would have had to come save you.

LIAM. Don't touch her!

(*A beat.* BOGGETT *stands, letting* PHOEBE *fall back into the water.*)

BOGGETT. Don't touch her? I *am* her.
You are looking at Phoebe, Liam. I am The Phoebe.
Be careful, that you do not become The Boggett.

LIAM. I'm dead. I don't have to be anything I don't want to be.

BOGGETT. In the past. That was true of the past. But we are entering a new age.

LIAM. Get out!

(BOGGETT *walks past* LIAM. *He goes to the bathtub, kneels by* PHOEBE. *In the door,* BOGGETT *hesitates.*)

BOGGETT. (*As close as she gets to apology:*) If I have been harsh—it has been for all of us. The world has become deeply disordered. I, as The Liam, could not repair the damage. You will like it, Liam, the new world that I will create.

LIAM. There will be nothing new in it.

BOGGETT. How can you say that?

LIAM. It will be old. Built on a ground that is old. Its bones and fastenings are old. There is no new world when the ones who build it are soaked in the blood of the old.

(*A long beat. This actually touches* BOGGETT *all the way down to bone. She hears it. He looks in her eyes and sees the weight of it. And then she shakes it off.*)

BOGGETT. I will be downstairs in the parlor when you are ready. I will be drawing up a new strategy. I will expect you to be present.

(*She goes.* LIAM *climbs into the bathtub. He holds* PHOEBE. *He strokes her hair back.*)

LIAM. This is how it will be, Phoebe.
We'll go South.
The ground will thaw. The sunny days will be longer. The air will heat. Just enough.
We will thaw.
And we will lay ourselves down in the earth, Phoebe. The warm moist earth. Just you and I.
We will lie together until our bones grow together.
And you will let me love you.
And it will be very quiet.

(A gigantic EXPLOSION, like the one that started the play, rocks the entire house. Lights flicker wildly, water in the bathtub spills, windows break, smoke shrouds our vision. Lights flicker into darkness.)

15.

(Lights up. The living room. As at top of play. The ultimate aftermath of a war zone. Everything is broken. Scattered. Shattered. The house is missing large parts of its walls. Snow has accumulated on the furniture and the floor. Winter has invaded the house, and everything is very very still.

BOGGETT perches on the pieces of Da Creedy's rocking chair holding a broken wine glass. DA CREEDY sits on another damaged chair, reading a charred book. ANTHER plays chess against himself with a single chess piece.

JEREMIAH crouches by the fireplace. All the men bleed heavily from their heads, just like Liam did. They are all dead except for BOGGETT.)

DA CREEDY. This is a fine passage.

ANTHER. I've just made a fine move.

DA CREEDY. This author displays a fine command of logic and causality.

ANTHER. But then when I play the other side, I make fine moves as well.

BOGGETT. Boggett, if you'd please, another glass of this fine wine.

JEREMIAH. There is no fine wine.

DA CREEDY. This is another fine passage.

ANTHER. And another fine move!

BOGGETT. Well then, bring me a fine glass of brandy.

DA CREEDY. I am becoming famished, little sister.

BOGGETT. *(To DA CREEDY:)* You always have such a vigorous appetite, Jeremiah.

DA CREEDY. That is because I am young and vicious and in my prime.

ANTHER. Boggett?
Boggett!
A fine glass of brandy for me as well.

JEREMIAH. There is no brandy, fine or otherwise, Master Anther.

ANTHER. But fetch it.

DA CREEDY. Boggett?
Boggett!
Bring me roast beast.

JEREMIAH. There is no roast beast.

DA CREEDY. But bring it to me!

BOGGETT. Little sister is catching a chill. There must be cracks in the walls.

JEREMIAH. You blew up the house. There are no walls.

DA CREEDY. I have such hunger and our Boggett is useless. Why must we always have such useless Boggetts?

ANTHER. Some day we will have a better one, brother.

BOGGETT. An apple! I demand an apple!

(*JEREMIAH fetches* BOGGETT *an apple.*)

JEREMIAH. Here, miss. Have an apple.

(*Just as* BOGGETT *takes a big BITE—*
CRASH!
The door is kicked open from the outside.
All turn their heads expectantly toward it.
Blackout.)

End of Play